Animals and Sacred Bodies in Early Medieval Ireland

Animals and Sacred Bodies in Early Medieval Ireland

Religion and Urbanism at Clonmacnoise

John Soderberg

LEXINGTON BOOKS
Lanham • Boulder • New York • London

Published by Lexington Books
An imprint of The Rowman & Littlefield Publishing Group, Inc.
4501 Forbes Boulevard, Suite 200, Lanham, Maryland 20706
www.rowman.com

86-90 Paul Street, London EC2A 4NE

Copyright © 2022 The Rowman & Littlefield Publishing Group, Inc.

All rights reserved. No part of this book may be reproduced in any form or by any electronic or mechanical means, including information storage and retrieval systems, without written permission from the publisher, except by a reviewer who may quote passages in a review.

British Library Cataloguing in Publication Information Available

Library of Congress Cataloging-in-Publication Data

Names: Soderberg, John (Professor of archaeology), author.
Title: Animals and sacred bodies in early medieval Ireland : religion and urbanism at Clonmacnoise / John Soderberg.
Description: Lanham : Lexington, [2021] | Includes bibliographical references and index. | Summary: "Clonmacnoise was among the busiest, most economically complex, and intensely sacred places in early medieval Ireland. In Animals and Sacred Bodies in Early Medieval Ireland: Religion and Urbanism at Clonmacnoise, John Soderberg argues that animals are the key to understanding Clonmacnoise's development as a thriving settlement and a sacred space"—Provided by publisher.
Identifiers: LCCN 2021046924 (print) | LCCN 2021046925 (ebook) | ISBN 9781793630391 (cloth) | ISBN 9781793630414 (paper) | ISBN 9781793630407 (epub)
Subjects: LCSH: Clonmacnoise (Ireland)—History. | Animals—Religious aspects—Christianity. | Rites and ceremonies—Ireland—Clonmacnoise. | Clonmacnoise (Ireland)—Church history. | Human settlements—Ireland—Clonmacnoise. | Monasteries—Ireland—Clonmacnoise. | Clonmacnoise (Extinct city) | Clonmacnoise (Ireland)—Antiquities. | Excavations (Archaeology)—Ireland—Clonmacnoise.
Classification: LCC DA995.C57 S67 2021 (print) | LCC DA995.C57 (ebook) | DDC 941.8—dc23/eng/20211012
LC record available at https://lccn.loc.gov/2021046924
LC ebook record available at https://lccn.loc.gov/2021046925

Contents

Acknowledgments	vii
Figures and Tables	ix
Introduction	1
1 Enclosure, Cattle, and Sanctuary Cities in Early Medieval Ireland	23
2 Excavating Clonmacnoise	57
3 Grounding the Archaeology of Religion	83
4 Animals and the Rise of Clonmacnoise	115
5 Animals, Tabernacles, and Towns: The Iconography of Sanctuary	141
6 The Animals of Clonmacnoise in a New Millennium	183
Afterword	207
Bibliography	211
Index	245
About the Author	249

Acknowledgments

I am grateful to the Irish Studies Program at Boston College for providing an opening to a career studying Ireland. Adele Dalsimer, Nancy Netzer, Phil O'Leary, Jim Smith and others created an atmosphere of joyous transdisciplinary inquiry that remains an inspiration. At the University of Minnesota, I found a community of American archaeologists who study Iron Age and medieval Europe with similarly broad-minded curiosity. Peter Wells is the group's foundation and animating spirit. Your patience and insight have been transformative for me and for many others. I would also like to thank Bettina Arnold, Theresa Early, Emily Weglian, Eric Bangs, Ora Elquist, Silas Mallery, Jenny Immich, Heather Flowers, Katie Erdman, Kristina Golubiewski-Davis and Brooke Creager. Terri Valois, you are in a class of your own. I am fortunate that the University of Minnesota was also home to archaeologists who ensured that I thought beyond Europe. Marth Tappen and Gil Tostevin provided an immense amount of support and clear-eyed advice. Stephen Gudeman, Gloria Raheja, Tim Dunnigan, Bill Beeman, and many others at the University of Minnesota were instrumental in helping me engage with the intellectual traditions of cultural anthropology. The foundation of the Evolutionary Anthropology Labs was an important turning point for me professionally and intellectually. My time there was rewarding in many ways, but the platform it provided for introducing me to biological anthropology is a foundation of this book. At the time, I could only see confrontation between my emerging interest in religion and the sensibilities of evolutionary biology. Opportunities for integration became apparent only after I left, but none of it would have been apparent without the intellectual worlds that Martha Tappen, Greg Laden, Mike Wilson, and Kieran McNulty opened to me. I would also like to thank the students who took my classes and worked in the Evolutionary Anthropology Labs, particularly Kevin Malloy and Lisa Delance. Keith Manthie, you are deeply missed.

One theme of this book is the importance of generosity in encounters between strangers. None of my work would have been possible without the generosity of people in Ireland toward an American stranger. John Bradley, Heather King, and Finbar McCormick were particularly open-handed in helping me to start research on Clonmacnoise. I wish John and Heather had been available to comment on this book. I am also grateful for the generosity of the faculty at Queen's University Belfast, Emily Murray, Tom Moore, Phelim McAleer, Con Manning, Conor Newman, Kieran O'Conor, Niall Brady, Terry Barry, Matt Stout, Aidan O'Sullivan, and others. The generosity of many American colleagues has also buoyed me over the years, particularly Pam Crabtree, Peter Bugucki, Tom Finan, Jimmy Schryver, Rachel Scott, Tom Herron, Karen Overbey, and Tom Sanders.

I am grateful to Denison University and the Department of Anthropology and Sociology, including Nancy Welu, for all the support since 2016. I am particularly appreciative of the opportunity to discuss ideas with Denison students, particularly those in Archaeology of Religion. Your questions and comments are inspirational.

Cookie Sunkle had the unenviable task of copy-editing an early draft of this book. Thank you. Kasey Beduhn, Ashleigh Cooke, and others at Lexington Books have been enormously helpful throughout the production process. I would also like to thank the anonymous reviewer. Your frank comments made this a much better book.

I am fortunate to have many friends who have encouraged the ideas presented here. Two have been particularly vital. Rick Brown, you are still one of my most insightful readers. Michael McNally, our conversations about religious studies and many other matters are the staff of life.

Above all else, I am deeply thankful for the layers of family that give my life shape. My siblings—Sigrid, Nancy, and Lars—are my guideposts. Melissa, my wife of thirty years, I could not wish for a better companion on life's journeys. Angus and Philip, my two boys, I am so proud of the humans you are becoming.

I dedicate this book to my parents. The longer I am a parent, the more I appreciate all you did. You are missed.

Figures and Tables

FIGURES

Figure 1.1: Map of Ireland, showing the location of key sites discussed. Created by John Soderberg.   24

Figure 2.1: Digital elevation map of the region around Clonmacnoise based on two-meter elevation data from the Ordinance Survey of Ireland. 1. Castle, 2. St. Ciarán's School excavations, 3. Tourist Office excavations, 4. Car Park excavations, 5. Bridge excavations, 6. Wastewater System excavations, 7. Steeple Garden excavations, 8. Central enclosure (location of St. Ciarán's Church excavations and High Crosses excavations, 9. New Graveyard, 10. Nun's Chapel. Created by John Soderberg.   58

Figure 2.2: View of Clonmacnoise from the Shannon callows. Photo by John Soderberg.   59

Figure 2.3: 3D digital model of the "Foundation Panel" on the Cross of Scriptures, from model created by The Discovery Programme, Center for Archaeology and Innovation Ireland.   65

Figure 2.4: View of the New Graveyard from the round tower in the central enclosure. Excavations occurred in the foreground of the white portacabin. Photo by John Soderberg.   73

Figure 4.1: Species ratio for Phase 1 and Phase 2 assemblages, based on the number of bone fragments identified to each taxon (number of identified specimens or NISP).   120

Figure 4.2: Comparison of Phase 1 and 2 cattle mortality patterns with those from rural sites (green) and Fishamble St.   123

Figure 4.3: Cattle fusion pattern for Moynagh, Dublin, and Clonmacnoise.   125

Figure 4.4: Comparison of pig mortality patterns from Knowth, Fishamble St., and Phase 2 (Knowth and Fishamble St. data after McCormick and Murray 2007).   131

Figure 5.1: View of the Cross of Scriptures (replica) from the west with the Cathedral in the background. Letters identify cross segments: A. cap, B. arm, C. ring, D. shaft, E. base. Photo by John Soderberg.   143

Figure 5.2: 3D digital model of the Cross of Scriptures, NW and SW corners) from model created by The Discovery Programme, Center for Archaeology and Innovation Ireland.   148

Figure 5.3: The base of the Cross of Scriptures (northeast corner) from model created by The Discovery Programme, Center for Archaeology and Innovation Ireland.   155

Figure 5.4: The base of the Cross of Scriptures (southwest corner) from model created by The Discovery Programme, Center for Archaeology and Innovation Ireland.   156

Figure 5.5: Schematic diagram of the directions figures face on cross bases. Created by John Soderberg.   159

Figure 5.6: The east and north faces of the Kells Market cross from model created by The Discovery Programme, Center for Archaeology and Innovation Ireland: 1. Sacrifice of Isaac (south arm); 2. Daniel in the Lion's Den (center); 3. Temptation of Anthony (north arm); 4. Raven feeding Sts. Anthony and Paul; 5. Canines flanking an animal-headed biped.   163

List of Figures and Tables xi

Figure 5.7: Cross of Scriptures at the northeast corner from model created by The Discovery Programme, Center for Archaeology and Innovation Ireland. 1. Foundation panel, 2. Musician with cats, 3. Prone figure with staff to eye. 165

Figure 6.1: Species ratio for all New Graveyard Phases, based on NISP. Created by John Soderberg. 187

Figure 6.2: Comparison of New Graveyard cattle mortality pattern with those from rural sites (Knowth, Deer Park Farms, Moynagh) and Fishamble St. Created by John Soderberg. 189

Figure 6.3: Cattle fusion pattern for New Graveyard, Fishamble St., and Moynagh (Fishamble St. and Moynagh after McCormick 1987). 189

Figure 6.4: Comparison of pig mortality patterns from Knowth, Fishamble St., and Phase 2 (Knowth and Fishamble St. data after McCormick and Murray 2007). Created by John Soderberg. 190

Figure 6.5: Phase 3 fragmentation rates (NISP/MNI) for assemblages from features in Phase 3 with an MNI over 20, in rank order by NISP with the largest at the left. Only bones from cattle, sheep/goats, and pigs are included. Created by John Soderberg. 192

Figure 6.6: Mean rates of fragmentation for cattle elements in Phases 2 and 3. Created by John Soderberg. 192

Figure 6.7: Percentage of unfused cat elements for Fishamble St. and the New Graveyard (Fishamble St. data after McCormick 1987). 194

Figure 6.8: Comparison of dog mandible dimensions for all New Graveyard phases. Created by John Soderberg. 195

Figure 6.9: Scatter plot of cat mandible dimensions for all New Graveyard phases. Created by John Soderberg. 195

Figure 6.10: Red deer antler to postcranial element ratio for selected Irish sites (Waterford data after McCormick 1997a; Deer Park Farms after McCormick and Murray forthcoming; Moyne after McCormick 1987a; Fishamble St. and Moynagh after McCormick 1987). Created by John Soderberg. 197

TABLES

Table 4.1: Statistics on species ratio, based on estimates of the number of individual animals in each taxon (minimum number of individuals or MNI), for a sample of early medieval Irish sites (after McCormick 1991: 43 and McCormick and Murray in press) and New Graveyard Phases 1 and 2.   120

Table 4.2: Age-at-death data for cattle from sites with cattle provisioning (after McCormick et al. 2011).   127

Table 5.1: Summary Statistics for the vertical and horizontal location of animals on the seven Muiredach crosses ($N = 238$).   149

Table 6.1: Statistics on species ratio, based on MNI, for a sample of early medieval Irish sites (after McCormick 1987, McCormick 1991: 43, and McCormick and Murray 2007) and Phases 1 and 2.   188

Introduction
Strangers, Animals, and Religion

Strangers[1] haunt human imaginations. Countless tales turn on a stranger appearing at the door. Their mystery is what will happen next. On the main, this book is an investigation of archaeological data gathered from excavations at Clonmacnoise, a medieval monastery in the midlands of Ireland. The goal is to shed light on the intersection between religion and the development of cities in post-Roman Northern Europe. But, equally, this book offers a tale about strangers gathering at Clonmacnoise: what drew them there, what they encountered as they crossed in, what transformations they hoped to find, what transformations they encountered.

Those people are of course long dead and, almost without exception, their lives happened outside the scope of texts. But, as Janet Spector defined decades ago in *What this Awl Means* (1993), archaeologists forget our dependence on tales about such people at our peril. Archaeologists working in early medieval Ireland are fortunate to have contemporary tales told in early medieval Ireland. Adomnán's *Life of Columba*, written circa 700, describes the activities of a holy man who left Ireland to found a monastery on Iona, an island off the coast of Scotland. In two tales, Columba crosses to the mainland and finds himself a stranger seeking hospitality at a poor farmer's dwelling for a night (Adomnán II: 20–21). Both times, Columba is welcomed and well provided for. During the course of the evening, Columba asks how many cattle the farm has. When he hears that each has only five, Columba blesses those cattle and the herd miraculously increases to 105. Columba guarantees such prosperity for three generations.

Scholars use Adomnán's account to create tales about how religion sat amidst the dynamics of early medieval Ireland. With Columba as an avatar of monasteries (and what they made sacred), the encounter points toward what monasteries brought to the world around them. To an extent, such interpretations are empirical investigations, but they also require an element of Janet Spector's imaginings to achieve coherence. Commentary on the tale of miraculous cattle typically focuses on class hierarchies and possibilities for movement among them (e.g., Sharpe 1995: note 255). An enlarged herd elevated the farmer's status by creating enough cattle to loan some out. Recipients were obligated to return the original loan, plus "interest" in the form of goods and services. Such "clientage networks" were pervasive and central to early medieval Irish society. Both secular and ecclesiastical forms existed. Networks of clients leveraged one's position into the upper echelons. Following the principle that "a man is better than his birth" the *Uriacecht Becc* indicates that such elevation can occur through diligent husbandry. Yet, for a full movement to upper echelons, prosperity had to be maintained for three generations (Kelly 1988: 12). Given the adherence to the details of clientage laws in the tale, Adomnán's miraculous cattle are often seen in the context of the consolidation of social inequalities and the role of religious ideology in fostering that process. The promise of miraculous increase facilitates recruitment of subordinates to the monastery with the promise of other-worldly rewards.

Interpreting the encounter in terms of exploitative clientage relationships is legitimate, significant, and ignored at peril. But, this interpretation also depends on assigning very particular character traits to strangers at the door. A very particular type of person triggers the transformations recounted in the above interpretation: obligations that disadvantage the recipient and yield subordination. Throwing open your door to such a stranger could only lead to an empty larder and escalating dependencies. If that stranger is offering religion, that character gives coherence to a particular tale about religion. It becomes ideology, an instrument wielded by both the saint and farmer to maximize wealth, status, control, and so on. Janet Spector's views are useful for highlighting ways that such interpretations require tales with very particularly drawn characters.

This book does not seek to discard such tales. They have been the source of numerous advances since Maire Herbert (1988) introduced such "political" perspectives on hagiography. Similar tales have driven insights in archaeology, anthropology, and a host of other disciplines from the mid-twentieth century onwards. In the mid-1980s, my introduction to social psychology was grounded in the tale of Kitty Genovesse: a woman in New York City murdered while neighbors did nothing. Those on-lookers were seem as not unlike the stranger and the farmer eyeing each other in calculation of self-interest. These characters were the foundation of how social scientists made sense of their views on human social dynamics. Scholars drew upon such tales because they have tremendous power to illuminate social dynamics lost to earlier functionalist tales with striving for the good of the group.

But, in the last decade or so, scholars working in a variety of fields have grown increasingly concerned with how devotion to one character occludes possibilities for different tales built around different characters. Even the tales about Kitty Genovesse have come under scrutiny. In 2015, a documentary film (*The Witness*) proposed that some neighbors were far more proactive than those filling tales I heard in the 1980s. Likewise, since 2010, the number of books focused on ways that people are often surprisingly kind to each other (in more technical terms, ways they act in a prosocial manner) has exploded. In 2013, Lee Cronk and Beth Leech published *Meeting at Grand Central: Understanding the Social and Evolutionary Roots of Cooperation*; in 2019, Nicolas Christakis published *Blueprint: The Evolutionary Origins of a Good Society*; in 2020, Brian Hare and Vanessa Woods published *Survival of the Friendliest: Understanding Our Origins and Rediscovering Our Common Humanity*. While it is too soon to fully understand the consequences of these books, they are part of a decades-long effort to recover alternatives lost in tales that drove inquiry from the mid-twentieth century.

The fundamental motivation of this book is to promote a similar change for perspectives on medieval Europe by using Clonmacnoise as a case study in applying such new alternatives. Elaborating the details will require examining research in a variety of fields, but, an indication of the direction my argument will take is available in Adomnán's tale of miraculous cattle. On my reading, prevailing interpretations neglect a key element of the tale. After conjuring one set of cattle, Columba stipulates that the herd cannot increase beyond 105, except those that "could be devoted to either the own needs of the household, or else to the use of charity."[2] This proviso sits uneasily within the interpretation of the tale in terms of aspiring cattle-lords. It seems directly opposed to that view. Use of the cattle for status enhancement or other personal gain was specifically debilitated. The herd could only grow beyond 105 if that increase sustained the household or were shared in a very different manner from the instrumental process identified in the above account of clientage: through charity.

This proviso creates a decision point on religion. It can be contained within the prevailing view, but doing so requires seeing the proviso—and by implication religion generally—as ideology masking the true intent /consequences of the encounter. But, as is discussed in subsequent chapters, new perspectives on the intersection of religion and economics increasingly view such views as explaining religion away more than actually explaining it. In essence, new perspectives suggest taking the charity proviso more seriously. But, doing so requires conceptualizing a stranger at the door less driven to empty the larder and create subordination. New developments in a variety of fields have created an approach to the intersection of religion and economics better able to account for the proviso in Adomnán's tale and the different social outcomes from encounters with strangers at the door. This book takes Clonmacnoise as a case study demonstrating the implications of these alternatives for understanding early medieval social dynamics and, more specifically, what role religion had in fueling the resurgence of urbanism.

The concise version of my answer is that animals made Clonmacnoise sacred and the process of transforming those animal bodies made Clonmacnoise a city. My decision to approach Clonmacnoise via animals is related to "Spectoral" imaginings. So far, I have used Janet Spector's views on tales to explore an early medieval text to sharpen sensibilities about what has been marginalized by the grounding assumptions of established perspectives. But, Spector developed her view for archaeological artifacts, with their articulations to lives and places absent from textual accounts. I am a zooarchaeologist, an archaeologist who studies animal bones. The field is well known as a means of defining how people reared, traded, and consumed animals. Such topics can seem very distant from the practices that made Clonmacnoise a sacred place. But, that perceived disjunction is a product of views about "sacred" and "secular" that are becoming increasingly discredited in religious studies. The rejection of sacred/profane dichotomies is part of a wider movement to move beyond Enlightenment-era tales about the split between mind/body or cognitive/material. In their place, practice-based accounts offer concepts such as embodiment and materiality. In lieu of sacred transformations as spirits animating inert material, practice-based approaches conceptualize sacred transformations as processes of gathering and articulation (bundlings). Bodies are not made sacred. They make sacred.

This perspective makes zooarchaeology a premier means of studying religion. The grubby business of rearing and slaughtering animals is not a profanity kept walled away from sacred precincts. Sacred bodies form in the relational fields created as such mundane practices are gathered and recontextualized. The transformation at the core of this book is the set of processes leading from slaughtering animals to the creation of a sacred place. How did transforming those animal bodies into food and raw materials make Clonmacnoise sacred. *Not* how they fed what made Clonmacnoise sacred, but how their bodies actually made Clonmacnoise sacred.

Monasteries are a particularly useful point of inquiry for emerging concepts of the intersection between secular and sacred. Monasteries are sacred places where people live. They are not sacred refugia surrounded by settlement. They are sacred settlements. Rather than being apart from the hurly-burly of human life, they become gathering points. The core insight of the perspective on religion offered here is that the settlement element of monasteries is not subordinate to, or separate from, whatever makes a locale sacred.

It is what makes it sacred. That argument involves taking an animal-eye view of the intersections between sacred and settlement that animated gatherings at Clonmacnoise.

Gatherings at Clonmacnoise return us to encounters with strangers. The most common question about settlement at Clonmacnoise is whether or not it was urban. Cities are places where population density, socio-economic specialization, and other factors create a settlement unable to feed itself. Urban dwellers have to secure food and raw materials from elsewhere. In other words, urban dwellers depend on strangers. Tales about the transformations rising out of those encounters give coherence to theories of urbanism just as they do in Adomnán's tales. Like the proviso Columba adds, Clonmacnoise is an oddity with religious overtones that does not sit easily within prevailing tales.

Clonmacnoise was in a set of monasteries known in contemporary accounts as cities of refuge (*civitas refugii*), or more colloquially: sanctuary cities. Since at least the 1980s—and perhaps back into the Middle Ages themselves—opinions have split over the validity of claims to urban status. Some see monasteries like Clonmacnoise as distinct trajectories of urban resurgence in post-Roman Europe. Others see claims of urban status as wishful thinking. While most participants agree that the debate concerns essential questions about religion and social dynamics in early medieval Europe, resolution has been elusive because the sides—with adherence to different tales—often talk past each other. One possibility for moving the debate forward is shifting its terms. To date, the primary locus of debate has been establishing criteria for what qualifies a settlement as urban. The challenge with establishing that Clonmacnoise was urban is that the monastery was in a locale without the accepted drivers of urbanism: aspiring elites founding urban centers as part of strategies for gaining control over agricultural and/or manufacturing economies.

By the turn of the millennium, calls for a wider range of drivers for urbanism (and social complexity more generally) were growing common. I first engaged with the topic in this period. Naively, I assumed that resolving debates about sanctuary cities was largely a matter of determining if the signatures of urbanism found elsewhere in Northwestern Europe from circa AD 700 could be identified at Clonmacnoise. Zooarchaeologists have repeatedly shown that early medieval urban centers were provisioned with animals drawn in from the surrounding country site. My assumption was that if I could demonstrate that Clonmacnoise was provisioned, clearly conceptions of what fuels urbanism need to change. Such was not the case.

I had not reconned with tales. Theories about early medieval European urbanism that coalesced in the mid-twentieth century depend on tales about religion that are very like the tales that make Adomnán's miraculous cattle a matter of clientage hierarchies. The growth of practice-based views of religion create an opportunity to develop a robust link between the sacred and settlement elements of Clonmacnoise. Accordingly, the following pages will approach Clonmacnoise via what might seem a particularly profane route: the remains of animal bodies slaughtered in quest of creating food and raw materials for manufacturing. In this case, rather than a stranger arriving at a farm, the tale involves people walking cattle from farms to encounter strangers at Clonmacnoise. As is discussed in chapter 2, a person would have walked into a spectacle. If you were driving cattle to the monastery along the esker ridges and bog trackways of Ireland's Midlands, winds carried smells from iron working hearths and tanning pits. As you came around the last bend of the road, sounds of squealing pigs and bleating goats surrounded you. Soon you were walking past bone cutters pulling antlers from dung heaps and houses looking like the ones at home.

Standing amid these spectacles and surrounded by strangers, you could look up the hill to stranger things: shrines holding relics and giant crosses swirling with vines, people, and animals. You probably knew the crosses—early on of wood, later stone—marked space to take sanctuary if something went wrong. Elders might have told you stories of a boat appearing in the air somewhere up the hill and about the abbot who knew that its travelers needed help. You might have heard about the miraculous powers of the cow skin left by Clonmacnoise's founding saint, Ciaran. But, you certainly knew that your cattle came to Clonmacnoise to be slaughtered for food and raw materials.

The tale hammered out in the following chapters tries to make sense of how our stranger bundled together all these encounters with Clonmacnoise. What transformations would she have expected to occur as the pole-axe hit her cow's forehead? Standing amidst the sights and smells, would she have anticipated them becoming just so much meat and raw material? Or would that transformation have resonated with those up the hill?

CLONMACNOISE IN THE CONTEXT OF MEDIEVAL ARCHAEOLOGY

Janet Spector intended such imaginings to be uncomfortable companions to empirical hypothesis-testing traditions in archaeological research. In the case of Clonmacnoise, I am setting my tale against theories of urbanism in post-Roman Northwestern Europe. The aim of that juxtaposition is to bring into focus the sorts of characters who give coherence to prevailing theories and to establish the need for alternatives.

In 1959, Philip Grierson set key terms of debate for early medieval socio-economics in his seventeen-page article "Commerce in the Dark Ages." He framed the period in terms of Marcel Mauss's *The Gift*, or, more precisely, the interpretations of Mauss that had developed within economic anthropology by the mid-twentieth century. Historians and archaeologists have been wrestling with the implications ever since. From the 1960s onwards, accounts of medieval urbanism and exchange networks proceed from Grierson's Mauss.[3] But, recently some scholars have shifted away from "commerce" in an effort to draw from other elements of *The Gift*. Of particular note for my approach to Clonmacnoise are several studies that use Mauss to revise the instrumental views of religion that have pre-dominated since the mid-twentieth century. Florin Curta (2006) argues that Grierson's Mauss drew too much attention to movements of goods and other such narrowly economic activities. He advocates more attention to the values animating those movements, which leads to an argument for a shift from economic strategies toward political phenomena, specifically the negotiation of religiously inflected "internal" associations (2006: 677 and 678). Frans Theuws (2004 and 2012) adopts a similar view of values/religion as vital for articulating the "imaginary worlds" of individuals and groups. Such articulations are essential for creating the production and movement of goods (i.e., what is often called the economy). Most recently, Roberta Gilchrist (2020) grounds her view of monastic religious practices in Mauss's views on embodiment (techniques of the body). In each case, religion is an animating force in ways lost to Grierson's Mauss.

The diversity of perspectives growing out of Mauss's work is a testament to its potential. But, it is also a testament to the maddening complexity of grasping his intentions. On one hand, many consider Mauss's work the most influential thinker in twentieth-century anthropology (e.g., Graeber 2001: 151). Likewise, no other anthropological text has been exported to other intellectual fields more commonly (for a review of its multifaceted influence on early medieval studies, see Curta 2006). But, on the other hand, explanations of what Mauss thought remind me of a comment a linguist once made to me about the experience of being taught Old Irish by three different professors: unless each had told him they were teaching the same language, he was not sure he would have known. One assessment of Mauss often seems discontinuous or even totally at odds with the next. Briefly tracing out several key turns in the use of Mauss will establish what motivated these new perspectives on religion and what my views about Clonmacnoise add to theories of post-Roman urbanism.

John Moreland (2000 [2010]) surveys three key legacies of Grierson's article for discourse into the 1990s. First, Grierson assumes that economies are divided into production and exchange spheres, which led him to envision what Moreland considers an oxymoron: an economy without production (Moreland 2010 [2000]: 88). This segregation led to a belief that exchange sectors were somehow more socially potent than production sectors. Essentially, it cast subsistence agricultural and localized manufacturing (autarkic economies) as minimal influences on social dynamics. While Grierson is a convenient metonym for this conception, such views were important to world-wide theories of social complexity in the mid-twentieth century (e.g., Brumfiel and Earle 1987). For Europe specifically, Fernand Braudel lavished attention on the Wheel's of Commerce, but passed over "subsistence" as a non-economy (Braudel 1979: 59–60). In zooarchaeological terms, animals become socially potent primarily as they enter trade cycles. Rearing and other matters of production have little place in economic "progress."

Second, socio-economic analysis focused on gift-exchange as an elite matter: "in its emphasis on elite exchange and consumption as the driving forces in structuring and transforming society, it perpetuates another, but equally stereotypical image of the early Middle Ages as a world of 'mead halls' and 'ring-givers'. . . an account that does little justice to the (archaeological *and* anthropological) evidence" (Moreland 2010 [2000]: 91). Here, *The Gift* is reduced to competitive gift exchanges in which escalating cycles of gifts and counter-gifts are fueled by the need to avoid unreturned obligations and subordination. Mauss's discussion of potlatching among post-contact Native Americans in the Pacific Northwest certainly describes such economies. But, they are only one among many examples. Capturing the spirit of the gift in that single case is reductive. Strangers at the door offer only empty larders.

Third, Moreland argues that Grierson's Mauss facilitated the sense of the early medieval period as *Other*, with processes and organizing principles fundamentally different from "Modernity" (market driven societies with Weberian modernity and rational spirits of capitalism). By the 1980s, various authors had established a variety of ways that early medieval socio-economic institutions operated on varieties to Modernity's commerce for profit (e.g., Astill 1985, Geary 1986, Hodges 1982).

Richard Hodges's work is particularly significant. He elaborated Grierson's views into a deeply influential theory of the socio-economics surrounding urbanism in post-Roman Northwestern Europe (e.g., 1982). Drawing from Grierson, Carol Smith (1976), and Fernand Braudel (e.g., 1979), Hodges combines Grierson's view of gift-exchange with excavation data on early medieval trade centers (emporia) to argue that, in the quest for prestige items, rulers established trade centers and long-distance trade networks to acquire rare and precious goods that would allow them, via continued gift-exchange, to enhance their own power. Hodges's attention to gift-exchange of prestige items was a much needed effort to advance beyond the limitations of earlier scholars (e.g., Pirenne 1925, Duby 1968, 1974), who found agricultural intensification a precursor to post-Roman urbanism (see Hodges and Whitehouse 1983: 106–8; Hodges 1989: 58–59).

Irish sanctuary cities occupy a revealing place in this narrative. The possibility of an urban Clonmacnoise represented a test of the model advanced in *Dark Age Economics*. At the time, power in early medieval Ireland appeared insufficiently centralized to fuel the exchange cycles that created urban centers (Hodges 1982: 195). Given the parameters of Dark Age economics, locales without significant social inequalities and the attendant exchange cycles should lack urban centers. Furthermore, if religion is an instrument of those powers, it is an unlikely driver. On both counts, the absence of urban qualities at Clonmacnoise affirms the model for Dark Age economics. Hodges unequivocally rejects the possibility of monasteries as centers for urbanization: "clearly these were not towns" (1982: 42).

But, at much the same time, R. A. Butlin (1977) and Charles Doherty (1985) made an argument that such monasteries indicated processes of urbanism not captured by models such as Dark Age economics. But, voices of concern did not coalesce into broadly accepted critiques and alternative models until closer to the turn of the millennium. Hodges's model remains deeply influential, particularly with recent updates (e.g., Hodges 2012). But, the focus on elite directed commerce and other legacies of Grierson's Mauss seemed increasingly ill-suited to the variability across early medieval Europe.

One of the most significant shifts is renewed attention to agricultural production. Partly, the shift is a matter of rejecting the separation of economic spheres Moreland discussed so that agricultural intensification becomes as socially potent as long-distance trade in luxury goods. Pam Crabtree views land as a key source of wealth in Anglo-Saxon England, as agricultural intensification allowed the mobilization of social surplus via tribute and food rents, with trade through early urban centers (and smaller trade centers) a secondary development (2018: 182–83). Wickham pursues a similar argument for Europe more generally (Wickham 2005). To an extent, this shift concerns a multi-generational debate over the importance of commerce or agriculture as sources of elite power (see Hodges 2012 for review).

But, to the extent that economic spheres are associated with different demographics, increased attention to agricultural production (and localized manufacturing) is also an effort to identify ways that groups other than elites define the course of social change. For theories of urbanism, that shift broadens the view of towns as nodes of control to include a view of them as gathering spaces. They become "points of contact" for the surrounding countryside; consequently, rather than towns as space for elites to dupe others into subordination, they also become spaces "where ideologies and identities are negotiated" (Crabtree 2018: 184). As a wider array of demographics become vital to those negotiations, the sources of urbanism become more diverse.

Theuws demonstrates how this perspective can offer a profound challenge to prevailing models of urbanism growing from Grierson's Mauss (Theuws 2004 and 2012). The source of the challenge is widening the scope of socially significant economic practices. Economies are systems of values that animate movements of goods, services, and so on. If both production *and* exchange are socially potent, value is generated throughout landscapes: "objects gain value "at the time of production, during circulation and at deposition . . . the value of things, even of commodities, is embedded in the imaginary worlds or the ideology of the participant in the exchange" (2012: 44). One key phrase here is *participant in the exchange*. This model does not reject the possibility that one partner will lose agency and become subordinated. But, it recognizes that outcomes are variable in ways obscured by Grierson's Mauss because the sources of value are dispersed and variable. The concept of value at play here is discussed in detail below. But, in general terms, it draws on the same practice-based views of religion that are the basis of my concept of sanctuary cities. In essence, Theuws's argument is that urbanism is as much about religion and as (neoclassical) economics (see also Curta 2006). Theuws uses the term *values* to identity how social and individual values (imaginary worlds) are entangled with economic values (costs/benefits of producing and exchanging goods). While this perspective emphasizes the variety of imaginary worlds cultivated in the whole economy, he also gives a role to central places such as towns in hosting "tournaments of value" a term Arjun Apadurai used to describe gatherings that were larger scale social values were negotiated and sanctified (2004: 125–26). Values are not maters for distinct sectors of the economy, nor are they segregated according to profane and sacred registers. As the range of imaginary worlds articulated in urban gatherings grows, urbanism varies in space and time.[4]

All participants create the imaginary worlds that establish human societies. Susan Oosthuizen (2016) builds a similar view of social dynamics in Anglo-Saxon England through a focus on shared pasture rights. Long-standing conventions around the rearing and consumption of animals becomes an animating social force in ways lost to mid-twentieth-century models. The "mutuality" of the relationships is deeply embedded and cannot be regarded as noise around elite commerce. Other scholars have developed similar approaches to craft and other sorts of production as essential for early medieval urbanism (e.g., Callmer 2007, Croix et al. 2019, Asby and Ashby Sindbæk 2020).[5] Bottom-up considerations of production have gained space alongside top-down elite exchange as a means of recognizing variable paths to urbanism (Crabtree 2018: 31).

My attention to animals at Clonmacnoise follows on these efforts to engage various demographic groups and a range of different value schemes economic sectors in fueling post-Roman urbanism and other facets of social complexity. As values are generated across landscapes, the farmer raising cattle and releasing some to feed urban dwellers has a far more integral role in creating cities than is encompassed by earlier models. In addition to asking how elites created Clonmacnoise, we must also ask how walking cattle created monasteries. The goal is to recognize that Clonmacnoise might have been a node of control, but it was also a gathering point. Understanding Clonmacnoise requires understanding it as both.

The problem with making that argument is that, as discussed so far variability, is an ill-defined concept. Terms such as bottom-up imply that more demographics gain agency. But, a concept of social dynamics in bottom-up circumstances that addresses problems with Grierson's Mauss remains elusive. Moreland reviewed efforts up to the turn of the millennium and offered suggestions for furthering the project (2001 [2010]). Since 2000, such approaches have become increasingly common. Strikingly though, Theuws concluded in 2012 that, despite resolute attention to variability, virtually all explanations still end up in the same place as in the 1980s: a "common theme is the idea that elites are crucial to the economic growth of the early Middle Ages" (2012: 33). Despite all the attention to varability, somehow the models end up the same.

Crabtree hints at the problem in her observation that Anglo-Saxon society was never egalitarian (2018: 182). In one sense, that statement reflects rejection of evolutionary models that posit linear movement over time from communal/altruistic societies to class-based/exploitative societies. It may be the case that no human society is usefully characterized as egalitarian. But, the weakness of the solution does not mean that the problem that gave rise to it is not important. While Anglo-Saxon England might not have been egalitarian, it was not simply hierarchical or class-based either.

A brief look at the history of the term in Anglo-Saxon archaeology will illustrate why it is important to keep trying to identify whatever circumstance words like egalitarian were grasping after. At a time when *Dark Age Economics* was at its peak influence, Jennifer Bourdillon used *egalitarian* to describe aspects of Anglo-Saxon urbanism that seemed discordant with elite directed commerce. She found the animal evidence from Hamwic "strangely egalitarian" (1988: 190). Ultimately, she explained away the strangeness and accepted elite directed control as the best available explanation. But, the echo of the issue across decades is illuminating. Bourdillon was right to be uncomfortable with the explanation as egalitarian. But, the more important issue is the sense of something strange about Hamwic in the context of Dark

Age Economics. The same concerns fuel much of the literature reviewed here from Doherty in 1985 to Theuws in 2012.

The issue is that mid-twentieth-century archaeology was spectacularly successful at describing the social dynamics of power and inequality. As Gil Stein observed at much the same time as Moreland was writing, by the 1980s, models for social complexity were mostly "attempts to document elites strategizing to gain and maintain hierarchical power through the manipulation of economics and ideology" (Stein 1998: 8). Egalitarian might not be the right word, but Bourdillon's strangely egalitarian animals at Hamwic are describing exactly the same problem that Theuws identified in 2012. All the attention to variability has been a long trip around back to the starting point unless we can better define the strangeness.

Calling Clonmacnoise a sanctuary city has a similarly strange quality. The degree of social inequality (elite control of values) in early medieval Ireland is unequivocally lower than Anglo-Saxon England and in turn early Anglo-Saxon England has less inequality than Frankish areas (see chapter 1). Urbanism growing from religious practices certainly seems strange from the perspective of elite-centered models. The challenge is finding ways to conceptualize that strangeness without explaining it away, as Bourdillon did, and without resorting to simplistic notions such as egalitarian (the sorts of brittle explanations that gave rise to Dark Age economics in the first place). The solution pursued in the following chapters begins in the same place as Curta and Theuws: updating conceptions of Mauss to establish a new intersection between religion and economics.

That process requires some additional background on the economic anthropology that created Grierson's Mauss and how its lingering influence still debilitates understanding fundamental variation in the social dynamics of urbanism. Greirson's Mauss took shape within the substantivist/formalist debates dominating mid-twentieth-century economic anthropology. When viewed through the lens of Karl Polanyi's *Great Transformation* (1944) and other substantivists, early medieval Europe seemed to offer an opportunity to discover the eighth- and-ninth century roots of the shift from ancient to modern social organizations. Much of the interest in Mauss's *The Gift* was based in a sense that "gift-exchange" created circumstances from which economies were "disembedded" from social conventions, allowing the emergence of market economies. By the time Moreland wrote his critique at the turn of the millennium, numerous studies had shown that historical and ethnographic data simply did not support dichotomies between gift economies and commodity economies. A firm consensus held that Substativist/Formalist debates operate from were unproductive distinctions between what Moreland calls Same and Other. But, little agreement existed on how to consider "other" economies (i.e., those prior to or otherwise distinct from market economies and other facets of Western Modernity).

Since the turn of the millennium, some have sought to reconcile the sensibilities of substantivism and formalism by concentrating on ways that all economies are "embedded" or "instituted" (elaborated within a social context). For example, the New Institutional Economics blends traditional economic concepts, such as transaction costs, with sensitivity to contextual variation in socio-political contexts (e.g., North 2005, see Crabtree 2018 for an application to early medieval Europe). David Graeber (2001) views such theories as recapitulating—not resolving—the problems that plagued substantivist/formalist approaches. In light of his perspective, approaches such as New Institutional Economics attempt a middle ground where Otherness is manifest in terms of institutional order and Sameness is manifest in motivational schema. What individuals seek varies according to context, but the value scheme that motivates them is invariant: people are always driven by a desire to maximize gain. The particular object of desire and the institutional order via which desires are satisfied are all that vary. Recent attention to heterarchy and dual processual dynamics in medieval Europe follow this path (e.g., Ray and Fernández-Götz 2019, but see also Crumley 1995).

Graeber's account of "post-substantivist" economic anthropology identifies why such approaches seemed to always circle to their starting point. Graeber's insight is that such solutions do not resolve the impasses of mid-twentieth-century economic anthropology. They look away from them, and, in doing so, recapitulate the problem that led to the original impasse they seek to resolve. Such theories cannot break free from working in circles because theories of economic variability have not established a revision to the essential and powerful economic tale of utilitarian individualism or maximizing individuals.

Here we return to the importance of Janet Spector's tales. Since the 1990s, a broad consensus has grown around the idea that lots of different people played a role in creating urban centers (and that elites could not simple direct change). The controversial issue is how significant that diversity is to the social dynamics that fuel urbanism. In some cases, the difference is epiphenomenal because the only characters end up involved are maximizing individuals. If—as is the case with prevailing interpretations of Adomnán's miraculous cattle—the wider landscape is populated with endless copies of that character, the variety of sectors contributing to urbanism grows, but the basic process remains the same: all one really needs to explain urbanism, or any other social phenomenon, is fully bounded units maximizing their own success, whether the aim is commercial profit or social status. In such circumstances, the strangeness of phenomena such as the charity proviso in

Adomnán or Bourdillon's strangely egalitarian cattle merely deconstructed as the elaboration of utilitarian individualism in varying institutional contexts. Grierson's Mauss is designed to do just that.

Graeber establishes an alternative through a fascinating and wide-ranging critique of anthropology that is beyond the scope of this book. But, the significance for the issues most relevant for medieval European urbanism is that the discipline can do economics or it can do anthropology, but post-substantivists are not doing both (Graeber 2001: 5–22). He argues that anthropology and economics were created around different objectives. Economics is driven by prediction, which requires a theory about the moods and motivations that impel action. In other words, they are grounded in "Spectral" imaginings: tales about what happens when strangers meet. Thorstein Veblen memorably characterized the only characters in neoclassical economic tales as "a lightening calculator of pleasures and pains, who oscillates like a homogeneous globule of desire of happiness under the impulse of stimuli that shift him about the area, but leave him intact. He has neither antecedent nor consequence" (Veblen 1898: 389–90). Neoclassical economic theories explain how the desires of Veblen's globules create the schemes of value that cause the movements of goods and services. Not coincidentally, prevailing interpretations make the stranger appearing at the farmer's door in Adomnán's tale looks very much like Veblen's globule.

By contrast, Graeber observes that anthropology seeks to understand what lies outside Modernity, which for economic anthropologists is manifest in market economics. But, anthropologists tend to avoid prediction of individual behavior, instead focusing on variation in institutional organization and cultural meanings. He takes mid-century-economic anthropology as a paradigm for such approaches. The decades between the 1940s and the 1980s yielded numerous taxonomies of variation in how goods are distributed. But, they offered little in the way of a counterpart to Veblen's globules: accounts of what motivated individuals to choose one good over another. Graeber establishes this logic in his characterization of the mid-twentieth-century formalist/substantivist debates that subsequent scholarship has sought to escape. He sees that substantivists offered anthropology without economics and formalists offered an economics without anthropology by marginalizing the significance of cultural variation. The objects of desire might vary—status or social power instead of financial profit—but utilitarian individualism remains the only motivational model.

Consequently, according to Graeber, confrontations between the two were unproductive because both sides were only capable of creating taxonomies of variation: formalists saw ways that Veblen's globules acted in different circumstances; substantivists saw circumstances where those globules were not useful, but either did not, or could not, establish an alternative models of individual motivation. Either way, mid-twentieth-century economic anthropology left "an empty space into which economistic theories were always trying to crawl" (Graeber 2001: 21). Without an alternative to Veblen's globules, economic anthropologists can do (neoclassical) economics or they can do anthropology. But, they cannot do economic anthropology. Without a scheme for individual motivations (what Graeber calls a theory of value), arguments about what lies beyond Modernity are either taxonomies or teleological narratives about the evolution of Modernity.

The narrowness of neoclassical economics cannot be resolved by accounts of institutional variation. Without an alternative to Veblen's globules, anthropology—and by extension anthropologically informed medieval studies—can describe circumstances where those globules were not useful or it can describe ways in which those seemingly "other" circumstances are actually the product of encounters between Veblen's globules. Sounding very much like Theuws assessing new models of urbansm, Graeber concludes his survey of "Current Directions in Exchange Theory" with the sobering conclusion that most post-substantivst/post-structuralist work is either "a warmed over economism that makes 'value' simply the measure of individual desire, [or it is] some variant of Sausserean 'meaningful difference.' . . . In either case, what's being evaluated is essentially static" (2001: 46). Without an alternative to Veblen's globules, taxonomies of variability will inevitably contain that open space for the globules to re-enter.

The pattern is evident in theories about early medieval urbanism. Taxonomies of institutional variation have proliferated, but most all keep a version of Veblen's globules at their core. Despite increasingly variable paths to urbanism, most ultimately rest upon the desires of maximizing individuals, whether the object of their desires is long-distance trade goods, agricultural surplus, or religious ideology. Hodges 2012 "new audit" of his seminal *Dark Age Economics* (1982) presents a fascinating and encyclopedic account of changing views since the 1980s. But, as Graeber would predict, each of the three major "challenging models" are dependent on the same maximizing behavior that guided the original model (Hodges 2012: 8–18). Even most divergent model Hodges includes (Theuws 2004) is not clearly disarticulated from concepts of agency that are reifications of utilitarian individualism. (For a review of such issues in agency theories, see chapter 3.) My own early efforts to escape from reliance on Veblen's globules are liable to criticism as taxonomies (e.g., Soderberg 2001). The stranger at the door is always the same.

Post-substantivist reconsideration of early medieval urbanism has gained tremendous sensitivity to variation in the variety of processes and institutional organizations that spur the development of urbanization. Agricultural intensification, craft production, and religious gathering are now well documented as important factors. But, to the extent that models of urbanism have traced out variable processes without a parallel account of how values work within individuals, they are liable to the same problem that Graeber associates with anthropology. Veblen's globules still crawl into the empty space Graeber identified in taxonomies of variation.

The scope and nuances of Graeber's solution to this problem far exceed the bounds of this book, but the essential point is evident in his assessment of Marilyn Strathern's concept of the partible person, which is among the most influential of the post-substantivist/post-structuralist efforts to build an alternative to neoclassical value schemes (Stathern 1988 and 1992, Graeber 2001: 35–43). It has fostered considerable interest in intersubjectivity and "non-Western" (i.e., strange) concepts of self (e.g., Danziger 2017). Mark Mosco (2015: 366) defines partible persons as:

> composite beings constituted of the gift contributions of the detached elements of other persons. Social life in this context consists in the reciprocal elicitive exchange and distribution of those transactable parts of persons with one another. Through lifetimes of such transactions, persons are cumulatively composed and decomposed of the elements of other persons; hence, social relations can also be seen as people's mutually embodied components.

Strathern's concept is immensely valuable as a description of what an alternative to Veblen's globule would look like. The open and permeable borders of partible persons are a response to the impermeable boundary that makes it possible for homogenious globules to calculate self-interest. Social meanings (values) go inside, but no account of what happens in there is provided. They do not identify what creates the moods and motivations (desires) that stimulate partible persons into action. Graeber argues such accounts leave individuals as black boxes.

Graeber calls such accounts of individual motivation *Theories of Value*. Values are a key source of vitality for economies, for societies, for people. They catalyze action from agricultural production to religious worship. They are a source of creativity and transformation that animates the movements encompassed by the term economy. Graeber's argument is that, without a matching theory of value, accounts of partible persons are not capable of offering alternatives to neoclassical accounts.

Graeber argues that the necessary theory of value is waiting in *The Gift* all along. Scholars have long recognized that the book is motivated by the quest for an alternative to British utilitarian individualism (e.g., Douglas 1990: x–xiv). The sense of opposition between commodities and gifts that led to Dark Age economics has roots in Mauss's objection to barter as the emblem of the "natural economy": two people meet, haggle over the price of desired goods, and then part without enduring association. In *The Gift*, Mauss sought an alternative paradigm in forms of exchange that entail enduring social relationships (people with histories). Countless scholars have sought to understand non-market or embedded social relationships in terms of Mauss's question about why gifts compel return. Graeber's distinctive contribution is that these explanations of the "spirit of the gift" have concentrated too much on taxonomies of exchange modes and their social consequences.[6]

Instead, he urges consideration of what Mauss has to say about ways that values catalyse desires (2001: 179). It is reductive to define Graeber's argument as just a theory of value for partible persons, but the example provides a useful illustration. Mauss draws his theory of value from Maori philosophy, in which gifts contained a portion of the giver (*hau*) that desired to return to its native land and owner. Graeber takes that point to mean that gifts are not just transfers of debts or social obligations (a foundation of Dark Age economics). Gifts are a useful counterpoint to commodities because they highlight ways that all economic activity—from production to trade—is about creating/transforming associations with other people. Graeber's emphasis on values is a reminder that such processes are not just outside individuals. Values create "certain sorts of persons" as desires are transformed and actions are catalyzed (Graeber: 2001: 211).

Following this logic, Graeber suggests reframing the various exchanges Mauss describes as creating associations that run from open to closed, not embedded to disembedded. The distinction between open and closed is temporal. Open indicates enduring commitment to the association. Closed indicates a contingent association that is wrapped up as speedily as possible. In this context, answering why gifts are returned is a matter of when they are returned. Values around which exchanges are negotiated are always entangled with the social relationships emerging via the exchanges. The "spirit of the gift" is the duration and extent to which a portion of the giver (*hau*) stays a part of someone.

Herein is the source of the creativity and transformation in Graeber's theory of value along the spectrum of movements described by economic anthropologists. Barter does not occur outside social space. Closed exchange is how one acts "with people towards whose fate one is indifferent" (Graeber 2001: 154). The objects moving between partners do not signal an absence of association, they establish a contingent and ephemeral association that keep boundaries in tact. Competitive potlatching is similarly a matter of shaping relations around indifference. In this context, the return is an effort to stave off subordination or to maintain fragile and competitive equalities (Graeber 2001: 221). Veblen's globules are useful for such value schemes. Open exchanges are those that delay return indefinitely, or even eternally. They are not more embedded or socially instituted than other exchanges, but they create more enduring associations and the people to match. If economies are about creating persons, whereas barter creates closed individuals (Veblen's globules), more open exchanges create open individuals. Such individuals are only strange if one believes only Veblen's globules exist. The spirit of the gift is most inexplicable if tales have only globules without precedent or antecedent.

One useful way of demonstrating the difference between Graeber's Mauss and Grierson's Mauss is to consider what Mauss wrote about medieval Europe and Modernity in the fourth chapter of *The Gift*. His goal is to demonstrate the utility of his scheme for understanding complex societies. The primary difference he identifies is the extent to which daily life is pervaded by associations with strangers. In smaller scale societies, the sorts of economies best described by neoclassical economics—barter—are those that happen across the edges of groups. In chapter 4, Mauss identifies a revealing quality to those encounters. They are not just barters simple outsiders where parties are indifferent to other's fate: "Over a considerable period of time and in a considerable number of societies, men [*sic*] approached one another in a curious frame of mind, one of fear and exaggerated hostility, and of generosity that was likewise exaggerated" (1925 [1990]: 81). Mauss is not describing diadic confrontations that maintain borders between globules or entanglements of partible persons. Mauss casts the encounter with strangers as both or neither because it happens in indeterminate space awaiting the creation of persons, associations, and exchanges. Values around which exchanges are negotiated are always entangled with the social relationships emerging via the exchanges.

That observation is important to post-Roman Europe because, urbanization—and social complexity more generally—is a circumstance in which encounters with strangers become pervasive. As was noted above, the basic definition of urbanism is a settlement with enough economic specialization and population density to require getting food and raw materials from elsewhere: from strangers. Mauss's emphasis on the "curious state of mind" evoked and required in such moments demonstrates how the entire spectrum traced out in *The Gift* is drawn into such moments. Mauss reaffirms why such circumstances cannot just be characterized at the rise of closed exchange (barter and commodity exchange). Other types are as necessary as ever. In fact, if anything, gifts and the people they create become more important than ever, as dependence on strangers grows more essential. In a sense it is a classic moment of closed exchange with an outsider, a party of unknown intention and reliability, but since life depends on an enduring association it is simultaneously an open exchange. As cities depend on strangers, the essential problem is how to solve this Maussian conundrum. And, theories of urbanism depend on the tales they tell about encounters with strangers. Complex exchanges will always require complex values. Veblen's globules are essential, but also insufficient.

From this perspective on Mauss, Adomnán's tales of miraculous cattle offer a paradigm for the challenges of understanding social complexity. To the extent that the stranger is an exploitative psychopath willing to deploy all manner of manipulative ideologies, much of the foregoing discussion of Maussian nuances is of limited impact. But, if we need to account for other possibilities (other types of strangers leading to other types of associations), Mauss is deeply aware of the indeterminacy and creativity of the space created as the farmer opens his door. In that circumstance we must let go of the coherence that Veblen's globules give to the encounter and develop tales populated with a more variable cast of characters. Saying that the farmer is also a psychopath or that encounters between psychopaths can yield variable socio-economic institutions is not enough. We need an account with greater sensitivity to the spectrum of values that may arise in such spaces. The account of early medieval urbanism provided in this book is written from a similarly "processual-plus" approach as Crabtree has recently applied to Anglo-Saxon England (2018). But, I approach the task with the same sense of dissatisfaction Graeber has with economic anthropology and the same conviction as Curta and Theuws that making economics more a matter religion is the way forward.

I am also not convinced that any of the literature surveyed here is sufficient to the task. I know economic anthropology was not for my own early efforts to understand Clonmacnoise as a sanctuary city. As will be detailed in chapter 3, to my sensibilities, full development of the alternative tale Graeber seeks requires moving beyond anthropological discourse on both religion and economics. Advances in biological sciences developing at the same time as the advances discussed above offer a more compelling account of the operation of Graeberian values under a person's skin. The fundamental assertion of chapter 3 is that accomplishing the tasks that Curta and Theuws define requires this step outside anthropological and humanistic discourse. In a sense, the objective is no more pairing archaeology's long tradition of associating with cultural anthropology with an association to biological anthropology. In the last decade, various biological sciences have documented with quantitative precision that exchanges between people involve something remarkably like the process Mauss describes with a piece of a person crossing to and dwelling in others.

But, before exploring the potential of recent advances in biological sciences, we need to define how the overall concerns of medieval archaeology play out in an Irish context. Chapter 1 surveys key aspects of early medieval archaeology in Ireland, with the goal of establishing important aspects of that landscape and how the interpretive trends discussed here have shaped understanding of early medieval Ireland. Chapter 2 surveys results from nineteen different excavations that have occurred at Clonmacnoise since the 1970s, including Heather King's New Graveyard excavations, which are among the most extensive of any excavations at the early medieval Irish monasteries known as sanctuary cities. Chapter 2 reviews prevailing account for what drove the development of Clonmacnoise.

Chapter 3 articulates the issues raised in the introduction with new developments in biological sciences. The chapter begins with a review of the new perspectives on religion hinted at in Curta's and Theuws's articles and the implications of practice-based approaches for reconceptualizing medieval urbanism in a manner that can more successfully accommodate urban qualities at monasteries like Clonmacnoise. The result resonates with Theuws's account of links between imaginary worlds and economics. One step necessary for realizing the value of these new views on religion is to move past the disciplinary divide that segregates biological and humanistic approaches to religion, both within archaeology and other fields of religious study. The result is a concept of religious practices as *bundlings*, in the sense developed by Theuws (and scholars such as Severin Fowles, María Nieves Zedeño, and Tim Pauketat), but with biological grounding missing from their approaches. As with Graeber's view of anthropology, I believe that the archaeology of religion needs to strengthen its account of what happens under the skin.

Chapter 4 explores the rise of Clonmacnoise as seen from the perspective of the animal remains collected during the New Graveyard excavations. Chapter 6 turns to the iconography of animals on the monumental crosses that defined areas of sanctuary at Clonmacnoise and implications for identifies how they define the nature of such sacred spaces. Chapter 7 considers changes in the roles animals played during the final centuries of intensive settlement at Clonmacnoise, between the eleventh and thirteenth centuries, a period of profound religious and social transformation in Ireland.

Ultimately then, this book explores ways animals create the assemblage of practices bundled together to form Clonmacnoise. How do animals become entangled in the life of this sacred settlement and what can the archaeology of those creatures tell us about how religion animated Clonmacnoise and early medieval Ireland?

NOTES

1. Additional materials related to this book are available on this book's webpage at rowman.com

2. "*aut in usus proprios familiae aut etiam in opus elimoysinae expendi poterat*" (trans. Anderson and Anderson 1961: 370–71).

3. Georges Duby is also an influential voice bringing economic anthropology to the study of medieval Europe (e.g., ref). But, to the extent that discourse on urbanism has followed Grierson's attention to commerce (as opposed to Duby's attention to production), Grierson has an outsized influence.

4. Chris Wickham develops a similar perspective on urbanism with his discussion of how *civilitas* or cityness changed from the Roman to the post-Roman period (Wickham 2005: 596).

5. In many respects, these models are reminiscent of Peter Wells's views on entrepreneurs, which presaged turn of the millennium interest in non-elite and productive activities (Wells 1984: 198). See Crabtree (2018: 14) for the divergence in views between Wells and Hodges.

6. The more nuanced version of Graeber's argument is that dominant voices in the discipline have marginalized the argument that Graeber puts forward. Stephen Gudeman, for example, has been making much the same argument since the 1980s. In fact, Gudeman sees such tensions as formative elements of socio-economic models back at least to the time of Aristotle. Gudeman's perspective is a foundation from which Graeber's view of economics rises. For review, see Gudeman (2001).

Chapter One

Enclosure, Cattle, and Sanctuary Cities in Early Medieval Ireland

INTRODUCTION

Clonmacnoise was founded in the mid-sixth century AD and remained a significant settlement into the thirteenth century and perhaps later. In terms of cultural periods, Clonmacnoise is primarily a phenomenon of the Early Medieval Period (~300 to ~1100). This chapter defines key aspects of the socio-economic dynamics in these centuries and the perspectives that archaeologists use to understand them. Since Clonmacnoise's roots extend back into the Iron Age, the chapter also addresses some elements of that period.

A full survey is well beyond the scope of this book. The surge of development-led archaeology that coursed through Ireland in the late 1990s and early 2000s exponentially increased the number of excavations/surveys and significantly broadened the range of voices contributing to discourse on Irish archaeology. Several recent volumes have achieved remarkable syntheses of new data and established key points of debate on early medieval Ireland.[1] This chapter is very much written from the shoulders of these studies.

One change emerging out of work since the turn of the millennium concerns settlement aggregation (high density settlement) and urbanism. For much of the twentieth century, early medieval Ireland was assumed to be deeply rural. Settlement patterns were thought to consist almost entirely of dispersed farmsteads. The primary exception were coastal trade centers that were generally accepted as urban from the 1980s. But, a sense that they had an uncertain relationship to wider "Irish" social dynamics is evident in their description as Viking towns early on and then from the last decades of the twentieth century onwards as Hiberno-Norse towns.

Monasteries were associated with dispersed settlements in that they were often small and spread widely. Larger monasteries were of course known, but they sat uneasily amidst conceptions of a rural landscape. Part of the sense of contradiction associated with sanctuary cities such as Clonmacnoise is that, if they were urban, they ran against the grain of settlement dynamics. To highlight tensions around understanding aggregated settlement and urbanism, this chapter will first examine smaller dispersed settlement and reserve discussion of urban settlement to the end. The goal throughout is to examine the early medieval period in terms of the tensions over social dynamics identified in the introduction: what tales do archaeologists tell about encounters among strangers in early medieval Ireland.

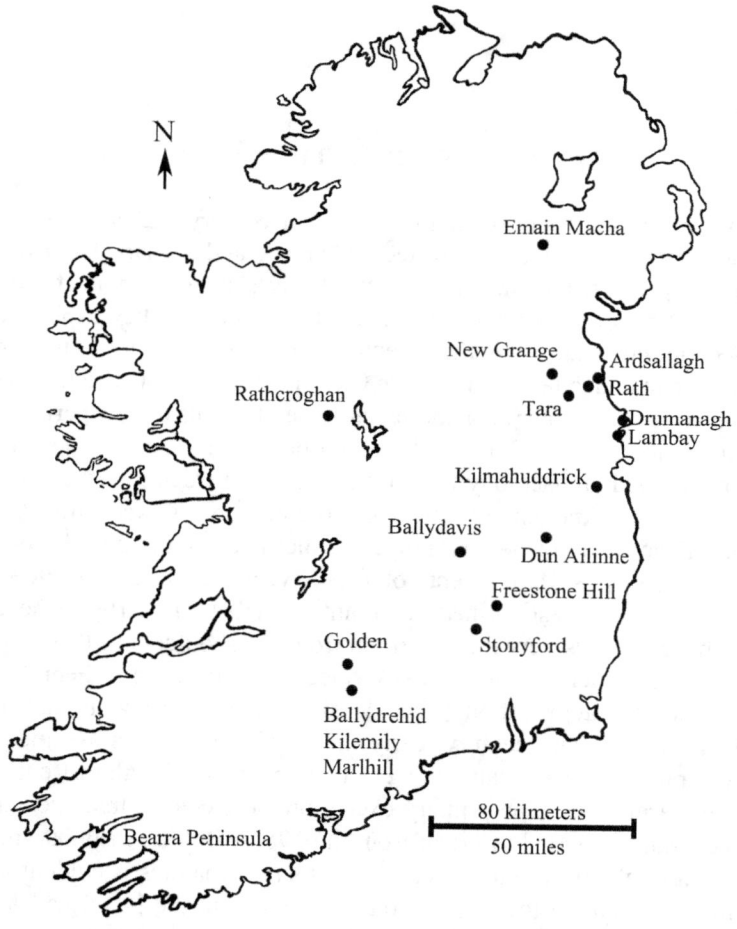

Figure 1.1. Map of Ireland, showing the location of key sites discussed. Created by John Soderberg.

THE LATE IRON AGE BACKGROUND

The Developed and Late Iron Age periods in Ireland extend between the final centuries BC and circa 400 AD (Becker 2012). These centuries held a number of remarkable developments. First, after millennia of expansion, evidence for agriculture drops and woodlands expand precipitously in many locations. This "Iron Age Lull" is most evident between 200 BC and 80 AD (McClung 2013 and O'Donnell 2018). One study from Co. Monaghan found that generally arboreal pollen declines and agricultural pollen rises from 2500 BC. Then, between 220 BC and 220 AD, levels drop back to those from 2500 BC (Chique et al. 2017: 12). Second, at much the same time that the palynological lull begins, evidence for settlement also falls away. To the point that, Barry Raftery famously described the population of this period as "the invisible people" (1994). Settlements from earlier eras were often abandoned, and, at least until recently, their replacements were quite scarce. Pottery also largely disappears from the archaeological record.

Third, the later Iron Age also yields evidence for architecturally dramatic gathering places known as ceremonial centers: Tara, Emain Macha, Rathcroghan, and Dún Ailinne. These stridently visible monuments include intriguing mixes of new construction and curation of ancient Neolithic and Bronze Age monuments. Large ceremonial centers are distributed among what became the provinces of Ireland in the medieval period. All reach their floruit in the centuries around the turn of the millennium and the first centuries AD.

Centuries later, these centers remained significant features of medieval imaginations. An introductory poem to the "Martyrology of Óengus" (circa 800) provides an origin story for Clonmacnoise and other such monasteries. Each is said to have taken the place of one Iron Age ceremonial center and gained sovereignty over secular rulers associated with those places. Clonmacnoise is designated at the successor to Rathcroghan (Chrúachán) in nearby Co. Roscommon: "Chrúachán has vanished along with Ailill, the scion of victory: but fair sovereignty over princes prevails in the settlement of Clonmacnoise."[2]

Understanding of the later Iron Age has been, and will continue to be, transformed by the surge of excavation in Ireland during the Celtic Tiger era and a number of ongoing research projects. A detailed survey of emerging perspectives is beyond the scope of this book. But, three elements are particularly relevant to understanding Clonmacnoise.

First, Iron Age ceremonial centers are increasingly recognized as phenomena involving flows of animals. Pam Crabtree (2003) considers the faunal assemblage from Dún Ailinne to represent remains of feasts associated with the gathering of regional populations. For Tara, the abundance of evidence for butchering and roasting horses has been interpreted in the context of rituals associated with sacral kingship (McCormick 2002a and 2005). At Emain Macha, the superabundance of pig is similarly associated with "the ritual of hospitality in the courts of kings and in the dwellings of the gods" (McCormick and Murray 2007: 32). Richard Madgwick et al. (2019) use isotopic data to demonstrate the movement of animals across Ulster to Emain Macha.

These studies of animal flows are part of a wider assessment of ceremonial centers as spaces in which elites sought to enhance their status and gain control over sacred practices (Newman 1998, Grogan 2009, Warner 2009, Johnston et al. 2014, and O'Driscoll et al. 2020). Conor Newman argues that the occupants of Iron Age ceremonial centers are "probably the closest to sacral kings or priest kings that Irish late prehistory has yet to offer" (1998: 132). He views these centers as reflections of large regional polities that began to fragment in the early centuries AD, a pattern that established the foundation for the early medieval period.

Second, the Iron Age Lull is no longer considered a time of collapse resulting from extended climatic downturn. The agricultural lull is now known to have persisted through different climatic conditions and to start/end at different times in different locations. Consequently, the dramatic activities associated with ceremonial centers can no longer be seen as responses of a desperate populace in the face of climatic deterioration. Lisa Coyle McClung and Gill Plunkett (2020) identify more complex interaction between cultural and climatic dynamics.

It has also become clear that people did not vanish. Development-led archaeology in the 2000s increased the number of sites associated with the period by several hundred-fold. Raftery's 1994 map of known settlements from the Late Iron Age contained just twelve locales. The Discovery Programme's LIARI project has identified one thousand monuments from four hundred fifty sites (Dowling 2014). Population numbers must have dropped, but people did not vanish. Based on new data, "invisibility" has to be considered in terms of how people engaged with their ecologies. Ways of altering landscapes via agriculture and settlement became less visible.

Third, Iron Age Ireland is no longer thought isolated from the rest of Europe. That sense of isolation fostered views of Ireland as, depending on intellectual proclivities, free from or left behind developments in the Roman world. Connections between Ireland and Romanized Europe are now recognized as far more than a matter of occasional lone traders venturing across the Irish Sea and raiders bringing back exotic memorabilia. Aspects of *romanitas* became features of the Irish landscape. As Andrew Heald comments, the evidence now clearly calls for "alternatives more diverse than trade yet subtler than warfare" (2001: 694). In religious terms, various scholars now argue that Romanized ritual practices took hold in Ireland and reflect substantial networks of communication across the Irish Sea (e.g., Daffy 2002, Ó Floinn 2000, Walsh 2012). Perhaps the most significant aspect of recognizing more substantial types of contact is that the networks clearly extended well beyond the dynamics of kingship at the out-sized ceremonial centers. Instead of a sacred landscape dominated by a few large ceremonial centers, a significant number of small localized centers are now recognized (e.g., Newman 1998, Newman et al. 2007, Prendergast 2012, O'Connell 2013). Recognition of such locales changes conception of the ritual landscapes of Ireland. Instead of sacred practices contained at a few large centers, sacred places are appearing across the land, which has fascinating implications for the associations that grew from them.

In some cases religious links parallel the long-distance associations thought to power the biggest ceremonial centers. For example, Ragnall Ó Floinn (2000) argues that Freestone Hill (Co. Kilkenny) was a *temenos* for imported Roman cult practices. Freestone Hill is a small rural shrine, not Dún Ailinne. Other locales present more highly localized associations. Enclosures in the Barrees Valley (Co. Kerry) reflect similarly localized sacred practices as at Freestone Hill, but without the long-distance connections to *romanitas* (O'Brien 2002 and 2009). At an even smaller scale, the surge of excavations in the 2000s revealed numerous locales in which Bronze Age ring-barrows were used for burial through the first millennium AD. Conor Newman and Andy Halpin memorably refer to such sites as "cuckoo-style" burial practices (2006: 18). Known more formally as *fertae*, these burial monuments are often located in prominent locations. Many locales are active from the Iron Age into the Middle Ages. Elizabeth O'Brien and Edel Bhreathnach (2011) see the continued use of "ancestral" grounds as introducing "guardians" for ancestral territories.

Elsewhere, I emphasized the importance of seeing equivalence between highly localized efforts at making connections and the "outward" looking connections associated with the influx of Roman goods in the period (Soderberg 2013). While *fertae* operated at a micro-scale relative to the largest ceremonial centers, they were no less ceremonial than Dún Ailinne. Nor were they less concerned with gathering the sorts of imaginary worlds Theuws discusses in the early medieval period. Localized associations should not be considered less socially potent than long distance ones.

Gabriel Cooney believes that localized monuments have been overlooked among those studying the Irish Iron Age. He writes that "the continuing importance of the past and the ancestors as well as the complex and subtle interweaving of ideas and places that people drew on in using the past and the dead in the affairs of the living" (2009: 384). As the sacred landscape of Iron Age Ireland grows increasingly crowded with different scales and types of sites, models depending on centralized control of sacred practices at a few "big" locales seems increasingly inadequate.

A host of different social constituencies were making themselves visible in the sacred landscapes of the Iron Age. As the landscape becomes filled with alternatives to large ceremonial centers, questions grow about the impact of sacral kings. For example, Brian Dolan has recently advocated for a shift to perspectives "beyond elites" towards a view of the Late Iron Age driven by "fundamentals in how individuals lived their lives" and the development of shared cosmologies (Dolan 2014: 370). In the sense of Heald's request for "alternatives more diverse than trade yet subtler than warfare," such perspectives are a useful compliment to accounts of Iron Age social dynamics in terms of maximizing elites.

ENTERING THE EARLY MEDIEVAL PERIOD

Traditionally, the early medieval period starts in the fifth century, when records of missionary activity in Ireland commence. A combination of new data and new perspectives supports pushing the start earlier. The "crisis" of the third century and its aftermath are now recognized as pivotal for Romanized Europe in social/economic/religious terms (see Brown 2013). New recognition of the crucial role of late Antique trade networks in bringing all sorts of influences to Ireland support arguments that such events may have also influenced Ireland. Palynologists also date the resurgence of agricultural activity back to the third or fourth century. Taking such considerations into account, Ger Dowling (2014) identifies the beginnings of early medieval settlement trends in the third century AD.

As the Iron Age Lull begins to fade in the third century, woodlands once again recede and agricultural landscapes expand. In the County Monaghan study noted earlier, arboreal pollen return to pre-lull levels between 220 and 440 AD (Chique et al. 2017: 13). As with the start of the lull, climate is no longer seen as the controlling factor. Linking climatic and cultural changes remains challenging, but two conclusions about relationships between agriculture and climate at the beginning of the early medieval period are well accepted at this point (McClung and Plunkett 2020). First, the trend toward intensification began in the Roman Warm Period, well prior to the climatic fluctuations of the Dark Ages Climatic Deterioration beginning circa 500. Second, the post-500 period had significant adverse periods, such as those associated with the Justinian plague circa 540, but it also had mild periods. It is also worth considering that agricultural strategies may not respond to one set of conditions. They may also respond to variability itself.[3]

The precise chronology and geography of Christianity's emergence remains elusive. Religious change was certainly well underway by the sixth century, but the earliest presence of Christianity is obscure. Linguistic studies of words associated with Christian sacred spaces provide some information about the locations and chronology of the earliest Christian institutions. *Domnach* (*the Lord's place*, pl. *domnaig*) is an Old Irish word that passed out of use circa 500, giving an indication of church foundations prior to that date. *Domnaig* locations are seen as seats of the first bishops in Ireland and centers in early diocesan territories (Doherty 1991 and Bhreathnach 2014: 169). They occur across Ireland, but concentrations exist in the north and east of the island.

Christian practices are likely to have arrived via a similar cultural spread as Raghnall Ó Floinn associates with the rural shrine at Freestone Hill. Matthew Stout points to the earliest written script in Ireland (a Latin-based alphabet known as *ogham*) as evidence for the circulation of ideas and technologies in the fourth and fifth centuries likely associated with the spread of new religious practices (Stout 2017: 23). Edel Bhreathnach pursues a similar argument in her emphasis on rural estates as a key mechanism infusing Christianity to Ireland (2014: 162–63). Garranes (Co. Cork) is a circular settlement surrounded by three enclosures which produced a rich array of Mediterranean pottery dating to the fifth and sixth century (Ó Ríordáin and Ryan 1941/1942). Bhreathnach views the settlement as a high-status farmstead acting as a "hub" for imported goods and craft production. Garranes is also the find spot for one of the earliest examples of Christian symbolism in Ireland: a mould with an inscribed cross. Garranes hints "at a community open to the reception of Christianity and literacy" (Bhreathnach 2014: 163).

In such circumstances, understanding Christianity's beginnings in Ireland requires knowing Ireland's relationship to the Roman and post-Roman world more generally and how such associations intersect with more local dynamics. Religious practices are likely one part of a larger spread of late Antique culture and sensibilities. One key impact of the Roman presence in northwestern Europe is the introduction of novel social institutions and their transformation as Roman institutions advanced and receded. Taxation and associated processes for the circulation of goods is a particularly important set of institutions that spurred the monetization of social relationships. As Patrick Geary observes, a key dynamic of the early medieval periods is the process by which Roman taxation systems and other institutions withered into the hands of local elites (1988). Peter Brown and others emend this view by observing that the defining characteristic of the late Roman period across the empire is dramatic escalation of socio-economic inequality and declining investment in public infrastructure. Robin Fleming details the expansion of villas and the decline of public structures in Britain from the third century onwards (2010). Much withering was underway by the third century.

This perspective sets up an interesting challenge for thinking about Ireland in the early centuries AD. On the one hand, the island is unequivocally outside the Roman sphere. Taxation and related institutions are not prevalent. As their implementation elsewhere is obviously consequential, their absence in Ireland is also consequential. But, equally, *romanitas* is a complex and partible set of identities known to obtain a significant presence in Ireland.

The tension between local (inward looking) and regional (outward looking) views of Ireland is challenging to negotiate because it is also tangled with modern European imperialism. From the time of the Anglo-Norman conquest in the twelfth century onwards, narratives about Ireland commonly frame Ireland in terms of indigenous/colonizer dichotomies with colonizers as agents of modernity and indigenous peoples as primitive, averse to progress, or otherwise stuck in the past. Such dichotomies run back even to late Roman times. In the first century, Pomponius Mela inserted Ireland into the classic Roman dichotomy between barbaric (*societas*) and civilized (*civitas*) in describing inhabitants of *Iuverna* as unrefined, ignorant, and lacking all sense of duty (quoted in Stout 2017: 14). Any discussion of Ireland as participating, or not, in *romanitas* or other continental trends must struggle with the weight of this long legacy and resist the attractions of its dichotomies.

These issues have been particularly troublesome for considering conversion to Christianity. While evidence of Iron Age (i.e., pre-Christian) activity is common on early medieval sacred sites, unambiguous evidence of religious continuity is rare (see Harney 2017 for review and discussion). But, as was noted above, the number of burial sites in use over millennia has grown in recent years. Tomás Ó Carragáin associates this local burial practice with the late Roman change in which burial/settlement boundaries are breached (Ó Carragáin 2009 and 2010b, see also O'Sullivan and McCormick 2017: 111–12 for discussion). Ó Carragáin's view resonates with recent conceptions of *romanitas* in terms of *glocalization*: simultaneously local and regional (Pitts 2008). The two traditions merge in Ireland, forming the conception of sacred enclosures in early medieval documents as places of religious and juridical sanctuary.

EARLY MEDIEVAL IRELAND: PART 1 (~300 TO ~800)

Archaeologically, the early medieval period is a time of enclosure. The prototypical settlements of the period (ringforts and monasteries) are defined by moving earth into ditch and bank or piling stones around a perimeter. Archaeologists now know that early medieval Ireland was not a land of just ringforts and monasteries (e.g., Coyne and Collins 2003, Coyne 2006, and Kinsella 2010). Yet for the most part, new site types remain variations on the theme of enclosure. Even those sites without enclosure are defined by its absence: unenclosed settlements.

Enclosure created space for much of life in early medieval Ireland. It defined domestic spaces where grain was stored, cattle housed, and bodies found a night's sleep. More abstractly, earth-moving was an assertion of social capital. Antoine Giacometti (2006), for example, has shown that the non-circular enclosure at Lusk was constructed so that the banks appeared largest as one moved through an entry bridge. Jonathan Kinsella notes the contrast between such elements and the otherwise modest material culture of the site and proposes "aspirational" earth-moving to project a status not otherwise apparent (2010: 121). As was noted above in the discussion of multi-period cemeteries, early medieval burials were set into earlier acts of earth-moving. Enclosure also defined sacred space and places of worship.

Seeing early medieval Ireland as a time of enclosure invites consideration of earth-moving as an economy in which all sorts of Graeberian values brought earth into motion. Each basket-load of earth shifted is an act of meaning making to be seen in context with other basket-loads. The challenge is understanding how economies of earth-movement contributed to the dynamics of early medieval Ireland. That process begins with a taxonomy of different types of enclosure.

Sacred Enclosures

The most obvious manifestation of religious practices in early medieval Ireland is enclosure. Caherlehillan (Co. Kerry) is among the earliest dated monasteries in Ireland (Sheehan 2009). The site is defined by a roughly circular enclosure thirty meters in diameter that contains the remains of the earliest dated church in Ireland (fifth/sixth century) and a grave marked with a later stone shrine, presumably venerating a founder. If enclosure is an important means of marking sacred space, an account of the economy of such enclosures is the foundation of understanding these institutions. Matthew Stout observes that church, enclosure, and tomb are "the three pillars upon which the physical existence of the early Church rests" (2017: 30). The early Church in Ireland is nothing if not variable. All three are not present in all locales. But, these "pillars" certainly demonstrate key aspects of economies for creating sacred enclosures.

But that scheme has an important lacuna. At Caherlehillan, the enclosure does not just encircle a church and burials. Those pillars only occupy the northwest third of the enclosure. Two-thirds of the space is devoted to very different activities: post-and-wattle houses, a grain storage structure, industrial/craft activities, and refuse pits (Sheehan 2014). The animal bone assemblage is too small to support detailed conclusions about husbandry at the site, but nothing about the assemblage distinguishes it from what is found at a routine farmstead. Giving Caherlehillan three pillars elides most of the enclosure.

Adding this fourth pillar is critical to stabilizing the concept of a monastery. The variety of forms compassed by the term is enormous. Their organization and architecture differ so much that the settlement category can seem incoherent. More technical alternatives—such as ecclesiastical settlement and cemetery settlement—have been proffered. While such neologisms are useful markers of variation, they also threaten to obscure the fact that monastery is also an entirely coherent category.

Leaving out the fourth pillar elides what gives the category unambiguous coherence: monasteries are sacred places where people lived. No matter how variable the manifestation of sacred practices, they represent the convergence of settlement and sacred. They are built around the tensions of bodies inhabiting sacred space. From this perspective, the variety from site to site is not a matter of fundamental difference. It rises from different ways of addressing the contradictions of inhabiting sacred space.

As will become clear in chapter 3, this debate concerns far more consequential matters than settlement taxonomy. The practice-based theories of religion that have come to prominence in recent years reformulate concepts of the sacred—and how religions sit within social dynamics—around just such entanglements of sacred and settlement. The concept is a key foundation for a robust understanding of the intersection of religion and urbanism at Clonmacnoise. It is also the beginning of explaining how animals can make Clonmacnoise sacred. They are part of the process of articulating sacred and settlement. Letting them into the sanctuary is necessary because, according to practice-based theories, it is how sanctuaries are created. In this sense, the debate about sanctuary cities is not fundamentally different from general debates about how sacred settlement sit within societies. As John Bradley suggested, perhaps all monasteries are sanctuary cities (1998: 42).

But, while these issues have important theoretical implications, clarity about their basis can grow from thinking about ways that Caherlehillan is defined by settlement. The majority of the enclosure is essentially a farmstead. The experience of entering the enclosure would have been entering a farm very like the rest of the enclosed farmsteads across the Irish landscape. In spatial terms at least, visiting Caherlehillan was as much visiting a farmstead as a shrine. Cattle walked there as elsewhere. Ignoring such settlement activities indicates that they are not part of what makes the site sacred. Striped of its theoretical armature, the argument to follow is that farmness is an integral part of those things bundled together at Caherlehillan. It, as much as any other element, is making the site sacred. As Theuws's emphasis on understanding economic totalities indicates, hiving off the settlement yields a limited account of animating values.

Reviewing the range of monasteries present in Ireland from the seventh century is beyond the scope of this work. But, many are elaborations of the bundlings found at Caherlehillan. Nendrum (Co. Antrim) provides a useful illustration of the form taken by monasteries larger than Caherlehillan (McErlean and Crothers 2007). The site has three enclosures. The innermost contained churches, burials, and shrine. The second enclosure held primarily domestic features and industrial activity. The outermost enclosure contained a corn-drying kiln and iron working. Agricultural activity is also likely a component of this outer area, but evidence is ambiguous. The oldest known tidal mill in Europe was identified in a nearby cove. Industrial activities are added to the farmness of Nendrum, but such changes are only elaborations of how settlement and sacred are brought together at Caherlehillan. The variability in how different monasteries engaged with sacred and secular practice is vast. Even though it is also built around a mill complex, High Island is remarkably different from Nendrum, as is Raystown (Seaver et al. 2016), not to mention monasteries without mills, such as Illaunloughan (Marshall and Walsh 2005). But all are exercises in bundling settlement and sacred.

The definition of monasteries as sacred settlements is also useful for understanding a newly recognized site type: settlement cemeteries. They are a notable category of monastery because they lack the markers of ecclesiastical affiliation found at most monasteries, such as churches and shrines. Appreciation of these burial-cum-habitation sites grew from research into diversity in burial practices from the Iron Age into the medieval period (e.g., O'Brien 1992, 2003). Terminology for these sites remains unsettled. Stout and Stout (2008) used the term secular cemeteries. Others view this choice as neglecting the role of habitation/manufacturing at the sites and have proposed alternatives, including settlement cemeteries (O'Sullivan et al. 2014) and cemetery settlement (Ó Carragáin 2009, 2010b). For general reviews and references, see Stout and Stout (2008), Kinsella (2010), and O'Sullivan et al. (2014: 306–12).

To date, much of the debate surrounding how to best conceptualize these sites has concerned their relationship to social and ecclesiastical centralization. Colmán Etchingham (2006) proposed that settlement cemeteries result from a two-tier system of pastoral care in which sites with ecclesiastical architecture are associated with intensive pastoral activities for the upper echelon and settlement cemeteries with minimal pastoral care for the rest of the population. To the extent that the Church allocated its pastoral care resources to elites, this perspective ties ecclesiastical institutions to articulating a centralized hierarchy spanning political and religious realms.

Tomás Ó Carragáin finds Etchingham's formulation too dependent on a top-down approach to how communities engage with religion (Ó Carragáin 2010b: 218–19). Instead, he suggested that the variation from site to site reflects different types of engagement with religion. In this context, settlement cemeteries become emblematic of local and familial engagements that counter extensive hierarchies. Ecclesiastical settlements are emblematic of a more fully articulated and expansive Church hierarchy. Working from evidence that settlement cemeteries become less common over time, Ó Carragáin argued that shifting burial activity to ecclesiastical settlements was a manifestation of an increasingly solid hierarchy. They become markers of changed social circumstances that become evident in the second phase of the early Middle Ages, which begins circa 800. (See below for discussion.)

The same basic narrative is also applied to the development of monasteries in general. In defining his view of Glendalough, a large monastery similar to Clonmacnoise, Etchingham stipulates that its key dynamic "was how elite families sought to exercise influence over Glendalough, bringing to its heart the political rivalries of north Leinster aristocratic dynasties" (Etchingham 2011: 23). Both are built along the same lines as the prevailing interpretation of Adomnán's miraculous cattle in terms of exploitative clientage. Understanding the logic of this narrative and how it came to dominate consideration of religious practices requires consideration of secular enclosures (enclosures without obvious sacred precincts).

Ringforts and Other Enclosures

Many people walking to a monastery would have started at a ringfort, a site type also known as rath, *ráth*, *líos*, *dún*, and cashel. Recently, efforts have been made to clear this terminological thicket by referring to them in generalized morphological terms (small circular enclosures) and reserving the above terms for variation in form and construction material (see O'Sullivan et al. 2014: chapter 3). Here, ringfort is retained as an umbrella term for all small circular enclosures (following O Ríordáin 1942). But, the term is used with recognition that it can obscure, rather than illuminate, variation within the category over space and time (see Fitzpatrick 2009).

An immense number of ringforts are known. Stout and Stout (2011) identify over forty-seven thousand ringforts. Many see 60,000 as a conservative number (e.g., O'Sullivan et al. 2014: 49). Ringforts are not found in village-like clusters. They are a dispersed and highly uniform settlement form. The most obvious variation in form is the number of enclosures. Stout estimates that 80 percent have one enclosure (univallate) (1997: 17). While the enclosed area of most univallate ringforts is at grade, a substantial percentage (perhaps 15 percent or 20 percent) have an elevated interior, either through tell-like accumulation of habitation layers or concerted earth-moving (O'Sullivan et al. 2014: 53). These are known as platform ringforts. The remaining 20 percent of ringforts consists almost entirely of bi-vallate ringforts. A very small number of tri- or multi-vallate ringforts are also known. The chronology of these various forms is critical for understanding change across the early medieval period. Details are considered below. Structural variation is also connected with regional and chronological variations that have important connections to key regional trends in early and late medieval Ireland (e.g., Hull and Comber 2008, Fitzpatrick 2009, Gibson 2012).

Dated occupation of ringforts currently extends back to the sixth century, though the existence of earlier examples remains a possibility (e.g., O'Sullivan et al. 2014: 48). Uni- and multi-vallate ringforts are concentrated in the period between 700 and 850 (Kerr 2007 and Stout 2017). That clustering should not obscure evidence of earlier and later occupation.[4] But the tight peak in construction for what is likely to be tens of thousands of ringforts testifies to the massive scale at which they were adopted in their heyday. Ringforts existed within a wider landscape of pasture, fields, and woodland clearance. Susan Lyons identified a shift in the species composition of charcoal from ringforts and other types of early medieval enclosures that testifies to the association with landscape changes (Lyons 2018: 276–78). Iron Age kilns show an orientation on hazel and oak. She found that from the fifth century kilns were fueled with a new diversity of species, particularly those associated with the woodland clearance and "scrubby" secondary growth. This pattern provides compelling evidence for anthropogenic factors in the reduction of woodland associated with the end of the Iron Age Lull.

As is discussed below, archaeologists now recognize that early medieval settlement in Ireland involves more than just ringforts. But, dispersed enclosed farmsteads appeared the right choice to an enormous number of people for several centuries at the beginning of the early Middle Ages. As Finbar McCormick notes, the protected and scattered nature of these farmsteads is also uncommon in western Europe: "they are a unique response to the value system of Ireland" (2008: 216). Understanding the values animating these settlements is a key aspect of understanding early medieval social dynamics. One way of delineating values of ringfort and other such settlements is to consider morphology.

As the name implies, generally ringforts have circular enclosures, but geometric precision does not seem to have been an overwhelming concern. Oval and other sub-circular variations are known (Edwards 1990: xx, Kinsella 2010). Given the enormous number known, ringforts are also remarkably uniform in size. One study of ringforts in the south-west midlands found that, 84 percent fell between 20 and 44 meters in diameter (Stout 1997: 15). The enclosed space is typically devoted to structures associated with a familial-scale farming enterprise: habitations, outbuildings, work zones, and livestock areas. A study of the insect remains from Deer Park Farms (Co. Antrim) confirms the presence of livestock (Kenward et al. 2011). Examples without structures are known and likely represent enclosures devoted entirely to penning livestock (McCormick 1995).

Over the past three decades, numerous studies have focused on social inequality as the animating value associated with ringforts. The basic argument is very similar to the prevailing interpretation of Adomnán's miraculous cattle as tools for consolidation of power over others. That similarity is not coincidental. Ringforts—as places for rearing and consuming cattle—are spaces where social stratification would have been elaborated.

Matthew Stout has demonstrated with statistical rigor that morphological and topographical variations in ringforts correlate with the divisions among the free social grades defined in early law tracts. Morphology and artifact assemblages vary in ways consistent with distinctions in legal status (Stout 1992 and 1997). Such analyses provide important support for the argument that ringforts were spaces for the elaboration of social inequalities. But, as with Adomnán's miraculous cattle, that interpretation must contend with ways in which they also do not.

The evidence for status differences is clear. But, equally, the gap between the highest and the average is miniscule compared to other regions of medieval Europe. Morphologically, little separates one from the next. Stout finds that the mean for the internal diameter of ringforts is approximately thirty meters and that higher status settlements do indeed have a somewhat larger internal diameter (forty-seven meters). Not an awe inspiring basis for establishing lordly dependency. As was noted earlier, number of enclosing banks is one of the few readily discernable differences in ringfort morphology; however, even this feature is not precisely correlated with other indicators of status (Warner 1988: 59).

Housing fits a similar pattern. C. J. Lynn's study of house construction in early medieval Ireland found no difference in style or quality of construction between high, ordinary, and low status sites as described in documents or as identified in excavation (1994: 91). Lynn did find correlation between the diameter of houses and site status, but—as with the diameter of enclosures—

the difference is small: the mode diameter is six meters. One particularly large structure, from Moynagh Lough, is ten meters wide. Compare such differences to contemporary Britain. The Moynagh house has somewhat less than three times the area of Lynn's mode house size. By contrast, the hall at Yeavering has six times the area of the middle-sized Chalton house. Differences in status were marked among Irish houses according to other markers of status, but neither Lynn nor Stout finds evidence for substantial inequality.

One possible solution is that inequalities are more evident elsewhere in the landscape and that exclusive focus on ringforts has obscured divisions. The best studied alternative sites are crannógs: lake settlements often on artificial islands but also along lake shores (see O'Sullivan 1998 and Fredengren 2002). High-status crannógs certainly existed (e.g., Henken 1950). Subsequent work has demonstrated that feasting occurred at crannógs (McCormick 2002b) and that some acted as redistribution and patronage centers (O'Sullivan 1998). But, other studies have shown that crannógs were also occupied by less exalted social strata (Fredengren et al. 2004) and that some were specialized habitations for metal-working (O'Sullivan 2009). But, the overall degree of inequality is not dramatically different from the pattern known from ringforts. Another long-recognized enclosure type, promontory forts, enclose headlands, or topographic heights along coasts and rivers, but also inland (e.g., Barry 1981). Over time, interpretation of promontory forts has shifted from a focus on military refugia to locales for organizing/controlling trade networks (O'Sullivan and Breen 2007).

Recent excavations have identified approximately one hundred enclosed settlements that do not fit the patterns found with ringforts and crannógs. These "irregular enclosures" are larger than typical ringforts and of a more variable shape (for review see Coyne and Collins 2003, Kinsella 2010, and O'Sullivan et al. 2014: 55–57). The group includes the settlement cemeteries mentioned above and sites without obvious sacred elements. Their size challenges assumptions that Ireland's settlement pattern is composed of dispersed familial-scale farmstead, consensus on their socio-economic identity is still emerging. On analogy with villages elsewhere in Europe, they could signify the presence of a subordinate class not marked by ringforts. But, Kinsella offers a compelling argument that, in social terms, these enclosures mirror the qualities of ringforts and monasteries more than they oppose them (Kinsella 2010). Unenclosed settlement remains something of an enigma and questions about the degree of inequality in early medieval Ireland certainly remain open. But, at least based on current data, little reason to expect radical differences from the patterns known from other sites.

The absence of significant inequalities in settlement morphology raises difficult questions about Ireland's relationship to wider European trends.

Frankish territories are usually seen as the most emblematic of key trends in western Europe. Here, the Roman empire withered into the hands of local elites, providing effective tools for establishing the social inequalities that lead to Merovingian and Carolingian kingdoms (Geary 1986, Hodges 2012, McCormick 2001, Wickham 2005). These locales provide hospitable terrain for seeing the workings of deep inequalities.

The problem is recognizing ways that Ireland is not Gaul without slipping into colonial dichotomies between primitive and advanced. Recognizing that Ireland is different from "core" areas of medieval Europe can collapse into views of Ireland as behind the times. Likewise, arguments for participation in Continental dynamics can flatten important contrasts so that differences become insignificant noise. Escaping the pull of these dichotomies is an ongoing challenge, but any account of early medieval Ireland has to recon with differences across medieval Europe between Ireland and Gaul.

The political units of early medieval Ireland are small compared to Merovingian and Carolingian realms. While over-kingdoms come into play from the seventh or eighth century through the first millennium, Ireland was divided into one hundred fifty kingdoms that average just over five hundred square kilometers. Stout makes several observations about these territories that bear on understanding inequalities within and among them (2017: 54). The Irish term for such a territory is *túath*, which Stout defines as a "community of farmers . . . sufficiently large and self-assured to refer to their leader as a king." He observes that if a typical *túath* were round, a ringfort at its center would only be thirteen kilometers from its border. Little evidence exists archaeologically for consolidation of such units into larger territories, particularly in the early centuries of the early Middle Ages. Stout puts such evidence in perspective by observing that, in 771, nine kings were in competition for an area 1/27 the size of the realm Charlemagne ruled for decades (Stout 2017: 124). One of the most celebrated high-status or royal sites in early medieval Ireland is Lagore (Co. Meath). It is rightfully and usefully understood in terms of social inequality. But, Lagore is also not Aachen. Understanding the significance of that fact is no less difficult than understanding Mauss's ideas about gifts. But, it is no less important. Closer examination of the values about cattle and the economics of ringforts will illuminate ways forward.

Cattle and Clientage Values

Coming to terms with Ireland—medieval and otherwise—has long been a matter of coming to terms with flows of cattle through its landscapes. The species looms large in imaginations about Ireland across millennia. Pomponius Mela, the Roman geographer noted earlier, comments on the extraordinarily high quality of Irish pastures, noting that animals could eat to bursting on them (Stout 2017: 14). More than a millennium later, colonial commentators in the Elizabethan era make a remarkably similar set of identifications between Ireland and cattle (Soderberg 2021). Conrad Arensberg and Solon Kimball (1940) define early twentieth-century Ireland in terms of cattle flowing from the west of Ireland eastward and, ultimately, to British meat markets.

Undoubtedly, this long history can imbalance interpretations of cattle in early medieval Ireland. But, even accounting for such issues, cattle are fundamental to first millennium Irish values and movements. Medieval Irish agriculture was heavily oriented on cattle production. Early medieval Irish value systems are anchored in cattle. Into the sixteenth century, cattle were an acceptable unit of wealth in parts of Ireland (McCormick 1991). They were a means to wealth and status. Contracts, tribute, and fines were settled in numbers of cows. Ringforts were constructed to protect cattle (McCormick 1995).

As Finbar McCormick observes, particularly in the period prior to 800, cows were "the core of the value system" (McCormick 2008: 211). The nature of that value system is evident in understanding ringforts as a product of the need to protect cattle from theft because cattle raiding is "more political competition than criminal activity" (McCormick 2008: 211). With political competition as the animating value, both earth and cattle are propelled from place to place by efforts to build social capital and prevent its loss.

The same logic organizes a less obviously violent form of cattle movement. Clientage involved the transfer of cattle and other goods with reciprocal obligations. Historians identify two basic forms of clientage: free-client relationships which could be broken and did not entail enduring subordination (*sóerchéile*); base-client relationships had heavy penalties if the terms were not met and required re-payment in terms of labor and hosting the lord (*dóerchéile*) (Kelly 1988: 29–33). Both lay and ecclesiastical forms existed.

As Donnchadh Ó Cróinín, writes, "The basis of [early medieval Irish] society is the institution of clientship" (1995: 141). Clientage animated the movement of crops, livestock, raw materials, labor, military service, and protection around the landscape. Cattle, as the highest status domestic species and a unit of wealth, were the premier basis of clientage transfers. Base-clientage has often been viewed as a fulcrum leveraging inequality in early medieval Ireland. Accumulating cattle guided status, as increased numbers of cattle created increased numbers of clients, which in turn increased the return flow of cattle in the form of renders. Likewise, the size of the grant given was linked to the legal status of the client. To the extent that clientage is identified with relationships of dependency, such cattle movements create cattle-lords, which in turn creates an important set of tools for centralizing wealth and power. If clientage is taken as the basis of early medieval Irish society, as the value animating economies, then cattle-lords with the power they gain via cattle movements become a synecdoche for early medieval Irish society.

But, that conclusion depends on the viability of equating clientage and subordination. Discourse on clientage is generally in accord with the prevailing interpretation of Adomnán's miraculous cattle. Fergus Kelly, for example, states that "It seems from the law-texts that by far the most important transfer of foodstuffs in early Irish society was the food-rent which a client (*céile*) paid to a lord (*flaith*) in return for a fief. . . . As far as we can judge from the texts, the system weighed heavily in favor of the lord" (Kelly 1997: 320). Nerys Patterson arrives at much the same conclusion: "the contract between lord and base-client had a number of features which tended to entrap the client in the relationship" (1994: 176). Through clientage, society becomes "divided into proto-classes by control of the distribution of cattle to farmers" (Patterson 1995: 132). Michele Comber observed that "Early Irish society was strictly hierarchical. . . . The whole of society was divided into social classes, each one tied to its neighbors by the circulation of goods and services" (Comber 2001: 76–77).

Such views are undoubtedly accurate but the problem with such views is that same as identifying power inequalities from the morphology of ringforts. Despite the compelling the logic of this argument about the values of clientage, at some point, it must bump up against the absence of significant inequalities. Scholars have certainly noted discordant qualities to clientage. Kelly describes numerous elements of clientage relationships that curb a patron's coercive power (1988: 26–33). Likewise, Stout identifies significant differences between clientage ties and the premier instrument of subordination in feudal economies: vassalage (2017: 100). Early medieval Irish clients were commonly kinsmen. Base-clients could enter into relationships with as many as three lords. Free clients could break client bonds with little penalty. He concludes that clientage fueled social dynamics similar to fosterage: both were "a cement which bound the individual members of a *túath* together" (2017: 100). Bart Jaski made such mutualistic or leveling aspects an important facet of his perspective on clientage (e.g., Jaski 2000: 89–112). Similarly, Dáibhí Ó Cróinín recognizes that the social dynamics associated with that core are simply dependency: "In a tribal economy where wealth is reckoned in terms of land and livestock, the standard of living among the aristocracy cannot have differed very much from that of the ordinary farmer" (1995: 142).

Such alternative clientage values contradict the argument that clientage creates inequalities in just the same manner as ringfort morphology (see Soderberg 2006). In both cases, it is difficult to identify how the supposed tools of subordination are used to bring about subordination. Patterson recognized the paradox when she asked "how lords, being possessed of coercive power, were not more oppressive to the peasants than they were" (1995: 133).

McCormick (2008 and 2014) provides a compelling resolution to Patterson's paradox. He begins by observing that law tracts are very specific about the foundation of the value system associated with cattle. Status and wealth did not depend on cattle. McCormick emphasizes that, for the dairy-oriented economy of early medieval Ireland, cows were the actual "unit of value" or even more specifically the unit is cows with calves, since cows would not lactate without a calf present (2008: 211). Cattle herds become a vehicle for sustaining cows and calves, which in turn are vehicles for maximizing milk production. Managing the production and movement of milk is the fundamental basis for wealth and social capital. McCormick sees them as milk-lords.

The point is to focus attention on the core of the value system. McCormick's discussion of milk leads to an argument that milk (and cows) functioned as a nascent form of commodity in early medieval Ireland. Building from his identification of ringforts as structures for protecting cows, he argues that milk functioned as currency in early medieval Ireland. Specifically, cows/milk filled all the roles that Daniel Snell (1995) defines for a primitive currency: standard of value, medium of exchange, means of payment, and a vehicle for accumulating/storing wealth.

Neither Snell nor McCormick use the term primitive. Snell prefers chronological terms such as early or ancient. But, his views on media of exchange are teleological in the sense that improvement occurs over time. In this formulation, cows/milk are inefficient commodities. They are expensive to store and their increase is limited by their biology. A given landscape can only feed so many. Cows die and milk spoils. In this context, relative to subsequent monetary economies, cows are "singularly ineffective as a means of accumulating wealth in the form of surplus" (McCormick 2008: 219).

This observation neatly resolves the conundrum Patterson raises about cattle-lords. As milk-lords, their inability to use the tools at hand becomes explicable. The problem is the tools, not the lords. Milk-lords were structurally inhibited from fulfilling lordly strategies of subordination. The value-movement arrangements associated with cattle and enclosure in early medieval Ireland offered both possibilities and limitations for gaining status and consolidating power.

In addition to resolving Patterson's paradox, McCormick uses the replacement of cattle currency with more efficient currencies after 800 as an explanation for lords gaining more centralized control in these later centuries. Before exploring that facet of his argument, it is important to consider the argument in light of Graeberian values and the quest for alternatives to Veblen's globules.

McCormick's milk-lords are animated by a single value system: maximizing lordliness. Within Snell's system, alternatives are either irrelevant or artifacts of a passing age. Either way the narrative is filled only with Veblen's globules. Variation over space and time only occurs in the extent to which players are able to full live into the role. The value scheme associated with milk-lords is liable to the concerns defined in the introduction. It may elide rather than explain discordant elements.

Consider A. T. Lucas views on cattle values. He was clear that "an extraordinary preoccupation" with "cows as yielders of milk" existed (Lucas 1989: 3–4). But, Lucas takes what we would now call a more semiotic or phenomenological approach to cows and their calves: They were "so interfused with the very concept of existence that they automatically presented themselves to the minds of the people of the time" (1989: 14). Because cattle were a common experience, they formed a basis for understanding and interacting with others. Lucas did not work in terms of anthropological concepts such as meaningscapes (imaginary worlds) and theories of value, but his view of cattle accords with the Maussian perspectives described in the introduction. Lucas catalogs all different groups who understood themselves and their engagements with others via cows. The values cattle acquire are a variable as any Graeber describes. St. Brigit's sanctity was marked by being bathed in milk, cattle mourned at funerals, good kings brought an abundance of milk, and poets cursed opponents with cows that gave no milk (Lucas 1989: 6–14). McCormick views cows and milk as an instrument for bringing about a particular social order. Lucas views cows and milk as a medium through which social dynamics are negotiated.

If clientage were simply vassalage, milk-lords would be sufficient. But clientage was not vassalage. The lending relationships motivating cattle movements are far more variable than subordination. That situation recalls Mauss's uneasy territory where partners remain strangers in the sense they are neither friend nor foe. In this context, it is also worth noting that such views of clientage tend to either avoid religion all together or to reduce it to ideology. Cattle are woven into many different facets of life in early medieval Ireland. Cattle value would also have been.

A fundamental motivation of the grounded approach to religion developed in chapter 3 is giving those everyday sorts of activities the same social heft as grand strategies for using religion as an instrument of control. But, Aidan O'Sullivan and Triona Nicholl (2011) highlight the key issue in an Irish context by approaching domestic architecture as theatrical spaces for the performance of social roles. As was noted in the introduction, a key insight of practice-based theories of religions is the entanglement of what earlier views saw as separate spheres of profane and sacred. As Richard Bradley's concept of ritualization emphasizes, houses are places of ritualization as much as a saint's shrine (Bradely 2005). Grinding oats, milking cattle, or any of the other activities set within an ordinary ringfort are sacral. They create Graeberian values.

This view opens an alternative solution to Patterson's paradox. The problem is not that lords failed to act lordly or that they lacked the proper tools to meet their lordly aspirations. The problem is casting social dynamics in terms of lords and peasants. People are not acting like lords and peasants because they were not just lords and peasants. Inhabitants of ringforts need not be defined as lords in ways they were clearly not. To the extent that people did act like milk-lords, considering milk as a commodity is enormously useful. The problem is also accommodating the circumstance that milk is always something other as well.

Pam Crabtree singles out the work of Susan Oosthuizen (e.g., 2016) as an effective alternative to top-down models for social dynamics in early Anglo-Saxon England. Oosthuizen builds her more mutualistic view of social dynamics through a focus on shared pasture rights. These practices foster horizontal forms of governance that compliment elite-directed models. This approach resonates well with the need for associating a variety of social dynamics with clientage. As will become clear in subsequent chapters, as cattle movements are a foundation of early medieval social dynamics, this variability cascades outward to all aspects of society, particularly the consideration of how walking cattle made Clonmacnoise sacred.

Early Medieval, Phase 2 (~800 to ~1100)

The discussion so far mainly describes conditions in the first centuries of the early medieval period. After the eighth century, the landscape begins to change considerably. Norse trading/raiding activities commence at the end of the eighth century. An associated surge in silver into Ireland increased market-style commodity exchange and, eventually, the emergence of coinage towards the end of the millennium (Sheehan 1998). Coastal trade settlements flourished, including Woodstown, Waterford, and Dublin. At a more modest scale, after centuries in which housing is circular, rectilinear housing makes an appearance in the ninth century and becomes the norm in some areas over the next several centuries (Lynn 1994).

A strong consensus exists that political centralization and social inequality grew significantly across these centuries (e.g., Graham 1993, Ó Corráin 1995, Doherty 1998, O'Keeffe 2000). Texts record provincial kings having increased success at expanding their spheres of control. Stout considers this period as the point when substantive high-kingship is established (Stout 2017: 134–39).

The growth of centralized rule, larger and territorially based kingdoms, and commodity-based exchanges are generally seen as related political-economic processes in which kin-based (socially constructed) cycles of exchange become increasingly oriented around a concept of gift-exchange as a mechanism through which elites gain control of exchange cycles through controlling the movement of socially valued goods (preciosities). The emergence of more monetized vehicles of exchange—silver bullion and eventually coins—is seen as providing less socially constrained cycles of exchange and greater possibilities for accumulation/storage of wealth (Doherty 1980, Sheehan 1998, Kerr 2009). Doherty captures the sense of profound social transition in his discussion of the disenchantment of rulership as sacralized models of kingship gave way to proto-feudal models of rule (Doherty 2005. See also O'Keeffe 2000). As was discussed in the introduction, these models of 'gift-exchange' fostering centralization and the emergence of centralized states have a long history in medieval studies.

For Ireland, colonial paradigms stunted consideration of such processes. For much of the twentieth century, Ireland was considered archaic until the advent of the Anglo-Norman conquest in the twelfth century. That process was considered to have introduced "Modernity" to the island. Cities, monetary economies, intensive agricultural strategies, and a host of other features were thought to have arrived in the twelfth century. Since the 1970s, scholars have repeatedly demonstrated that traits once thought absent were present in Ireland well before the twelfth century. For example, in 1980, Charles Doherty argued that market style socio-economies date well back into the early medieval period. A major orientation in the discussion of urbanism in Ireland has been countering suggestions that early medieval Ireland was inimical to cities (see below). Attention to hoards in early medieval Ireland has been similarly oriented toward tracing the emergence of fully monetary forms of exchange (Sheehan 1998 and Valante 2008). While in some sense it might seem trivial to show that Ireland is experiencing the same processes at much the same time as elsewhere in medieval Europe, given the wider discourse about the island, such arguments have been—and continue to be—entirely necessary.

This background is an important part of the context for McCormick's view that cattle lost their role as the unit of socio-economic value. McCormick and Murray observed that, after circa 800, the uniform dominance of cattle in faunal assemblages starts to fracture (2007: figure 5.3). The exact nature of the change varies from location to location. In some areas, pigs become more prevalent; in others, sheep do. Variability in species composition suggests growing variability in agricultural strategies.

This shift in animal agriculture coincides with significant changes in the settlement pattern. As was noted earlier, between 15 percent and 20 percent of known ringforts have raised central areas. They are largely a phenomenon of this second phase of the early medieval period. By contrast, univallate construction peaked in the seventh century. Thomas Kerr (2007) defines two contrasts between univallate and raised settlements: (1) raised raths tend to be occupied at the scale of centuries, and univallate ringforts are occupied on a scale of decades; (2) raised raths are associated with concentrations of arable land and univallate ringforts are not. McCormick amplifies the contrast between these settlement types by noting that the raised interior made the original defensive function of ringforts obsolete. They could not effectively protect cattle. He sees the switch from flat to raised forms at sites such as Deer Park Farms and Knowth as abandonment of such defensive capabilities as the value of cattle shifted (2008: 220–21).

The discussion of association of raised raths is part of a wider reconsideration of arable agriculture in the early medieval period. For much of the twentieth century, arable agriculture was thought to be relatively insignificant prior to the Anglo-Norman conquest (e.g., Duignan 1944). Research over the past decade has proven conclusively that arable agriculture is a pervasive component of early medieval Irish strategies (McClatchie et al. 2015). The best evidence for intensification of arable agriculture occurs with crop processing technology. Kilns were used to speed the drying process and reduce spoilage, a particularly important innovation in relatively cool and cloudy areas such as northwestern Europe. Corn-drying kilns are present in Ireland from the Iron Age, with a steady rise in their numbers up until perhaps the seventh century, when numbers decline. Reasons for this decline are uncertain—particularly given a general impression of intensifying agriculture in this period—but Mick Monk and Orla Power (2012) suggest that it may be related to the introduction of a more efficient variety of kiln and reorganization of control. At roughly the same period, water mills also become an increasingly common phenomenon in Ireland. Niall Brady identifies the peak period of mill construction between 775 and 850 (Brady 2006).

In sum, beginning circa 800, Ireland experiences a decline in the prevalence of cattle in faunal assemblages, the decline in construction of flat ringforts, and the increase in raised raths. McCormick sees this convergence in the context of other arguments that a proto-feudal socio-economy developed in this second phase of the early medieval period. He grounds the logic in the values associated with agriculture. Whereas cattle were a "singularly ineffective" mechanism for accumulating wealth, arable agriculture had far greater potential because it is more easily stored and transported (2008: 218). Taken in combination with the expansion of bullion in this period, he associates the shift with a step toward a value system better suited to establishing centralized control. As Stout writes: "Grain-growing and the grain trade became the economic drivers of this modernizing Irish economy" (2017: 162).

Pollen studies often create problems for assertions that arable transformation occurred in this period. Pollen studies have found abundant evidence for increased woodland clearance in this period (Hall 1993, Hall 2005, Newman et al. 2007). Perhaps most notably, Valerie Hall (1993) found evidence of extensive woodland clearance in Co. Antrim in this period, which is in the area where Kerr established the connection between raised raths and soil suited to arable agriculture. McClung and Plunkett present evidence that a surge in cereal production is evident in the mid-ninth century (2020: 24). But, it is important to recognize that significant regional variation exists. As will be discussed in the next chapter, one of the best studied bogs in Ireland is near Clonmacnoise. A different pattern holds there.

Similarly, the change in the prevalence of cattle in faunal assemblages also has significant regional variability. As with the pollen data, the model works best for Ulster, where from the eighth century onwards, sheep and pigs predominate. In Meath, assemblages do not diverge from the early pattern until the eleventh or twelfth centuries. Patterns from the west are a bit more complex to assess due to sample size issues, but McCormick argues that they match patterns observed for Ulster, with cattle declining and sheep/pig increasing as the centuries pass. Data from the northwest and the south are too sparse. (For discussion, see McCormick et al. 2011.)

McCormick understands the cultural displacement of cattle in terms of ecological and social processes fostering regional difference in early medieval Ireland before the Norse arrived. Ecological differences encourage different means of "accumulating wealth" in different regions (McCormick 2008: 219). From this perspective, the displacement of cattle as the central measure of value is a key aspect of the transformation to social centralization and a commodity economy. If cattle are "ineffective as a means of accumulating wealth," shifting to arable agriculture and other more easily commodified products provided the means for maximizing efficiency (2008: 219 and McCormick 2014). Antrim and Galway are better suited to alternative means of accumulation: sheep grazing. But, the grasslands of Meath foster enduring cattle grazing (McCormick et al. 2011: 95).

McCormick's argument is an extension of Charles Doherty's work on the prevalence of commodified exchange in early medieval Ireland (e.g., Doherty 1980), which, in turn, is an extension of Philip Grierson's 1959 integration of Marcel Mauss's *The Gift* into medieval European archaeology. Kerr et al.

provide a thorough history of the impact that Grierson's Mauss had (2013: 41–71). In general, they are an effort to explore social dynamics in early medieval Ireland along the same trajectory that Hodges describes for early medieval Europe: Aspirant elites manipulate gift-exchange processes, such as clientage, in an effort to gain control. The control situates them to take advantage of more disembedded forms of exchange as they arise and they increasingly shuck social constraints.

While such narratives yield considerable insights, advocates have not reckoned with the ways they depend on a misreading of Mauss. They do not recon with the range of values that the dependence on strangers that accompanies the development of social complexity entails. Just as seeing lords constrained by economic modes pre-800 is inadequate, defining the later centuries only in terms of expanding lordliness is inadequate. This issue is particularly clear in discourse on one of the most significant changes to Ireland in the second part of the early medieval periods: the proliferation of urban centers.

URBANISM IN EARLY MEDIEVAL IRELAND

I have deliberately limited discussion of aggregated settlement and urbanism thus far. The chronology and causes of urbanization remain among the most contested aspects of medieval Ireland. For much of the twentieth century, early medieval Ireland was considered ineluctably rural (i.e., having no aggregated settlements and a subsistence oriented agricultural economy). As Daniel Binchy wrote: "urban civilization . . . remained quite foreign to the Celtic-speaking peoples of these islands until it was more or less imposed on them by foreign conquerors [in the twelfth century]" (Binchy 1962: 55). Since the 1960s, efforts to push urbanism into the first millennium and into the workings of indigenous society have been both relentless and highly successful. A stable consensus now exists that urban settlements and other forms of aggregation prospered at least from the ninth century and that, while Norse activities were an important factor, they were entwined with Irish society (Bradley 1988, Bradley 2010, Wallace 2008).

Less consensus exists on the question of whether urbanism also grew around monastic centers such as Clonmacnoise. Since the 1970s some scholars have argued that another path to urbanism existed in Ireland. Whereas Dublin was seen as fueled by commodity production and international trade, Clonmacnoise was seen as fueled by sacred practices.

When I entered the debate about the possibility of monastic urbanism circa 2000, I assumed that disagreements were primarily evidentiary: if we could get some excavation data parallel to what had been discovered at Hiberno-

Norse settlements, then the debate would be settled. But, as evidence for urban qualities at early medieval monasteries accumulated and rejection remained strong, I learned that scepticism about monastic urbanism ran deeper.

To many, the very possibility of urban qualities at monasteries was illegitimate. Beyond did not, urbanism could not develop there. With that conceptual divergence, no matter what evidence becomes available, opponents are stuck talking past each other about what qualifies a settlement as urban. Reflecting on this circumstance, Edel Bhreathnach has observed that discourse on urbanism in early medieval Ireland would "make more sense" if it were to move from taxonomies of urbanism to "a more universal and anthropological approach" (2014: 26). This section is an effort to facilitate that effort.

The first step involves gaining clarity on the tales built into the anthropological approaches that have been central to understanding medieval urbanism since at least the mid-twentieth century. As was discussed in the introduction, a dominant model for urbanization involves gift-exchange mediated centralization (e.g., Hodges 2012). Understanding of Hiberno-Norse urbanism grew from this context.

The first Viking raids in Ireland are recorded in 795. By the 840s, records indicate the development of relatively permanent settlements, such as Woodstown 6, where a D-shaped enclosure contained evidence of intensive settlement and manufacturing evidence. Finds include rivets for ship repair, bone and amber working, silver ingots, and more than two hundred lead balance weights (Russell and Harrison 2011). Such finds signal the profound social and economic changes spreading through Ireland in the ninth century. As Stout observes, "Pre-Viking Ireland was made up of communities of farmers. This description, still apt in 800, no longer applied a century later" (Stout 2017: 163). During that century, Norse settlements became fully enmeshed with the wider Irish landscape and grew into fully urban centers during the course of the ninth century (Wallace 2008).

As was discussed in the introduction, this model of urbanism owes a great debt to Richard Hodge's *Dark Age Economics* (1982) and Philip Grierson's views on Mauss (1959). But, gaining perspective on this model for urbanism—and its rejection of the possibility of urbanism at Clonmacnoise—requires setting the concept within a longer history of debates on urbanism. It's relationship to Max Weber's views on urbanism is particularly important. For Weber, cities emerge from the combined forces of a market economy and a highly centralized social organization, a combination which gives rulers strong coercive powers (e.g., Weber 1958). In essence, Weber defines power as "the probability that one actor within a social relationship will be in a position to carry out his will despite resistance, regardless of the basis on which the probability rests" (Weber 1964: 152). For Weber, urban centers foster a "complex of domination" (Graham 1987: 3).

With the growth of that complex, cities become walled realms foreign to rural communities. The basic cause of the division is a consumer/producer dichotomy. Weberian cities are the province of consumers: priests, politicos, and tradesmen who could not feed themselves. City dwellers had to consolidate control over a rural hinterland to secure food and raw materials. Urbanism becomes practices that subsume "ruralism" into the rationality and social dynamics of the city. Participation requires becoming subsumed into the urban economy as subordinate producers. This formulation led Moses Finley to characterize Weber's cities as having a "parasitic" relationship with hinterlands (Finley 1985: 125).

Such models of the values animating urbanism have been enormously valuable at illuminating evidence from excavations at coastal trade centers in Ireland. Considerable attention has been given to evidence for intensive craft production and exchange as evidence for the emergence of commodified exchange mechanisms. One house from the Fishamble St. excavations in Dublin contains remains from working Baltic amber into jewelry (Wallace 2016: 290–96). Others were devoted to manufacturing bone combs. The intensity of production suggests a strong focus on production for exchange. As was the case at Woodstown, Hiberno-Norse towns yield large numbers of balance weights, silver ingots, and coins. John Sheehan places the 108 known hoards dating between 800 and 1000 in the context of "establishment of a commercially orientated economy" through exchange of silver by weight (Sheehan 1998: 197). Dublin has the earliest recorded coin minting in Ireland.

Dublin also produced vivid evidence for the commodification of land, with a series of twelve trapezoidal plots consistently marked through twelve reconstruction events in the Fishamble St. excavations (Wallace 2004). Similar evidence of plot boundary was found in the Temple Bar area of Dublin (Simpson 1999). Wallace contends that the fixed nature of each "plot"—through at least two hundred years and twelve different building episodes—indicates that "the plots were the products of an ordered society in which urban property was respected and its regulation possibly controlled" (1992: 36). Archaeological indicators for "control of access" and documentary evidence for the conception of plots as units of owned property bolster this contention (Wallace 1992: 40–43). Elsewhere in later periods, such developments are linked to profound social and economic changes associated with the emergence of a market economy (e.g., Leone 1988, Johnson 1996). The Dublin plots delimited a parcel of land and suggest that each unit of land had an existence independent of its owner. The consistency of the boundaries over time and the lack of good parallels in earlier periods suggest a profound social change associated with the emergence of Dublin and the advancement of a market economy.

Seeing Hiberno-Norse towns as centers for such transformations also led to consideration of how such Weberian centers might have transformed their hinterlands. As was noted in the introduction, cities cannot feed themselves. They must find outsiders to supply food and raw materials. Zooarchaeology has a long tradition of investigating how such associations worked (see Zeder 1988). I decided to become a zooarchaeologist after reading Finbar McCormick's account of provisioning Dublin and the transformations triggered (1983).

People in Hiberno-Norse towns could have kept some goats and pigs, but the bulk of animals needed to walk into the city from elsewhere. Archaeologists have shown that Hiberno-Norse towns were provisioned with elderly female cattle and other animal products such as deer antler from the surrounding countryside. Details about these discoveries are provided in chapter 4, but the core conclusion is that farmers in early medieval Ireland focused on dairy production and herd maintenance, which lead to cattle herds dominated by reproductive females and their calves. The cattle remains excavated from such sites are usually composed of a large number of elderly female cattle who had come to the end of their productive lives and a significant number of young male cattle culled after weaning.

Excavations of Hiberno-Norse urban centers yield mostly elderly female cattle. McCormick concludes that Dublin was supplied by cattle raised elsewhere in what he calls "a modified dairying economy" (1983: 261). This term refers to a transitional organization between a subsistence-oriented dairying economy where meat is an incidental product and a specialized cattle economy where production focuses on "large quantities of cattle for the Dublin meat market" (264). Rhoda Kavanagh's study of the horse in Viking Ireland associates reliance on the horse with a process of economic specialization as well (1988). Shiobhán Geraghty (1996) has identified other products brought to Dublin through her analysis of botanical remains from Fishamble Street excavations. Based on data from latrines, Patrick Wallace estimates that the early medieval Dubliners would have required twenty tons of moss each year to clean themselves (Wallace 2016: 207).

Getting elderly cattle and moss to flow requires establishing relationships—values—that redirect earlier flow patterns. Urbanism requires a theory of strangers. From a Weberian perspective, rural farmers are outsiders to the socio-economic dynamics of the urban center. These strangers are transformed into producers increasingly dependent on urban dynamics as they increasingly produce for urban markets. For early medieval Ireland, this Weberian perspective completes the transformation of the cattle-lords discussed earlier. Cattle-based clientage fostered economic inequality as cattle-lords gained control over clients. That dynamic grew as cattle-as-currency gave way to more "efficient" exchange media during the eighth century. McCormick emphasizes that arable products are better suited to centralized control. Such developments are the core dynamic of Weberian models. They provide the thin end of the wedge marginalizing the social constrains of "gift-economies" and opening space for socio-economic transformation to "disembedded" economies of the market. "Primitive valuables" created "the moment when a socially embedded economy became disembedded" and, via that process, market towns became "the hallmark of a non-kin-based political strategy" rulers in the mold of Charlemagne used to consolidate power via collections of currency-based tribute and taxes (Hodges 2012: 6).

Here we arrive at the second sense in which Bhreathnach offers a way forward in observing that Irish urbanism makes more sense if scholars take "a more universal and anthropological approach" (2014: 26). The possibility of sanctuary cities only makes sense if one is willing to acknowledge inadequacies in the narrative of urbanism just reviewed. Many have found the concept of monastic urbanism incoherent or a retrograde turn to outdated models (e.g., Graham 1987, Valante 1998, Etchingham 2011, Ó Carragáin 2014. But also see Maddox 2016). This sense of incoherence and misplaced nostalgia results from not recognizing how monastic urbanism fits into the anthropological discourse on urbanism reviewed in the introduction.

The term monastic town derives from medieval documents describing monasteries as having urban qualities and associating them with sanctuary cities described in Joshua and other Deuteronomic histories. Biblical sanctuary cities were an influential concept in medieval Ireland, as elsewhere in medieval Europe (Shoemaker 2011: 54).[5] A seventh- or eighth-century Irish text "De civitatibus refugii" assembles biblical, patristic, and other practices for taking sanctuary. A map of the Promised Land (*terre repromissionis*) with sanctuary cities marked is inserted into a ninth-century edition of the text (see O'Loughlin 2006). Offering sanctuary has long been recognized as an important role for Clonmacnoise and other monasteries (e.g., Stokes 1898). An entry in the *Annals of Clonmacnoise* for 1060 describes how two groups "came to prey Clonvickenos, and tooke certaine captives from the place called the Crosse na Streaptra and killed twoo there, a layman and a spirituall" (Murphy 1896 [1993]: 178). These outrages were quickly avenged, and the people returned.

Perhaps the most referenced contemporary comment on cities in Ireland is Cogitosus's observation on Kildare circa 700: "Since numberless people assemble within it and since a city gets its name from the fact that many people congregate there, it is a vast and metropolitan city. . . . [T]ogether with all its outlying suburbs, it is the safest city of refuge in the whole land of the Irish for all fugitives" (Connolly and Picard 1987: 26).

Two features of Cogitosus's perspective stand out as contrasts to Weberian urbanism.[6] First, the city is a place of congregation, not alienation. Sounding rather like a modern archaeologist arguing about the nature of urbanism, in at least one edition of the text, Cogitosus, notes that Kildare had no walls, asks if walls were necessary to qualify a settlement as a *civitas*.[7] Cogitosus points to a different relationship between rural and urban peoples than found in Weber.

Second, Kildare was a place of sanctuary. Frequently in discussions of medieval concepts of sanctuary, fugitives are identified with criminals. Sanctuary offered a safe harbor from punishment until wrongs can be properly adjudicated (e.g., Shoemaker 2011). But, as will be discussed in detail in chapter 6, some studies have recognized that such criminals are unlikely to have been the majority of those seeking sanctuary. T. B. Lambert (2012) finds that in Anglo-Saxon England sanctuary is entangled with hospitality, age-old and pan-human practices guiding how guests are treated in the household. Charles Doherty (1985) makes a similar set of associations by connecting medieval sanctuary with prehistoric practices of encircling communal gathering spaces with a ditch. That focus provides the basis for a different theory about strangers and urbanism that came to prominence in the 1970s and 1980s.

At the same, Charles Doherty used this intersection of urbanism and sanctuary to craft an alternative approach to urbanism from the perspective then emerging for *emporia* (Doherty 1985. See also Butlin 1977). International commodity trade was a raison d'etre for emporia. For monastic towns, religion was. Doherty elaborated his argument using Wheatley's concept of cities as "replicas of the cosmos," which makes them an image of a cosmogony (*imago mundi*) and a means of bringing about its accomplishment (*axis mundi*). For Christian settings, this general formulation is familiar from the concept of the celestial and the earthly Jerusalem, a metaphor found in the earliest descriptions of churches, in Bede, and in early medieval Irish iconography.[8] Doherty connected Cogitosus's description of Kildare as a *civitas refugii* with Wheatley's concept of the sacred center: "[the Church] was an institution in a way that early medieval kingship could never be. . . . [S]uch islands of asylum prevented the power of the kings from totally embracing all of their subjects" (Doherty 1985: 55 and 70).

Wheatley wrote from a sense that prevailing theories of urbanism were drawn from a narrow range of "Western" thinkers and case studies, which he saw as unduly influenced by Weber. Wheatley developed his concept of ceremonial centers as an alternative. Unfortunately, Wheatley drew heavily on esoteric Eliadian cosmologies. One enormous problem for appreciating Wheatley's theory of urbanism is that, Eliade's concept of the sacred has collapsed as a viable project in religious studies. But, that issue need not distract from Wheatley's wider project to create an alternative to Weber. Stripped of Eliadian esoterica, Wheatley's ceremonial centers become a means to reject the Weberian break between city and hinterland. Oddly enough, Wheatley begins at the same point as Cogitosus: his cities do not need walls. Wheatley adopted the concept of an "extended boundary city" which defines the 'population' as the entire community using the center as a focal point (1971: 339–51). Wheatley writes (1971: 389):

> And, by their presence at the ceremonial cities during the great festivals of the year, countrymen, no less than town dwellers within the complex, played their parts in ensuring the effectiveness of those rituals designed to regulate the cycle of time and to ensure the fertility of the earth.

Inhabitants of ceremonial cities might not feed themselves, but their life remained integrated with the "rhythm of the seasons" (1971: 479).

Readers should not be distracted by the seemingly poetic nature of this observation. Wheatley is not engaging in woozy Age of Aquarius sentimentality. This observation is a precise statement about non-Weberian socio-economics: "Unlike migrants to the modern city ... those entering ceremonial cities were ... not confronted with new and often alarming experiences [or] ... an unfamiliar value system" (1971: 479). In Weber's scheme, hinterland producers are transformed into subordinates. In Wheatley's they remain strangers in the sense of being from somewhere else but also engage with the center without becoming subsumed into alienating producer/consumer dichotomies.

From this perspective, Wheatley is making the same critique of Weber as Finley, who wrote:

> the economic relationship of a city to its countryside ... can range over a whole spectrum, from complete parasitism at one end to full symbiosis at the other. ... The question then is whether ancient cities were, as Max Weber thought, primarily centers of consumption. Stated differently, how did the cities pay for what they drew from the country? (Finley 1985: 125)

Finley derives his alternative to alienation from Aristotle, specifically the economic significance of *koinonia* (κοινωνία): "exchange relations within the framework of the community" (Finley 1970: 8. See also Polanyi 1968.) Both Wheatley and Finley elaborated their alternatives via the sensibilities of midtwentieth-century economic anthropology. While subsequent developments have shown the liabilities of that approach, Wheatley's concepts retain considerable value if they are reconceptualized in terms of Graeberian values. For example, Wheately's concept of rural visitors is quite similar to the long-term engagements with strangers that Mauss places at the core of Modern societies.

Likewise, Theuws's concept of religious activity as articulating disparate imaginary worlds and economic processes is reminiscent of Wheatley's ceremonial centers. Colin Renfrew (2013) has drawn attention to sanctuaries as centers of congregation.

In sum, Wheatley's ceremonial centers—with their unperturbed rural visitors—reformulate Weber's model of the relationship between city and hinterland. This point is deeply transgressive. Since the nineteenth century, theories of social complexity have been based on assumptions about sea changes in social dynamics. The "unfamiliar value system" in Wheatley's model is a cagey attack on Weber's (and consequently most models of medieval urbanism) tendency to see urbanism springing from only alienation and an escalating complex of domination.

The foregoing highlights elements of Wheatley's thinking that deserve ongoing attention in scholarship on religion and urbanism. But, building a functional concept also requires confronting weaknesses. The greatest weakness in *Pivot of the Four Quarters* is that, despite presenting profound challenges to "Western" thought, ultimately Wheatley leaves ceremonial cities as a fleeting anomaly of initial urbanism. Having spent hundreds of pages detailing a counter-intuitive model that demands re-examination of dearly held presumptions, suddenly, Wheatley's alternative urbanism morphs into an abortive step preceding development of Weberian urbanism.

Space is not available for describing all reasons for this turn, but the most important for monastic towns is founding ceremonial cities on Mircea Eliade's view of the sacred. Eliade defined "traditional society" as entwined with the sacred and Modernity as a time of desacralization. Paralleling Weber, his Modernity brings alienation from the sacred. Ultimately, Wheatley chose not to disaggregate his notion of sacred practices from this fixed trajectory. His cosmo-mythical symbolism remained petrified as "an almost universal concept in the traditional world" (Wheatley 1971: 429). With this stance, Wheatley abandoned his challenge to Weber's narrative, leaving ceremonial centers trapped *in illo tempore*. Doherty's monastic towns fare little better. He believed they evaporate in the face of advancing Modernity. Due to Eliade's sense of desacralization, sacred cores disintegrate in the face of Modernity.

Chapter 3 will explain the details of how emerging perspectives on religion resolve such problems. But, first, with this introduction to the concept of sanctuary cities, it is necessary to complete the review of settlement in Ireland with a survey of the only potential sanctuary city that has been extensively excavated: Clonmacnoise.

NOTES

1. See particularly, Ó Carragáin (2010), McCormick et al. (2011), O'Sullivan et al. (2014), Bhreathnach (2014), and Stout (2017).

2. See Stout (2017: 120–21) for text and translation.

3. McClung and Plunkett (2020) use the discontinuities between climatic and cultural patterns to urge a shift away from climatically deterministic models of social change. They say repeatedly that the discontinuities suggest cultural factors are predominant. But, climatologically-oriented archaeologists working in other parts of the world have recently found that adaptability to variable climate conditions may be more important than adaptation of any one set of conditions (e.g., Potts and Faith 2015).

4. See Corlett and Potterton (2012) for potential Iron Age examples. See O'Conor (1998) and Fitzpatrick (2009) for later medieval examples

5. I am generally limiting discussion to Ireland, but the phenomenon is a recurrent one in medieval Europe. For a discussion of sanctuary cities in Anglo-Saxon England, see John Blair (2005).

6. The notion of Weber and Cogitosus "in dialogue" about urbanism is not entirely fanciful. Weber's theories emerge from M. L. Morgan's ideas about *civitas* transforming *societas*. Morgan's concepts draw from distinctions made by the Roman writer Horace. One contribution of anthropology, and perhaps the most significant way that it helps make sense of urbanism, is recognizing ways that debates about urbanism are very long arguments (see Soderberg 2017a).

7. Cogitosus, Vita S. Brigidae, c. 32. For text and translation, see Charles Doherty (1985: 55–56); Seán Connolly and J. M. Picard (1987: 26). Not all editions contain the question about walls, e.g., Migne (1849: 788).

8. For churches, see Doherty (1985: 48). This topic is taken up in detail in chapter 7.

Chapter Two

Excavating Clonmacnoise

INTRODUCTION

The experience of walking into Clonmacnoise today is quite different from what a medieval visitor would have encountered, but Clonmacnoise remains a sacred landmark. Burial and religious events are ongoing. Clonmacnoise is also among the most visited heritage sites in Ireland, with over 150,000 visitors per annum (Bowers 2019). Numbers have grown substantially in the past several decades, but such "cultural tourism" extends back to at least the nineteenth century (McGettigan and Burns 2001). Standing monuments from the Middle Ages are lead attractions, but the landscape itself is also an important draw. The area around Clonmacnoise preserves rare habitats that have been the subject of EU funded research projects on the intersection of wildlife conservation, farming, and tourism (Tubridy 1987 and 1998). One study found that the area was home to twenty percent of Ireland's *Lepidipotera* species (Bond 1989). One motivation for all this curation work is a hope for glimmers of what drew medieval travelers there and what they would have encountered.

As the only potential sanctuary city in Ireland that, first, was not extensively disturbed by post-medieval building and, second, has been extensively excavated, Clonmacnoise has the potential to yield considerable insight on conditions in the Middle Ages. The previous chapter identified key elements of the early medieval Irish landscape and the value of identifying space in that landscape for sanctuary cities where strangers could find refuge. The goal of this chapter is to begin defining how that circumstance is manifested archaeologically. It surveys what is known archaeologically about Clonmacnoise and its relationship to surrounding landscapes in the medieval period. This book began with a request to imagine walking into Clonmacnoise. This chapter surveys what archaeologists know about what that visitor would have encountered. The goal is to define the general layout of the monastery and the range of structures discovered.

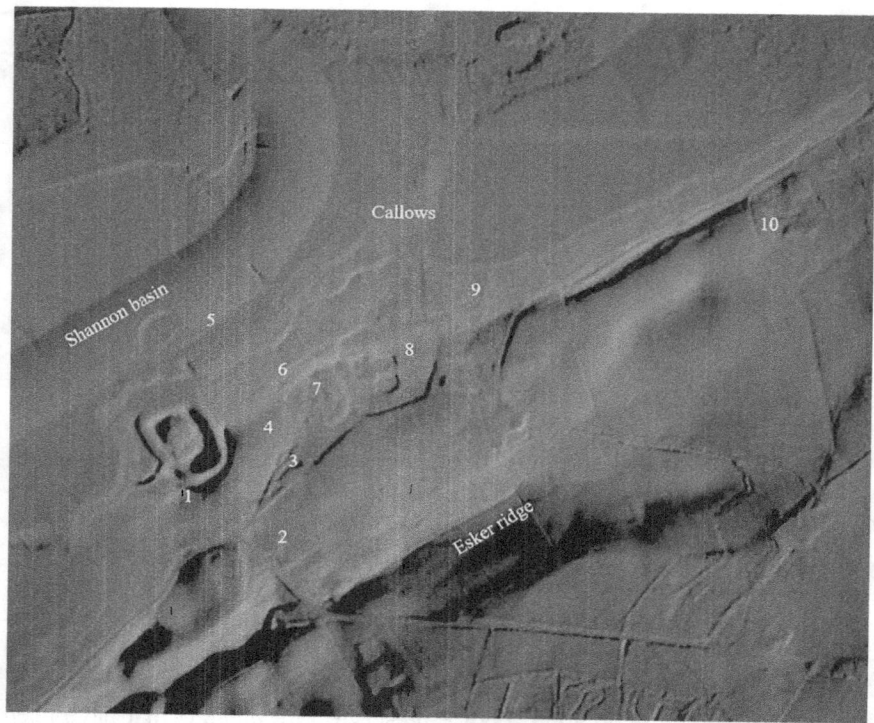

Figure 2.1. Digital elevation map of the region around Clonmacnoise based on two-meter elevation data from the Ordinance Survey of Ireland. 1. Castle, 2. St. Ciarán's School excavations, 3. Tourist Office excavations, 4. Car Park excavations, 5. Bridge excavations, 6. Wastewater System excavations, 7. Steeple Garden excavations, 8. central enclosure (location of St. Ciarán's Church excavations and High Crosses excavations, 9. New Graveyard, 10. Nun's Chapel. Created by John Soderberg.

THE LANDSCAPE OF CLONMACNOISE

Clonmacnoise occupies an elevated promontory facing northwest over the Shannon River (figure 2.1). The Shannon—Ireland's longest river—is a major north-south communication route. It opens into the Atlantic with a vast estuary that articulates with oceanic trade routes. The tenth-century Latin *Life of Ciarán* links Clonmacnoise with settlements in the Shannon estuary, with a tale about a robe being miraculously carried to an island at the mouth of the Shannon and a reference to Gallic merchants bringing wine (Bradley 1998: 47). The Shannon also formed the border between two early medieval provinces: Mide to the east and Connacht to the west. Clonmacnoise did not develop enduring links to a particular lineage or region (Ryan 1940: 507). Over the centuries, affiliations with royal dynasties shifted from links to the east in Mide, to the west in Connacht, and to the south in Munster (Kehnel 1997: 90–132).

Clonmacnoise's location on the Shannon rightfully draws attention to possibilities for regional and international connections. But, the river also shaped Clonmacnoise in a much more local fashion. One version of the Life of St. Ciarán, the monastery's founder, notes that the Shannon was an abundant source of fish (Plummer 1925: 211. See Kehnel 1997: 91 for discussion). The floodplain of the river also provided significant terrestrial resources. In the immediate vicinity of Clonmacnoise, the lands along the Shannon are called callows: riverine meadows seasonally enriched by winter floods (figure 2.2). Callows would have provided rich summer grazing land. At least since the nineteenth century, one section of callows to the northwest of the monastery has also been used for saving hay, a practice which has facilitated habitat for the endangered corncrake (Turbidy 1998). In the winter, the callows support populations of migrating birds such as geese and swans.

Figure 2.2. View of Clonmacnoise from the Shannon callows. Photo by John Soderberg.

A second dominating feature around Clonmacnoise are eskers: gravel ridges formed by water flowing under glaciers. The term is derived from the Irish word for a sand and gravel hill (*eiscir*). These ridges formed important routeways across the bogs and damp lowlands of the Irish midlands. Prior to modern drainage work, seventy percent of County Offaly was bogland (Turbridy 1998). Clonmacnoise sits on the *Eiscir Riada*. A major early medieval routeway east-west from Dublin to the west coast, *an tSlighe Mhór* (the Great Road), ran along the *Eiscir Riada*, meeting the Shannon north-south routeway at Clonmacnoise (Ó Lochlainn 1940, Comber 2001, Doran 2004). As Heather King writes, Clonmacnoise's "position at the crossroads of Ireland provided all the ingredients for a successful and powerful ecclesiastical and commercial center that flourished for over six centuries" (2009: 333).

As with the Shannon, eskers are not just routes for getting through the midlands. The well-drained soils on eskers foster species-rich grasslands (Pilcher and Hall 2001) that made valuable winter pasture for livestock and patches of arable land. They also provide a boundary to settlement. About five hundred meters to the south of the Shannon, a section of esker rises above the river plain, separating the Shannon landscape from the bogland to the south.

While bogs might seem to offer little opportunity for passage and habitation, bogs throughout Ireland were crisscrossed by wood and gravel roads. Dry "bog islands" also create what Valerie Hall and Dmitri Mauquoy call "honeycombs of fertile land" (2005: 1087). Wetland survey in the region around Clonmacnoise has identified hundreds sites of various periods (Maloney 1998). Bogs were also a source of iron ore and other raw materials.

Several sections of a gravel road run into a large expanse of bog island at the center of Bloomhill bog. The road was an impressive two to three meters wide, constructed of gravel and large flagstones, and maintained from the mid-sixth to the late eighth centuries with an additional layers of timber, dendrochronologically dated to the thirteenth century (Breen 1988). Conor McDermott (1995) considers this path part of a regional network for the communities in and around Clonmacnoise. Fitzpatrick and O'Brien (1998: 7) associate the road with pilgrimage.

Palynological studies provide insights about the impact that Clonmacnoise had on its surroundings. Hall and Mauquoy (2005) present data from a core in Mongan bog, located two kilometers from Clonmacnoise. The earliest layers in the core date to approximately 350 AD and indicate drier over the succeeding centuries, particularly after the twelfth century. Evidence for mixed farming is present throughout, with increased emphasis on grazing between 590 and 870, then increased cereal farming from the twelfth century. A second core from Mongan bog provides broadly similar results, as does a core from Clonfert bog, located ten kilometers further west in County Galway (Hall 2005).

The introduction of monasticism is often associated with agricultural innovation in medieval Europe. Other parts of Ireland saw woodland clearance and agricultural transformation though the early medieval period. Cores from the Bann Valley in Northern Ireland show substantial woodland clearance in this period (Hall et al. 1993). Clonmacnoise is different. The advent of the monastery may be responsible for an increased emphasis on grazing, but mixed farming is prevalent from the base of the core (circa 350 AD) through the Middle Ages. Likewise, no changes are associated with the expansion of Clonmacnoise into a large settlement after 700. For the environs of Clonmacnoise, Hall sees "a landscape of scrubby woodland and damp pasture" across the entire period (2005: 5). Hilda Parkes and Fraser Mitchell (2000) found some evidence of woodland decline circa 800, but Hall and Mauquoy discount that conclusion on methodological grounds (2005: 1091).

Hall is sensitive to the limitations of her data. Bog cores are not likely to register activity closer to the monastery. Data from excavations (see below) demonstrates substantial amounts of grain were processed at the site. But, even accounting for such concerns, Clonmacnoise seems to have grown into an established landscape management regime, rather than founding a new one. Palynologically, Clonmacnoise is nearly a non-event just a few kilometers away.

The landscape itself offers one explanation. The area offers a valuable mix of resources, including iron from bogs and pasture-land in the callows (Mytum 2003: 43–45). But, as is often the case in the midlands, the landscape offers little opportunity for intensive arable agriculture or extensive grazing (Soderberg and Immich 2010). But, these qualities should not be taken as a weakness for Clonmacnoise. While perhaps not useful for intensive production, the landscape was also a source of affluence because the mix of resources and links to other regions established a significant measure of economic independence for Clonmacnoise.

CLONMACNOISE IN DOCUMENTS AND ARCHITECTURE

The stretch along the banks of the Shannon near Clonmacnoise is likely to have been significant prior to the Middle Ages. Fording spots across the Shannon are known to the north and south of the monastery. Heather King's excavations in the New Graveyard revealed substantial Iron Age activity beneath the monastic settlement (see below).

The earliest known medieval monument at Clonmacnoise is an ogham inscribed stone. Perhaps as old as the fifth or sixth century, the stone could predate the monastery. The text is largely indecipherable (Manning and Moore 1991). Annals record that Ciarán founded the monastery during the 540s but died shortly afterwards in the plague of 549. Edel Bhreathnach observes that Ciarán is one of five members of the founding generation of monasticism in Ireland said to have died in this plague. While skeptical of the accuracy of the obits, she suggests that this cluster of individuals is different from the network of foundations associated with the *domnaig* churches of an earlier era (Bhreathnach 2014: 185). Annette Kehnel (1997) provides a review of the foundations associated with Lives of Ciarán and other texts.

Clonmacnoise is the earliest recorded pilgrimage destination in early medieval Ireland (Harbison 1995: 51). The *Annals of the Four Masters* note the death of a pilgrim there in 606. The *Annals of Clonmacnoise* mention pilgrims at Clonmacnoise in 617, 754, and 832. References to Clonmacnoise in texts such as Adomnán's *Life of Columba* and Tírechán's *Life of Patrick* indicate that, by the beginning of the eighth century, the monastery had become both a substantial settlement and a significant feature of the Irish sacred landscape. Numerous studies have shown that Clonmacnoise prospered for the next four or five centuries, becoming among the most important Irish monastic centers (e.g., Bhreathnach 2014).One manifestation of its significance is the development of patronage with royal lineages. Raghnall Ó Floinn (1995) has traced the vicissitudes of patrons via the distribution of cross-inscribed slabs and other artwork.[1] Other studies have traced shifting patronage via the familial origin of individual officeholders (e.g., Kehnel 1997). In return for supporting building programs and other endeavors at Clonmacnoise, royal patrons would have received burial rights and other forms of legitimization.

Clonmacnoise also became the head of a large federation of sacred sites (*paruchiae* or *familiae*). To an extent these federations would have operated via an ecclesiastical version of the clientage relationships discussed in the previous chapter. Kehnel observes that the Registry of Clonmacnoise—a seventeenth-century document thought to derive from a pre-twelfth-century account of land holdings—describes that churches in Co. Leitrim were obliged to pay a yearly rent of two cows and one pig to the abbot of Clonmacnoise, who would come to collect the rent every St. Martin's day (Kehnel 1997: 52). St. Martin's day is November 11 and associated with harvest feasts. As with secular clientage, the temptation is to see such relationships in terms of dependency. But, as with clientage generally, the existence of such ties do not simply signal subordination. Kehnel is careful to note that such arrangements are likely to have offered advantages to dependent churches, including supply of priests and protection. Kehnel also observes that Clonmacnoise is often linked with churches far away and suggests that such long-distance contacts may have been useful in navigating local quarrels (Kehnel 1997: 52–53).

Federations were a source of considerable conflict among leading monasteries, as each sought to lure away churches from rivals. Tirechán, for example, complains that Clonmacnoise had hold of Patrician foundations in Connacht. On two occasions Clonmacnoise fought battles with other monasteries, Birr in 760 and Durrow 762. Two hundred men were slain in the conflict with Durrow (Mac Airt and Mac Niocaill 1983). Maire Herbert suggests that the conflict arose from tensions between the *familiae*. Kehnel suggests that the Durrow battle may also have been fueled by secular dynastic struggles (1997: 108). Such layered motivations for large-scale conflicts seem likely, but no matter the balance of ecclesiastical and secular motivations, the very fact of monastic warfare is a salutary moment to reflect on ways that early medieval monasticism challenges concepts of the sacred.

Bhreathnach reflects on these wars in terms of secularization, offering a developmental scheme for transforming the "sacred landscape . . . from a prehistoric place of worship around the wells of Sine and Slán to the *túath* bishopric of the Temenrige, and then to a tribute-paying church subject to Clonmacnoise" (2014: 186). This model correlates Clonmacnoise with the motivations and social dynamics that McCormick associates with transformation of milk-lords into feudal lords. Notably, the eighth and ninth centuries are a key threshold for both. The sense of monastic entanglement with profane politics becomes clear as Bhreathnach bifurcates Clonmacnoise: one part joined in secular violence and another remained isolated in the contemplative life (2014: 187).

Kehnel expresses reservations about bifurcating Clonmacnoise between secular and sacred spheres: "The question, therefore is, whether the distinction between the secular and the ecclesiastical or spiritual is a valid concept underlying an analysis of political history in medieval Ireland" (1997: 90). While she notes that such distinctions were used in contemporary texts, it is also the case that Clonmacnoise's participation in war did not impair its sacred qualities: "On the contrary, spiritual authority was the means by which secular power was claimed and in fact held" (1997: 90). Kehnel points to a decidedly different relationship between secular and sacred, and one that resonates well with perspectives emerging in archaeology currently (see chapter 3).

Whatever the sources of its growth, Clonmacnoise was at its peak through the early centuries of the second millennium. Clonmacnoise grew into an important population center, as suggested by a record of 152 houses being burned in 1179 (King 2004: 458). In 1082, the *Annals of Clonmacnoise*, record the destruction of houses in the churchyard of the Nuns (Bradley 1998:

46). Its affluence is indicated by a raid in 1023 in which "many hundred cows" were taken (Fitzpatrick and O'Brien 1998: 25). These references do not address when such features first appear, but they do indicate significant complexity in settlement at Clonmacnoise at least in its later centuries.

Standing remains at Clonmacnoise include two round towers, nine churches, three monumental stone crosses, and a late medieval castle. (For a review of the standing remains, see Manning 1994a/b, 1998, 1995; O'Brien and Sweetman 1997: 89–95.) A radiocarbon date with a calibrated range of 660 to 980 AD has been obtained on one church (Teampall Chiaráin. Berger 1995: 169). The largest of the churches, the Cathedral, was initially constructed in AD 909, but was extensively remodeled in successive centuries (Manning 1995). Approximately a third of a mile along the "Pilgrim's Road" to the east of the main enclosure lies the Romanesque Nun's Chapel. A reference to a nunnery at Clonmacnoise in *The Annals of the Four Masters* dating to 1026 indicates the presence of a community in the area by that time (O'Brien and Sweetman 1997: 93).

Monumental stone crosses (High Crosses) are among the most iconic monuments at Clonmacnoise. High Crosses often stand over three meters tall and were inscribed with a complex mix of biblical, patristic, secular, and decorative imagery. At Clonmacnoise, the cross originally located at the western doorway of the Cathedral is likely to have been the Cross of Scriptures identified in medieval annals. An inscription on the cross implies that the cross was erected during the reign of Flann Sinna (879–916 AD). One panel on the cross is often interpreted as showing a king and an ecclesiastic founding Clonmacnoise by planting a rod (figure 2.3). The Cross of Scriptures has long been considered an emblem of sanctuary (e.g., Stokes 1898). As was discussed in chapter 1, the *Annals of Clonmacnoise* describes people taking sanctuary around the Cross of Scriptures. Doherty (1985: 70) identifies such spaces for sanctuary as the core of monastic towns.

In the twelfth century, Clonmacnoise began to slip from prominence. It was marginalized in the Church reforms of the period. An Anglo-Norman castle was constructed to the west of the central precinct in 1212. A letter records that the bishop of Clonmacnoise was compensated for lands and other goods lost to the castle. But, as with Anglo-Norman control in the area more generally, its duration was short. The castle was unoccupied by the beginning of the fourteenth century (O'Conor and Manning 2003). Settlement at Clonmacnoise declined precipitously in this period. As Kehnel writes, "the once majestic city of St. Ciarán was transformed into the bishop's seat of one of the smallest and poorest diocese in the Irish [Church]" (Kehnel 1997: 2).

Figure 2.3. 3D digital model of the "Foundation Panel" on the Cross of Scriptures. Created by the Discovery Programme, Center for Archaeology and Innovation Ireland.

SURVEY OF EXCAVATIONS AT CLONMACNOISE

For many monasteries the above review is the extent of information available because subsequent development has disturbed most early medieval deposits. The lack of extensive settlement at Clonmacnoise after the Middle Ages preserved extensive early medieval deposits. The remainder of the chapter reviews results of excavations at Clonmacnoise since the 1970s. The locations for each excavation is listed in figure 2.1.

St. Ciarán's School (Ó Floinn and King 1998)

The modern series of excavations at Clonmacnoise commenced in 1979, when schoolchildren discovered a Hiberno-Norse coin hoard while removing goalposts on the playing field of St. Ciarán's National School (Ó Floinn and King 1998: 119). The find spot is a few hundred meters to the southwest of the central enclosure. Raghnall Ó Floinn excavated a four-meter square cutting in the summer of 1979. Between 1992 and 1994, Heather King excavated eight cuttings further to the south from the hoard location. St. Ciarán's School is located at the base of the east-west esker ridges discussed above, making the area a likely area for the southern extreme of settlement around Clonmacnoise.

The 1979 excavations demonstrated that the hoard pit had been disturbed by both the insertion of the goalposts and earlier cultivation activity. Twenty-seven complete and three fragmentary coins were recovered. Numismatic analysis suggests a deposition date circa 1095 (Kenny 1998). The hoard also included a copper-alloy ingot and a segment of plaited gold likely from a finger-ring. The hoard is noteworthy for the inclusion of non-numismatic material, a combination unusual for the late eleventh century.

In addition to the hoard, the excavations also revealed evidence of ferrous and non-ferrous metalworking: a furnace bottom, crucibles, tuyères, moulds, and copper alloy strips. The stratigraphic relationship between such evidence for metalworking and the hoard is unclear, but Ó Floinn concludes that the area reflects short-term manufacturing activity with a noteworthy absence of habitation evidence.

King's excavations in the early 1990s also provided some evidence for metal working to the south of St. Ciarán's School in the form of a bowl furnace fifty centimeters in diameter and lined with burnt clay (Ó Floinn and King 1998: 130–31). The furnace is located in the cutting farthest south from the hoard pit. The remaining seven cuttings are spread between. They produced very little evidence of medieval activity in this area, helping to confirm that this area was on the margins of settlement through the medieval period, appropriate for stashing valuables, sporadic manufacturing, and perhaps grazing.

The upper layers in many of the cuttings around St. Ciarán's School contain U-shaped cultivation furrows running north-south. While this set produced no clear dating evidence, other excavations at Clonmacnoise indicate that these furrows are either very late medieval or early modern (see below for discussion). Stratigraphically, they mark the terminus of the extensive settlement at Clonmacnoise.

Steeple Garden (Manning 1985, 1987, 1990)

Construction of a new visitors' center on the southeast edge of the central enclosure led to a series of excavations along a ridge in the esker and adjacent hollow to the north. Occupation deposits in the hollow extended down two meters. Conleth Manning identified four phases of early medieval activity. In contrast to cuttings at St. Ciarán's School, the Steeple Garden produced ample evidence for intensive settlement. The earliest layers contained a series of stake holes and a dump of furnace waste. This layer was sealed by an archaeologically sterile layer. The succeeding layer contained two scatters of stakeholes and occupation refuse, separated from each other by a gravel pathway. Manning's excavations also uncovered crucible fragments associated with a hearth, a layer containing large amounts of iron slag, and a series of superimposed stony layers, the latest of which appears to date after the twelfth century.

While the standing monuments at Clonmacnoise signal the power and prestige the monastery held, the Steeple Garden excavations demonstrated the intensity of domestic and manufacturing activities in the early medieval period. Substantial re-organized also seems to have occurred over time, as suggested by an archaeologically sterile layer of humic soil intervening between the two archaeologically productive layers. While the relationship between reorganization in the Steeple Garden areas and the reorganization King found beneath the Cross of Scriptures is uncertain, the cessation of housing and manufacture at the core of the monastery circa 700 certainly resonates with the intensity of habitation activities just tens of meters to the west through the early medieval period. As at other locations, north-south cultivation furrows seal deposits associated with pre-thirteenth-century activity.

High Crosses (Manning 1992, King 1992b, 1993, 1997, 2001, 2004)

The three monumental crosses (often called high crosses) located to the south, west, and north of the Cathedral were moved into the Visitor Center in the early 1990s and replaced by resin copies. Small cuttings were excavated in the area around the base of each cross. Excavations under the North Cross revealed that the base of the cross was a millstone with steps and other modifications added. A similar arrangement is known from a cross at Iona. Two burials were located directly under the cross. One was dated to 600 AD at the latest. No *in situ* settlement deposits were identified, but recovered artifacts include amber, bronze, and slag.

Remains under the South Cross were less disturbed. King found evidence that this cross was inserted into a pre-existing post-hole, but the shape of that earlier marker was unclear. The excavation exposed twelve medieval burials, all of which were male. King dates the earliest burial, located below the central pit, to the seventh century. Others range up to the eleventh century (O'Brien 2020: 204–205).

The West Cross, also known as the Cross of Scriptures, produced similar evidence of burial and a marker preceding the cross. The predecessor was rectangular and made of wood. As was noted above, this excavation also produced evidence for a reorganization of the area circa 700. The burials were cut into settlement deposits including a hearth, post-holes, and ash deposits containing iron objects, a bone pin, bronze tweezers, a mould fragment, a hone, and cut antler.

King emphasizes three conclusions from these remarkably productive excavations (2004). First, the area was initially used for habitation, presumably in association with the early years of the monastery. Beginning as early as the seventh century, habitation ceased. The area became devoted to burial (apparently for males) and other activities. Wooden markers, perhaps pre-cursors to the existing stone crosses, were added circa 700. Burials extend across the semi-circular area defined by the three crosses, indicating that it did not define a burial precinct. King argues that the north cross, which was set further from the Cathedral than the other two, is likely to have been moved in antiquity and that evidence of a similar marker may exist closer to the Cathedral. The current stone crosses are likely to have been implanted circa 909.

Clonmacnoise Bridge (O'Sullivan and Boland 1997 and 1999; O'Sullivan et al. 1998; Moore 1996)

Underwater survey in the Shannon River adjacent to the monastery uncovered remains of a bridge, dated by dendrochronology to 804 AD. The bridge was five meters wide and ran at least one hundred twenty meters across to the Roscommon side of the Shannon, with paired supports driven into the river mud at five- to six-meter intervals. Mortised crosspieces kept the posts from sinking further. At the time of discovery, the Clonmacnoise bridge was heralded in *Science* "the largest wooden structure from the early medieval period ever found in Europe" (Duke 1998: 480). Finds associated with the bridge include nine dugout canoes, axes, a copper basin, iron slag, and animal bones. Three of the dugouts were found with carpentry tools on their bottoms, encouraging speculation that they were sunk during bridge construction (O'Sullivan and Boland 1999: 36). The copper basin is a ninth- to tenth-century type of ecclesiastical metalwork known from Norwegian Viking graves, but otherwise rare in Ireland (O'Sullivan and Boland 1999: 36).

On the far side of the Shannon, the bridge connected with a gravel road through bog land. The road is three to five meters wide and thirty centimeters deep. The line of the road has been traced heading westward for 1.5 miles (O'Sullivan and Boland 1999: 35). Maloney estimates that sixteen hundred cubic meters of gravel would have been transported for constructing that distance of road surface (1998: 9). Additional survey upriver from the bridge located no additional structures but did find two more dugouts and other artifacts. No evidence of reconstruction was located.

The bridge provides testament to the sophistication of engineering and wood-workings skills in early medieval Ireland. Prior to this discovery, little evidence for large bridges existed in Europe between the end of the Roman period and the late medieval period. Initially, the bridge was associated with a textual reference to a bridge at Clonmacnoise in 1198. The dendrochronological date pushed the construction date backward by well over three hundred years, providing an important reminder that, as John Bradley observed, "the Dark Ages were not so dark" (Duke 1998: 480). On a smaller scale, the date also supports arguments that the eighth and early ninth century was a period of profound reorganization and construction at Clonmacnoise (see below).

The bridge also highlights the importance of Clonmacnoise as an interstitial locale. The situation of Clonmacnoise at the intersection of trade routes was well recognized prior to the discovery of the bridge. But, the level of investment highlights how central communication and transport must have been. The Clonmacnoise Bridge would have rivaled any other monument visitors would have encountered.

Harold Mytum speaks to this point when he notes that the bridge fed directly into Clonmacnoise's ritual core (Mytum 2003: 47). Mytum makes this observation in the context of observing that the area north from the central monuments to the riverbank held some of the densest habitation and manufacturing at the site. But, Mytum astutely avoids the temptation to identify bridge and secular commerce. It equally led to the central core. Whether or not this entry point is an accident of topography or an intentional design, the arrangement makes the bridge and all it represents an essential element of Clonmacnoise. The bridge calls attention to the challenges of seeing both sacred and settlement at Clonmacnoise.

Tourist Office (Murphy 2003)

An area of approximately five hundred square meters was excavated in advance of construction for a tourist office approximately one hundred meters from the 1979 excavations associated with the hoard. Donald Murphy identified four phases of activity, the earliest of which is a ditch, roughly six meters wide and four meters deep, running east-west through the cutting. Murphy argues that the ditch articulates with evidence for a ditch found just to the west of the castle and evidence identified to the east via subsurface survey. These three sections form an arc that suggests the extent of an enclosure ditch for the monastery. Documentary evidence for such boundary markers is common, as in the boundary crossed in Adomnán's tale of Columba's visit to Clonmacnoise (Anderson and Anderson 1961: 214–219). Murphy estimates that the ditch would have enclosed an area of approximately thirteen hectares (Murphy 2003: 22), which matches Mytum's estimate of ten hectares of intensive settlement based on his topographic survey (Mytum 2003: 56).

No evidence is available to date the opening of the ditch. The absence of significant silting/slumping suggests either that the ditch was recut shortly before being filled or that it was filled soon after being dug. The fill at the bottom of the ditch returned a radio-carbon date with calibrated range of 714 to 873 (Murphy 2003: 13). The homogeneity of the deposits suggests that the ditch was back-filled in a single episode, likely from an adjacent bank. Murphy observes that this date range coincides with other evidence for massive reorganization of Clonmacnoise in the eighth and ninth centuries. Additional research is necessary to determine whether this boundary was simply erased or moved further south to accommodate settlement expansion.

The remaining three phases identified in the Tourist Office excavations include two burials dating to the twelfth or thirteenth centuries (Phase 2), nine pits and iron working likely of late medieval date (Phase 3), and a series of cultivation furrows running north-south. The form and orientation of the furrows match those from the St. Ciarán's National School excavations. A sherd of post-medieval pottery provides some dating parameters.

Wastewater System (King 2002, 2003)

Replacement of a septic system led to test excavations to the north of the Visitor Center. One cutting measured fifteen by four meters. Material from the demolition of a school master's house in the 1980s sealed the earlier sod layer and "an agricultural horizon." A layer of black soil below yielded iron, slag, charcoal, a fragment of rotary quern, cut antler, and animal bones. The cutting also revealed two medieval pits. One contained a single layer of fill with a stud-headed pin (eleventh to thirteenth century), iron nails, bronze fragments, and animal bones.

A test trench one meter wide and forty meters long was dug for an outflow pipe leading north to the Shannon. The northern third of the trench crossed the floodplain and contained no archaeological deposits. In the middle third, the ground level had been built up and used for occupation activities including stone-revetted structures, hearths, and pits. The southern third of the trench contained evidence for iron working "on a massive scale" (King 2009). A thirteen-meter stretch contained ironworking remains almost a meter deep, including furnace bottoms, slag, and charcoal.

T. P. Young conducted a study of the iron working material from the Wastewater excavations (Young 2005). He concluded that the material "comprised residues from all parts of the iron processing chain" and that "those processes were physically associated and indeed located very close to the excavation site" (Young 2005: 4). Iron working evidence is ubiquitous in excavations at Clonmacnoise. But, this section of the settlement seems to have been a locus for particularly intense iron working.

St. Ciarán's Church (Murphy 2008)

A cutting 3 meters by 2.4 meters was excavated in advance of a burial. Excavation located three coffin burials (dating between 1928 and the 1940s) and five truncated burials (likely dating between 1810 and 1950). An extension of the cutting to determine the stratigraphic relationship with St. Ciarán's Church located a burial cut into esker gravel extending under the church foundation. The body is likely to have been redeposited just in advance of the construction and was radiocarbon dated between 710 and 890, which agrees well with a date from mortar from the church mentioned above.

Car Park (Murphy 2019)

Fourteen test cuttings were examined in advance of improvements to parking facilities. Six produced no archaeological features. Three produced only evidence of cultivation furrows. The remaining five exposed a section of ditch matching the size and arc of the enclosure ditch from the Tourist Office excavations, two smaller ditches (one meter wide and less than half a meter deep) running parallel to each other, and several road surfaces potentially of medieval date.

Other Excavations

Test trenches in the following locations produced no archaeological features:

- five hundred meters east of the central area and two hundred meters north of the Nun's Chapel produced no archaeological features (Murphy 1999).
- South-east of central enclosure in garden of domestic property; five trenches revealed modern debris on esker gravel (Murphy 2001).
- South of the New Graveyard and east of the central precinct; house extension. Sand and gravel of esker directly under sod (King 1993)
- South and west of the central precinct; house construction; half a meter of sod and brown soil on esker sand/gravel. (King 1994).
- Monitoring for an extension to St. Ciarán's National School identified no archaeological deposits (Carey 2007).
- Test trenches were dug in advance of construction for an agricultural shed at a house "within sight of the castle and monastic complex"; the site is land rising to the esker ridge; small amounts of redeposited slag were found in several cuttings; no in situ deposits were located (Carey 2008).
- Test excavations associated with a new water well for the Visitor Center seventy-five meters to the south-east of the center and fifty-six meters from the outer bank of the castle (Keegan 2011a).
- Two pits less than one meter in diameter were dug in replacing the gate to the south-west of the Nun's Chapel. (Keegan 2011b)
- A cutting nine meters by ten meters was excavated in advance of reconstructing St. Kieran's Well, located a half mile to the southwest of the central enclosure; all identified remains and structures were post-medieval.
- Demolition of out-buildings and construction of an extension to a house near Clonmacnoise yielded architectural fragments and inscribes stones; excavation of foundation trenches yielded no archaeological deposits (Quinn 2003).

Monitoring of areas prepared for planting around the Visitor Center revealed pits with cut antler, iron fragments, and slag to the west of the center and a portion of a rotary quern in the Steeple Garden (King 1993).

New Graveyard (King 2004 and 2009)[2]

Heather King directed the most extensive excavations at Clonmacnoise in an area called the New Graveyard, just to the northeast of the central enclosure. Between 1990 and 1999, King excavated more than fifteen hundred square meters and recovered, excluding animal bone, more than six thousand artifacts, including iron, worked bone, bronze, lignite, glass, silver, and gold.

The area is divided from the central precinct by a rectilinear wall dating to at least to 1658 (Manning 1994a: 18–20). Scholarly consensus holds that the wall is a post-medieval construction. No evidence of an earlier boundary has been identified, but the possibility remains that the division existed in earlier centuries. Based on the arc of excavated sections of the ditch from the Tourist Office excavations, the New Graveyard area would have been within the enclosed area.

The landscape in this area slopes down sharply from the esker ridge toward the Shannon. In flood stage, the Shannon can advance quite close to the wall along the northern and western extent of the graveyard. The graveyard is bisected by the "Pilgrim's Road," which is currently visible as a flagstone path running from the central enclosure through the New Graveyard and continuing beside the modern road to the Nun's Chapel. The *Annals of the Four Masters* record this section of the road as constructed by Abbot Breasal Conailleach in 1026 (O'Brien and Sweetman 1997: 94).

The excavation area remains an active graveyard, and archaeological remains have long been exposed during the digging of new graves. In May 1990, an ogham stone, dating to the fifth or sixth century, was discovered during rescue excavation in advance of a burial (Manning 1998: 48). Follow-

Figure 2.4. View of the New Graveyard from the round tower in the central enclosure. Excavations occurred in the foreground of the white portacabin. Photo by John Soderberg.

ing this discovery, with funding from the Office of Public Works, Heather King opened the first two cuttings to determine the extent of undisturbed archaeological deposits. She continued excavating in this area through 1998, opening a total of seventeen cuttings. The dimensions of each cutting were often constrained by the presence of occupied graves or plots for which the owners were unwilling to grant permission for excavation. By 1998, King had exposed approximately 1,350 square meters, with archaeological deposits averaging one meter deep. Monitoring of grave digging has confirmed the existence of similar deposits across the New Graveyard (King 1993: 66).

Under the topsoil and the ploughed horizon, excavation revealed stratified deposits stretching from the thirteenth century back to the final centuries of the first millennium BC. After the first season of excavation, King commented that the "lack of [post-thirteenth-century] pottery on the site in an area so close to the Anglo-Norman castle would seem to suggest that the site was abandoned before the arrival of the Normans and that it remained unused since then" (King 1991: 50). While subsequent excavation did turn up some evidence for activity in the thirteenth century (mainly ploughing), this initial conclusion remains largely intact. The dearth of post-thirteenth-century material exists in both the disturbed topsoil and in stratified deposits.

King grouped the stratified deposits into five phases of activity, three of which pertain to the monastic settlement. Based on radio-carbon dates and diagnostic artifacts, King established the following five phases of activity:

- Phase 4: post-thirteenth century (agricultural furrows sealing occupation deposits).
- Phase 3: late eleventh and twelfth centuries.
- Phase 2: ninth and tenth centuries.
- Phase 1: seventh and eighth centuries.
- Late Iron Age: final centuries of the last millennium AD.

The New Graveyard excavations still await full publication. The following description represents a synthesis of my personal experience on the excavation, preliminary excavation reports, unpublished material, and conversations with Heather King. The absence of a final excavation report makes evaluating the above chronology difficult. While the artifacts recovered provided King substantial dating evidence (particularly for Phase 3), a more robust radiocarbon dating program would allow for more precision in dating the various phases of occupation. The analysis presented in the subsequent chapter is based on those contexts that King could confidently place within stratigraphically defined occupation, but, the boundaries of those phases are only broadly defined.

The Iron Age layers are comprised of sandy soils atop the glacial esker deposits. Identified features include a pit in cutting 6 filled with partially burned timber (F505: S237). The timber yielded an uncalibrated radiocarbon date of 330 (± 25) BC. This feature appears associated with a further thirty-four pits that form a double arc. They range between 0.5 and 1 meter in diameter and 0.5 and 0.7 meter in depth. King suggests that the presence of packing stones in many of the pits indicates that they were post-pits (King 1995: 76). Additional features believed to date to the same period include trenches and, possibly, a spread of broken limestone in cutting twelve (King 1996: 92). Unfortunately, these features produced no diagnostic artifacts, and the only firm date is the radiocarbon sample noted above. The proposed contemporaneity of these features is based largely on stratigraphy. A band of alluvial peat seals the Iron Age features from medieval deposits.

The alluvial peat appears to represent material deposited over much of the site by flooding from the Shannon River. Archaeological deposits in the peat could date to any point between the final centuries BC and AD 600. Radiocarbon dates, however, suggest that—as elsewhere in Ireland—"lull" in settlement appears to exist. Three radiocarbon dates for features in upper layers of the peat suggest a substantial break in intensive occupation: F184–AD 620 (± 20), F888–AD 635 (± 44), F1495–AD 632 (± 52). Diagnostic artifacts from peat and sod layers also suggest a similar break in occupation.

King divided the peat deposits into lower and upper segments. The upper peat layers are interspersed with archaeologically rich sod layers that probably represent periodic drying. These occupation deposits are beneath another series of layers which are similar in terms of artifacts, except that they do not include peat deposits. Taken together, these two sets of layers suggest the onset of intensive occupation in the area. While the soils are distinct, in terms of occupation evidence, Phase 1 deposits are homogeneous and generally consist of layers containing stake holes, burned areas. Stake holes are thought to represent structures, but no individual floor plans were evident. Artifacts include nails, bone pins, iron slag, and animal bone.

The radiocarbon dates and diagnostic artifacts from Phase 1 in the New Graveyard suggest that this occupation sequence falls into the period of time between 600 and 800 AD, and probably the century surrounding 700 AD. That date range matches the range King has identified for the reorganization of the central enclosure, on the basis of the switch from habitation to burial evidence in the excavations under the Cross of Scriptures (see chapter 7 and King 1997a). At this time, it is not possible to conclude that Phase 1 in the New Graveyard and the transition in the central enclosure were precisely contemporaneous, but Phase 1 in the New Graveyard likely reflects the same general period of reorganization.

Phase 2 layers mark the onset of an intensive building program. Phase 2 contains nearly all the structural remains identified in the New Graveyard. Structures include two grain drying kilns, and five structure (three round houses built on stone-revetted platforms, one rectangular, and one D-shaped). Uncalibrated radiocarbon dates for layers immediately below the platforms are: 667±37 AD, 709±34 AD, 658±34 AD, 707±44 AD. These dates combined with dates for diagnostic artifacts suggest that Phase 2 layers date to the ninth and tenth centuries. The correspondence with the construction of the bridge and the enclosure ditch is noteworthy.

The round platforms consisted of yellow sand surrounded by a ring of boulders and are seven and a half meters by eight meters in diameter. Both round platforms contained hearths and are likely to have been house foundations. No evidence for superstructure survived. The D-shaped structure was not built on a raised platform, but six courses of wall stones survived. A small out-building with a metaled surface was attached.

One round house had a large external hearth. One yard held remains of four posts and a hollow King identified as a grain storage structure. Phase 2 also yielded two grain drying kilns and implements used in arable agriculture, including quern stones and reaping hooks, testifying to an agricultural emphasis (King 2003).

Phase 2 also produced substantial evidence for precious metal, and stone working, in the form of crucibles, lignite, a silver ingot, droplets of molten glass, glass bangles (Carroll 2001), two grades of bronze wire, and hundreds of copper objects some with enameling and silver (King personal communication). Excavation located a circular hearth surrounded by more than a meter of burnt clay containing charcoal, crucibles, and molds. A cache of scrap metal was nearby (King 2009).

These structures flanked a road running from the central enclosure downhill toward the Shannon callows. The beginnings of the road may date back the seventh/eighth century, but the evidence is ambiguous. Clearly identified portions include thirty layers of sand, gravel, and peat. The road was approximately three meters wide and remetaled frequently. On its downhill side, the road rested on natural sandy esker soils. On the uphill side, it rested on Phase 1 deposits and was capped by disturbed topsoil. The road went out of use during the eleventh century, based on evidence from a pit cutting through the road that contained artifacts dating to this period, including a crutch-headed pin (AD 1000–1075).

Downhill from the structures, a revetment ran to the east of the road. This revetment may have been linked to the road, but a modern grave is situated between the road and revetment, obscuring the stratigraphic relationship. The extent of the revetment is unclear as it runs out beyond the limits of the excavation. The side closest to the settlement was faced with boulders set end to end. The revetment itself consisted of heavy clay that may have been quarried from the callows. King concluded that the revetment was introduced to provide a dry surface for a low section of the settlement. The area also includes a possible docking area (King 2004). A large hearth (3.5 meters by 4 meters) was located to the north of the platforms. A timber structure may have surrounded this hearth. The lack of metalworking artifacts suggests that this area was used for cooking or other food processing (King 1997b).

Phase 3 is the final period of intensive occupation in the New Graveyard. In several cuttings, a thick deposit (F1013) containing large amounts of animal bone marks the transition from Phase 2 to Phase 3. The radiocarbon date from an animal bone in this feature is 757 ($\pm$ 45) AD. The calibrated range for this date is 687 to 960 AD. The deposit also produced a coin dating between 924 and 939. In combination with the evidence for the end of the road, this evidence suggests that Phase 3 commenced circa 1000 AD.

Phase 3 includes several pits cut into earlier features as well as some features deposited after the abandonment of the Phase 2 structures. One such pit yielded an uncalibrated radiocarbon date of 1090 ($\pm$ 20) AD. Phase 3 pits are lined with various materials including peat, stone, and timber. One likely storage pit had a wooden cover. They appear to have been used as wells and storage pits. The fill of the pits typically includes manufacturing debris such as iron objects, worked bone, cut antler, and antler shavings. King writes that the fill of one pit appears "to represent the clearing out of a workshop floor" (1996: 77). Stratigraphy, diagnostic artifacts, and radiocarbon dates suggest that these features date between the eleventh and twelfth century.

As in other excavations, evidence for activity dating to the following centuries is sparse in the New Graveyard and consists mainly of furrows and occasional artifacts. King rejects the suggestion that occupation evidence in this period has been destroyed, as post-thirteenth-century artifacts are also rare in the disturbed layers.

SYNTHESIZING THE ARCHAEOLOGY OF CLONMACNOISE

The past four decades of excavations around Clonmacnoise offer an unparalleled view into the workings of a large monastic center in medieval Ireland. The large pits from the Iron Age located in the New Graveyard excavations demonstrate that at least one example of monumental architecture was present in the New Graveyard during the final centuries AD. The absence of similar evidence in other excavations around Clonmacnoise may suggest that other areas were not as intensely occupied, although medieval activity could well have obliterated other Iron Age deposits. At least in the low ground of the New Graveyard, an occupation hiatus occurred in the early centuries AD, introducing discontinuity between Iron Age and early medieval activities.

Palynological research has yet to offer insights on the Iron Age landscape. Published cores from the area only reach back into the early centuries AD. But, those cores do indicate that the emergence of Clonmacnoise is not associated with major changes to the local ecology. As with many areas in Ireland, the intensity of agriculture grows from circa 300 AD and the balance of pastoral and arable strategies shifts though the end of the millennium. But, those patterns should not obscure Hall's emphasis on continuity. She repeatedly rejects earlier studies suggesting that any substantial woodland clearance occurred in the medieval period. Scrubby woodland perdures well into the second millennium. Clonmacnoise grew into an established landscape and did little to fundamentally alter it as the settlement grew.

The earliest evidence of medieval occupation at Clonmacnoise is concentrated on the high point of the ridge adjacent to the Shannon, in what became the monastery's central precinct. Up until some point in the seventh century, this area housed a range of activities including habitation, manufacturing, and burial. Available evidence for this area is limited and dates primarily to the seventh century, but it matches what is known from more extensive excavation at smaller monastic settlements, such as Caherlehillan. A heterogeneous mix of activities occurred, including habitation, manufacturing, agricultural processing, burial, and other sacred practices. Understanding of Clonmacnoise in this early period is very limited, but available evidence does indicate that—prior to reorganization circa 700—both habitation and worship activities occurred in this central zone.

That circumstance provides a crucial context for understanding the reorganization of Clonmacnoise into the form that would endure into the second millennium. The expansion of settlement into the New Graveyard does not reflect secular encroachment or some form of desacralization. From the earliest period, Clonmacnoise was settlement and sacred. Reorganization circa 700 is a matter of reconfiguring the relationship between the two. Burial and other sacred practices continue in the central region, as habitation and manufacturing move outward to surrounding lands sloping toward the Shannon. But, that arrangement is not fundamentally different from Caherlehillan or somehow un-monastastic. From its earliest days through to the later medieval period, Clonmacnoise is a monastery with all the uneasy linkages between settlement and sacred that term designates. It was always a sacred settlement.

The earliest intensive occupation in the New Graveyard and the Steeple Garden is comprised of occupation layers containing scatters of stake holes too complex to resolve into individual structures. Finds from Phase 1 in the

New Graveyard are similar to those from the early occupation deposits under the crosses, suggesting that, while the location and scale of activities may have changed, the range of activities is similar to what was occurring in the central precinct earlier.

Clonmacnoise attained its full monumental status in the ninth and tenth centuries, with the construction of the bridge, filling the enclosure ditch, and, somewhat later, placement of the High Crosses and construction of stone churches. This is also the period when intensive habitation and manufacturing grew around the settlement. If one were unaware that burial and other sacred practices were occurring adjacent to the New Graveyard, one might reasonably characterize it as a mixed-use habitation site with smithies, docks, and abattoirs.

The organization of Clonmacnoise changed once again circa 1000. In the New Graveyard, the road and other structures go out of use. A substantial layer of redeposited material was spread over much of the area. The most common feature in eleventh- and twelfth-century layers are pits used as wells and storage, then filled with debris. Pollen cores indicate drier conditions and an increased orientation on arable agriculture after the turn of the millennium. Burials appear in the area of the filled ditch. A hoard of coins and metal was deposited.

Another transformation of Clonmacnoise began in the thirteenth century. The relationship between the two events is unclear, but, archaeologically, the most notable features are the construction of the castle and, in subsequent decades, the cessation of intensive habitation and manufacturing. All excavations at Clonmacnoise suggest that the end was decisive in terms of the loss of intensive settlement. Very few artifacts dating after the thirteenth century have been found. For the next few centuries, agricultural furrows are the primary activity attested archaeologically outside the central area. But, Clonmacnoise may well have remained a significant location well into the Late Medieval period.

CONCLUSION

In chapter 1, urbanism was identified as a key point of debate about monasteries such as Clonmacnoise. As reviewed so far, archaeology has certainly demonstrated that considerable socio-economic complexity and population aggregation occurred there at least by the second phase of the early medieval period when urban settlements such as Dublin were thriving. The intensity of iron working certainly suggests the degree of specialization associated with urbanized economies. But, such evidence does not settle crucial questions about urban/hinterland relationships. Chapter 4 examines the animal remains excavated from the New Graveyard to determine if and when Clonmacnoise became a settlement unable to feed itself. It and subsequent chapters also consider changes across the centuries and if links with hinterlands are better understood in Weberian or Wheatlian terms: were the visitors bringing cattle able to find sanctuary for strangers?

But, the sorts of people who reared cattle and walked them to Clonmacnoise have gained little purchase in narratives about Clonmacnoise. As with the aspects of early medieval archaeology reviewed in chapter 1, research on Clonmacnoise since the 1970s has been particularly attentive to the roles that secular elites seeking centralized control had in shaping the Irish landscape. These interpretations have made Clonmacnoise a place very inhospitable for those bringing cattle.

For example, the implantation of the High Crosses is often read in terms of the affiliation of the monastery with a king called Flann. The Cross of Scriptures includes an inscription stating: "A prayer for Flann, son of Máel Sechlann . . . and for Colman who made this cross on[?] King Flann."[3] The text likely refers to Flann Sinna—high king of Ireland 879 to 914—and Colman Conaillech—abbot of Clonmacnoise and Clonard from 904–926. They are credited with construction in 909 of the adjacent Cathedral. Manning has dated its construction to 909 and suggested that the Cross of Scriptures was erected in line with the Cathedral's west doorway (1995: 30–33).

The panel directly above the inscription shows a royal figure (secular dress with a sword) and an ecclesiastical figure (clerical dress and tonsured) jointly holding a stake (figure 2.3). These figures are an emblem of the partnership of Flann but are also probably intended to evoke an earlier partnership between Ciarán—the founding saint of Clonmacnoise—and Diarmait—a royal ancestor of Flann (Williams 1999). A tenth-century *Life of Ciarán* describes the pair planting the first stake for the first church at Clonmacnoise. As Heather Pulliam writes, "The interplay of the panel, inscription, and vita indicates that the collaboration between Colman and Flann was purposely framed as an imitation of the cooperation of their celebrated precursors, Ciarán and Diarmait" (Pulliam 2020: 10). Such perspectives situate Clonmacnoise in the context of ascendant royal power in the tenth century and its association with an equally ascendant ecclesiastical hierarchy. The stake becomes an emblem of the bargains Clonmacnoise made.

Heather King grounds her interpretation of the High Cross excavations in that narrative (King 1997a). As was noted above, the basic chronology of settlement in this area is habitation until the seventh century, then a shift in emphasis to burial, then circa 700, a re-orientation of burials to match the wooden precursors of the stone crosses, and finally the stone crosses are planted in the tenth century.

King matches that information with interpretation that the South Cross was dedicated to Flann's father, Máel Sechnaill, in the mid-ninth century to form a hypothesis about the origin of the stone crosses (King 1997a: 130):

> One could therefore succumb to the temptation that, in preparation for the dedication of the new cathedral, King Flann re-ordered the area to the west of the cathedral by removing the older wooden crosses and replacing them with the north cross, his father's cross to the south of the cathedral and placing his own new cross, the Cross of Scriptures, directly in front of the west door.

Bhreathnach's account of Clonmacnoise is similarly oriented on the doings of secular powers (2014: 183–92). She adopts Matthew Innes's *reichklöster* model in which monasteries are "dominated by kings and aristocrats, nodal points in the topography of power" (Innes 2000, quoted in Breathnach 2014: 183). As was noted earlier, Colmán Etchingham pursues the same perspective in his assessment of Glendalough. As was quoted in the introduction, for Etchingham the key dynamic "was how elite families sought to exercise influence over Glendalough, bringing to its heart the political rivalries of north Leinster aristocratic dynasties" (Etchingham 2011: 23).

Such perspectives have generated significant advances in understanding early medieval Ireland. But, they also tend either to elide the sacred or subordinate it to other social dynamics. Much of the above consideration of Clonmacnoise is demonstrating the significance of creating sacred space at Clonmacnoise for social dynamics. But, the animating values are those of maximizing elites. They are offering the same account of how religion sits among social dynamics as prevailing views of Adomnán's miraculous cattle. Sanctuary at Clonmacnoise is space where aspiring milk-lords can more efficiently execute their desires.

In the introduction, I noted that Florin Curta and Frans Theuws were drawn to Graeber by an urge to seek a more expansive view of the intersection between religion and economics. Roughly speaking, both argue that Dark Age economics generally, and theories of medieval urbanism specifically, have been too much about economics and not enough about religion. My sense is that they are pointing to conclusions from a broad-based rejection of mid-twentieth-century sensibilities about religion that parallels in both chronology and motivation efforts to reformulate economic anthropology into a "post-substantivist" footing. Within archaeology, renewed efforts to create archaeologies of religion are focused on escaping "instrumental" views of religion as ideology. Edward Swenson characterizes these "instrumental" approaches as tending "to reduce ritual to a political game played between generically conceived superordinate and subordinate agents" (Swenson 2015: 332. See also Swenson 2011). In failing to identify a broader role for religion, they—consciously or inadvertently—obscure elements of social dynamics in the same way that viewing cattle as tools for subordination does.

Such perspectives have essentially the same motivation that spurred Wheatley to propose ceremonial centers and Doherty to propose monastic towns. They are compelling arguments for articulating economies with the moral and cosmological "values" encompassed by the term religion. But, as with economic anthropology for Graeber, that project requires careful delineation of how religion sits within people. Skipping that step leaves space open for the very economics all are trying to escape to creep back in.

This chapter has discussed the enormous amount of evidence that archaeologists have recovered from Clonmacnoise. Particularly when taken in conjunction with the otherwise highly dispersed settlement pattern in early medieval Ireland, archaeology at Clonmacnoise has unambiguously established that Clonmacnoise was a large, economically complex settlement that merits consideration along the terms of the monastic towns debate. Even before weighing in the evidence that will fill the final chapters of this book, it is no longer possible to say that clearly Clonmacnoise was not urban. But, before settling whether zooarchaeology supports claims that Clonmacnoise was a sanctuary city, it is necessary to identify how new archaeologies of religion define an alternative view of the sacred space at Clonmacnoise.

NOTES

1. For an alternative view, see Swift (2003).
2. See also King 1991, 1992a, 1993, 1994, 1995, 1996, 1997b, 1998.
3. This interpretation of the inscription follows Stalley (2007) and Henry (1980). For an alternative view, see Harbison (1979).

Chapter Three

Grounding the Archaeology of Religion

INTRODUCTION

A number of different scholars have called for renewed attention to religion as a key factor in the socio-economics of medieval Europe (see introduction). One motivation is to enrich conceptions about the drivers of social change, including the growth of post-Roman urbanism. This chapter advances that project by articulating debates about urbanism with new perspectives on religion that have emerged in archaeology in the past decade or so.

Religion has been a vexed subject for archaeologists. Lars Fogelin writes, "I study the archaeology of religion for the same reason that I made gunpowder when I was 12—because I was told not to" (Fogelin 2008: 129). For much of the mid-twentieth century, the physical objects from which archaeological insights are built seemed ill-suited to topics like religion. But, in the 1990s, attention to embodiment and materiality spurred fresh approaches (e.g., Hill 1995, Brück 1999), as Fogelin's assessment of his own turn to the archaeology of religion suggests, new approaches were still coalescing after the turn of the millennium. The early sections of this chapter described the rise of these new approaches and examines how they are useful for developing a concept of sanctuary cities beyond Wheatley. The later sections argue that archaeologies of religion must take on-board radical new accounts in biological sciences of how Graeberian values work under the skin.

MOVING RELIGION OFF THE LONG FINGER

One challenge to creating an account of urbanism that includes sanctuary cities is that, as perspectives on urbanism were coalescing, the archaeology of religion seemed a fool's errand. David Macaulay's *Motel of the Mysteries* captures the ethos well (Macaulay 1979). The book imagines archaeologists in AD 4022 who discover a site, the Toot'n'C'mon Motel, from the ancient Usa culture. Imagining they found a temple, toilet seats become sacred collars, and "sanitized for your protection" seals becomes a sacred headbands. Macaulay's book is light-hearted satire, but his point is trenchant: How can archaeologists hope to understand ancient religious practices when all the people are dead? Their practices and beliefs seemed to have become part of a dead past. From that perspective, archaeologists can only offer airy speculation about religions in the past, what Lewis Binford derisively referred to as "paleopsychology" (Binford 1965). That perspective is an example of the skepticism anthropologists have about accounts of culture within individuals. And, as Graeber predicts, that stance creates an empty space.

Macaulay's parody is faithful to the spirit of Hawkesian processual archaeology that shaped perspectives on religion from the 1960s (e.g., Hawkes 1954 and Binford 1965). For Hawkes, "cognitive" aspects of the human experience—such as religion—float free from the practical/material concerns of subsistence and are therefore less accessible from (i.e., encoded within) material remains (see Robb 1998 for discussion). Essentially, Descartian divides between mind/body are being mapped onto ways of living so that sacred activities seem to be segregated from or fundamentally different from mundane activities (Brück 1999, Jones 2007, Fogelin 2007b). If archaeology is a discipline best suited to mundane realms, dropping religion from a research agenda seems reasonable. Deferring it into some unspecified—and likely unattainable—future circumstance when the practicalities of life are understood, seems broadminded. To use an Irish idiom, religion gets "put on the long finger."

When such perspectives are entrenched, archaeologists tend to take two options to *Motel of the Mysteries* style. One option was embracing Hawkes's full split of secular from sacred so that archaeology can fully focus on secular/material concerns. For the study of monasteries in medieval Europe, the second half of the twentieth century saw a surge in attention to farming techniques and methods for handling various sorts of settlement logistics (e.g., Greene 1992). Such work yielded valuable insights into the operations of monasteries and ways that they were integrated into surrounding ecological and social landscapes. The second option maintains more direct interest in religion. As was discussed in the introductory review of medieval urbanism, during the 1970s and 1980s, strategies for power consolidation became central to understanding social dynamics (Stein 1998: 8). Where sacred matters entered discussion, religion was largely a matter of ideology and power consolidation. As was noted at the end of chapter 2, from this perspective, the concept of a sanctuary city seems an artifact from a "more deferential age" that defined sacred centers as separate from profane political hurly-burly (Etchingham 2011: 23).[1]

One task defined at the end of chapter 2 is demonstrating that instrumental approaches to religion are responsible for making theories of urbanism that include sanctuary cities seem incoherent. Weberian cities are space for subordinating hinterlands. Rural visitors should been estranged there. In that context, Wheatley's visitors who feel at home entering the city are either befuddled—presumably with religion as the means—or the city is not really a city (i.e., not really functioning as a city). In other words, either sanctuary cities are a mistake or they are of marginal use for examining essential processes. Sanctuary cities require different sensibilities about religion.

Fortunately, the new archaeologies of religion emerging since the turn of the millennium have done just that. They are based on a sense that, while mid-twentieth-century approaches certainly did explain a lot about sacred practices (and the problems with prior approaches), they also explained away significant aspects. To get religion off the long finger, new approaches must show that, while rural visitors certainly should be afraid, but, they also recognize how there are also genuine reasons to feel at home too. The gist of what the rest of this chapter argues is that emerging views of religion make it possible to see the experience in terms of Mauss's fear and generosity.

These new perspectives on religion begin with shucking the view of material culture that made *Motel of the Mysteries* seem so trenchant. As Lars Fogelin observes, new perspectives transform "archaeological studies of religion from mercurial to 'conceptually simple' once we get beyond untenable dichotomies between praxis/doxa or body/mind or mundane/spiritual or profane/sacred" (Fogelin 2008: 13. For detailed reviews of these developments, see Arponen and Ribeiro 2014, Fogelin 2007a, Fowles 2013, Meier and Tillessen 2014, Swenson 2015, Gilchrist 2020). The first step in making the archaeology of religion conceptually simple is breaking the equation between religion and belief. The "simple" part of Fogelin's transformation is recognizing that religions occur in physical spaces and involve physical bodies engaged with material objects. If these material and embodied elements are integral, archaeology has an obvious path into religion. Religion becomes about doings, not thinking (Boivin 2009, Fowles 2013).

"Beyond belief" views of religions emerge from rejecting dichotomies between belief (*doxa*) and practice (*praxis*) (Bourdieu 1977). Catherine Bell's approach to ritual has been influential for understanding religions as embodied and material doings (1992, 1997). Bell founds her approach in Henri Hubert and Marcel Mauss's attention to sacralization in rituals as building from everyday (i.e., secular/mundane/profane/material) communicative activities

(1992: 15. See also Charles S. Peirce [e.g., 1982]). For Bell, sacred activities are not a bounded category distinct from other human activities. All activities can have the reflexive meaning-making quality typically associated with sacrifice and other religious rituals: "Rather than impose categories of what is or is not ritual, it may be more useful to look at how human activities establish and manipulate their own differentiation and purposes—in the very doing of the act within the context of other ways of acting" (1992: 74). To illustrate, she references Rappaport's example of a person kneeling. Posture does not communicate submission; it constructs submission (1992: 100).

Three of Bell's insights are particularly important to recent archaeological work on religion. First, bodies and material culture are no longer vessels for meaning analogous to the page on which words are written. Rather than being somehow "in" objects, meaning emerges through interaction among humans, the object, and the wider material world (Jones 2007. See also Renfrew 2001a, 2004, Preucel 2008, Boivin 2009). Matthew Champion (2015) adopts this view to show that graffiti in late medieval English churches was was part of creating the Church itself. Similarly, Pauketat and Alt (2004) similar views a cache of stone axes at a village outside Cahokia marked Cahokian ascendancy. In both cases, material culture becomes what Meier and Tillessen call "witnesses of patterned action" via ritualization (Meier and Tillessen 2014: 118).

Second, religious doings become entangled with mundane or "everyday" doings, not separated from them. As Bell writes: "Practice theory claims to take seriously the ways in which human activity, as formal as a religious ritual or as casual as a midday stroll, are creative strategies by which human beings continually reproduce and reshape their social and cultural environments" (Bell 1997: 76). Bell asserts a reflexive quality to any and all doings. Rituals are not fundamentally different if they involve lots of gold regalia inside exotic architecture or a ceramic pot of mush over a home fire. Rather than the opposition to the mundane world, ritualization is a matter of how parts of the world are articulated (Fowles 2013: 103. See also Bradely 2005, Swenson 2015, Højbjerg 2007, Renfrew 1994, Smith 1987, Turner 1967). Discussion of middens as structured deposits anticipates this perspective (e.g., Richards and Thomas 1984, Hill 1995, and Garrow 2012). Patrick Geary also anticipated many of these concerns as he interprets the emplacement and exchange of relics in medieval Europe in terms of founding/altering relationships between peoples, places, and things (Geary 1986). See also Bintliff 2014, Brück 1999 and 2005, Emerson and Pauketat 2008, Grant 1991, Herva 2009, Price 2008, Renfrew 1994, Whitehouse 2004, and Whitley and Hayes-Gilpin 2008.

A third consequence of practice-based approaches is increased attention to agency and identity. As everyday life becomes increasingly filled with practices that situate and generate meaning, earlier attention to social solidarity is replaced by attention to social interactions as processes of self/other definition. Individuals become self-conscious agents tactically elaborating a pastiche of identities signaling affiliations (e.g., Jones 1997, Wells 1999 and 2005). Inomata (2006), for example, examines plazas in Mayan settlements as spaces where Maya worlds and power relationships were negotiated. Scholars have also emphasized conversion and syncretism as negotiated processes involving selective adoptions and strategic reformulations that build into new hybrid identities (e.g., Ferguson 1992, Webster 2001).

Pilgrimage has often provided a useful opportunity to understand how religion sits in people's lives (e.g.,McCorriston 2011, Dubisch and Winkelman 2005, Kantner and Vaughn 2012: 66–68). In recent years, various archaeologists (e.g., Silverman 2016, Van Dyke 2007 and 2018) have seen pilgrimage as a useful means of considering the relationships between meaning and movement. This research draws from scholars such as Michel de Certeau with the concept of walkers actualizing (de Certeau and Randall 1984), Jane Bennett with the concept of enchantment (2001), and Tim Ingold with the concept of wayfaring (2007). In summarizing the intent of such perspectives on pilgrimage, Ruth Van Dyke notes that Chaucer's *Canturbury Tales* are not famous because of events at the destination; the story is the journey and its relationships (Van Dyke 2018: 351).

Jacob Skousen (2018) draws together many of these emerging themes in his consideration of relational approaches to pilgrimage at the Cahokian center in Illinois known as The Emerald Acropolis. He is particularly interested in how Bennett's enchantment (lively and intense engagement with the world) occurs during "crossings" (times/spaces when phenomena come into relationship) (2018: 262–63). Earlier research at the Emerald site identified pre-Cahokian lunar observances based on a ridge that aligns with the maximum lunar standstill once every 18.6 years and the "co-opting" of the locale with emphatically Cahokian architecture (Pauketat et al. 2017). Skousen emphasizes the movement of thousands of people between Cahokia and the Emerald site as essential for "the complex, affective gathering of people, places, things, substances, emotions, beliefs, memories, and more" that created Cahokian worlds.

Skousen's sense of gatherings creating Cahokia derives from Tim Pauketat's use of *bundling* as a framework for elaborating practice-based views. Pauketat's perspective on Cahokia bears some detailed consideration because his approach is remarkably similar to Theuws's and Curta's perspective on Graeberian values. Bundling refers to a complex of practices among North

American indigenous peoples involving wrapping objects together in concert with social, ecological, and cosmological relationships. For María Nieves Zedeño (2008), bundling calls forth concepts of the sacred because bringing two or more elements into relationship and alters the wider field of relationships to which the elements also connect. Bundles are "objects as active and influential components of a dynamic system of human-environment relations" (Zedeño 2008: 376).

Like Graeber's values, bundling provides Pauketat a framework for understanding how institutional orders catalyze individuals to action. The goal is to escape the same sort of excessive reliance on utilitarian individualism that Graeber identifies in economic anthropology (see introduction). Pauketat defines bundling as "nothing more or less than particularly intimate sensations of one's position in a larger field of moving cosmic powers" (Pauketat 2012: 190). From that point of view, questions about religion cannot be extricated from questions about agency (2012: 28). As tales about individual decision making, theories of agency have considerable difficulty avoiding something very like Veblen's globule: agents maximize their ability to assemble identities and navigate structure (see Dornan 2002). Not coincidentally, Pauketat's bundling relies on the same anthropological literature as Graeber used for defining values associated with distributed and relational concepts of individuals (e.g., Strathern 1988 and Gell 1998).

Also following Ingold's emphasis on relational fields and "meshworks" (Ingold 2011), Pauketat urges redefinition of both agency and religion in relational terms: "By bringing otherwise distinct people, places, and things into relationship with each other, bundling creates nodes in a larger field or web of relationships. . . . Such bundles might also be considered as agents if or when such entities link and mediate relationships in ways that alter the course of history" (2012: 27). Pauketat adds that the specifically religious qualities of bundles arise from linkages that "transfer agency and translate experience across dimensions and scales" (2012: 27). Rather than humans and not-humans simply having agency, with bundling, linkages among entities afford agencies.

This account of religion converges nicely on Theuws's account. Pauketat's attention to the wider cosmos emphasizes ways that religions both create and collapse boundaries among otherwise disperate individuals. From this conception, Pauketat argues that pilgrimages built Cahokia via bundling and unbundling the experience of a rising moon with habitual activities, objects, and places of daily life, with earlier Hopewellian bundlings, and with bundlings at contemporary settlements as far away as Wisconsin. "[The] generation-long patterns of the moon . . . may have initiated great pilgrimages, flooding the [Cahokian] region with human bodies and, ultimately, affording a grand religious movement that built Cahokia" (2012: 198). If one were to swap in medieval Christian practices, one would arrive at Theuws view of central places as spaces for tournaments of value, where "objects gain value "at the time of production, during circulation and at deposition . . . the value of things, even of commodities, is embedded in the imaginary worlds or the ideology of the participant in the exchange" (Theuws 2012: 44). The sense of life as pilgrimage is very similar in both. The primary difference is that Pauketat is more deliberate about articulating his theory of religion.

Pauketat's account is also helpful to understanding sanctuary cities because bundling is also intended to redress problems with the concept of the sacred in Eliadian traditions of religious studies, the same tradition that is a basis of Wheatley's account. As many religious studies scholars have observed, Mircea Eliade's views on *hierophany* (the experiential context through which his Sacred is made manifest) aim at a universal concept that flattens the varieties of human experience (e.g., Smith 1987). Pauketat rightly sees Eliade's work as the epitome of overly-structuralist (top-down) and abstract symbolist views of religion (2012: 13–15).

RELIGIONS AS CROSSING AND DWELLING

The theory of religion I have found most helpful for redressing the concerns that animate these investigations of religion is from Thomas Tweed, a religious studies scholar of Cuban and Cuban-American religion. My view of the values animating sacred space at Clonmacnoise—and where my views diverge from the archaeologies of religion discussed so far—are built from his views on crossing/dwelling and recognition of ways that Tweed's insights converge on Graeber's concept of values.

Tweed defines religious practices as "confluences of organic-cultural flows that intensify joy and confront suffering by drawing on human and suprahuman forces to make homes and cross boundaries" (2006: 54). This definition focuses on religions as processes of orientation. They create 'dwelling space' in the sense of constructing/maintaining identities through the elaboration of self-other boundaries. Many anthropologists have built similar perspectives. Tweed's distinctive contribution emerges from his attention to two aspects of how humans inhabit spaces. First, dwelling is not static. For Tweed, dwelling involves three distinct sorts of movement: mapping, building, and inhabiting. These movements are directed at creating a sense of timelessness and stasis (2006: 81–82). In this way, Tweed twists James Clifford's designation of travel and routes as central metaphors for understanding cultural processes (e.g., Clifford 1997). Dwelling establishes a distinct phase of movement that is lost when emphasis is purely on travel and the contingent nature of any defined place. Similarly, Benedict Anderson's concept of imagined communities usefully emphasizes the constructed-ness of communities and their traditions (Anderson 1991). But, as with Clifford, Anderson lends a troubling placeless-ness to the idea of seeing communities as merely invented. Crossing and dwelling addresses that lacuna.

The second key feature of Tweed's account is that dwelling is not distinct from crossing. Dwelling requires crossing. Crossing requires dwelling. Consequently, Tweed's account of religion challenges the common association of religion and the creation/maintenance of boundaries. Boundaries established during dwelling are thresholds as much as barriers. While that observation might seem trivial, it leads Tweed to make a very important observation about what occurs in dwelling/crossing. Thresholds do not simply lead to somebody else's dwelling nor do they just link one dwelling to the next. Thresholds are spots from which dwelling breaks out to foster wider scales of dwelling. Crossing/dwelling becomes a process of establishing common ground from which ever larger dwellings are built and transcended.

Tweed illustrates the process via a fifteen-inch statue representing Our Lady of Charity, which three men are said to have rescued from the sea off the Cuban coast in 1611. She was declared the patron of Cuba in 1916. Exiles smuggled the statue out of Cuba in 1961 to Miami. After spending six years collecting nearly half a million dollars mostly in small donations from recent exiles, the community built a shrine in 1973 to house Our Lady of Charity. The core of the shrine is a six-sided object, with soil and stone from each of the six Cuban provinces, mixed with water from a raft on which fifteen refugees had died. Her feast day remains an important focal point for the Cuban community in Miami. Tweed's ethnography describes the charged emotional atmosphere at such gatherings, with fathers lifting children, smiling, shouting, weeping. Some participants greet her as Oshun, a Santería orisha; others call her Mary.

This series of crossing/dwellings runs from bodily orientations to the creation of "intimate spaces for dwelling" to a group's shared space and out to "the wider terrestrial landscape and the ultimate horizon of human existence—the universe and the beings that inhabit it (Tweed 2006: 97–98). Crossing/dwelling is cognate with what is usually thought of as "making sacred" or meaning making. Here, Tweed joins a long tradition in religious studies. Emile Durkheim's effervescence is the foundation for Tweed's attention to "flows that intensify joy and confront suffering." But, critically, Tweed does not see consensus and solidarity as the goal. The objects through which the practices occur are as heterogeneous as the participants. Our Lady of Charity is Oshun and Mary.

Tweed's conceptions resonate well with the approaches developed in archaeology recently. Crossing/dwelling addresses the same concerns as bundling and sacred doings. Tweed also offers a helpful means of establishing sacred space that can accomodate the volatile mix of fear and generosity Mauss associates with social complexity. It accommodates the possibility that Wheately's rural visitors are not just being duped into feeling at home.

But, for all its strengths, Tweed acknowledges that his account is incomplete in one critical way. For all his success with understanding religions as orienting bodies, he has essentially nothing to say about what happens in bodies. Without that account, it is difficult to tell if anything like crossing/dwelling occurs in people. While Tweed details the workings of higher order dwellings, individuals are left as black boxes. But, to his credit, he does not see that lacuna as a badge of honor. Recognizing that his account covers religion as "institutions working," Tweed acknowledges that "neurons firing" accounts exist, but that they are also essential for a robust account (2006: 91).

Anyone who has worked in a discipline spanning humanistic and scientific disciplines will recognize how little crossing/dwelling occurs around such borders. Mostly they are observed with grim silence or thoughtless acrimony. These two realms of inquiry about religion have proceeded with remarkably little interchange. Humanistic perspectives—such as the practice-based theories reviewed above—tend to see biological theories as products of Enlightenment assumptions and imperial agendas (cf. Asad 1993). Biological theories are often seen as essentialized accounts that do more to affirm dubious assumptions than to generate valuable insights (e.g., Smith 2009, Cho and Squier 2008). As Joseph Bulbulia and Edward Slingerland observe, constructionist scholars often assume "that scientific approaches are undesirable, incoherent, or even morally wrong" (2012: 564).

Pauketat's account of bundling follows this tendency to discount. Pauketat's bundling is impressively semiotic and contextually sensitive. But, he specifically avoids an account of what happens under the skin of agents. Pauketat's identifies important ways that Eliade missed the profound implications of situated experience. Pauketat recalls Bruce Trigger's stinging dismissal of Eliade: all the evidence Eliade assembled on supposedly pan-human experiences of the sacred is simply the result of "the basic sensory dynamics of how *erect primates* view the world around them" (Trigger 2008: 64, emphasis added). Those sensory dynamics are elaborated via each person's engagements with particular landscapes. Sacred practices are products those ongoing engagements.

Similarly, Meier and Tillessen (2014) provide a wide-ranging account of archaeological engagements with religion that helpfully integrates English and German scholarship, but they dismiss biological perspectives entirely:

"it remains doubtful whether evolutionary biologism is an appropriate approach to describe and explain cultural developments" (Meier and Tillessen 2014: 53). Commonly cited review articles on the archaeology of religion pass biological research largely in silence (e.g., Fogelin 2007a and Swenson 2015). Nicole Boivin (2009) creates an important and effective argument that, in order to escape the limits of linguistic models of engagement with material culture, archaeologists must pursue models built from material, emotional, and sensual engagements. Yet, biologies of those engagement are absent.

Leaving biological workings as undefined "in there" processes undercuts the central project of practice-based theories: religion as embodied and material practices. It is attempting an account of embodiments without fully physical bodies. The absence of an account engaged with "erect primates" implies two unfortunate circumstances: one, dualism (two realms in and out) simply exist at the most intimate level; and two, that the body is important only as inscription animates its physical matter. Both alternatives foster the equation of religion with abstractions and imply that the skin is an absolute barrier between self and other.

Severin Fowles's *An Archaeology of Doings* (2013) comes closer to including a place in religions for "erect primates." As Fowles emphasizes, the damage done to Durkheim's theory when it is reduced to assertions such as gods are projections of society or religion serves to evoke social solidarity.[2] Fowles sees these characterizations as missing the significance of effervescence: a "vivifying action" that emerges in gatherings when participants are "open to outside impressions" (Durkheim 1965 [1915]: 240–47). Building from a distinctive view of Durkheim as a counter-Enlightenment figure opposed to equating religion with belief or other abstractions, he argues that the effervescence of social experiences is not solidarity, but "duality of personhood—the sense in which they are simultaneously unique agents and also parts of a larger social whole" (Fowles 2013: 146). Such effervescence is not integration, a loss of self, or a tool for enforcing solidarity. It is a feature of people and their gatherings. Fowles is emphatic that experience of the sacred is not loss of difference. Effervescent doings are significant precisely because they are simultaneously of difference and similarity. Like Pauketat's bundlings, Fowles's effervescent doings converge very closely on Tweed's views. Both fix attention on crossing/dwelling along the blurry edges of self at intimate and extended scales. Fowles writes: "To be aware of this process—to be engaged in the act of overtly tracing out the worldly relations that make all things what they are—is to be in the province of doings" (2013: 148).

While Ruth Van Dyke is a strong advocate of such movement oriented perspectives on culture is also sensitive to their limitations. She observes that an exclusive focus on crossing can slide into unhelpful assertions that everything is connected to everything else (2018). I take her concern as a recognition of the ways that practice-based approaches can end up reifying boundaries between individuals by privileging individual experience. If such is the case, chasms of experience divide one from another. Archaeologists certainly need the fluidity and nuance of crossing to counter excessively *still* concepts such as solidarity, integration, and structure (see Van Dyke 2007). But, without at least a contingent sense of coming to rest, no shared experience of pilgrimage is possible. That opens the same sort of space where Graeber finds maximizing individuals creeping back in. The reluctance to engage with biological accounts has the same consequences for archaeologies of religion as Graeber saw with anthropology relationship with economics. The perspective is a persuasive expression of the need to replace uniformitarian assumptions about human behavior associated with Enlightenment intellectual traditions (utilitarian individualism). But, reluctance to provide a similarly "internal" account limits what the account can accomplish. The same crossing/dwelling that Tweed sees as the core religious practices also need to be part of academic practices.

BIOLOGY AND THE ARCHAEOLOGY OF RELIGION

Most recent archaeologies of religion work from a humanistic perspective, but some do adopt "neurons firing" perspectives. Engagement takes a variety of forms. Boivin's attention to material, emotional, and sensual engagements derives partly from George Lakoff's theory of cognitive metaphor (e.g., Lakoff and Johnson 1999), which seeks to establish bodily sources for more abstract or linguistic modes of thinking (Boivin 2009). Scott Ortman's pioneering efforts to revitalize archaeologies of religion are also founded in Lakoff's Cognitive Metaphor Theory (Ortman 2000 and 2008. See also Culley 2008 and Wiseman 2015).

The most enduring effort to bring the concerns of biological sciences to bear on archaeology has grown from Colin Renfrew's cognitive archaeology (Renfrew 1985, 1994, 2007). Cognitive archaeology is an effort to adapt Hawkes's and Binford's processual archaeology to constructivist concerns with semiotics. It gives emphasis to physical experiences of working with symbols in material settings (Fogelin 2008: 64). Jean Clottes (2016), for example, concentrates on the environmental context and physical experience of creating rock art to develop an account of religion in such contexts in terms of trance states. Robin Skeates (2007) takes a similar approach to understanding the development of underground worship spaces in prehistoric Malta. Though Christopher Tilley and other scholars arrive via a different intellectual route—Heidegger's phenomenology—they end up with a similar emphasis on the significance of experiencing and conducting religious activities with shared bodily structures (e.g., Tilley 2004, Insoll 2004). Joanna Brück (2005) provides extended discussion of phenomenology and religion. Cognitive archaeology and phenomenology come together in neuro-phenomenological approaches to archaeology (e.g., Dornan 2004 and Malafouris 2007).

Other research takes inspiration more directly from evolutionary theory. Evolutionary archaeologies grew in the 1990s but tended to be framed in opposition to humanistic modes of archaeological thinking (e.g., Spenser 1997, Lyman and O'Brien 1998). More recently, biologically oriented archaeologists have found more opportunities for mutual engagement. John Kantner and Kevin Vaughn (2012) recognize the value of humanistic discourse on pilgrimage for exploring specific instances of pilgrimage, but they also argue that such theories are of very limited utility for understanding the long developmental context of such doings or cross-cultural relevance of pilgrimage concepts. Kantner and Vaughn's draw in biological perspective by emphasizing ways that pilgrimage involves "individual decision-making in group settings" (2012: 68).

They consider pilgramage via biological theories about "costly signals." A key feature of pilgrimage journeys are the difficulties they present. And, to the extent that they involve other pilgrims, pilgrimage is socially visible. For Kantner and Vaughn, such "costly signals" serve to mediate relationships among participants and among the wider relations implicated in pilgrimage. Kantner and Vaughn also identify signaling qualities in pilgrimage destinations and interesting tensions between signaling associated with the ceremonial center and individual participants. They employ this view to illuminate two classic archaeological case studies in pilgrimage: Chaco Canyon in modern New Mexico and the Nazca center of Cahuachi.

Archaeologists have also sought a more physical account of cognitive processes by focusing on emotions (e.g., Tarlow 2012). David Whitley valiantly takes up Tweed's challenge to work across disciplinary boundaries in his account of emotions and religion (2008). Whitley reconciles an icon of constructivist thinking—Michel Foucault—with recent cognitive psychology. Whitely argues that David Lewis-Williams's *Altered States of Consciousness* as too oriented on abstract ideas (e.g., Lewis-Williams and Clottes 1998, Lewis-Williams 2002). Whitley suggests shifting to a more physically engaged concept: *Altered Emotional States*. Drawing insights from cognitive psychology, he asserts that humans need institutions to modulate their emotional states. Referencing pervasive drug use across cultures and association of religious practices with changing cognitive states, he asserts that humans "have a strong innate drive to alter their state of consciousness" and that "[r] eligions 'work' . . . because of the way they make people feel" (2008: 96 and 98). Whitley (2009) explores this perspective further with an emphasis on his own struggles with emotional stability. Whitley articulates such biological insights with humanistic accounts. Instead of leaving "feeling together" as a simple integrative urge, he connects the physiological need for "feeling together" with Foucault's insight that madness is socially constructed. That disciplinary crossing/dwelling yields investigation of how rituals do far more than promote social solidarity.

Severin Fowles raises legitimate questions about the universalizing tendency of Whitely and other biologically informed scholars (2013: 35). But, I share Tweed's sense of a lost opportunity when those objections are used as a reason to simply ignore the work. When I began thinking seriously about these issues, I had conviction that connecting the two approaches were important, but the stout border dividing them seemed uncrossable. But, around 2010, a surge in transdisciplinary approaches breached science/humanities boundaries in dramatic new ways (e.g., Slingerland 2008, Bulbulia and Slingerland 2012, and Teske 2013). The key was a new willingness to take on board humanistic concerns about ascribing universal traits, particularly utilitarian individualism, which if anything had been an even more crucial foundation in biology than in economics. Though I have found no one who cites Graeber, the effort is similar to the objective that Graeber set for economic anthropology: creating a model for the internal workings of religion that accommodates the variability humanistic scholars expose and an alternative to Veblen's globules.

GROUNDING RELIGION

To understand the significance of the change, it is necessary to provide some background on earlier biological approaches to religion that depend entirely on Veblen's globules. Religion has often been presented as a quality that sets humans apart from other species. Such views are as gauntlets thrown down before generations of biologists. Darwin responded by founding his theories about religion on a dog mistaking a parasol moving in the wind for "the presence of some strange living agent" (Darwin 1871: 64–65). As with much else, Darwin set the terms of debate: understand religion in terms of processes that shape life for all species on Earth. In this sense, biological perspectives on religion have a similar motive to the practice-based approaches described earlier in this chapter. But, the sensibilities about bodies are vastly different (see Sofaer 2006). Particularly since the mid-twentieth century, biological inquiry into all human activities—

religious and otherwise—has been dominated by the effort to account for human behavior via the assumption that it is always guided by the desire to maximize individual reproductive success. The process of establishing alternatives within biology has been contentious and long. Even by an optimistic reading, alternatives remain emergent. But, over the last decade or so, as understanding of cognitive processes has become more fine-grained, researchers have learned that cognition is not just a process occurring under the skin of atomistic individuals. Cognition—religious and otherwise—is deeply entangled with our environments. To borrow Tweed's vocabulary, it crosses and dwells with our surroundings. These discoveries encourage new accounts that run from the level of neurons, to individuals, to populations, to lineages of species (e.g., Slingerland 2008, Slingerland and Bulbulia 2012, Teske 2013, and Sapolski 2017).

Space does not permit full discussion of the biological accounts, but, by the turn of the millennium, two strains of research were prominent (Boyer and Bergstrom 2008 and Tremlin 2006). The first defined cognitive processes that were implicated in making religion possible. One is a set of capacities that enable organisms to detect threats/opportunities that other agents present. Justin Barrett argues that Hypersensitive Agency Detection Devices fostered a sense of a world populated by agents at and beyond the edges of perception (Barrett 2000). Metacognition (a.k.a. theory of mind or knowing about knowing) is another key capacity. Metacognition is the ability to attribute different states of knowledge to different minds (Premack and Woodruff 1978). A long line of research has shown that humans devote considerable attention to what is happening in others' minds (for review, see Schlinger 2009). Following Guthrie (1993), Barrett paired metacognition with profligate agency detection to create an account of religion focused on beliefs about agents who may well know things that we do not (Barrett 2004). In this context, a shaking bush goes from representing a surprising opportunity/danger to a presence trying to tell us something we do not know.

Evidence for the association between religious practices and such cognitive processes is becoming increasingly abundant. Brain imaging studies, behavioral experiments and surveys have all provides empirical support for links between such cognitive processes and religious practices (e.g., Kapogiannis et al. 2009; Norenzayan et al. 2012). A perennial problem with cognitive experiments is the over-representation of white, North American/European, college-educated populations. But, attention to cross cultural variation is growing and, at least based on current evidence, not altering fundamental conclusions (see Rochat 2009: 215–17)

The second strain of biological research at the millennium rejected defining religion in terms of the architecture of the brain as insufficient because it does not explain why people believe and how beliefs motivate behavior (e.g., Norenzayan and Shariff 2008, Cronk 1994, Irons 1996, Whitehouse 2004). Instead the primary interest is articulating religion with evolutionary theories about group dynamics (see Purzycki et al. 2014). The basic motivation is a sense that religious practices run counter to the basic currency of natural selection: individual reproductive success.

The signal achievement of evolutionary biology in the mid-twentieth century was demonstrating with mathematical rigor that apparently altruistic behaviors—costly actions without obvious benefits to individuals performing them—were best explained as strategies for individual reproductive success. In the 1960s, George Williams published an influential critique of the idea that individuals act unselfishly or for the betterment of their group (group selection, Williams 1968). In its place, he saw competition between genes as the relevant mechanism (what Richard Dawkins [1976] popularized as the selfish gene.[3]

As with the economic theories discussed in the introduction, the goal of these theories is exclusive dependence on Veblen's globules. Altruism fails due to the free-rider problem. Imagine a scenario in which a group of altruists exists. The appeal of everybody helping everybody else is obvious: everyone benefits. But, what happens if some individuals cheat in an effort to get a free-ride: enjoying benefits of others' altruism while skipping out on the costs. Herein lies the supposed "tragedy of the commons" (Hardin 1968). From this perspective, the emphasis on altruism and self-sacrifice in many religious traditions becomes a ripe target for deconstruction. One possibility is that apparently altruistic behaviors are actually fostering an individual's reproductive success (Hamilton 1964, Trivers 1971). The stranger at the door always has the same desire.

A large body of research has explored how religious practices/beliefs serve to trigger a sense of being watched, implying that "all seeing" gods will catch cheaters. Famously, the addition of a picture of eyes next to a psychology department's coffee pot significantly reduced theft (Bateson, et al. 2006. But see also Carbon and Hesslinger 2011). In a more rigorously designed experiment, casually mentioning rumors that the ghost of a former student haunted the lab in which subjects met for a task significantly reduced cheating on a rigged computer test (Bering et al. 2005).These approaches emphasize "stick" approaches to cooperation. Others pursue "carrot" methods for inducing trust. One is based in signaling theory, which explains apparently altruistic behaviors such as standing sentry as actually demonstrating vigor and reliability, which in turn enhances their reproductive opportunities (e.g., Zahavi 1975, Zahavi and Zahavi 1997). From this perspective, religion can become "elaborate rituals that are costly in time and sometimes in other ways" that signal reliability as a cooperative partner (Irons 2001: 293, see also Bulbulia and Freen 2010). Notably, religious displays often involve emotional expressions. Studies have shown that emotional/physical reactions are more difficult to fake. Hence, the honesty of signals often requires physical, not verbal, work (Bulbulia 2004: 671). Joseph Henrich (2009) refers to such signals as credibility enhancing displays. Numerous studies have supported the connection between honest advertising and religion (e.g., Sosis and Alcorta 2003, Sosis and Bressler 2003, Sosis and Ruffle 2004, Bulbulia and Mahoney 2008, Soler et al. 2014).[4]

Currently, one of the most influential biological perspectives on religion are "Big Gods" theory. The theory is particularly relevant to Clonmacnoise because it focuses on the role of religion in complex societies. Big Gods theories combine theories about "big eyes" and "honest signals" to explain "the massive expansion of cooperation in some societies over the last 10 millennia" (Atran and Henrich 2010: 1). Advocates see them as paired mechanisms for ensuring the stability of cooperation by thwarting free-riders. The result is a theory that focuses on Big Gods as a means of solving free-rider problems via biological mechanisms evolved in the general context of social cognition.[4]

As was discussed in earlier chapters, social complexity presents a series of problems related to dependence on strangers. These theories present Big Gods as a means of stabilizing networks of strangers. The logic begins with a Maussian perspective that, as cities and specialization grew, humans had to figure out new means of cooperating once communities got too large for the means used in smaller "face to face" groups. Essentially, this account of religion sees the emergence of social complexity as a significant break from the structure of human societies up until the last few thousand years. According to this account, more than ninety percent of human history—that is, the environment in which *Homo sapiens* evolved—is dominated by kin-based interactions in small groups (i.e., in circumstances where other agents are known). If such is the case, social complexity presents profound and novel problems with strangers. But, no alternative to Veblen's globules is necessary.

Norenzayan demonstrates their workings with an example of coconuts being delivered to the Maa Tarini Temple in the Indian state of Orissa (2013: 56). Fifteen thousand coconuts arrive at the temple daily. This remarkable logistical feat begins with devotees leaving coconut offerings in donation boxes or giving them to local bus drivers, who deliver them as far as they are going and then pass them along to the next driver. Norenzayan and co-authors see the network of coconut delivery as costly signaling in an effort to ward off the punishing potential of gods with all-seeing eyes. Big Gods provide a means of extending in-group dynamics across the sprawling networks of social complexity. This type of prosocial religion dampens competition among individuals within groups by both compelling trustworthy behavior and, via costly demonstrations of that trustworthiness, signaling the reliability of cooperation with strangers.

Big Gods provide the sprawling communities of social complexity "amalgams of beliefs, norms, and rituals (belief–ritual complexes) that most effectively increased internal solidarity, elevated in-group cooperation in expanding groups, and promoted success in outcompeting or absorbing rival groups" (Norenzayan et al. 2016: 14). The salutary effect is that borders of groups become effectively policed so that free-riders are punished and enough trust is established among members that cooperation becomes more rewarding than defection.

DIFFICULTIES GETTING THE BIOLOGY OF RELIGION BACK OUT OF SKINS

Such bio-inflected approaches to religion make important additions to understanding religious practices. Consider how Big Gods theories can shape understanding of Adomnán's tales about Columba. Adomnán presents Columba as all-seeing: "by divine grace he had several times experienced a miraculous enlarging of the mind so that he seemed to look at the whole world caught in one ray of sunlight (Adomnán I.1, trans. Sharpe 1995: 112). He rewards those who are honest partners and rejects gifts from the unworthy. From a Big Gods perspective, the miraculous cattle become a means of strengthening the farmer's commitment to Columba and his followers. But, Big Gods do not offer much of an explanation of why he gave Columba hospitality in the first place. The farmer's prosocial action (offering a stranger hospitality) is only note-worthy because he has no idea who the stranger is. Offering a place to spend the night would hardly be remarkable if the farmer knew who Columba was from the start.

Luke Galen addresses the core issue with his observation that the theory is only useful for limited forms of prosociality (2016: 29–30). This "parochial prosociality" is directed at other group members: those from whom one can dependably expect a return. In other words, these partners are not true strangers, who require open or extended prosociality. Big Gods work only with clearly bounded in- and out-groups. Big Gods promote in-group solidarity, which is evolutionarily valuable because it provides an edge in competition with Out-groups. But they offer no account of the uneasy balance of fear and generosity in the territory where strangers at the door exist.

Consider the account of how coconuts get delivered to the Maa Tarini Temple. Big Gods give participants a sense of being inside a group: those under the purview of a deity. Membership makes the coconuts flow. Such cooperation is parochial in the sense that it operates within known social borders and, consequently, has an obviously calculable utility. People are not really giving coconuts to strangers. They are giving them to others who are part of the temple complex: co-religionists. Within a Big Gods perspective, the instabilities and ambiguities of Tweed's crossing/dwelling have little relevance. By definition, the borders between Big Gods groups are fixed and need to be impermeable. Out-groups can be engulfed; in-groups can shrink. But, the border is unambiguous either way.

Such accounts are ill-suited to the ambiguities that Mauss highlights in his description of encounters between strangers in terms of both fear and generosity. To the extent that social complexity involves the contradictions of dependence on strangers, encounters are defined by uneasy tensions between in and out, between self and other. These theories only account for atomistic individuals seeking their own enhancement. Such individuals operate with a solid sense of self that is unshaken by the tensions and ambiguities of Tweed's crossing and dwelling. Groups become no different because they are assumed to be individuals writ large.

Tweed's account of religion is far better suited to spaces where self/other boundaries are unstable. For Tweed, religions are about the evanescence of self/other borders, engagements between self and stranger. Keeping biologies of religion under the skin fosters and creating taxonomies prosociality obscures these qualities. As Graeber comments about post-structuralist economic anthropology, with no alternative to Veblen's globules, all that emerges is "a warmed over economism that makes 'value' simply the measure of individual desire" (Graeber 2001: 46). As was noted in the introduction, prevailing interpretations of Adomnán's tale of the miraculous cattle emphasize its role in facilitating a monastery's efforts to subordinate farmers into disadvantageous clientage relationships: acceptance of the cattle establishes debts to be repaid. Big Gods theories accomplish much the same result as the farmer becomes a member of Columba's in-group. To the extent that the charity proviso is relevant at all, in both cases, it remains instrumental ideology facilitating the monastery's control. For all their strengths, in this respect, they have not moved very far from the starting point on religion, economics, and social complexity. Establishing a robust account of sacred space at Clonmacnoise requires more.

Biological researchers have been sensitive to such issues for some time but, solutions have rarely endured. One hundred ten years after Veblen identified a pressing need for an alternative to globules, Boyer and Bergstrom find little has changed. They observe that humans "are more altruistic than expected utility would predict. Why is that the case?" (2008: 116).

For decades, biologists have seen over-reliance on maximizing individuals as a problem. Alternatives include multi-level selection and dual-inheritance theory (Wilson 2003, Henrich and McIlreath 2007). To say that such proposals have been met with skepticism is an understatement. One veteran of such battles, Frans de Waal, describes his career via an analogy with an Australian phenomenon in which frogs are found clinging to the inside of a toilet bowl, no matter what falls on them (de Waal 2013: 38–39). de Waal endured decades of unpleasantries for suggesting that humans, primates, and other mammalian species are more than Veblen's globules. Interestingly though, de Waal describes that a few years ago, he stopped feeling like a toilet frog. In the late 2000s, rigid defense of individual reproductive success faded, and openness to alternatives emerged. That shift created an opportunity to move beyond the limitations of biological approaches to religion reviewed above.

Accounting for this sea-change is complex. A host of different factors undoubtedly fosters increased acceptance of the views that de Waal and others are putting forward. The most important for the account of religion offered here is that de Waal and others focus on ways that the boundaries of self are permeable. They are not suggesting that in some special circumstances individuals stop acting like Veblen's atomistic globules. Rather, they are developing a biologically sound account of intersubjectivity: ways in which the boundary between self and other does not exist in any absolute sense. Rather than rejecting the logic of atomism, they are exploring an irony of the process. People might attempt to calculate self-interest, but entanglements of self and other mean that no reliable basis exists for those calculations. We are always inviting strangers inside.

de Waal gives biological shape to the workings of an intersubjective self by defining a cognitive process that under-cuts self/other distinctions that form the basis of mid-twentieth-century models: empathy. He writes, "the whole point of empathy is a blurring of the line between self and other. This obviously makes the difference between selfish and unselfish motives rather hazy" (de Waal 2013: 33). Here we arrive at a key value of approaching such topics biologically. In de Waal's view, the origins of empathy are not a recent development to cope with post-Neolithic social complexity. Empathy runs deeper: into our hominin, our primate, and even our mammalian lineages (de Waal 2008).

de Waal is not alone in taking this turn. Another primatologist, Sarah Hrdy, finds engagement with others equally essential to the entire span of human history, not just the last few thousand years. She writes, "what worries me is that by focusing on intergroup competition, we have been led to overlook such factors as childrearing that are at least as important. . . . We have underestimated how important shared care and provisioning of offspring by group members other than parents have been in shaping prosocial impulses" (2009:

20). As the title of her book, *Mothers and Others*, suggests, Hrdy finds a key turning point in human evolution to be the development of alloparenting, taking care of somebody else's offspring. Instead of deconstructing that care into self-interest, she sees intersubjectivity as a pervasive primate proclivity that is significantly elaborated and sustained in humans.

Hrdy offers a rare example of crossing/dwelling between humanistic and biological views when she observes that her biological account matches with the perspective that Marcel Mauss offers in *The Gift*. In building her argument that profligate prosociality is an evolved human trait, she notes that "the point is not to share but to establish and maintain social networks" (Hrdy 2009: 12). In this sense, one could read her argument as identical to Graeber's. The point is to cross/dwell with strangers.

Similarly, Marco Iacoboni characterizes his research in cognitive psychology as "a major revision of widely held beliefs [about] . . . self-serving individualism" (Iacoboni 2009: 666). *The Annual Review of Psychology* recently featured an article focused on alternatives to theories based on diadic competition: "Survival of the Friendliest: Homo sapiens evolved via selection for prosociality" (Hare 2017). These accounts require more than Big Gods blowing in a few thousand years ago and more than Veblen's globules.

These various strands of research operate in very different ways, but they share a common interest replacing theories dependent on atomistic individuals with something very like Tweeds's crossing/dwelling. All recognize that the boundaries between self and other are evanescent to support theories working only from individual reproductive success calculations. Firmly grounded in evolutionary theory, they do not reject the insights of mid-twentieth-century biology. But they bring into the foreground a mammalian irony of that process: the self does not exist in any absolute sense. It is always emergent, its borders collapsing into its surroundings. An agent might seek its own self-interest. But, self-interest is difficult to pursue if boundaries around the self keep dissolving.

In essence, de Waal and others are suggesting a biology of crossing/dwelling for individuals and groups. Tweed's theory is emphatically not about in-group solidarity, or a means by which in-group identities are maintained. Dwelling is not merely a process for individuals or other bounded units. Likewise, crossing does not establish just an aggregate of bounded units calculating costs and benefits in the same way as individuals. Crossing/dwelling collapses borders as much as it erects them. In doing so, such work of accomplishes Graeber's call for a value scheme (an economics) to animate the variability associated with partable persons and other such anthropology.

GROUNDING ARCHAEOLOGIES OF RELIGION

The account these researchers provide for the crossing/dwelling of values in individual can be identified with a version of embodiment known as grounded cognition (Barsalou et al. 2005). The term embodiment refers to a loosely connected set of theories united over the proposition that the physical context of cognition—both in terms of the body and its environment—has a significant impact on cognition. One important source of energy for advocates of embodied cognition has been philosophical discourse about building alternatives to the divided mind and body associated with Descartes (e.g., Lakoff and Johnson 1999, Noë 2009). Embodied theories see cognition entangled in the material world, both in and outside the body.[6]

Barsalou uses the term grounded cognition to describe a version of embodiment oriented on intersubjectivity. Grounded cognition is simulative and modal:

> When someone hears the word "chair," for example, a subset of the modality-specific states experienced previously for chair are simulated (i.e., reenacted) to represent the word's meaning . . . [the] idea of a chair is not represented by amodal symbols transduced from experiences for chairs—instead it is represented by modality-specific states experienced while interacting with them." (Barsalou et al. 2005: 23)

From grounded perspectives, bodily experiences with chairs become active components of thinking about chairs. A substantial body of research demonstrates that simulation is pervasive and significant, although debate continues about the balance between transductive and simulative processes (see Rizzolatti and Craighero 2004, Lewis 2006, and Barsalou 2008). To reformulate Wordsworth's classic statement that we are born into "the world trailing clouds of glory," for grounded cognition, at minimum, thoughts are born trailing clouds of the world.[7]

The most straight forward grounding of cognition is in the body. For example, moral decisions—once thought of as a set of abstract (disembodied) principles guiding behavior—have been shown to operate via "gut" level emotional responses (e.g., Haidt 2001). Notably, de Waal cites Haidt's article as a catalyst for the sea-change that released him from toilet frog status (2013: 41–42).

In addition to breaching mind/body barriers, grounded cognition also articulates cognitive processes with various aspects of the environment. The material world—both in terms of the body and in terms of its wider ecologies—becomes an integral component of thought, not just a repository of or conduit for things to think. For a parlor-trick level of evidence, one can place a rubber hand on a table and one's own hand under the table out of sight. Have somebody else rub both hands at the same tempo. After a few seconds of watching, subjects typically start to "feel" touch in the location of the rubber hand. More rigorous efforts at exploring this sort of embodiment have attended to the distinction that people make between the space around their bodies that is near (the area within reach) and that is far (the area beyond reach). Berti and Frassinetti (2000) show that holding a stick causes remapping so that near space now extends out to the end of the stick.[8] "The machinery of mind, if this is correct, is not simply the biomachinery contained within the ancient skinbag" (Clark 2011: 76).

Objects are not the only relevant feature of environments. People are there too. Having cognition involve others is a profound challenge to the borders among "skinbags." The most challenging aspect of grounded cognition is that it incorporates other people (strangers) just as much as the carpenter's hammer. As Merlin Donald writes, "Collectivity has thus become the essence of human reality. Although we have the feeling that we do our cognitive work in isolation, we do our most important intellectual work as members of cultural networks. This gives our minds a corporate dimension that has been largely ignored until recently" (Donald 2011: 84). Grounded cognition requires crossing/dwelling at boundaries among individuals as much as the boundaries between objects and bodies.

Here, a precise physical account begins to emerge for the behavioral insights that Hrdy and de Waal present with alloparenting and empathy. Crossing/dwelling is a fundamental dynamic both under skins and among skins in ways lost to perspectives based in Veblen's globules. As George Lakoff writes: "The mind isn't what we thought it was. . . . The new view of mind changes everything, in an almost shocking way" (Lakoff 2003, 49).

Evidence for extended minds run so counter to assumptions about individuals, that experimental results can seem like science-fiction. Mirror systems, for example, were discovered in the 1990s during an experiment on macaques designed to define neurons associated with movement.[9] Researchers found that the same neurons fired both when doing and seeing an action. Subsequent research identified similar structures in human brains (Rizzolatti and Craighero 2004). One researcher concludes that "the human mirror neuron system does not simply provide an action recognition mechanism, but also constitutes a neural system for coding the intentions of others" (Iacoboni et al. 2005: 530). In another in fMRI study, Krämer et al. (2010) found that simply watching pictures of emotionally charged situations led to increased activity in brain regions for both emotional processing and social cognition. Another study—with the riveting title "Pupillary Contagion"—found that reactions to sad faces were "simulated" to the extent that the dilation of subjects' pupils occurred in synch with those in images of sad faces (Harrison et al. 2006). Such effects have led some researchers to connect mirror systems with simulative approaches to cognition (e.g., Gallese and Goldman 1998, Gallese and Sinigaglia 2011). Cecilia Heyes summarizes the significance of that connection: "Mirror neurons seem to bridge the gap between one agent and another; to represent 'my action' and 'your action' in the same way" (Heyes 2010: 575).

This quality of simulative cognition undermines the most basic self/other distinctions. Individuals becomes strangers to themselves. In a precise bodily sense, people do not always distinguish between something I do and something you do: between self and other. As Simon Baron-Cohen concludes from studies in which observers own pain regions were activated by seeing images of a needle piercing another's hand: "we must be putting ourselves in the other person's shoes, not just to imagine how we would feel in their situation, but actually feeling it as if it had been our own sensation (Baron-Cohen 2012: loc 508).

Research on empathy and mirror systems comes together in studies of synesthesia. Vision-touch synesthesia, for example, is a condition in which seeing someone touched yields a sensation of touch. Significantly, no such phenomenon occurs when seeing an object touched. The phenomenon is keyed to people. Studies links such synesthesia to hyperactive mirror systems (Blakemore et al. 2005, Fitzgibbon et al. 2009). Banissey and Ward (2007) tested whether or not individuals with vision-touch synesthesia also had higher than average levels of empathy. They compared results from an empathy test between vision-touch synesthetes and those with non-mirroring forms of synesthesia (e.g., seeing colors associated with numbers). The vision-touch population scored significantly higher in emotional reactivity than the control population. This anomalously strong form of contagion suggests to Banissey and Ward that empathy and other forms of social cognition build from embodied simulation. Empathy is based in grounded cognition.

Here we have arrived at the most significant way that biological perspectives converge on crossing/dwelling. Extended cognition—particularly socially directed cognition—reveals the limitations of understanding social dynamics via atomistic individuals or diadic self/other confrontations between groups. As the retention of perceptual mode breaks down the barrier between mind/body and body/environment, mirroring and simulation breach boundaries among individuals. Mirroring is crossing/dwelling among individuals. Connecting with others becomes both an inevitable and essential human social dynamic.

To illustrate how this conception provides an alternative to Veblen's globules, I will conclude this section with a summary of how several different scholars demonstrate the workings of such grounded and relational values internally. Each accords remarkably well with Mauss's vision of encounters charged with both fear and generosity.

Philippe Rochat (2009) refers to simulative cognition as having "others in mind." He intends the phrase as a challenge to classic metacognition (theory of mind). Drawing from Mead and other intersubjectivity theorists, Rochat argues that a more unbounded concept of self is necessary. He changes the basic Descartian definition of self from "I think, therefore I am" to "We think, therefore I am" (2009: 37). The turn of phrase leads to a redefinition of metacognition from "solipsistic" to into the "negotiation of shared experience" or "what should be called our co-conscious experience" (2009: 55). This recognition of a certain "in-betweenness" to individuals creates what Rochat calls a cloudiness to self-identity, a lack of fixed boundaries (2009: 203). The experience of self is fundamentally an experience of seeing ourselves as evaluated by others, or what Rochat sees as the tension between 1st and 3rd person accounts.

In *The Science of Evil*, Simon Baron-Cohen builds research on mirroring, theory of mind, and empathy into an argument that the sorts of behaviors commonly called "evil" are best understood in terms of empathy being withdrawn or otherwise disabled. He defines empathy as "our ability to identify what someone else is thinking or feeling and to respond to their thoughts and feelings with an appropriate emotion" (2012: 16). He suggests that all humans fall along a spectrum, with the "evil" acts of warmongers and psychopaths resulting from empathy erosion that debilitates the capacity to view others as more than objects. Baron-Cohen's account provides ample illustration of the disastrous effects that occur when empathy either fails or is withdrawn, making a compelling reminder of why finding better conceptions of strangers at the door is critically important. The capacity for empathy—the ability to cross/dwell—is both critical and gossamer.

Lee Cronk and Beth Leech (2012) pursue yet another route to seeing humans as supercooperators. Cronk, an evolutionary anthropologist, and Leech, a political scientist, use data from game theory experiments to explore the dilemmas of cooperation. They are far less strident than Baron-Cohen and Tomasello in criticizing the mid-twentieth-century surge in attention of self-interested explanations for cooperation. But the basic thrust of their analysis is that cooperation needs to be understood as a crucial factor in solving the coordination problems that human societies present.

Cronk and Leech center their concept on the term *focal point*. The classic example of a focal point is a 1960 study asking people in New Haven, Connecticut, where they would meet somebody in New York City if they had forgotten to identify a specific location (a problem of pre-cellphone days).

A majority of respondents said "Grand Central" because it is where the train arrives (Schelling 1960). Such emergent common understandings derive from common experience, not instilled belief. The lost commuters of New Haven do not find each other because they all believe one thing about Grand Central. They meet up through shared embodied experience.

In more formal biological terms, Grand Centrals are an example of niche construction. The concept derives from ecological observations that species do not just adapt to the activities of other species, they also adapt to the ways that their own species has changed its environment. For human ecology, intense sociality is commonly flagged as the key project in niche construction. Humans live in the "cognitive niche" (Tooby and DeVore 1987). As Cronk and Leech write: "humans stand out for the varied and innovative ways in which they have created their own social worlds. These structures include everything from informal rules and cultural norms to organizations, laws, and the state" (Cronk and Leech 2012: 101).

ENLARGED MINDS AND RELIGIONS

The preceding sections argue that new biological perspectives on religion can enhance emerging practice-based archaeologies of religion. The tendency in those accounts to avoid "under the skin" accounts is liable to the same problems that Graeber found with economic anthropology. An accounts of intersubjectivity without an account of "neurons firing" is either taxonomy or doomed to circle back to maximizing individuals. Grounded cognition provides the alternative value scheme Graeber seeks.

The next step is building this general account of grounded cognition and social dynamics into a specific account of religious dynamics. In the past decade, an increasingly large group of scholars have become dedicated to that project. As Bulbulia and Slingerland observe (2012: 582):

> [Research on] the social interactive and ritual dimensions of religious cognition ... forms an important, distinctive new direction for the cognitive science of religion, what we call the "next generation" in the cognitive science of religion. Importantly, next-generation research is seeing classically-trained scholars of religion playing leading roles in collaboration with classically trained life-scientists, with impressive early results.

For such scholars, coconuts do not just get to temples because people are worried about divine punishment. The urge for profligate prosociality runs deeper and creates the possibility of *Meeting at Grand Central*. These connections led de Waal to notice that primatologists had spent too much attention on chimpanzee violence and not enough on care of others. He builds his sense of religion from profligate prosociality in bonobos (de Waal 2013).

Grounded cognition is essentially creating an ecological view of thinking as organism-environment couplings (Teske 2013: 772). From this perspective, religious studies and ecology are a natural fit. Some might associate ecology with functionalism and concepts of culture as an extra-somatic means of adaptation. But, ecological theory is increasingly working with intersubjective agents and semiotically structured systems. One might call it a biology of imaginaries.

One approach uses the Weberian concept of charisma to develop a concept of religions as "charismatic ecologies." The basis is niche construction theory. In basic terms, niche construction recognizes that organisms do not just adapt to an external environment. Organisms also create the environments to which they are adapting (see Day et al. 2003). This perspective has led to the development of 'dual inheritance' theories for human evolution that establish how built elements of our physical and cognitive environments become paired with genetic inheritance (e.g., Richerson and Boyd 2005). This line of thinking has yielded a significant amount of research into how distinctive features of the human lineage—a high degree of sociality, symbolic thought/language, religion—result from constructing a socio-cognitive niche (cf. Lakoff and Johnson 1980, Tooby and DeVore 1987, Deacon 1998, McBearty and Brooks 2000, Pinker 2003, Tomasello et al. 2005, Boyd et al. 2011, Stuz 2014, Marean 2015). While significant differences exist, researchers see symbolic communication and associated cognition as creating semiotics that structure human evolution recursively.

As research highlights the significance of cognitive processes occurring beyond the mind, researchers have begun developing increasingly grounded ecologies. Charismatic ecologies are one (e.g., Bulbulia 2008, Bulbulia and Freen 2010, Bulbulia and Sosis 2011). Researchers begin with the observation that signaling establishes trustworthiness (see above). But, traditionally, signaling required direct contact. Signals had to be seen to be effective. Bulbulia and co-authors consider the same problem described with Big Gods theories: complex urban settlements require extended dependence on strangers. They offer charismatic ecologies as a means of fixing the inability to address profligate prosociality. Traditional signaling theory is not of much use in that case because partners are not in direct contact. But, if the inclination to cooperate sits deeper "under the skin" profligate prosociality becomes very useful (Bulbulia and Freen 2010: 260–63). For Bulbulia and Sosis, the pervasiveness and automaticity of human cooperation derive from a specific form of niche construction: *charismatic ecologies*. The term *charismatic* is borrowed loosely from Weber and means an exceptional quality that motivates behavior: "[C]ooperative niche construction at the 'charismatic' level will tend to be both 'embodied', from factors that express strong cooperative dispositions without second-guessing them, and 'embedded', in salient features of those natural (including social) habitats by which partners synchronise their concordant expectations" (Bulbulia and Sosis 2011: 376). Ecologies become charismatic as structures align orientations and synchronize the expression of orientations. In this sense, *Meeting at Grand Central* is a charismatic ecology, as is the empathy that characterizes human interaction for Baron-Cohen, and others in mind for Rochat.

Recent work on awe provides a vivid demonstration of bodily participation in the charismatic ecologies that resonate with ideas about *Meeting at Grand Central* and empathy from the previous section. Piff et al. (2015: 883) define awe as "an emotional response to perceptually vast stimuli that defy one's accustomed frame of reference" and associate it with the feeling of being "in the presence of something greater than the self." Our goosebumps rise when we feel awe in the presence of a mountain range, a temple, a surging crowd. What intrigues psychologists about awe is its association with particular definitions of self and tendency to induce prosociality.

A substantial body of research has shown that feeling awe is associated with what some researchers call the small self or the integrated self, which is opposed to the inflated self. For example, studies show that people who feel lots of awe (but not pride) are less likely to define themselves as "special" or "one-of-a-kind" (e.g., Shiota et al. 2007). One experiment found that people who stood next to a T. rex skeleton gained an expanded self-definition as part of universal social categories. Another found that watching a nature video led participants to feel more connected to others.

Piff and colleagues surveyed 1,500 individuals from around the United States on a series of questions about how much awe they felt. Subjects were given—supposedly as a participation gift—ten lottery tickets. But, the experimenters mentioned that another participant had not gotten any and the subject could share their tickets if they wanted to. Those reporting frequent experiences of awe gave away 40 percent more tickets than those who felt it infrequently. Even more interestingly, a tiny moment of awe seems to have an effect. The researchers brought participants into a grove of two hundred foot tall Eucalyptus trees on the UC, Berkeley campus. They randomly assigned half of the group to look up into the trees for one minute. The other looked at a nearby tall building. Then, an experimenter who was handing out a survey "accidentally" spilled a box of pens. Those who had looked up into the trees picked up significantly more pens, had lower scores on indexes of entitlement, and had higher scores indexes of ethical behavior.

Our goosebumps rise when we are in the presence of something big and sense the possibility of connecting. Piff and colleagues propose that our capacity for awe has developed to facilitate the complex social groups in which we and our ancestors have lived. Awe fosters "a diminished emphasis on the self and its interests and a shift to attending to the larger entities one is a part of (e.g., small groups, social collectives, and humanity." They conclude that awe enhances "prosociality by causing people to be more willing to forego self-interest in favor of others' welfare." (Piff et al. 2015: 883 and 884–85). These are moments suffused with Mauss's fear and generosity.

RETURNING TO ADOMNÁN'S MIRACULOUS CATTLE

A biologically enhanced version of Tweed's crossing/dwelling provides the foundation for a fine-grained and biologically engaged account of Mauss's paradigmatic encounter in social complexity with its "curious frame of mind, one of fear and exaggerated hostility, and of generosity that was likewise exaggerated" (1925 [1990]: 81). They establish the sort of internal terrain that can account for how the values Strathern identifies with partible persons can catalyze action. They account for Theuws's assertion that religions articulate disparate imaginary worlds.

Consider the implications for Adomnán's farmer with a stranger at the door. Rather than an encounter only drawing farmer from out-group to subordinate, the encounter becomes a *Meeting at Grand Central*, with its associated charismatic ecologies and awe. Without discounting the possibility that the stranger might be a psychopath, they engage with other possibilities. Such a space is well suited to exploring the layered crossings and dwellings of the encounter where all are tangles of self and other crossing/dwelling from neuron to institution.

In terms of issues raised with medieval Ireland in chapter 1, these accounts also strengthen the case for revisiting such topics as Patterson's paradox with clientage, as the partners in those cattle movements become more and more entangled. In terms of monasteries, these accounts of religion provide alternative process of creating space that matches the state of monasteries as sacred and settlement. For Clonmacnoise, specifically, these accounts help make sense of sanctuary cities by grounding them in practices for rearing cattle as much as elite power consolidation. Bundling gives clarity to ways that Clonmacnoise gathered doings from around the Irish landscape and provides a basis for arguing that the farmer herding cattle and the antler worker cutting combs are on the same footing at the officiant lifting the Eucharistic chalice.

ANIMALS AND GROUNDED COGNITION

The next step is to examine the lives of the counterparts of Adomnán's miraculous cattle that were excavated from Clonmacnoise. This chapter aims to enrich the range of possibilities for the tales about what a person who raised those animals encountered at Clonmacnoise. That change widens the possibilities for what led those animals to their death and burial there. The next chapter presents what we know of those animals and defines how they helped make Clonmacnoise a sanctuary city

The foregoing discussion provides the general disciplinary context for an archaeological assessment of religion at Clonmacnoise. But, it has not yet defined why zooarchaeology is specifically useful to that process. As reviewed so far, the archaeology of religion has been a very human affair. Where do animals fit and how is it possible to learn about sacred practices from zooarchaeological data (piles of animal bones)?

This book began with an assertion that the bodies of animals slaughtered at Clonmacnoise need to be a foundation for understanding how religious practices animated Clonmacnoise. The particular challenge of Clonmacnoise's animals is that none are likely to have been brought as sacrifices in the Classical sense of the word. They are not slaughtered on the altar. They died in mundane service to the dinner table, the tanner's pit, and the bone cutters workshop.

The archaeologies of religion that have grown out of practice-based perspectives are calculated to examine exactly that circumstance. Practice-based concepts of ritualization make "sacred" a repositioning or intensification of "profane" activities. They are designed to collapse barriers between farmyard and sanctuary. As Tweed emphasizes, sacred becomes a reconfiguration of the relationship of various scales of activity from neurons to institutions. What have previously been considered the unique or special qualities of religion become matters of scale or setting, not kind. The opposite of sacred becomes disarticulated, not profane.

The concerns raised earlier in this chapter about defining religion via dichotomies between sacred and profane and via Enlightenment concepts of rationality have had significant impact on zooarchaeology. J. D. Hill highlighted concerns with viewing ritual as set apart from other sorts of semiosis in his reconsideration of trash middens (1995). He drew attention to certain waste disposal contexts as special deposits, not in the sense of being guided by specific religious beliefs, but in the sense of an emphasis on meaning-making. Hill's articulation of semiosis with everyday practices is part of a wider semiotic turn in zooarchaeology growing after the turn of the millennium (e.g., Pluskowski 2007 and Campana et al. 2010). Neill Wallis and

Meggan Blessing (2015) regard the placement of animals in a Mississippian-era feasting pit in terms of the relational ontologies associated with bundling practices. Garbage disposal begets ontologies.

For medieval European archaeology, research on hunting practices has been particularly productive for understanding the roles animals have in meaning-making. Both Naomi Sykes (2005, 2006, 2007) and Richard Thomas (2007) see the rituals of deer carcass disbursement—the "unmaking" of the deer at the conclusion of the hunt—as performances of social order associated with the Norman conquest. The deer bones are fundamental parts of the ritualizations creating Anglo-Norman identities.

Hawkes (1999) assesses links between foodways and ethnic identity with indigenous reactions to Romanization in northwestern Europe. Albarella (2007) also presents evidence for resistance to Romanization in species ratios from Iron Age Britain. Pavao-Zuckerman uses faunal assemblages to track the impact on animal management of contact between European colonists and indigenous North Americans (Pavao-Zuckerman and LaMotta 2007, Pavao-Zuckerman 2007). Such works demonstrate the ability of zooarchaeologists to explore with dexterity issues related to the transformation of animals into material culture and the implications that process has for human identities.

In such a context, herd management is no less ritually charged than sacrifice at an altar. Here is the essence of what it means to let animals into the sanctuary. As physical engagement with the material world becomes cognitively significant, herding and milking can become as socially significant as more obviously 'symbolic' activities like lifting a chalice at an altar. More than a matter of entangling profane and sacred, it opens sanctuary to the wider world. Sacral transformations do not just occur at the altar. They do not just occur when cattle arrive at Clonmacnoise. Each and every entanglement of human and animal is a bundling, a ritualization. And, the animals have a role in the meanings made from forest to barnyard to alter. The scale of bundling might be different, but the basic nature of these doing is not.

Achieving that view of animals is just as conceptually simple as any aspect of the archaeology of religion. Conceptions of animals have to follow the same shift as material culture. They need to get beyond untenable dichotomies body and mind or profane and sacred. Johanna Sofaer (2006) explores how such dichotomies have structured the study of human bodies. She argues that archaeologists are polarized between biophysical and cultural views of the human body, with biophysical signaling an emphasis on the body as a biological organism and cultural signaling an emphasis on the body as a social construction. She provides trenchant criticism of how emphasis on the constructed body has paradoxically elided actual bodies, concluding that both functionalist (processual) and constructivist (post-processual) approaches failed to effectively incorporate bodies (2006: 25).

On the one hand, work on physical bodies is often segregated from theoretical concerns, creating an unfortunate circumstance in which some supply data on bodies and others supply cultural meanings. On the other hand, constructivist approaches tend to ignore that "people have common experiences, or are situated in contexts with common social values, bodies may have common expressions (albeit to different degrees)" (2006: 76). Drawing from Ingold (1998), Sofaer seeks to move beyond this division via appreciation of the materiality of the body, which proceeds from the inhabited experience for a given body in a given context.

Zooarchaeology can productively take the same approach to animal bodies. If the boundaries between mind and matter are as porous as these works suggest, herd management is no less ritually charged than slaughter at an altar. Here is the essence of what it means to let animals into the sanctuary. More than a matter of entangling profane and sacred, it opens sanctuary to the wider world, animals included. Sacral transformations do not just occur at the altar. They do not just occur among the cattle arriving at Clonmacnoise. Each and every entanglement of human and animal is a bundling, a ritualization. And, the animals have a role in the meanings made from forest to barnyard to alter. The scale of bundling might be different, but the basic nature of these doing is not.

NOTES

1. To keep David Macaulay's books as an emblem of perspectives on religion, his *Cathedral* is a useful marker for instrumental views of religion (Macaulay 2010 [1973]). Unlike *Motel of the Mysteries*, it is not a parody. *Cathedral* is an earnest attempt to understand medieval religion as a manifestation of "profane" social practices around the construction of a cathedral.

2. Fowles is not alone in returning to Durkheim for inspiration. Neo-Durkheimian views have been a common feature of recent work on religion in a variety of disciplines (e.g., Inglis 2016, Rosati 2016, and Throop and Laughlin 2002).

3. For discussion in the context of religion, see Wilson (2003).

4. For critical appraisals of this signaling research, see Bader et al. (2006) and Hoffmann (2013).

5. For a synthesis with critical commentary, see Norenzayan et al. (2016). See also Norenzayan and Shariff (2008), Atran and Henrich 2010, Norenzayan and Gervais (2012), and Norenzayan (2013).

6. While most of the research discussed here is critical of dualistic views that separate mind and body, it is important to note that other evidence supports a biological basis for dualism (e.g., Forstmann and Burgner 2015). As is discussed below, the ul-

timate question is not whether cognition is embodied or abstract, but how it proceeds via the tension between the two. Attention here is focused on embodiment—or more specifically grounded cognition—because it has been the more marginalized recently.

7. William Wordsworth. *Ode: Intimations of Immortality from Recollections of Early Childhood*. Though pursuing the topic is well beyond the scope of this work, Romantic literature, neoclassical economic theory, and evolutionary theory all converged on atomistic views of the individual at much the same time and place. For experimental evidence supporting grounded accounts, see Kirch and Maglio (1994), Proffitt (2006), and Longo and Laurenco (2007).

8. See Lewis (2006) for a review of research on the incorporation of tools as extensions of bodies. For additional discussion of extended mind theories, see Sutton (2010) and the special volumes of *Phenomenological and the Cognitive Sciences* (2010, vol. 9) and *Philosophical Transactions of the Royal Society B* (2008, vol. 363).

9. I use the term mirror systems instead of mirror neurons because we still await consensus on the exact brain structures involved and some research suggests that mirroring may recruit a range of different brain regions (e.g., Keysers and Gazzola 2009).

Chapter Four

Animals and the Rise of Clonmacnoise

INTRODUCTION

Heather King's excavations in the New Graveyard provide an unparalleled opportunity for exploring ways that animals got bundled into Clonmacnoise.[1] The excavations yielded one of the largest faunal assemblages from any monastery in Ireland. This chapter focuses on the assemblages from the first two phases of the New Graveyard excavations, as Clonmacnoise grew into its full prominence. Phase 1 dates to the seventh and eighth centuries; Phase 2 to the ninth and tenth. Very little of this chapter addresses topics that often dominate discussion of monasteries: worship, artistic productions, ecclesiastical organization, and political dramas. On the main, the animals buried in the New Graveyard reflect processes for obtaining food and raw materials. The challenge this chapter faces is approaching them in a manner that recognizes their role in making Clonmacnoise sacred.

One way to accomplish this task is re-defining what created sanctuary at Clonmacnoise. Chapter 2 summarized ways that the actions and aspirations of King Flann did so. As with political approaches generally, that approach tends to marginalize the wider array of social dynamics fueling Clonmacnoise. The New Graveyard animals—if approached from a grounded perspective—create an opportunity to examine Clonmacnoise as animals intrude on Flann's sanctuary. That perspective is the foundation of understanding Clonmacnoise as a sanctuary city.

Defining Clonmacnoise around animals can seem idiosyncratic or even trivial. But, the perceived disjunction between animals and what is important about Clonmacnoise emerges from the sorts of mind/body disjunctions that fuel problems discussed in earlier chapters. Animals would have dominated the lives of most people engaged with Clonmacnoise. Encounters with Clonmacnoise would have involved animals.

Grounded approaches to religion give urgency to learning how animals made Clonmacnoise sacred, not how they fed whatever made Clonmacnoise sacred. Precisely because they seem to represent the profane, farm animals are a useful means of approaching the sacred. The following pages, with their discussion of skeletal part frequencies and dental wear patterns, might appear quite disconnected from concerns of the previous chapter. The animals buried in the New Graveyard were not offerings at an altar. They were slaughtered to feed people and yield raw materials just as they would have been on any other site in early medieval Ireland. But, such practices only seem distant from sacred practices if sacred and secular are bounded from each other.

Grounded perspectives, with their attention to simulative cognition, bring into focus ways that animals would have been a defining presence in the lives of most—if not all—people in early medieval Ireland. They structured people's days. They defined engagements with others and wider landscapes. They filled imaginations. Human lives were grounded in animals. Clonmacnoise was grounded in animals. If sacred practices are matters of intensification and recontextualization, if the sacred is entangled with the secular right down to the workings of bodies, the routine, the mundane, the everyday nature of the animals lives detailed in this chapter are crucial for making Clonmacnoise settlement *and* sacred.

For small monasteries, such as Caherlehillan, the grounded perspective drew attention to ways that the monasteries were sacred and settlement; shrines and farms (chapter 1). For larger monasteries, "settlement" activities are more multifaceted, but the intersection of sacred and settlement is just as crucial. Zooarchaeologists working on such complex socio-economies examine how management and movement of animals changes as complexity grows. In urban contexts, two processes are particularly significant: provisioning and commodity manufacturing. Socio-economic specialization and the social practices that make such interdependence possible both fuel and are fueled by the transformation of animals into food and raw material.

Zooarchaeologists studying urbanism in post-Roman Northwestern Europe, have three primary means of ascertaining whether a settlement was provisioned: the majority of cattle were killed at an advanced age, pigs were killed at a wide variety of ages, and an unusually large number of goats are present. The elderly cattle on provisioned sites were animals that had reached the end of their productive lives on hinterland farmsteads. As Pam Crabtree vividly describes, "the inhabitants were supplied with older cattle which may have been culled due to barrenness, to bad character, or for economic reasons" (1994: 47). They walked to their demise at the provisioned settlement. Unlike cattle, pigs and goats can live within the confines of an urban settlement, providing a useful fallback in vicissitudes in getting materials imported.

Deducing information about commodity production from animal bones is more complex than is the case with provisioning. A few other possibilities will be discussed below, but the most reliable signatures for medieval Irish towns are: cats and dogs killed prior to maturity, an unusually high prevalence of goats, and deer antler assemblages composed almost entirely of antler. Each of these qualities reflects specialization in the production of raw materials for manufacturing, including leather, bone pins, and antler combs.

The presence or absence of such patterns in the New Graveyard assemblage has implications for Ireland's position in Northwestern Europe. The post-Roman resurgence of urbanism in Britain is generally dated to the end of the seventh century (Crabtree 2018, Holmes 2014). As was discussed in chapter 1, Ireland is typically thought to represent a secondary expansion of urbanism. Zooarchaeological signatures of urbanism are well known at coastal urban settlements, such as Dublin, from the ninth century (McCormick and Murray 2007). Their presence in Phase 1 would push their origins a century or two deeper into the early medieval period. That possibility is particularly intriguing because it both brings the Irish chronology into line with other European areas and fixes it prior to the second phase of the Irish early medieval period (i.e., post-800) when centralization and other conditions thought to fuel these changes become more prevalent.

Debate about the resurgence of urbanism in early medieval Europe has been dominated by consideration of distinctly secular forms of socio-economics (chapter 1). To the extent that religion is addressed at all, instrumental roles for facilitating the development of centralized hierarchies and market economics are dominant. Previous chapters explore alternatives to instrumental views grounded in a broader array of social dynamics, both within and among individuals. The challenge of the remaining chapters is demonstrating that grounded approaches are more effective.

This chapter discusses the animals from Phases 1 and 2 of the New Graveyard excavations. Phase 2 corresponds to the time when coastal centers such as Dublin had become urban and other changes associated with the ninth century were well underway. Various excavations show that Clonmacnoise was a substantial and complex population center, but questions remain if the complexity of the site matches what is known of coastal urban centers. Phase 1 correspond to the century or so before coastal urban centers grew. The artifact assemblage and the proliferation of stake-holes suggest that Clonmacnoise was far from an isolated retreat in this period. But, the absence of identifiable structures makes understanding the nature of settlement in this period difficult. The animal remains provide critical data for learning about the state of Clonmacnoise through both periods.

General Features of the New Graveyard Faunal Assemblage

Heather King assigned approximately 270 features containing animal bone samples to one of the phases discussed in chapter 2. That number includes virtually all features containing more than five hundred identifiable fragments and many smaller samples. Excluding ribs, vertebrae, and undiagnostic long bone fragments, the total number of identified specimens (NISP) in this sample is more than twenty-six thousand. The bones were hand-collected, washed, and stored after each season of excavation. Analysis of the assemblage was done during several periods between 1997 and 1999 in Finbar McCormick's faunal lab in Queen's University Belfast. Sheila Hamilton-Dyer prepared a report on bones of fish and birds (Hamilton-Dyer n.d. See also Hamilton-Dyer 2007). The goal of this chapter is to provide a survey of key conclusions in a manner accessible to non-specialists. Soderberg (2003) provides a full report.[2]

Each species has a known number of bones in its body. One key aspect of zooarchaeological analysis is calculating what sorts of bones are missing from an assemblage to determine if any segments of bodies have been systematically removed or destroyed. Bones show little evidence of weathering, abrasive wear, or destruction from soil conditions. Elements from all sections of the skeleton are present, suggesting that trade in haunches or other desirable parts was not common (exceptions are discussed below). Evidence of dog gnawing is prevalent, but butchery and other bone processing by humans is the dominant factor shaping preservation. The frequency of elements preserved is well correlated with the nutritional utility of different carcass sections. Particularly in the case of cattle, skeletal elements tend to be present according to the amount of meat, marrow, grease, and other products associated with a given element.

While numerous features yielded sufficiently large assemblages to provide evidence of intrasite variation in carcass processing and disposal, the differences among assemblages are subtle and generally do not suggest substantially different deposition histories. This conclusion is notable for Phase 2, which contains a greater variety of features including houses, hearths, and midden deposits than Phases 1 and 3. The most distinct feature in Phase 2 is a large hearth that was slab-lined and located inside a graveled area measuring 3.2 by 1.7 meters. A perimeter of small stones outlined the graveled area. King refers to this configuration as located in "an occupation area" adjacent to Round House 1 and adds that the area "may have been enclosed and roofed although no definite evidence of walling or roofing was found" (King 1993: 54). The finds from the Hearth include bone points, cut bone, slag, several iron nails, an iron staple, an iron knife, and unidentified iron objects (Heather King. Pers. com. 1998). Analysis of fragmentation rates for this assemblage shows that pig and cattle elements tend to be less fragmented than is typically the case for Phase 2 assemblages (Soderberg 2003: 385–90). But, skeletal elements associated with high concentration of meat and marrow (the mandible, and tibia) are fragmented at higher than normal ranges and evidence of carnivore gnawing is low, a pattern that is likely to suggest intensive processing for food (Soderberg 2003: 393–95). The Hearth also has an unusually high concentration of limb elements from young cattle, which are more palatable than older animals (Soderberg 2003: 403–07). Such variations could reflect a domestic orientation different from other features. But, given the small size of the assemblage (MNI = 21), such conclusions are tentative, and, in any case, do not reflect radical departures from the general pattern of Phase 2. Furthermore, the same patterns are not evident in other habitation related features. Individual features in the New Graveyard assemblage provide little evidence of internal differentiation in the New Graveyard.

The Types of Animals in Phases 1 and 2

Figure 4.1 illustrates the prevalence of the different species identified in Phases 1 and 2. Cattle are the most common species, by a considerable margin, followed by pigs and then sheep/goats. Sheep bones are often indistinguishable from goat bones, leading to their classification in a single taxonomic category. The remaining species constitute just a few percent of the assemblage. In this figure, abundance is calculated on the basis of individual fragments of bone (number of identified specimens or NISP). This method tends to exaggerate the prevalence of large animals such as cattle, whose relatively large and robust bones yield more diagnostic fragments than those of smaller animals. Table 4.1 uses a method that estimates the minimum number of animals necessary to account for the bones in an assemblage (minimum number of individuals or MNI). This method tends to exaggerate the prevalence of less common animals. The best estimates of species prevalence fall between these two alternatives. But, whatever the method used, the values for cattle, sheep, and pigs in Phases 1 and 2 are near the mean values for the early medieval period. The New Graveyard assemblage has a typical range and prevalence for sites in early medieval Ireland.

The only exception is red deer. Typically, this species is only a few tenth of a percent of the fragments identified or entirely absent. At Clonmacnoise, red deer are the most common of all the "minor" species. Monastic sites in early medieval Ireland often have a super-abundance of red deer (see below for discussion). Aside from this one anomaly, the prevalence of species

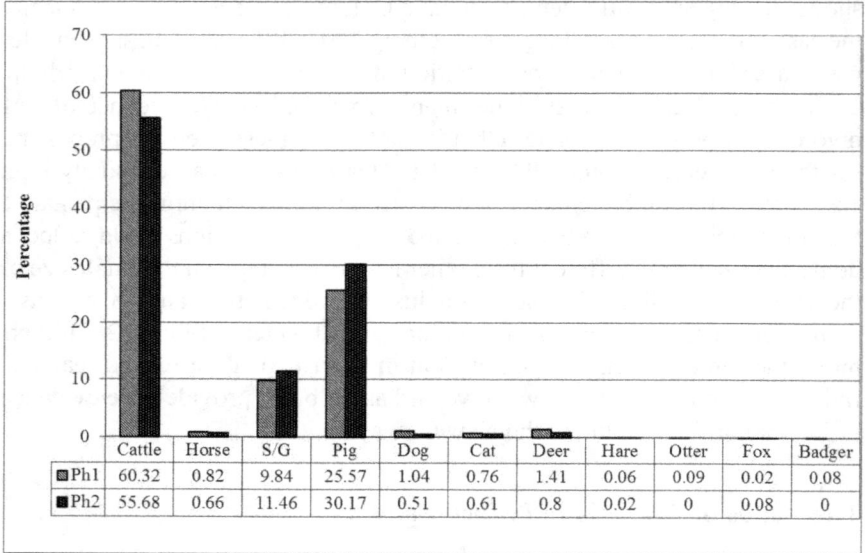

Figure 4.1. Species ratio for Phase 1 and Phase 2 assemblages, based on the number of bone fragments identified to each taxon (number of identified specimens or NISP). Created by John Soderberg.

Table 4.1. Statistics on species ratio, based on estimates of the number of individual animals in each taxon (minimum number of individuals or MNI), for a sample of early medieval Irish sites (after McCormick 1991: 43 and McCormick and Murray forthcoming) and New Graveyard Phases 1 and 2.

	N	Cattle	Sheep/Goat	Pig
Minimum		19	9	8
Maximum		71	51	57
Mean		46	23	31
Standard Deviation		14	13	14
Phase 1 (agg MNI)	244	48	21	32
Phase 2 (agg MNI)	336	44	22	34

encountered at Clonmacnoise would have been typical of any other site in early medieval Ireland.

As was discussed in chapter 1, much attention has been directed recently to questions about the "decline of cattle" circa 800. Running from the mid-seventh through the tenth centuries, Phases 1 and 2 in the New Graveyard span the period when McCormick has identified reduced numbers of cattle at settlements such as Knowth and Moynagh Lough, where cattle drop from over 50 percent down to well below. Phases 1 and 2 do not participate in such extreme changes. While figure 4.1 and table 4.1 do show a small drop in cattle and a corresponding rise in pig between Phase 1 and 2, the degree of change is not significant. Furthermore, there is no indication of any change through the course of Phase 1. The stratigraphically lowest Phase 1 deposits rest on the alluvial peat deposits sealing Iron Age deposits. These basal early medieval deposits are covered by a second set of features that Heather King designated "upper peat" layers. The species ratios for these two sets of features are essentially the same. Cattle remain a fixed majority at Clonmacnoise through the tenth century, well after the decline of the socio-economy of the cow appears in other sections of Ireland. Cattle values are at variance with those associated with milk-lords in chapter 1.

CATTLE

As was discussed above, the frequency of different skeletal elements in the Phase 1 and Phase 2 assemblages suggests that cattle were slaughtered on site and that carcasses were processed to extract meat, marrow, and grease. Bones, sinew, and hides were also used for manufacturing. Clonmacnoise produced some of the key manuscripts of the early Middle Ages. The New Graveyard assemblage has little evidence that animals buried there were a source of vellum for the scriptorium. Since calves yield the most sought-after hides for vellum, concentrations of young elements are a likely consequence of intensive vellum production. Bones from very young cattle are present in the New Graveyard assemblage, but are rare. As is discussed below, the distinguishing feature of the New Graveyard assemblage is abundance of elderly cattle.

Calves could have been slaughtered elsewhere and only hides would have been brought to Clonmacnoise. Hides were often transported with horns attached, leading to a concentration of horn elements where skins were processed. Such trade can create a superabundance of horn cores (the visible portion of horns is a sheath surrounding a core of bone). No superabundance is present in the New Graveyard. Cattle horn cores are just under two percent of the New Graveyard cattle assemblage in Phase 1 and Phase 2. This frequency is typical of early medieval Irish sites.[3]

The absence of evidence for an orientation on vellum is instructive. Manuscripts are a key component of modern imaginaria about medieval monasteries. It is certainly likely that some of the New Graveyard cattle were brought for vellum production. But the overwhelming majority were not. New Graveyard cattle were mostly present at Clonmacnoise for more prosaic activities than fueling a scriptorium. Encountering cattle in the New Graveyard is likely to have concerned everyday practices around getting food or securing raw materials to make leather, knife handles, and bone pins. The grounded approach to religion urges considering such practices as significant to the full life of the site.

Age-at-death patterns are a key tool zooarchaeologists use to gain a more detailed view into the forces shaping lives of animals. The primary means of assessing age-at-death uses eruption and wear patterns on teeth, both of which occur in predictable patterns through an animal's life. The method used for the New Graveyard assemblage follows McCormick's procedure for scoring mandibular (lower) tooth rows with the most distal tooth *in situ* and loose mandibular third molars (M3), which are always the most distal tooth row (see McCormick and Murray 2007: 12–13). Data are reported here as the age at which different changes typically occur. Individual and ecological variation influence the precise age at which changes occur, meaning that the categories represent a dental stage more than exact ages. The age ranges are provided to give a sense of the life-cycle of different species.

Age-at-death data provide key evidence for variation in the roles cattle had between consumer sites and farmsteads fully enmeshed in the production and consumption cycles of agricultural economies.[4] Figure 4.2 compares data from Phases 1 and 2 with data from a sample of farmsteads and Hiberno-Norse Dublin. Farmsteads have an early slaughter peak between fifteen and twenty-four months that reflects culling of "adolescent" animals weaned and reaching an optimal meat-weight (the point at which an animal reaches a body-size at which further feeding maintains rather than adds weight). These animals are likely to be male since only a few males are necessary for reproduction, but establishing the sex of young cattle is difficult. Rural sites have a second slaughter peak with cattle over thirty-six months. The mandibles and teeth used to assess age-at-death are not diagnostic of sex in cattle. But, the assemblages of adult cattle are known to be primarily female based on measurements of other skeletal elements. Metrical studies of metacarpals (bones in the lower fore-limb just above finger bones) show that these elderly individuals are primarily female in early medieval Ireland (McCormick and Murray 2017). This demographic represents individuals who have lived out their working lives producing milk and calves.

Dublin's Fishamble St. assemblage has a very different pattern. No slaughter peak for prime-aged cattle exists. The majority are elderly and female. This pattern is common to other coastal urban sites developing in Ireland during the ninth and tenth centuries and emporia in Britain such as Ipswich and Hamwic from the beginning of the eight century (for Ireland, see McCormick and Murray 2017; for Britain, see Crabtree 2018). The pattern is a

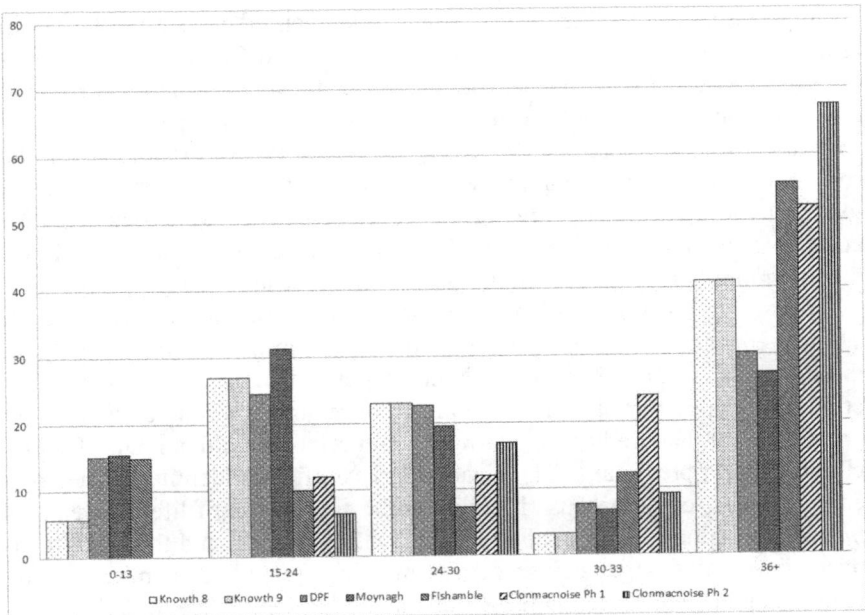

Figure 4.2. Comparison of Phase 1 and 2 cattle mortality patterns with those from rural sites (green) and Fishamble St. Created by John Soderberg.

key signature of separation from the production/consumption cycles of the general rural landscape. Dublin was not engaged in production of cattle. Elderly cattle who had passed through their productive lives within rural production/consumption cycles walked to their demise in Dublin. This pattern is a cornerstone of arguments that Hiberno-Norse coastal trade centers were provisioned urban settlements.

The Phase 1 and 2 cattle have the same age-at-death profile as Fishamble St: young cattle are very rare, and the majority of cattle are females well more than thirty-six months. The distal breadth of metacarpals indicates that, in Phase 1, 67 percent of the cattle are female ($N = 24$), and, in Phase 2, 74 percent are ($N = 34$). The only substantial difference between the Fishamble St. and the New Graveyard cattle age-at-death patterns is the complete absence of very young cattle from the New Graveyard assemblage. While young calves are an appreciable presence in the Fishamble St. assemblage, none were identified in dental data from Phases 1 and 2.

The absence of the youngest cattle in the dental age estimates could be an artifact of the method used to calculate age. The method depends on knowing which tooth is the last in the row. It is the most recently erupted and so provides definitive age data. Determining the last tooth in whole mandibles is simple because all remain in relationship to each other. But most teeth in assemblages are loose. While all teeth can be scored for wear pattern, only the third molar (M3) is included in age-at-death estimates because it is the only one known to be the last in the row. But, M3 is unerupted through the first two years, meaning that, for young cattle, a different tooth is last in the row. Theoretically, the aging method used for the New Graveyard could fail to register the youngest individuals if their mandibles were shattered. To complicate matters further, younger individuals have more gracile mandibles that are more likely to shatter than those from older individuals.

One way to test for such bias is to analyze the wear stages of loose teeth. These teeth cannot be reliably integrated into the primary aging method, but the degree of wear they show provides a general indication of age. Early erupting teeth that are lightly worn are from relatively young animals. Late erupting teeth that are heavily worn are from relatively old animals. The deciduous fourth premolar (dP4) is particularly useful for identifying the presence of young cattle because it erupts in the first weeks of life and remains *in situ* until approximately the time when M3 is in wear and the more-than-thirty-six-months stage begins. If the primary aging method is undercounting young animals, the assemblage should contain large numbers of dP4 teeth in early wear stages and few permanent fourth premolars in wear (P4). If young cattle are indeed rare, the assemblage should have mostly dP4s in advanced wear stages and P4s in wear. Tests using deciduous lower fourth premolars and other teeth do indicate some undercounting of young cattle in the New Graveyard. But, the degree of undercounting is very small. The vast majority of loose teeth are from very mature cattle, confirming the similarity to the age-at-death pattern from Fishamble St. and other urban provisioned settlements (Soderberg 2003: 108–18).

One additional age-at-death related point bears mentioning. It is also possible to obtain age-at-death estimates from other parts of the skeleton. In young individuals, bones have growth plates. As an individual matures, different plates fuse at different ages. Unfused elements in an assemblage indicate that the individual died prior to the age of fusion for that element. Since postcranial elements (skeletal elements located below the neck) are more liable than teeth to destruction and since rates of destruction vary from element to element, fusion estimates are both less precise and less reliable than dental estimates. But, they are useful for gaining perspective on dental data.

Figure 4.3 shows the percentage of unfused elements from Moynagh, Dublin, and Clonmacnoise, with elements grouped into categories by month of fusion. Fishamble St. has a far lower percentage of unfused elements in each category than the Moynagh Lough assemblage. In the New Graveyard assemblage, the percentage of unfused elements is closer to values from

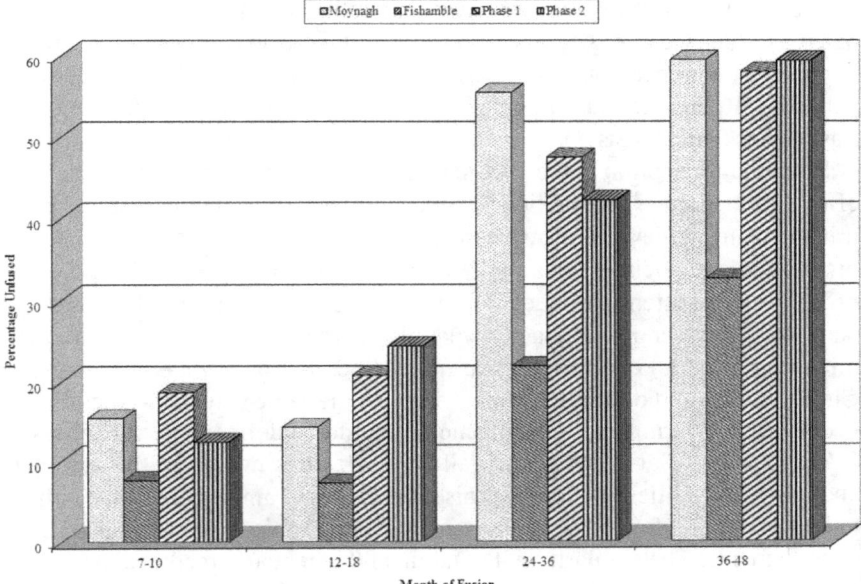

Figure 4.3. Cattle fusion pattern for Moynagh, Dublin, and Clonmacnoise. Created by John Soderberg.

Moynagh Lough than Fishamble St in each category. The implications of this pattern are unclear. They may indicate little more than variation in destruction and recovery between the various sites. Brian Hesse and Paula Wapnish (1985: 105) also argue that the percentage in each stage is less significant than the changes from stage to stage. In this context, it is notable that the Moynagh assemblage has a steep increase between the twelve to eighteen month and the twenty-four to thirty-six month stages, whereas the increase is less dramatic at Fishamble St. By this measure, the Phase 2 assemblage is more similar to Fishamble St. and Phase 1 is intermediate. Nothing in the fusion data warrants a whole re-interpretation of the dental age-at-death pattern as indicating cattle provisioning. But it does provide intriguing suggestions that the circumstances of provisioning are not the same as found at Dublin. As shown in figure 4.2, dental age data indicate that the New Graveyard has more cattle than Fishamble St. slaughtered in the "moderately" old categories: twenty-four to thirty months and thirty to thirty-three months. This difference could be a factor influencing the difference in fusion data, but other factors, including processing intensity and dog gnawing, cannot be rejected as sources of the differences.

Differences between the Fishamble St. and New Graveyard assemblages are noteworthy and merit additional consideration, but, they do not detract substantially from the core conclusion that both cattle assemblages are dominated by elderly cattle. At Moynagh Lough, 66 percent of the cattle are under 30 months. The percentages at Fishamble St., Phase 1, and Phase 2 are 33 percent, 24 percent, and 23 percent, respectively. The farmstead/urban contrast is stark and consistent.

From their inception in the 1980s, theories about sanctuary cities have been efforts to challenge assumptions about the association of the resurgence of urbanism in medieval northwestern Europe with market-based commodity production and social inequality. While Charles Doherty's 1985 article was probably not written with questions about elderly cattle in mind, their abundance at Clonmacnoise is exactly what his theory of monastic towns predicts: mirroring of urban qualities known from Hiberno-Norse trade settlements at Clonmacnoise and other such monasteries. In the same way that Caherlehillan is defined by "farmness," Clonmacnoise should be defined by "urbanness."

The cattle age-at-death pattern all by itself does not settle the argument about urban qualities at Clonmacnoise, but it is also among the best available means of making fine-grained assessments of the socio-economic functioning of settlements. The similarity with Dublin and other early medieval trade centers demonstrates significant socio-economic complexity at Clonmacnoise at the same time as such evidence appears in Britain (circa 700) and a century or two before its identification at Dublin.

Understanding the significance of Clonmacnoise's elderly cattle depends on the analysis of other aspects of the New Graveyard faunal assemblage to determine if they also reflect similarities with Dublin. But, as was discussed in chapter 1, understanding the significance of the age-at-death pattern also requires untangling such data from questionable assumptions about urbanism and the social forces that generate it. The slaughter pattern is not an item on a checklist for determining presence/absence of a city. The pattern is evidence of cattle movements. The values fueling them can vary. Ultimately, I see those values in the context of tensions between Weber's and Wheatley's concepts of urbanism. But, at present, it is most useful to recognize that Clonmacnoise received cattle from elsewhere in the manner typical of early medieval urban centers in Ireland and Britain.

The presence of cattle provisioning at Clonmacnoise suggests that these socio-economic arrangements were more deeply embedded in early medieval Ireland than if they were confined to coastal trade centers. Recent zooarchaeological discoveries have further embedded provisioning by yielding evidence of cattle provisioning at sites which have no claim to urban status. Table 4.2 summarizes data from other sites in early medieval Ireland that have age-at-death patterns dominated by elderly cattle.[5] Significantly, all of the sites listed are from the enigmatic category of enclosed settlements dis-

Table 4.2. Age-at-death data for cattle from sites with cattle provisioning (after McCormick et al. 2011).

Name	Site type	N	0–13	15–24	24–30	30–33	36+
Baronstown Ph 1	Enclosure-complex	112	1	18	14	11	56
Baronstown Ph 2	Enclosure-complex	16	0	0	25	0	75
Dowdstown Ph 2	Enclosure-complex	58	17	24	10	9	40
Dowdstown Ph 3	Enclosure-complex	34	0	15	18	9	59
Roestown 1a	Enclosure-complex	23	0	9	9	26	57
Roestown 1b	Enclosure-complex	11	0	18	18	0	64
Roestown 2a	Enclosure-complex	25	4	8	16	20	52
Roestown 2b	Enclosure-complex	27	0	0	0	7	93
Roestown 3a	Enclosure-complex	30	3	3	10	10	73
Roestown 3b	Enclosure-complex	4	0	0	0	0	100
Roestown 4	Enclosure-complex	8	0	13	13	38	38
Johnstown	Settlement-cemetery	12	25	42	25	0	8
Raystown 2	Settlement-cemetery	33	12	18	39	0	30
Raystown 3	Settlement-cemetery	15	7	23	23	7	40
Raystown 5	Settlement-cemetery	12	8	21	21	0	50

cussed in chapter 1 that have perturbed assumptions that early medieval settlement is composed of isolated farmsteads with a few pockets of aggregated settlement. The list is also striking because it includes both sacred settlements (settlement-cemeteries) and sites without overly sacred practices (enclosure complexes). These settlements are clearly very different from Clonmacnoise and Dublin. They are not usefully described as "urban." But, they do suggest a similar break from the rural production/consumption cycles. The presence of provisioning at these sites matches well with Bhreathnach's call to back away from check-list approaches to urbanism. It is a social phenomenon with implications across the settlement landscape.

Two additional sites bear consideration. They do not have the dearth of young cattle that is an essential quality for identifying a full provisioning process, but they do have an unusually high concentration of older cattle than could suggest another instance of urban qualities at a non-urban settlement. The first is Knowth. McCormick and Murray view the data from all stages at Knowth as reflecting engagement with production/consumption with an emphasis on dairy products as is typical of ringforts such as Moynagh Lough. Both are fundamentally farmsteads. But McCormick and Murray also see important distinctions between Knowth and typical farmsteads: fewer cattle in the youngest stage (5 percent vs. 15 percent) and more cattle in the oldest age stage (41 percent vs. 27 percent), leading McCormick and Murray to conclude that, like Scandinavian Dublin, Knowth was fed by "outside producers on a commercial basis" (McCormick and Murray 2007: 54–58). Notably, the faunal assemblage from the tenth century (Stage 9) also has qualities typically associated with urban centers: cat bones show evidence of skinning (see below and McCormick and Murray 2007: 49–50). With a total of fifteen houses and a large number of hearth sites in the surrounding area, this aggregated site is clearly not the same as Dublin, but Knowth does seem to have been enmeshed in a wider socio-economy where rural and urban distinctions were filling the landscape.

The second site is Clonfad (Co. Westmeath), located approximately fifty kilometers from Clonmacnoise along the same glacial ridges that formed important east/west routeways through medieval Ireland. Excavations in advance of road construction during 2004 and 2005 revealed evidence for a large and economically complex sacred settlement dating from 500 to 900 (Stevens 2009 and 2010). Paul Stevens found evidence of concentric enclosures. Like Clonmacnoise, habitation occurred in the central area early on, but the settlement was substantially reorganized at some point in the eighth century. As at Clonmacnoise, a manufacturing zone developed adjacent to a central area devoted to the most obviously ritual activities at the site: worship and burial. Clonfad yielded even more evidence for iron working than the New Graveyard excavations. Stevens places particular emphasis on evidence for techniques associated with the manufacture of iron handbells, one of most potent liturgical implements from the period. Some were enshrined as saints' relics. A tale recalls that Ciarán of Clonmacnoise used a bell to recall a murdered king from the dead (Stevens 2015: 135, see also Bourke 1980, 2008, and Devane 2013). In addition to large amounts of raw materials, bell production also requires considerable technical skill, including application of a bronze or copper brazing to the exterior.

The Clonfad assemblage yielded a substantial body of data on age-at-death for cattle ($N = 37$). Unfortunately, several factors militate against comparing Clonfad slaughter data with data from other sites. The method used for the Clonfad assemblage is different from that used for the other assemblages. Loose teeth are also excluded from calculation, which depresses the prevalence of older cattle. But, even accounting for these factors, the assemblage has parallels to Knowth. Emma Miller (2009) reports that no cattle under eight months of age were identified, 40.5 percent were from cattle ages eight to eighteen months. This pattern matches the rural slaughter pattern with a peak for prime aged cattle, as at both Moynagh Lough and Knowth. But, at Clonfad, approximately 38 percent of the cattle were more than thirty-six months. That figure matches the anomalously high figure from Knowth Stage 9, particularly if the not including loose teeth in the Clonfad age estimates depressed the number of elderly cattle registered. Both sites appear to have

PIGS

Pigs are the second most common species in the New Graveyard assemblage. At 25 percent and 31 percent respectively of the Phase 1 and Phase 2 assemblages, the New Graveyard values are typical for early medieval Ireland. The plots from the Fishamble St. excavations in Dublin are substantially different. This assemblage has among the largest proportion of pigs in all early medieval assemblages: 55 percent. McCormick (2013: 5) suggests that the high prevalence of pigs in the Fishamble St. plots is explained by the fact that, unlike sheep and cattle, pigs could be reared within settlements. In support of that conclusion, the assemblage included large numbers of neonatal pig bones (McCormick 1987: 136). The excavations also yielded evidence of a pen for pigs (Wallace 1992: 124). Dependence on pigs is best understood as a counterpart to cattle provisioning. Pig rearing gave town-dwellers a measure of independence from hinterland producers. As McCormick writes, Dublin "was surrounded by a politically unstable and often hostile hinterland leading the inhabitants to produce a reliable source of home-grown protein" (McCormick 2013: 5). Following this line of logic, it is notable that the prevalence of pigs fluctuates considerably among the different levels of the Fishamble St. excavation. McCormick identifies change from values between 40 percent and 50 percent in the early layers to values between 60 percent and 70 percent in three middle layers. In the uppermost levels, the percentage returns to the values of the early layers (McCormick 1987: 125–26 and McCormick and Murray 2007: 225). Although fluctuations could result from a variety of causes other than instability in the supply of cattle, changes are correlated with the prevalence of cattle, and, with the exception of one of the uppermost layers, the sheep/goat percentage remains fairly constant. This pattern of linked prevalence supports viewing pigs as counter-balancing dependence on cattle provisioning. As was discussed earlier, no such intrasite variation is evident in the New Graveyard. As with cattle, pigs remained a stable presence through Phases 1 and 2.

The degree of reliance on pigs found in the Fishamble St. assemblage is rare in early medieval Ireland. High percentages of pigs are not found in assemblages from other coastal urban sites. McCormick notes only one other assemblage with percentages similar to those of Dublin: Castlefarm, a settlement cemetery in Co. Meath, where the prevalence of pigs also reaches 50 percent in the eighth- to tenth-century assemblage (McCormick 2013: 5).

This pairing of Castlefarm and Dublin is intriguing because Castlefarm is among the settlement-cemeteries with evidence of cattle provisioning, further deepening association of such sites with the types of socio-economic complexity associated with "urban" economies, yet the absence of heavy reliance on pigs at all the other sites with evidence of cattle provisioning highlights the variable forms these animal economies can take in different settings.

Age-at-death data provide additional insights on the roles pigs play in different settings. The primary product pigs provide is meat, which fosters a tendency to slaughter when individuals reach mature size (between eighteen months and two years old). As figure 4.4 shows, slaughter patterns on rural sites are highly concentrated in this age category, with more than 60 percent of the individuals in the seventeen to twenty-three month category. At Fishamble St. and Clonmacnoise, under 40 percent are. Slaughter is dispersed across a variety of ages. McCormick and Murray emphasize the secondary slaughter peak between six months and a year, as a result of efforts to keep populations at a manageable level in an urban setting (2007: 61–64). But, the assemblage does not only differ from rural assemblages in this one category. The Fishamble assemblage also has more pigs considerably older than two years than farmsteads. Whereas Fishamble St. has 26 percent in twenty-three plus age categories, Moynagh has 16 percent and Knowth Stage 9 only 9 percent. Deer Park Farms matches Fishamble St. in having 26 percent in the oldest two age categories, but, with 62 percent in the seventeen to twenty-three month category and only 14 percent in the youngest age categories, Deer Park Farms does not have the fully dispersed pattern from Fishamble St.

The Phase 1 and 2 assemblage from Clonmacnoise has the same dispersed age-at-death pattern found at Fishamble St. While they lack the very high percentage of the youngest pigs found in Fishamble St., the assemblages have a similar concentration under seventeen months: Phase 1 = 34 percent, Phase 2 = 29 percent; Fishamble = 33 percent. As was discussed in chapter 2, the landscape around Clonmacnoise was dominated by scrubby woodland through the middle ages. That landscape could have provided a variety of farrowing locations not found around Dublin, which in turn could reduce the number of the youngest pigs at Clonmacnoise. But, pigs in their first year and a half of life died at similar rates on both sites. Slaughter rates for the eldest two categories (more than twenty-three months) are also similar: Fishamble = 26 percent, Phase 1 = 26 percent, Phase 2 = 34 percent.

A variety of factors could foster these dispersed slaughter patterns. The pattern could be in response to extended periods of shortage at provisioned settlements and/or a more generalized need to supplement food resources (as opposed to a more seasonally concentrated need/use at sites such as Knowth). But, it is also worth remembering that pigs can be driven across landscapes in

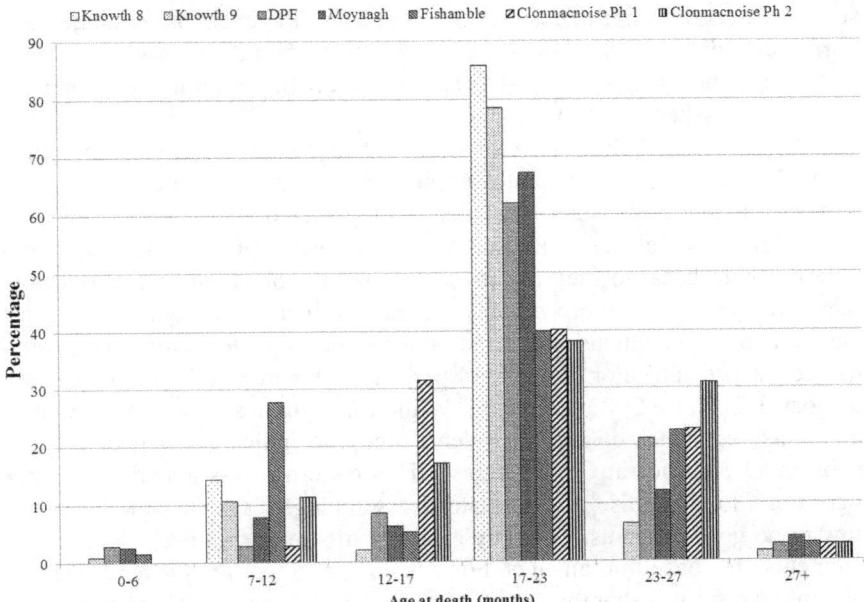

Figure 4.4. Comparison of pig mortality patterns from Knowth, Fishamble St., and Phase 2 (Knowth and Fishamble St. data after McCormick and Murray 2007). Created by John Soderberg.

a manner not dissimilar to cattle, although historical accounts of pig drovers do suggest that pigs were more recalcitrant participants than cattle. As with cattle, it is possible that the increased number of older pigs at Fishamble St. and Clonmacnoise also reflects provisioning with pigs.

Unlike evidence for cattle provisioning, dispersed slaughter patterns are not common at settlement-cemeteries and enclosure complexes. The only sites with cattle provisioning that also have less than 50 percent of pigs in the seventeen to twenty-three month category are: Raystown (3 and 5), Dowdstown (Phase 2 and Phase 3), Rathoath, and Roestown 3a.[5]

SHEEP AND GOATS

Separating sheep from goats is a difficult matter zooarchaeologically. Jennifer Bourdillon and Jennie Coy refer to the various anatomical features that distinguish sheep from goats as "an elaborate muddle" (1980: 109). While diagnostic shape differences do exist, isolating them in an assemblage is complicated by other sources of variation such as state of preservation, age, sex, and the prevalence of castration. In the New Graveyard assemblage, only horn cores, distal humeri, proximal radii, and metapodia showed consistent distinctions between sheep and goats, based on the criteria established by Joachim Boessneck (1969).

Goat post-cranial elements are a small but consistent presence in the Phase 1 and 2 assemblages. The small sample size for many of the diagnostic elements causes the measured prevalence of goats to fluctuate considerably from element to element. Proximal radii probably provide the most reliable estimate because they are present in reasonably large numbers (more than twenty) and are more reliably diagnostic than other elements (i.e., the percentage of specimens with ambiguous features or too much damage to categorize is small). For Phase 1, 14 percent of the proximal radii are classed as goat. For Phase 2, 8 percent are. While these figures should not be taken as precise estimates of goat prevalence, they do indicate that goats were a substantial presence at Clonmacnoise. This pattern marks a stark difference between Clonmacnoise and farmstead assemblages, which generally have few to no goat elements. The only category of site to routinely contain goat elements are coastal urban sites. For example, in a tenth to eleventh-century assemblage from Fishamble St. (Plots 2 and 3), 17 percent of the radii were from goats (McCormick and Murray 2007: 230). Such figures are typical of early medieval urban assemblages (see McCormick and Murphy 1997: 203 and McCormick 1997: 343–44). Like pigs, goats have very flexible diets and can be kept in densely settled areas. In addition to meat and hides, they would also have been a source of milk and other products for city-dwellers otherwise dependent on provisioning relationships.

Goats are also significant because they provide clear evidence of trade and specialization. While goats represent no more than 10 percent or 15 percent of the post-cranial elements, they provided the majority of horn cores. In Phase 1, 67 percent of the horn cores were from goats ($N = 12$). In Phase 2, 64 percent were ($N = 11$). This pattern is common at coastal urban sites, including Dublin (McCormick and Murphy 1997: 203), Drogheda (McCormick 1984: 211), Limerick (McCormick 1984: 324), and Waterford (McCormick 1997a: 343–44). The superabundance of horn cores in comparison with the goat post-cranial elements, suggests that these sites were specializing in horn-working and hide-working, because hides were transported with horns/head attached (Serjeantson 1989).

The disproportionate abundance of horn cores in Phases 1 and 2 suggests that intensive trade-based manufacturing was also occurring at Clonmacnoise, but, as with cattle provisioning, several centuries before the period when it becomes common at coastal urban centers. The Fishamble St. Plot assemblage—which is roughly contemporary with New Graveyard Phase

2—shows no such contrast between horn core and post-cranial elements. Among assemblages dating to the earlier centuries of the medieval period, the only other site to produce a substantial number of goat elements is Deer Park Farms, a ringfort in Co. Antrim, with 77 percent of horn cores from goats ($N = 13$) (McCormick and Murray 2011: 477–78). None of the settlement cemeteries or enclosure complexes produced significant concentrations of goats, either in the form of horn cores or post-cranial elements.

The sample size for sheep/goat mortality data in Phases 1 and 2 is small. Phase 1 has only ten specimens yielding age-at-death estimates (Stage 1 = 10 percent, Stage 2 = 80 percent. Stage 3 = 10 percent). Phase 2 has eleven specimens (Stage 1= 0 percent, Stage 2 = 36 percent, Stage 3 = 64 percent). The contrast in the number of individuals in the oldest age category might suggest an increased orientation on wool over time. But, any conclusions are very tentative because the sample sizes are small and the data may include both sheep and goats, which confuses understanding of management strategies.

OTHER ANIMALS

Horses are a small, but consistent, feature of the New Graveyard assemblages. Estimates of withers height range between 130 and 135 centimeters, which is typical of early medieval faunal assemblages. Dogs are 1.12 percent of the total NISP in Phase 1. Dogs are somewhat less common in Phase 2, at 0.53 percent. The difference, however, might be inflated by differences in the number of teeth. In Phase 1, teeth comprise 31 percent of the dog assemblage. In Phase 2, teeth are only 21 percent of the assemblage. All but a few of the dog elements are fused. In terms of body size, all elements yielding height estimates indicate that New Graveyard dogs fall into the two size categories identified among early medieval dogs (McCormick 1991: 44–45). Both dog sizes are present in Phase 1. Phase 2 contains only the small size. The prevalence of cats follows the pattern with dogs. Phase 1 has a slightly higher percentage than Phase 2 (Phase1 = 0.82 percent, Phase 2 = 0.45 percent, calculated in terms of NISP).

Mark Maltby (1979) and others (e.g., Hatting 1990; McCormick 1988) have suggested that cat and dog assemblages in urban setting have several distinctive features: high percentages of unfused elements, high concentrations of bones in single features, and the presence of skinning marks. In Ireland, evidence for both young age-at-death and skinning cutmarks is particularly strong at Waterford (McCormick and Murphy 1997: 833). These patterns are generally interpreted as indicating an emphasis on pelt production and less salutary conditions in dense settlements (e.g., McCormick and Murray 2017:

206). Rural cats and dogs presumably lived longer lives as pets, scavengers, guards, hunting aids, and pest exterminators. Neither the dog nor the cat assemblages from Clonmacnoise yield such evidence for specialization in dog or cat pelts. Pelt production does not seem to have been a major concern.

One additional point about the cat and dog assemblages bears mentioning. Mandibles suggest that two distinct morphologies existed at Clonmacnoise. The two relevant dimensions are the length of the cheek tooth row (vdD #5) and the length of the carnassial alveolus (the opening in the mandible that receives the tooth root (vdD #7) in New Graveyard cats. Carnassial teeth are the shearing cheek teeth that give the order *Carnivora* its name. Based on these dimensions, the New Graveyard cats segregate into two clusters: one shorter in length and smaller carnassial teeth and a second with longer mandibles and often larger carnassials. Most of the Phase 2 individuals fall into the larger of the two groups. Dog mandibles have a similarly bifurcated distribution when comparing the height of the mandible at M1 (vdD # 14) and the length of the carnassial alveolus (vdD #19). Further discussion of this morphology is deferred until chapter 5 to include Phase 3 elements as well.

The red deer assemblage for Phase 1 contains ninety-nine elements, of which forty-nine are antler fragments. Excluding cranial fragments and teeth, 43 percent of the assemblage is post-cranial. These numbers are noteworthy for two reasons. First, red deer comprise 1.87 percent of the total NISP for Phase 1. While not as high a percentage as found at Moyne ecclesiastical enclosure (McCormick 1987), the prevalence of red deer in the New Graveyard is substantially higher than is typical for early medieval sites, which provides some support for McCormick's (1997b) suggestion that red deer had a particular association with ecclesiastical settlements. Second, the Phase 1 red deer assemblage is evenly split between antler and post-cranial elements (see figure 6.10). Medieval Irish assemblages from urban centers typically have very few post-cranial elements, suggesting that the red deer remains derive primarily from antler imported into sites. The Phase 1 pattern is more typical of farmsteads, where carcasses were more commonly brought to site. In support of this suggestion, the assemblage contains four examples of antlers cut from skulls, which indicates that at least part of the carcass arrived with the antler. The assemblage also includes eight specimens of shed antler, which can be collected from the landscape without harming animals. In the Fishamble St. assemblage, by contrast, all five of the antler bases were from shed antler (McCormick 1987: 151). The Phase 2 assemblage has the same characteristics as Phase 1: red deer are over 1.2 percent of the NISP total ($N = 100$) and the assemblage has a balanced antler/post-cranial ratio. Excluding cranial fragments and teeth, 51 percent of the assemblage is post-cranial. The

Phase 2 assemblage contains two examples of shed antler and four broken from the skull.

The divergence between Dublin and Clonmacnoise suggests that deer had a different role at the two sites. They were a significantly larger presence at Clonmacnoise and were present equally in the form of antler and carcass portions. Their presence at Dublin and other coastal urban sites reflects intensive commodity production with antler. Deer had a more variable role at Clonmacnoise. In Phases 1 and 2, Clonmacnoise maintained access to red deer bodies in ways more similar to rural farmsteads than coastal urban settlements.

Understanding the significance of this divergence is complex. The pattern matches the cat and dog assemblages in not indicating intensive commodity production as is found at coastal urban settlements. Each of these three species diverges in the same way. But, these species also comprise only a few percent of the total assemblage. Otherwise, the Phase 1 and 2 assemblages have precisely the patterns one expects to emerge from an urban settlement in northwestern early medieval Europe. As was discussed in chapter 2, manufacturing with iron and other metals was clearly a significant presence at Clonmacnoise in these early centuries. But, the deer remains do suggest that these animals had not been pulled into commodity manufacturing processes in ways seen at coastal trade settlements. Given the extent to which those coastal settlements are understood as the consequence of the social dynamics of producing and exchanging commodities, the deer of Phases 1 and 2 provide intriguing evidence that Clonmacnoise had a different orientation in these centuries.

CONCLUSIONS: CONCEPTUALIZING MONASTIC ECONOMIES

The animal bone assemblages from Phases 1 and 2 in the New Graveyard demonstrate that Clonmacnoise was not a farmstead in this era. From circa 700, the monastery was not fully enmeshed in the production/consumption cycles that typify ringforts and other such farmsteads. As was discussed in chapter 1, many monasteries were. Visiting Caherlehillan was as much visiting a farmstead as a shrine. Such sacred settlements intensified and recontextualized farms. Visiting Clonmacnoise was different. The experience would have been more like entering Dublin in terms of ways that animals and people were bundled together from the surrounding countryside. Visitors walking into Dublin and Clonmacnoise would have found the same range of animals as a farmstead, but they would also have experienced divergences from the farmstead as well. For both sites, visitors would have walked mostly with their elderly cows, leaving the most valuable animals at home. They might have noticed the wider variety of pigs and the strange presence of goats.

In short, both sites have the three primary signatures of provisioning: the majority of cattle killed at an advanced age, pigs killed at a wide variety of ages, and high prevalence of goats. The similarity between Dublin and Clonmacnoise is particularly striking for Phase 1. Clonmacnoise has an urban provisioning pattern from circa 700, a century or two earlier than Dublin. The houses and other structures identified in Phase 2 suggest a density and permanence of settlement not unlike Dublin in the same period. The circumstances in Phase 1 are less clear. The numerous stakes holes and other occupation debris suggest intensive occupation, but numbers of structures are unknown. It is also possible that occupation was not year-round. But, the animal bones do not indicate any substantial change in the economies between the two phases. Urban-style provisioning is present from the earliest deposits onward. New evidence from settlement-cemeteries and settlement enclosures indicates that such socio-economic complexities were common-place in early medieval Ireland.

As was discussed in the introduction, socio-economic complexity in early medieval Europe, including urbanism, have often been viewed in terms of a wave of advance rolling out from Merovingian lands. That logic supports a relatively late emergence for urban qualities in Ireland in the form of coastal trade settlements in the ninth century, a century or more after Anglo-Saxon trade settlements such as Ipswich and Hamwic. The elderly cattle of Phase 1 walking to Clonmacnoise perturb that model. They are showing up in the wrong place, a monastery, and the wrong time, circa 700. Two solutions to this anomaly are possible. The requisite conditions—social centralization and commodity production—could be more prevalent than has been assumed. Or, dynamics outside the models of political approaches are responsible.

Both are undoubtedly correct. Perhaps as far back at the Roman period, and certainly since the Middle Ages, colonialist assumptions have fostered a sense that Ireland is behind or otherwise distinct from other area of medieval Europe. Since the mid-twentieth century, discovery after discovery has shown that qualities once assumed absent in the first millennium were in fact prevalent. Urbanism was once thought to be a post-Norman introduction. Since the 1980s, excavations in Dublin and elsewhere have demonstrated that cities were present by the ninth century. The animals of Phase 1 fit this trend by demonstrating the economic complexities deep inland circa 700. As was discussed in chapter 1, recent studies have also demonstrated relatively long-distance movements of animals into Iron Age ceremonial centers (e.g., Madgwick et al. 2019). That pattern suggests that whatever fueled cattle movements at Clonmacnoise may have roots extending back into the Iron Age.

But, the fact that both Dublin and Clonmacnoise are provisioned settlements does not mean that the same values aminated the movements of cattle. Cattle arriving at Clonmacnoise were walking into a very different settlement from Dublin or Hamwic. Clonmacnoise is an inland monastery, not a coastal trade depot. The balanced antler-to-post-cranial element ratio in the red deer assemblage suggests that different contexts facilitated different intensities of manufacturing. The challenge is figuring out how zooarchaeological evidence of provisioning links with the concept of a monastic town and the wider concept of ceremonial centers. How is it associated with the Wheatleyan notion that a rural visitor would be not be confronted with an alien environment?

A brief tour of views on the relationship between provisioning and urbanism will help answer that question. From the mid-twentieth century, perspectives were dominated by political approaches to what has been called the "be-cattling" of early medieval towns (Bourdillon and Coy 1980: 109). Weberian models of towns subordinating hinterlands understanding of provisioning. Wietske Prummel (1983) identifies supply farms at the edge of Dorestad (Neatherlands) as evidence of elite organization of supply. Steen Hvass (1979) concluded that Haithabu (Germany), which records describe as a royal foundation, had a more dispersed hinterland than at Dorestad, but one no less centrally directed. In Britain, Hamwic and other trade cities yielded similar evidence of provisioning, but evidence for highly organized hinterlands was harder to identify.[6] Reasoning that the lack of variation implies a central organization for distribution, Bourdillon concludes that movements of animals were organized by royal authority, presumably based in Winchester (Bourdillon 1988 and 1994). While she does ultimately support an elite directed model of provisioning, the support is quite equivocal. Against that conclusion, Bourdillon writes that "the feeding, the refuse-disposal habits, and even the animals of Hamwic are strangely egalitarian" (1988: 190). The strangely egalitarian be-cattling of Hamic signals a serious point of concern with what that model obscures. It seeks an account of a "co-operative of equals" to balance reliance on "some external power" (1988: 190). I take Bourdillon's concerns as parallel to those that motivated Charles Doherty (1985) to write about monastic towns as a counterbalance to prevailing theories at much the same time.

Changes in Pam Crabtree's views on urbanism illustrate how Bourdillon's concerns have blossomed into a robust account of the variable social dynamics associated with provisioning and other socioeconomics processes. In the 1990s, her assessments of material from Ipswich arrived at similar conclusions: provisioning was fueled by royal renders separating urban consumers and hinterland producers (see Crabtree 2018: 104–5). But, more recently, Crabtree has reconsidered that explanation (e.g., Crabtree 2016). First, zooarchaeological data from later periods when rural and urban contacts were not operating via royal renders show no changes. Second, other research has shown that markets and fairs were common presences from very early, suggesting that consumer and producer populations would have had ample opportunities for direct contact. These observations led Crabtree to stress the variety of ways that urban centers would have been articulated with their surroundings, which in turn facilitates diverse processes for the growth of towns. As was noted in chapter 1, Crabtree singles out the work of Susan Oosthuizen (e.g., 2016) as an effective alternative to top-down models for social dynamics in early Anglo-Saxon England (2018: 82–83). Oosthuizen builds her more mutualistic view of social dynamics through a focus on shared pasture rights. These practices foster horizontal forms of governance that compliment elite directed models. As does Frans Theuws (2012), Oosthuizen seeks an account that will capture such variation in fundamental desires, variation that is not driven by simple utilitarian individualism.

I resort to grounded theories of religion for provisioning at Clonmacnoise. But, Oosthuzien's orientation on the need for a better account of what she calls "mutualities" is similar. In a sense, we are both pursuing a means to explain the strangely egalitarian aspects of be-cattling of Hamwic and other points in the landscape. It is also much the same orientation reflected in Wheatley's rural visitors. Pursuing the likelihood of such alternatives for Anglo-Saxon England is well beyond the parameters of this study. But, it does help bring into focus the utility of Wheatelyan perspectives for Ireland. If the strangely egalitarian qualities that Oosthuzien to mutualities is an important facet of Hamwic or Ipswich, it is even more so for Clonmacnoise.

As was discussed in chapter 2, Clonmacnoise's rise is usually examined in terms of elite stratagems for control. Narratives about the core of Clonmacnoise—particularly its reorganization circa 900—encompass a variety of strategies, but maximizing elites still animate change. The High Crosses and the sanctuary they define are usually seen as results of Flann's efforts to consolidate control. This chapter has highlighted the roles that animals had across these same centuries. The intent is to pursue the concerns that Bourdillon's strangely egalitarian animals raised and to reconfigure their "strangeness" around grounded approaches to religion.

Sanctuary cities in Ireland are of enduring interest because they flourish away from the centers of gravity for these social dynamics. During Phases 1 and 2, Clonmacnoise lacks the abundant evidence for weights, coinage, property boundaries, and other such signatures of commodification that define coastal centers such as Dublin. Parallels to the estate centers yielding control over agriculture are more difficult to identify in Ireland than in early Anglo-Saxon England. Yet, Clonmacnoise clearly shows that it was drawing together people and processes just as were other early post-Roman towns. In this sense, Clonmacnoise provides yet another demonstration of the variety of urbanisms that grew in post-Roman Europe.

The critical next step though is establishing a means to keep explanations for what is fueling such variation from collapsing back into utilitarian individualism. In terms of Theuws's concern about a common theme from the days when Bourdillon first discussed Hamwic onwards, the challenge is to find an alternative to "the idea that elites are crucial to the economic growth of the early Middle Ages" (2012: 33).

It would be perverse to argue that sanctuary cities and Dublin are results of entirely different dynamics. But, their locales are different in terms of the prevalence of sanctuary and commodification. Wheatley created his concept of a ceremonial center to give social significance to just this sort of everyday religious experience. As chapter 3 demonstrated, a considerable amount of work is necessary to square Wheatley's concept with advances in religious studies, but bundling and crossing/dwelling can define the relationship between a city and its hinterland Weber established. Wheatley's visitors were "not confronted with new and often alarming experiences" or "an unfamiliar value system" (Wheatley 1971: 389). In contrast to the Weberian city, where the experience of a rural stranger is one of alienation, "the mores of the ceremonial city were essentially those of the village in more refined form" (Wheatley 1971: 479). They are strangers finding sanctuary. The cattle afford that process of bundling and crossing/dwelling. Provisioning becomes a generative social dynamic in which strangers create a sacred settlement.

The sanctuary cities of early medieval Ireland present an opportunity to bring these dynamics into focus. In this sense they remain just the counterpoint to settlements such as Dublin which Doherty proposed decades ago. To see how, we just need to afford visitors with their cattle a place in creating sanctuary.

NOTES

1. Data tables related to this chapter are available on this book's webpage at rowman.com.

2. For a detailed summary, see McCormick and Murray (2007: 209–17).

2. The ratio of horn cores to total NISP values are as follows: Phase 1 = 54/3178 (1.7 percent); Phase 2 = 64/4731 (1.4 percent), Knowth 8 = 13/723 (1.8 percent), Knowth 9 = 61/2900 (2 percent), Moynagh D = 87/4739 (1.8 percent), Fishamble St., Plot 2 = 196/12276 (1.6 percent).

3. This description avoids the term self-sufficient because trade and exchange are an element of essentially all settlements. Cattle and other animals would have moved among farmsteads.

4. In addition to the sites included in the table, two other settlement-cemeteries produced age data dominated by elderly cattle, but the data is reported in a form that cannot be correlated with the age categories used for other sites. At both Rathoath and Castlefarm (II and III) very few prime-aged cattle were present and the strong majority of the cattle were elderly.

5. The Roestown 3a assemblage has only five specimens, which makes this conclusion suspect. The other phases have larger assemblages and a single slaughter peak.

6. Subsequent research has identified the locations of provisioning farms. For a review of these issues, see Crabtree 2018: 97–133.

Chapter Five

Animals, Tabernacles, and Towns
The Iconography of Sanctuary

INTRODUCTION

The previous chapter took animal bones as a point of entry for understanding Clonmacnoise. The aim was to reframe discourse about Clonmacnoise as a sanctuary city in terms of the grounded approaches to religion developed in earlier chapters. This chapter maintains an orientation on animals but shifts to a different medium: iconography. The goal is to explore how representations of animals on the best-known monument to sanctuary at Clonmacnoise—the Cross of Scriptures—demonstrates similarly grounded concepts of religion. As with the last chapter, centering analysis on animal iconography, rather human iconography, is intended to shift narratives about what creates sanctuary at Clonmacnoise dominated by the foundation panel showing Flann and Coleman planting. Looking at all the animals swirling around the Foundation Panel invites consideration of what else animated sanctuary emanating from the Cross of Scriptures.

The effort is an extension of art historical studies that focus on discordant marginalia as a means of demonstrating the multivocality of iconography (e.g., McDonald 2006). The Cross of Scriptures has many voices, some offering arguments for and others rejections of Flann's stratagems in reconstructing the core of Clonmacnoise. Shifting attention to animal iconography is a means of attending to those other voices. But "vocality" is also a limiting metaphor for iconography. Phenomenological approaches to iconography reject notions that observers simply decode knowledge "spoken" from the iconography. In the terms from chapter 3, simulative models of cognition emphasize deeper entanglements between image and person. Iconography is not an external storage device.

As was observed in the previous chapter, animals are probably the most common point of contact people would have had with Clonmacnoise. For many, if not most, being amidst the butchery and bone-working along the banks of the Shannon was being at Clonmacnoise. Approaching the Cross of Scriptures via animals is an effort to articulate that experience of Clonmacnoise with being at the Cross of Scriptures. As with zooarchaeology, this iconographic study is another medium for articulating settlement and sacred.

The chapter begins with an account of the animals portrayed on the Cross of Scriptures and select other crosses. Patterns in these animal representations are then linked to the role the Cross of Scriptures had in creating sanctuary at Clonmacnoise. The core questions are what roles animals had in defining that manifestation of sanctuary and whether those roles help make sense of sanctuary cities as an element of post-Roman urbanism.

In a sense, the previous chapter brought sanctuary to the New Graveyard, and this chapter brings the New Graveyard to sanctuary. Somewhere among those crossing/dwellings a sanctuary city should emerge.

APPROACHING HIGH CROSSES

Roger Stalley (2020) estimates that well over two hundred high crosses currently exist in Ireland, with ten or fifteen percent having the elaborate iconographic program associated with the Cross of Scriptures. Most were carved from sandstone, although granite and other types of stone were occasionally used. Most crosses were constructed in three or four sections which, when assembled, form a variety of zones for iconography: base, shaft, transverse arms, ring, and upper arm/cap (figure 5.1).

Their most iconic feature is the ring encircling the arms of the cross. Rings probably had a mix of structural, aesthetic, and symbolic functions. They also indicate the cosmopolitan context in which the iconography developed. Clear parallels for a ring encircling the center of a cross exist in a sixth-century textile from Egypt now held by the Minneapolis Institute of Arts. It shows a cross fixed into a base with a wreath of fruit and other vegetation circling arms, presumably drawn from earlier associations of wreaths with victory. Similar depictions are found around the Mediterranean from at least the fourth century. Building from concepts of the cross representing the four axes of the cosmos, ringed crosses are thought to mark transformations associated with Christ's sacrifice (Roe 1965. See Stalley 2020: 10–11 for review).

In addition to marking out a sanctuary, crosses also marked the locations of significant events and perhaps stations in liturgy. They do not appear to have been burial markers, although burial did occur around them (e.g., King 1997a,

Figure 5.1. View of the Cross of Scriptures (replica) from the west with the Cathedral in the background. Letters identify cross segments: A. cap, B. arm, C. ring, D. shaft, E. base. Photo by John Soderberg.

chapter 2). Stalley (1996: 40) suggests that they are likely to have been focal points for liturgical ceremonies, prayer, and penance. The association of high crosses with various sacred practices makes them an important locus for exploring the value of grounded approaches to religion. If concepts such as sacred as intensification of mundane were important at Clonmacnoise, the concerns about food and raw material that dominate New Graveyard zooarchaeology should be entangled with cross iconography. Given the role of the Cross of Scriptures in defining sanctuary, the iconography should offer a border around which those walking cattle to slaughter along the Shannon cross/dwell with liturgy and worship.

Recent art historical scholarship is attentive to this sense of being at crosses. Phenomenological perspectives have promoted attention to ways that bodies would have engaged with iconography (e.g., E. Ó Carragáin 2011). Heather Pulliam (2020) argues that, if attention is only focused on decoding prescribed meanings, analysis misses ways that observer's experience is an essential part of creating meaning. She quotes Marilyn Stokstad's observation that "art history needs to widen the objects of its obsessions, beyond visual culture and media, outwards towards the human and other-than-human vectors that animate the planet and its ecosystems" (Stokstad 2004: 93 in Pulliam 2020: 8). That assertion is fundamentally the same as was discussed in the context of the contrast between transductive and simulative models of cognition. Viewers encountering iconography are not accessing meanings held there as if objects were some sort of external storage device. Meanings emerge from engagements.

Working from the biological twist given practice-based approaches to religion in chapter 3, I consider Pulliam to argue for a grounded approach to understanding iconography. In these terms, she advocates an ecological orientation on crossing/dwelling among viewer, object, and the wider associations of both. In this sense, Stokstad's orientation resonates with charismatic ecologies and other such biological concepts.

Pulliam's reading of the foundation panel on bottom of the shaft of the Cross of Scriptures demonstrates the potential of this phenomenological/ grounded approach (figure 2.3). She notes that the panel faces east and would have been illuminated by the rising sun bringing different elements to visibility as light moved upward from the base to the foundation panel and upward to the peak of the cross. Such dynamics lead her to consider relationships among the different elements gradually becoming visible to observers. As was discussed in chapter 2, a consensus holds that the iconography of the panel addresses the role of secular patronage in fueling Clonmacnoise. Pulliam's phenomenological approach emphasizes relationships among different panels that significantly reframe conclusions that the Cross of Scriptures is a monument to Flann's patronage and control over Clonmacnoise (Pulliam 2020: 10–12). The Last Judgement is above the foundation panel. To Christ's left, the damned are sent into the company of demons. To Christ's right, the saved are sent into the company of a trumpeting angel. To someone standing in front of the cross, the royal figure in the foundation panel is directly below the region of the damned (i.e., to Christ's left). The abbot is below the saved. For Pulliam, that relationship suggests that the iconography undercuts secular power as much as it celebrates Clonmacnoise's bargain with it.

Pulliam also notes evidence that worshipers are known to have moved around crosses, creating horizontal relationships among panels on the different faces of the cross. The king stands to the north of the abbot in the foundation panel. Building from a general association of the north with temptation, Pulliam argues that the panels on the north face of the cross depict the wages of worldly sins. The north face of the cross also faces the Shannon and the area of the site most connected to commerce and manufacturing. An observer moving northward around the cross toward the Shannon would next encounter the abutting panel showing a seated figure holding a book in one hand and a staff topped by a bird in the other. The figure is stabbing the staff into the eye of a prostrate figure with legs in the air (figure 5.6). Stalley notes that, while the exact references are obscure, the scene reflects generally victory over heresy or other such failings (Stalley 2020: 170). Pulliam describes the figure as "admonishing a sinner" (Pulliam 2020: 12). By contrast, the panel around to the south from the abbot is an interlace pattern Pulliam identifies as the Greek letter chi, a symbol of Christ's redemptive sacrifice.

That pairing further emphasizes Pulliam's sense that the royal figure is falling onto the side of Christ one hopes to avoid on Judgement Day. Biblically, that day involved separating sheep from goats (Matthew 25:31–46). Flann seems headed off with the goats. As Pulliam observes, "Given the king's involvement with the creation of the cross and church, his position—beneath the damned, on Christ's left, next to a sinner, and north of the abbot—requires some explanation" (2020: 12). Pulliam's explanation highlights tensions between sacred and secular authorities in manner very reminiscent of Doherty's assertion that sanctuary cities served to keep royal authority in check.

Pulliam's goal is to demonstrate the significance of an embodied approach, which trains her attention on a generalized experience of being at the cross. Rather than simply creating the sanctuary space, this and other monuments mark the tensions and anxieties of making such spaces. Though she does specifically cite the relationship of the cross to the wider settlement that dominates archaeological concerns, the people—and animals—of that settlement remain a distant presence. This view threatens to reduce the significance of taking a phenomenological approach by only identifying added complexity to the "meaning" encoded in the cross. In Graeber's terms, the danger is having a limited account of how the values of the cross catalyze desires in those encountering it.

Other phenomenologically inspired approaches have placed more emphasis on the contribution of demographics likely to have walked their cattle to Clonmacnoise. Karen Overbey (2011) draws attention to pilgrimage as a means of considering the wider population's engagement with and creation of holy space: "The space of medieval pilgrimage was . . . perspectival, and produced in the local encounter of pilgrim with *place*. . . . The saints were fully, simultaneously present both in heaven and their relics, and so their tombs were sites of *potential* where the miraculous was manifest" (Overbey 2011: 4). Overbey is particularly interested in the portability of relics as means for creating multivalent sacred spaces.

As with Pulliam, Overbey recognizes that the discourse of power which has dominated consideration of Clonmacnoise's sanctuary has a role. But she emphasizes that reliquaries "in their special polytopic space complicate those operations. . . . [The] relationships between container and contained, and between relic, reliquary, and audience . . . are constantly shifting and re-placed" (2011: 9). Reliquaries were certainly a means of establishing territorial authority, but, equally, they also create the possibility for "unofficial, contradictory, or differential geographies" (183). Overbey is particularly interested in how such possibilities are manifest in pilgrimage, which she describes as this primary context in which the general population engaged with holy places. Essentially, Overbey is moving further out into the wider ecologies that Pulliam recognizes as vital to creating crosses but does not specifically explore. Overbey's perspective aligns well with the archaeological approaches to pilgrimage described in chapter 3.

If Pulliam's and Overbey's arguments are reframed in the terms of grounded approaches to religion, they provide a means of expanding beyond the instrumental views that characterize views of the sanctuary at Clonmacnoise. As simulative views of cognition emphasize, meanings are not simply contained in iconography. Depicting a king and abbot cannot simply demonstrate or create centralized authority. At a proximate level, the iconography circumscribes royal authority as much as it affirms. More generally, if meanings are produced with engagements, the locus of meaning becomes dispersed beyond the narrow agendas of king, abbot or anyone else. The cross becomes a focal point for crossing/dwelling. The challenge is to articulate the pan-demographic sorts of engagements of Overbey's reliquaries with the sacred/secular tensions in Pulliam's Cross of Scriptures. The next section engages that process by bringing zooarchaeological sensibilities to the iconography of the Cross of Scriptures.

ANIMAL ICONOGRAPHY ON HIGH CROSSES

To explore the significance of these engagements, this section considers the portrayal of animals on the Cross of Scriptures (figure 5.2) and six other crosses that Roger Stalley believes are the works of the same artist, whom he calls the "Muiredach Master" (Stalley 2014). While the argument that all seven are products of a single artist/workshop remains under debate, at minimum, they form a coherent and iconographically rich group that provides contextual depth for the Cross of Scriptures. In addition to the Cross of Scriptures, the Muiredach Master crosses includes two crosses (the Market cross and the Tower cross, also known as the Cross of Patrick and Columba) from Kells (Co. Meath), two crosses (Muiredach's cross and the Tall cross) from Monasterboise (Co. Louth), a cross from Durrow (Co. Offaly), and one from Duleek (Co. Meath). All are dated to circa 900.

Four of the seven Muiredach crosses are available as rotatable 3D models, produced by the Discovery Programme (see Devlin and Shaw 2017 for discussion). Posting these models with open access is a tremendous gift to scholars.[1] They allow unrivaled precision of inspection, particularly for those segments getting little direct sunlight. Photographs, drawings, and direct inspection were also used.

The complete list of animals identified is available in Appendix II.[2] For this study, the term "animal" is used as a label for figures that are not human or related anthropomorphic forms (i.e., angels and demons). In some cases, the details of the carving are sufficiently well preserved and/or the context sufficiently unambiguous to allow for precise identifications, such as horse or dog. Hybrid forms are labeled with common terms (i.e., griffon) or by description of the different elements (i.e., lion with wings). In other cases, figures can only be confidently identified to a larger taxonomic category (i.e., quadrupeds or birds). Where elements suggest the possibility of a more specific identity, an additional description appears in the second ID column with an associated degree of certainty (1 = very likely, 2 = more likely than not, 3 = a possibility to consider). Cases where a shape is not clearly either human or animal are listed as "figure."

The location of each animal is registered horizontally by face (the cardinal direction each side faces) and vertically by cross segment. The different segments are: base, shaft, arm (the two lateral extensions outside the ring), arm up (the vertical extension of the cross above the ring), cap (a decorated replacement or addition to "arm up" often in the form of a building), ring curve (the segment of the ring extending between arms), arm under (the downward facing section of the cross arm), and arm cap (the north and south facing ends of the cross arms). Since shafts are divided into individual panels, shaft

148   *Chapter Five*

locations are also given a panel number with one indicating the bottom register. The segment identifications should be considered a tool for describing the distribution of figures, rather than markers for absolute divisions. Adjacent segments often have ambiguous borders.

A total of 246 animals were identified on the seven Muiredach crosses. This number represents a minimum estimate, particularly for crosses as yet unavailable as 3D models (the Monasterboise Tall cross, the Durrow cross, and the Duleek cross). But, in all cases, a degree of ambiguity is inevitable, and perhaps even intended. For example, interlace patterns present substantial difficulties for isolating individual bodies, even when the design is well preserved. A millennium of exposure to the elements makes the challenge more severe.

Figure 5.2. 3D digital model of the Cross of Scriptures, NW and SW corners. Created by the Discovery Programme, Center for Archaeology and Innovation Ireland.

The Cross of Scriptures has at least thirty-four animal figures, which is close to the average number for the group (thirty-five). The Kells Tower cross has the largest number (fifty-eight). Durrow has the fewest (eleven). The majority of the animals on the Cross of Scriptures are located on its base (52 percent). An additional 33 percent are located on the shaft. Each face on the shaft has three panels and a lower edge decorated in low relief (identified as "sub" in the table). Most animals are located on either the bottom edge or the lowest panel of the shaft (64 percent). No animals are depicted on the top registers of the Cross of Scriptures's shaft. Only five animals, 15 percent of the total, are present above the shaft.

Animals are also more likely to appear on the narrower north and south faces of the cross, than the more programmatically central east and west faces, which feature the Crucifixion and Last Judgement respectively. The north face has 44 percent of the animals, and the south 31 percent. The east and west faces have 22 percent and 3 percent respectively. In sum, animals are mainly a matter for peripheral regions of the Cross of Scriptures. They are mainly denizens of the lowest regions and, where they emerge in upper regions, they remain to the side.

Table 5.1. Summary statistics for the vertical and horizontal location of animals on the seven Muiredach crosses (N = 238).

Segment	#	%	Face	#	%
Base	61	26			
Shaft	92	39	E	53	22
Arm under	17	7	N	69	29
Ring curve	7	3	W	42	18
Arm cap	11	5	S	73	31
Arm N	6	3			
Arm S	6	3	**Shaft Location**		
Center	21	9		#	%
Ring face	4	2	High	30	33
Arm up	7	3	Middle	24	26
Cap	6	3	Low	38	41

Table 5.1 provides summary statistics for the Muiredach Master group. They suggest that the distribution of animals on the other crosses is generally similar to the Cross of Scriptures but also hint at significant differences among the seven. As at Clonmacnoise, a strong majority (65 percent) are located on the base and shaft. But that figure is smaller than the Cross of Scriptures, where 85 percent of the animals are on the base or shaft. As a

group, animals are also more evenly distributed around the four shaft faces, indicating that some of the other crosses have significantly more animals at the top of the cross and on the east or west faces. Table 5.1 also indicates that, as a group, animals tend to be far less common on bases, than is the case with the Cross of Scriptures (26 percent vs. 85 percent). To an extent, that difference is exaggerated by the fact that not all of the crosses have decorated bases. The Monasterboise Tall cross and the Durrow cross bases have only geometric designs. The Duleek base is below ground level. But, even in comparison to only those crosses with "inhabited" bases, the Cross of Scriptures has an unusually large percentage of its animals on the base. The Cross of Scriptures has 52 percent. The Kells Market cross has 41 percent. The Kells Tower cross has 19 percent. Muiredach's cross has 25 percent. Interestingly, the Clonmacnoise South cross—which pre-dates the Muiredach Master crosses significantly but was likely moved to its current location when the Cross of Scriptures was implanted—has an even larger percentage of animals on its base than the Cross of Scriptures (69 percent, $N = 16$).

Given the variation in base preservation/decoration, the best means of assessing the extent to which the Muiredach Master crosses keep animals to the lowest regions of the cross is to determine the distribution of animal on the different shafts.

The Monasterboise Tall cross has a distribution very similar to the Cross of Scriptures. Seventy-six percent of the animals are located on the north and south faces. While no animals are present on the base (it contains only geometric designs), 53 percent of the animals on the shaft are located in the bottom two levels of the shaft. Under 20 percent of all the animals are located in the upper half of the shaft. Since 75 percent of all the animals on the cross are on the shaft, animals are primarily features of the lower regions.

On Muiredach's cross at Monasterboise, the arrangement is more complex, but, ultimately, also emphasizes the presence of animals in lower regions. A smaller percentage of the total occurs on its base (28 percent). But attention is drawn to animals at the base of the shaft by pairs of feline quadrupeds carved in dramatically high relief on all sides except the north face, where the same space is occupied by two seated men pulling each other's beards. The only animals on the east are in this space. The east face has only those two. The west face also includes three animals held in the paws of the cats. In terms of percentages, animals are equally prevalent on the upper and lower halves of the shaft. But the only animals located in the upper half are found in a single interlace panel on the south side. It has at least six quadrupeds and two birds. In sum, since many "upper shaft" animals are in a single interlace pattern and the gaze of observers would have been drawn to the high-relief animals at the base of the shaft, an argument can be made that animals are a stronger presence in the lowest registers of the shaft, as on the Cross of Scriptures.

The two crosses from Kells in the Muiredach group also have similarities with the Cross of Scriptures. Most animals appear on the north and south faces of the shaft. The two crosses also have a visually strong presence of animals on their base. But the distribution of animals is different from the Cross of Scriptures. On the Kells Tower cross, only 19 percent of the animals are on the base. The north face of the shaft is a single interlace pattern making zone delineation more difficult than with other crosses, but individual bodies are most visible in the upper half of the panel. On the south face, the animals are distributed evenly over the face, although the top two are the largest and most easily discerned. On the Kells Market cross, 39 percent of the animals are on the base. Similar to the Tower cross, 78 percent (seven of nine) of the animals are in the top half of the shaft. The remaining two animals occur in the bottom panel on the south face.

The Durrow and Duleek crosses have a stronger version of the skew in animals on the Cross of Scriptures toward the north and south faces. No animals appear on the east and west faces of these crosses. But the vertical distribution of the animals is more similar to the Kells crosses than the Cross of Scriptures. On the Durrow cross, all animals are on the south face, with three of five animals on the top of the shaft. On the Duleek cross, four of the eight animals are in the bottom register, two in the middle, and two in the top.

In sum, all crosses show a preference for placing animals on the north and south faces of the shaft. Three of the crosses (Cross of Scriptures, Monasterboise Tall, and Muiredach) show strong tendencies to confine animals to the base and the bottom half of the shaft. The other four have a more even distribution of animals, with animals split evenly between the upper shaft and the lower shaft/base.

The top portion of the crosses includes the following zones on the east and west faces: a central area (the crossing between the horizontal and vertical sections), two arms extending north and south, a ring ("ring face"), and a cap extending off the upper arm of the cross. On the north and south faces, the top portion includes the ring curve running between the arms ("ring curve"), three faces of each arm—two of which are commonly decorated ("arm under" and "arm cap")—and the lateral faces of the upper arms ("arm up").

On the Cross of Scriptures, five animals are distributed across these top areas (12 percent of the total). The only one to occur on either the east or west faces is a quadruped in a diadem over the Crucified Christ, presumably representing the Agnus Dei (Lamb of God), a symbol of Christ's role in taking away the sins of the world, on the west face. While this animal is both literally and figuratively central to the iconography of the cross, the remaining animals are considerably less so. The ring curve on the south face has two serpents interlaced around two human heads. The ring curve on the north face has a single serpent interlaced around two human heads. The fifth animal is just above the serpent on the underside of the North arm. It is a cat-like quadruped holding prey (Pulliam identifies the prey as a human limb [2020: 16]). While the iconography of these four animals is certainly intriguing and their location on less central or well-lit segments of the cross raises questions about their relationship with iconography on the central areas, their presence in the topmost reaches of the Cross of Scriptures demonstrates that animals are not merely denizens of lower realms.

The Cross of Scriptures is similar to the rest of the Muiredach Master group in that the average percentage of animals in the less prominent regions of the top sections (arm under and ring curve) is 9 percent. Only the Monasterboise Tall and Duleek crosses have no animals in these areas. But the Cross of Scriptures differs from the norm for the group in having almost no animals in the other top regions. The average for the group is 36 percent. The only other cross with less than 35 percent of all its animals in the top regions is the Monasterboise Tall cross (21 percent). The maximum percentage is Durrow (55 percent). Generally for the Muidedach Master crosses, animals are a significant presence in these upper regions. That pattern runs counter to standard secular/sacred or body/spirit dichotomies.

Their importance to the iconography of these regions is emphasized by the fact that animals are typically concentrated on the most visible and most programmatically significant east and west faces of top segments. The average for the group is 18 percent. The Market and Durrow crosses have 24 percent and 36 percent of their total number of animals on these key east and west faces. Other than the Cross of Scriptures, the only other cross with less than ten percent is Duleek (8 percent). While animals are common in these areas, they generally do not appear on east and west faces of the ring (ring face). The only cross of the seven that clearly has animals in this region is the Kells Market cross, which has a zoomorphic interlace in each of the four segments.[3] As was discussed earlier, the Mediterranean analogs are composed of vegetation and fruit, which could explain the dearth of animals.

In sum, the upper regions of the Muiredach Master crosses are consistent in creating space for animals on the lateral undersides of the cross and, with several noted exceptions, the east and west faces. The only area of real variability occurs with the prominent segments of the north and south faces (arm cap, arm up, and cap). The Monasterboise Tall cross and the Durrow cross are similar to the Cross of Scriptures, with no animals. Three other crosses have a small percentage of animals in these regions: Muiredach (6 percent) and Kells Market (8 percent), and Monasterboise Tower (16 percent). The Duleek cross is the only one of the seven with a substantial percentage of its animals on the top lateral sides: 31 percent. As was note above, the total percentage of animals on the top segments of the Duleek cross is average and none occur on the adjacent undersides, meaning that the location—not the number—of animals is noteworthy. They are pushed upward and laterally more than on any of the other crosses.

The prevalence and distribution of animals across the different zones of high crosses indicates that they are a significant component of the iconographic program. That program covers a wide array of different subjects. Some are devoted to the Crucifixion or other core aspects of Christology. Others portray Old Testament and patristic events. Many possess no obvious connection to any Christian subject matter. The presence of animals across these different topics creates both a point of visual unity among the segments and an opportunity to understand the relationship among them. Ways that animals are, and are not, present across different areas of the cross provide a key locus for organizing encounters with these monuments.

The first step to understanding this process is a more detailed consideration of what types of animals appear and what patterns exist in the distribution of the different types. The 246 animals can be separated into four different categories: mundane, exotic, hybrid, and uncertain. Mundane animals are those that occupied the previous chapter: in other words, the sort of animals that filled daily life in early medieval Ireland, both domestic and wild. These represent 41 percent of all the animals shown. The majority of mundane animals are found on the base and the lowest registers of the shaft (62 percent). Interestingly, however, while few mundane animals appear on the upper shaft registers or the under and lateral section of the top, 25 percent are located on the east and west faces. In other words, mundane animals are confined to the lower regions, unless they are not. Then, they tend to appear on the most visible and most theologically central areas. This pattern is discussed further below.

One other notable feature of the mundane species is that the most common species in faunal assemblages—cattle, sheep, and pigs—are rare. The most common mundane animals on the crosses usually account for no more than one or two percent of the remains in faunal collections. Horse, birds, and dogs each account for 20 percent of the mundane animals. Deer are as common as sheep.

"Exotic animals" are 16 percent of the total. These are animals that travelers to other lands could have seen or that are describes in texts. The most common types are lions and serpents (that famous lacuna in Irish fauna). These animals have a contrasting distribution to mundane animals. None are located on the base. 82 percent are on top segments, split almost evenly between the undersections of the arms and the east and west faces. Exotics are animals of the upper regions.

Hybrids are those that combine features from the previous categories. Ten percent of animals are in this category. The group is evenly split between animal hybrids ("hybrid A"), which combine aspects of different types of animals and anthropomorphic hybrids ("hybrid H"), most of which combine a human body and an animal head. These two types are present in similar numbers. But they have different distributions. Sixty-seven percent of the anthropomorphic hybrids are on the east and west upper faces. The other 33 percent are on upper shafts. Animal hybrids, by contrast, have the same distribution as mundane animals. Most are found on the base and lowest register of shafts (62 percent), but a significant minority (23 percent) is in upper sections.

One significant concern with the validity of these patterns is that 34 percent of all animals identified are classed as unknown. Presumably, most of these would fall into one of the previous categories if they were less damaged or if modern observers were better able to read the iconography. But patterns among the previous three groups could be spurious if, for example, a large percentage of the unknowns were hybrid animals appearing on top segments. Several factors make that circumstance unlikely.

The majority are located in interlace patterns (fifty-one of eighty-two). At times, it is possible to differentiate among birds, serpents, and quadrupeds based on head shape and/or the presence of limbs. Approximately half of the "unknown" interlace patterns (i.e., those with figures as opposed to abstract shapes) are quadrupeds. 16 percent are likely to be birds. A further 24 percent are zoomorphic but the animal type is unclear. For 14 percent, the inhabitants of interlace panels are not clearly either human or zoomorphic.

Context and iconographic details such as ear shape also facilitate identifications, particularly when taken in context with the conventions of more easily decoded animal interlace in manuscripts. But this study is cautious about applying these materials to the crosses. With mundane animal and hybrids, in the absence of damage, the species is generally quite obvious. By definition, interlace distorts bodies. They are a different category.

Most of the remaining animals in the "unknown" category are quadrupeds but due to damage the identification is left uncertain. For example, deer are most easily characterized by antlers (i.e., stags). In several cases, adjacent animals have the same general proportions, but it is unclear if they have antlers. Though such animals are not included in the above counts, their distribution does not contradict the patterns known from more precisely identified quadrupeds. In other cases, the depiction itself is quite clear, but certain elements make classification as either a mundane, exotic, or hybrid unadvisable. For, example, the Muiredach cross is famous for the pairs of animals carved in high relief on the base of the shaft. Two are clearly domestic cats. But two others have feline faces with elongated necks.

The primary conclusion drawn so far is that the distribution of different animal types is not random. Mundane animals and animal hybrids are most common on the lower regions. By contrast, exotic animals and anthropomorphic hybrids are found in upper regions. Understanding the significance of that pattern requires a closer examination of each section.

CIRCLING THE BASE

On the base of the Cross of Scriptures, the most common of the seventeen animals are horse (35 percent) and deer (29 percent). The others include dogs, griffons, and two quadrupeds. The animals are divided among upper and lower panels on each face. The west face is so damaged that little can be said with confidence, other than that the upper panel has a central biped with three flanking bipeds on each side who are all converging to center. The

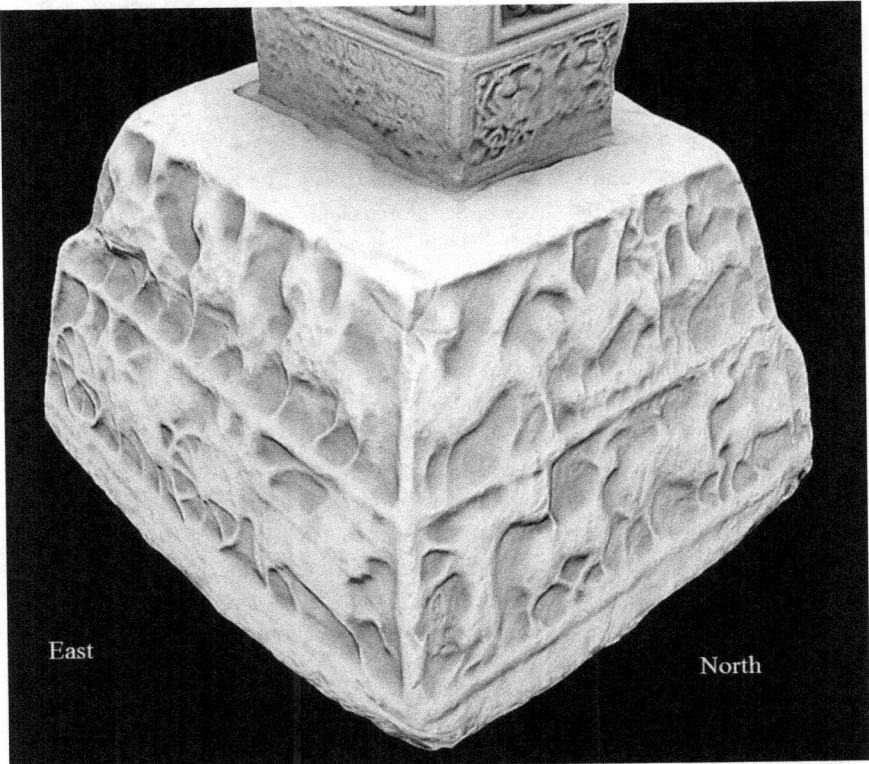

Figure 5.3. The base of the Cross of Scriptures (northeast corner). Created by the Discovery Programme, Center for Archaeology and Innovation Ireland.

Figure 5.4. The base of the Cross of Scriptures (southwest corner). Created by the Discovery Programme, Center for Archaeology and Innovation Ireland.

lower panel has additional figures but is largely undecipherable other than three bipeds facing the same direction as above.

The other three faces are better preserved. Each has a procession moving laterally across its face. The upper panel on the east face has three horses with riders moving southward. The lower panel has two chariots, each with two riders, headed north. No weapons are evident in either scene. Similar processions of unarmed horsemen are found on the other three bases in the group that also possess figures. The south face of Muiredach's cross has two riders and a chariot in a single panel. The west face of the Kells Tower cross has riders and a chariot also in a single panel (with a dog). The posture of the animals in each procession conveys a sense of intent movement, as if the processions are racing or on parade.

The east face of the Kells Market cross has a similarly dynamic procession of four horsemen, but, in this case, violent conflict is specifically cited. Each rider carries a shield. The procession heads southward toward a battle scene depicted on the south face. It shows two men with spears and shields faced against three crouching figures with shields and other weapons at the opposite end of the panel.

The north face on the Cross of Scriptures also has two processions of animals, but the animals are unaccompanied by humans. The upper row has two griffons and an indeterminate quadruped, heading east. A fourth figure may appear under the feet of the central griffon. The lower register has four quadrupeds. Three are headed west. Each has the body form of deer or perhaps cattle, but their type is uncertain. The one at the rear of this procession has a thicker neck and is rearing upwards, with its hindlimbs on the "ground" and its fore limbs braced against the eastern rim of the panel. This figure disrupts the otherwise linear direction of movement in the panel and opposes the charioteers around the corner to the east.

The Cross of Scriptures is the only cross in the group with griffons on its base, but a different type of hybrid animal (two centaurs) appears on the north face of the Kells Market cross. One has an arrow notched into its bow and has a bird on its back. The other holds the shaft of an implement that widens above its head. The centaurs appear with a diverse collection of other animals. A dog appears between them. All are headed toward two birds facing each other and holding animals in their talons. The larger of the birds holds what may be a fish and faces the same direction as the other animals. The smaller bird is in an oppositional position reminiscent of the thick-necked quadruped on the Cross of Scriptures. Both occupy the northeast edge of their base and confront the direction of the other animals in the scene. The north face of Muiredach's cross also has two centaurs who hold the same implements as on the Kells Market cross. The rear-most animal is a horse with rider. The animal at the head of the procession is likely a horse without a rider, although that identification is not certain. Few interpretations of these scenes have been well accepted.

Dogs might provide a clue. One appears in the horse procession on the Kells Tower cross. One appears between the centaurs on the Kells Market cross. Dogs are also a fixture of hunting scenes on crosses. The hunting scene on the Cross of Scriptures appears on the south face. The upper panel has four human figures heading east toward a pair of engaged figures in the posture of wrestlers. The lower panel has two deer heading west with two dogs and two humans in pursuit. The west face of the Kells Market cross has a very similar scene with an armed human and dogs pursuing two deer and a boar. The Market cross also echoes Clonmacnoise in having wrestlers appear above the dog on the north face, although in this case the wrestlers are in the bottom panel of the shaft. Dogs also unify the east and west faces of the Kells Tower cross. The east face of the base has at least three dogs and an armed human pursuing a deer and a boar. It is unclear if the large bird in the center is hunter or prey.

In short, dogs visually link the centaur scenes with the hunting and processional scenes. The horse bodies of the centaurs work in a similar way. Linking centaurs and hunting pulls forward the association with sylvan or other wilderness settings, the territory of deer and boars. Given the association of centaurs with wine and other bodily pleasures, the centaurs add to the overwhelmingly worldly orientation of the iconography on the cross bases. Not only are these the realms where most mundane animals appear, their wider iconographic context locates them with the concerns of this world.

Scholars have remarked on the dearth of overtly Christian symbols on these cross bases (e.g., Stalley 2020: 169, 174, and 180). As I have argued elsewhere, perhaps that absence is a reflection of an effort to identify the base as a place of temporal concerns (Soderberg 2004). Notably, the North cross at Clonmacnoise, which is older than the Muiredach Master crosses, has a millstone as its base. On the Cross of Scriptures, Pulliam has argued that a millstone appears around the neck of an individual on the top panel of the north face of the shaft as a symbol of the weight of worldly temptations (Pulliam 2020: 15).

The cross bases are certainly areas where figures travel horizontally, not upwards. Panels with figures direct the gaze sideways to the adjacent base panel, rather than upwards to the vertically oriented panels of the shaft. Base figures mostly go sideways. As will be discussed below, cross shafts have a distinctly vertical orientation, directing the gaze upward.

The worldly and horizontal orientation of cross bases also probably engaged the human bodies that gazed on them by establishing direction of movement. The South cross at Clonmacnoise is older than the Muiredach Master crosses, and so may provide a piece of the context from which the iconography of the Muiredach Master crosses was built. No animals appear on its north or south faces. But the east face has a collection of horsemen (and other figures obscured by damage) heading south. The west face has three panels with bosses and geometric interlace patterns in the corresponding location, but the horizontally-oriented panel above has a procession of five quadrupeds heading north. The animal at the front of the procession is certainly a deer and the next two have similar body forms. The remaining sections are too damaged to make out clearly. But the panel has the elements of the hunting/sylvan scenes from other crosses. The Muiredach crosses follow this same pattern on their east and west faces.

As shown in figure 5.5, the direction of the figures on east and west faces is almost completely uniform. Each also opposes horsemen with hunting or other animal processions. With the notable exception of the nearby Cross of Scriptures, all crosses match the Clonmacnoise South cross in terms of processional direction and content: west faces have figures headed north;

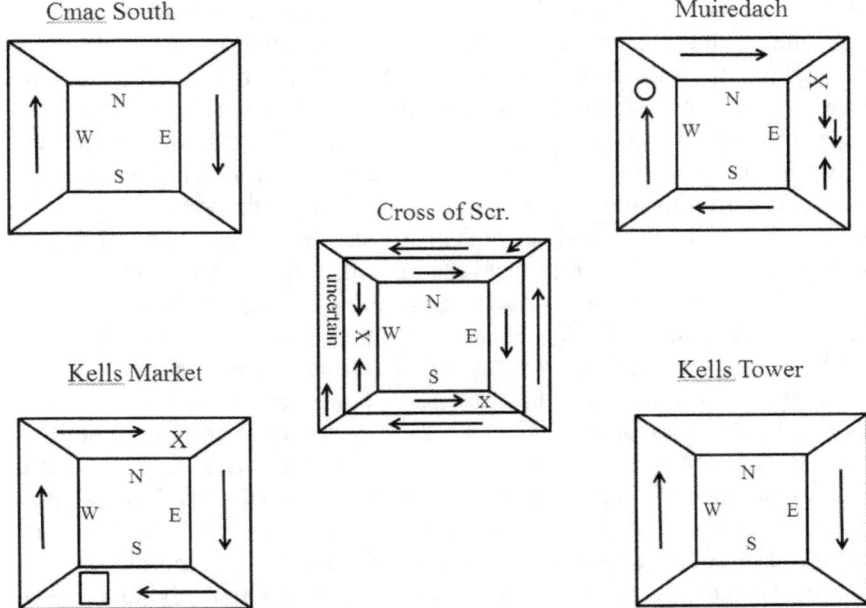

Figure 5.5. Schematic diagram of the directions figures face on cross bases. Created by John Soderberg.

east faces have figures headed south, although on Muiredach's east face two quadrupeds head south and one heads north.

Horsemen and hunting scenes are not found consistently on west and east sides. The Kells Market cross follows the Clonmacnoise south pattern, but the Kells Tower cross has the scenes reversed. But, irrespective of content, the direction of the figures is the same. If these figures are intended as pointers for how to move around the cross, all suggest a sunwise cycle of movement: E>S>W>N>E (clockwise as viewed from above).

Given that the Clonmacnoise South base is the earliest of the five, the four later Muiredach Master crosses may represent elaborations of an established pattern. The Kells Tower base swaps scene locations, with hunting on the east and horsemen on the west, but the processional directions are the same. The Muiredach cross adds figures to the north and south sides that continue the same circling pattern. It also adds figures that interrupt the direction of movement on the east and west faces. The west face has a figure (bird?) in a diadem. The east face has two facing figures on the opposing side of the east face and a quadruped opposing the direction of movement on the south end. The Kells Market cross matches the placement of scenes on the Clonmacnoise South cross. It includes figures on the north and south faces, as on Muiredach's cross, and has figures that interrupt the flow. But, unlike the Muiredach cross, they appear on the north and south faces, so that movement flows from the shield-bearing figures on horseback through the three crouched warriors on the south face and into confrontation with the two spear-bearing warriors on the far side of the south face. Likewise, movement flows from the hunting procession on the east face through the centaurs and other figures on the north face and into opposition with the two facing birds on the far end of the panel (or perhaps to just the farthest bird holding the quadruped since the first bird faces the same direction as the other figures).

The Cross of Scriptures has the most complex organization of all five. Each face is divided into two registers of figures that face opposite directions on the north, east, and south faces. The horsemen on the upper register on the east face head the same direction as the horsemen on the east face of the nearby South cross: south. The chariots in the lower register head north. A second difference with the South cross occurs on the west face. Instead of figures moving in the opposite direction from those on the east face, as on the South cross, the Cross of Scriptures has converging figures. The face is too damaged to preserve details, but the bipedal figures in the top register converge on a central figure who appears to face outward. In the bottom register three bipedal figures also converge on the center. The rest of the figures are unclear, although the south corner may hold two opposed figures.

The north and south faces add further complexity. On the other four bases, the majority of figures move in a sunwise direction. The north-facing chariots of the east face on Cross of Scriptures counters by going anti-sunwise. The north and south faces add additional types of contrary movement. On the north and south, the figures in the upper and lower panels move in opposite directions. The two sides are mirror images of each other. In both, the upper figures head east and the lower figures head west. But, since the faces are pointed in opposite directions, figures on the upper register of the north go sunwise, but those on the upper panel of the south face go anti-sunwise.

This mirroring also has consequences for movement of figures across the corners. With the exception of "oppositional" figures on the Kells Market and Muiredach crosses, movement of figures continues around each corner. The organization of the Cross of Scriptures creates a set of convergences and divergences.

At the northeast corner, the direction of movement flows around the corner with the upper going sunwise from the north and the lower going anti-sunwise. But, at the southeast corner, figures converge in the upper register and diverge in the lower register. Finally, the lower register on the north and the upper register on the south also include oppositional figures that block movement.

One can see the confusing variety of movements from face to face on the base of the Cross of Scriptures as an elaboration of the various interruptions to movement on the other crosses. In that case, not only do the base figures lead to circling, but they also impede that movement, perhaps to train the gaze upward and/or to emphasize the confusions of circling in mundane realms.

Moving Upward

The base is also structurally distinct from the upper regions. It anchors the cross itself to the ground. The cross rises from the base. As was noted above, that transition is also marked by a change from horizontal to vertical organization. If the base trains the gaze sideways, the shaft trains it upwards. Following this logic, both the base of the shaft and the base itself are the points of articulation between earthly and heavenly realms. This sense of the shaft as connecting lower and upper realms is enhanced by a tendency for the iconography on the low registers of the shaft to match the worldly orientation of the base. Significantly, this pattern holds for crosses with figures on the base, for crosses with non-figural bases, and for crosses without a base.

For the purposes of this study, the most notable manifestation of worldly orientation at the base of shaft segments is that mundane animals predominate in the lower shaft panels, just as they do on the base. Setting aside interlace patterns, half of the animals in the lower panels of shafts are mundane. They also often occur in similarly prosaic settings as on the base. The best known example is the two cats holding prey on the west face of Muiredach's cross. Carved in high relief on the very base of the shaft they are among the most mundane animals found in early medieval Irish sculpture, and, as with animals on the base, they contrast with the Christian iconography above. These animals appear to have crawled in from the surrounding settlement to enjoy a meal on the sunny western face. To make the contrast with higher realms starker, these animals are the only mundane animals found on the shaft of Muiredach's cross. No animals of any sort are located in middle panels. The only animals in upper panels are interlace zoomorphs on the south face.

A similar pattern occurs on the Kells Market cross. As was noted earlier, the bottom panel already has a link to the base, via the wrestlers on the north face. Stalley notes that their clothing shows they are not "biblical" figures (e.g., Jacob wrestling an angel) but worldly people (Stalley 2020: 182). The bottom panel on the south face (i.e., opposite to the wrestlers) has more explicit ties to base iconography. It is a hunting scene depicting a human driving a spear into a deer's back. A dog appears between the two. The fact that the deer on the shaft is in the process of being captured is a significant difference with base hunting scenes, where all deer are shown in flight with hunters far behind. That contrast is discussed below. At this stage, the significant point is the replication of elements commonly seen on cross bases replicated on low shaft panels. Both are home to mundane animals in a worldly setting.

A second significant point about the Kells Market shaft iconography is that, unlike Muiredach's cross, it also has mundane animals in the upper reaches of the shaft. But their context is very different from those below. Mundane animals higher up appear in explicitly Christian contexts: two fish shown with loaves in "Feeding of the Masses" panel on the west face. The animals themselves might be familiar, but they have been transformed by their setting into something miraculous. This pattern is common on other cross shafts, such as ravens feeding St Anthony.

This transformation in the animals between segments is also manifest in the types shown. The majority of mundane animals are on bases and bottom panels of shafts. By contrast, no exotic animals and zoomorphs in interlace appear on cross bases. Yet, animal hybrids—such as griffons—have much the same distribution as mundane animals: the majority are found on bases and the bottom registers of shafts (60 percent), none are in middle shaft zones, and the rest are on top segments (shaft high = 20 percent, upper lateral sides of the top = 20 percent).

Anthropomorphic hybrids take two forms. Those with animal bodies and human heads (centaurs) are located on the base. All other hybrids, with one exception, are located on the top segment of an east face (Kells Market, Kells Tower, and Monasterboise Tall). The most obvious are hybrids with human bodies and animal heads (demons tempting St. Anthony with worldly pleasures), presumably of the sort shown on lower segments (e.g., Kells Market cross: figure 5.6 #3).

The other examples require some stretching of definitions, but are at least worth considering as anthropomorphic hybrids. They appear in association with Sacrifice of Isaac scenes, as for example appears on the east face of the Kells Market cross opposite to the Temptation of Anthony scene (figure 5.6 #1). Just below the ram is a human figure bent into a quadrupedal position, making its hindquarters mirror those of the lions surrounding Daniel in the center of the cross. A very similar figure appears in the same location on the Kells Tower cross. In one sense, this human quadruped manifests the tensions between human and animal sacrifice inherent to the story of Isaac. But, on the Kells Market cross, that human/animal tension is magnified by the pairing with the Temptation of Anthony.

Notably, the Tower cross also pairs the Sacrifice of Issac with another animal-oriented St. Anthony scene: the Raven Feeding Sts. Anthony and Paul. That scene evokes a different animal/human relationship in demonstrat-

Figure 5.6. The east and north faces of the Kells Market cross: 1. Sacrifice of Isaac (south arm); 2. Daniel in the Lion's Den (center); 3. Temptation of Anthony (north arm); 4. Raven feeding Sts. Anthony and Paul; 5. Canines flanking an animal-headed biped. Created by the Discovery Programme, Center for Archaeology and Innovation Ireland.

ing how worldly creatures—a raven—can bring sustenance if one is properly oriented. This same scene occurs around the corner from the Temptation of St. Anthony on the Kells Market cross on the end cap of the north arm (figure 5.6 #4). The Kells Tower cross has a dramatic, if enigmatic, scene of animal/human conflict on its north arm cap: a figure grappling with a quadruped (canine? lion?) who also holds a sinuous figure that might be a serpent.

The only other hybrid with human head and animal body appears on the Kells Market cross, just below the Temptation of Anthony on the top panel of the north shaft face (figure 5.6 #5). The panel shows a horned and bearded figure with arms entwined around the forelimbs of two canines in bipedal posture.[4] The central figure's horns gain emphasis via their extension beyond the panel's upper frame. The figure's hands grasp sinuous forms that extend up to the canine's shoulders.[5]

No consensus exists as to the exact referents for this striking scene, but, given multiple mirroring relationships to scenes just above, it clearly represents a different animal/human relationship to the Feeding of Sts. Anthony and Paul and to the sort resisted in the temptation of Anthony, both of which are just above. If those higher scenes represent successful resolution of worldly circumstances, the horned figure represents a failed resolution: the mundane animals do not sustain. They attack. Or, perhaps, they jump up to embrace (the left canine seems to have an extension from its mouth to the horned figure's face, which may represent a tongue).

As was discussed earlier, the Cross of Scriptures is unusual among the Muiredach Master crosses in having very few animals on its east and west faces. With the possible exception of the stave/serpent in the foundation panel at the bottom of the shaft, the only animals of any kind are mundane: a horse with rider and a bird in diadems above and below the Crucifixion on the west face. The Crucifixion is, of course, the paradigm of Christian transformations of worldly conditions. From this perspective, the dearth of animals on the east and west faces emphasizes, rather than undercuts, the transformational iconography of other crosses in placing mundane animals adjacent to the Crucifixion. They present the same result as in the Feeding Sts. Anthony and Paul. The low panels on the east and west faces of the shaft also maintain an emphasis on worldly concerns, just without animals. Whether or not the staff in the foundation panel is also a serpent, the location of the panel directly above horsemen and chariots ties it to the concerns of the base. The royal figure is poised between circling horizontally and rising upward. The corresponding scene on the east face shows guards at Christ's tomb, with the shrouded body emphasizing worldly states.

Mundane animals are present on the north and south faces of the cross at rates typical for the group. The emphasis on failed and successful of animal/human tensions is as insistent as on the Kells Market cross. Both the north and south faces of the Cross of Scriptures's shaft have interlace zoomorphs on the bottom margin. On the south side, the first panel has additional interlace zoomorphs. The middle panel shows David playing a lyre while seated on a lion, iconography which, like the Temptation of St. Anthony, reflects resolutions in which mundane animals support.

Animal iconography on the north face depicts a similar juxtaposition as seen on the Kells's Market cross (figure 5.7). The northern counterpart to David seated on a lion also shows a musician, but the animals in this scene have a very different character. The musician's feet rest uneasily on two feline quadrupeds whose rear limbs and tails interlace, but whose bodies are not

Animals, Tabernacles, and Towns

Figure 5.7. Cross of Scriptures at the northeast corner: 1. foundation panel; 2. musician with cats; and 3. prone figure with staff to eye. Created by the Discovery Programme, Center for Archaeology and Innovation Ireland.

zoomorphic. The contrast to David's stability on the other side is emphasized by the musician's right knee extending higher than the left.[6] A third quadruped appears in the top corner adjacent to the musician's head. Its general body proportions match those of the figures below, suggesting it is feline. But the upper quadruped is pulling its hindlimbs back and burying its head in its hindquarters. To those familiar with Irish sculpture, the figure will evoke (probably) later female human "exhibitionist" figures who similarly expose their genitals (often called Sheela-na-gigs). Pulliam notes that early medieval Irish art has other figures signaling such auto-erotic activities (Pulliam 2020: 14). It is also difficult to avoid an association with the cats on Muiredach's cross holding their prey. That association is made all that much stronger by the presence of the cat just a few panels higher that, according to Pulliam, is either consuming or vomiting up a human leg (2020: 16). It also has an unnervingly rat-like tail. This disturbing figure would have been hidden in the shadows of the underside of the north arm. Its counterpart on the underside of the sunnier south arm is the redemptive hand of God. The valence of being on one side or the other is plain.

Taken as a whole, the Cross of Scriptures matches the iconography of the other Muiredach cross in dwelling upon the challenges of worldly temptations and alternative paths for resolving them. The tumultuous animals of the north face carry similar connotations as the horned figure on the Kells Market cross. As Pulliam writes, "The north side of the cross provides a meditation on the temptations of worldly pleasures, the nature of sin, and the necessity of correction and penance in a physical and visceral fashion. The top panel envisions a sinner with 'a great millstone hung around his neck,' while the lowest one presents a man who has fallen, been appropriately admonished, and is entering 'into life with one eye'" (Pulliam 2020: 15).

This iconography provides an important context for the foundation panel with Flann and Coleman. The fallen figure taking a staff in the eye is just around the corner from the bearded, sword-bearing figure representing King Flann and secular powers more generally. The replication of the linear staff shape invites comparison. Robed figures grasp the staff in both panels, but in the north panel the other figure is on the receiving end of the staff, having lost his grip. The foundation panel also sits just above the horsemen charging north and south on the base, circling but not rising.

GROUNDING THE ANIMALS OF THE CROSS IN THE ANIMALS OF THE NEW GRAVEYARD

Taken on their own, the foundation panel and the accompanying inscriptions are certainly monuments to expanding elite control. In this sense they are usefully understood as an outcome of the social dynamics associated with the decline of the cow and the rise of Flann. But, that explanation cannot encompass all that gave rise to sanctuary at Clonmacnoise. One step forward is seeing the foundation panel in terms of secular/sacred tensions. Different qualities in the panel then come forward. The two figures might seem to struggle over controlling the staff. The robed figure literally has the upper hand and the royal figure should be concerned about ending up on the north side of the cross. The north side indicates one outcome of not recognizing that circumstance. From this viewpoint, the whole cross undercuts as much as it asserts royal powers.[7]

But such "wages of sin" or worldly temptations orientations yield several problems for taking a fully grounded approach to the iconography. They can lead to exactly the concept of the sacred that was rejected in earlier chapters in which sacred is opposed to profane as body is opposed to mind/spirit. If staying off the north shaft involves rejecting the world, then the cross would seem to advocate exactly the sort of Durkheimian view of the sacred that motivated what earlier chapters thoroughly rejected. The "wages of sin" view does not create much space for crossing/dwelling, grounded cognition, and other concepts from earlier chapters.

Likewise, it presents cross iconography as dominated by an argument between ecclesiastical and secular elites: abbot versus king. Earlier chapters argued that focusing on elite stratagems is insufficient. They are not enough to explain the miraculous cattle in Adomnán's tale. They are not enough to explain urban provisioning in early medieval northwestern Europe. Defining the foundation panel as a struggle between ecclesiastical and secular power is equivalent to seeing the urbanism as requiring subordination of a hinterland.

Most importantly for this book, the worldly temptation view also disengages with all the activities that would have been happening a few hundred meters away to the north along the banks of the Shannon. It slips back into just being the settlement. As was discussed in chapter 2, consensus interpretations of the cross and associated architectural features assert that Flann caused the reimplantation of the earlier crosses (now known as the North and South crosses), the implantation of the Cross of Scriptures, and the construction of the Cathedral. They create and controls the sanctuary marked by these crosses. The visitor imagined in the introduction bringing her cattle to slaughter in the New Graveyard still does not matter very much. If she managed to make her way up to the cross, perhaps an abbot besting a king would have offered some comfort, but her visit and her cattle still do not really matter in terms of an account of what created sanctuary at Clonmacnoise.

Each of the previous chapters is fundamentally an exploration of how such views are insufficient. The basic premise of this book is that animal bodies made Clonmacnoise sacred. If such qualities leave no mark on a monument dedicated to the creation of sanctuary, the premise has a problem.

Happily, the resolution of that problem is simple: look to the animals. The worldly temptations view does not explain why mundane animals still occur in the top reaches of the crosses. Their confinement to lower realms makes sense: contain the secular/profane/bodily. Their creeping up the north shaft makes sense: a warning to embracing the secular/profane/bodily. But their presence on the most sacred east and west top regions seems odd. Odd, in the same way that calling Clonmacnoise urban seemed odd according to prevailing theories of urbanism: wrong place and wrong time.

Some animals in odd places may simply be a function of available Christological symbols. The *Agnus Dei* is a lamb iconically, but actually being a lamb need not be relevant. Even if actual flesh and blood animals are relevant, such icons could be specifically intended to educate those visitors used to only thinking of actual farmyard lambs, as they discover that the symbol over Christ's head is not "really" a lamb. In both cases, actual lambs are not very important.

But here is where the concept of grounded cognition can help fully realize the aim of Stokstad's embodied/phenomenological perspective: engaging iconography "outwards towards the human and other-than-human vectors that animate the planet and its ecosystems." Focusing purely on ways that the figure over Christ's head is not really a lamb ignores the basic insights of grounded cognition. It is inordinately transductive. Simulative cognition demands far greater entanglement between experiences a viewer would have had with actual animals. Visitors bring animals to the cross in ways that transductive accounts of the cross as a didactic tool cannot encompass. In iconographic terms, simulative cognition demands that base animals cross/dwell with those above.

This perspective opens additional elements of the iconography. While on other crosses an *Agnus Dei* icon appears over the Crucifixion, on the Cross of Scriptures, the icon has far more obvious ties to "base" animals: a horseman. The presence of "base" animals is more obvious on other Muiredach Master crosses. The upper regions of the Muiredach crosses are filled with figures that reference "base" qualities. The Kells Tower cross does have a lamb above the Crucifixion, but on the south face of the upper arm a cattle is entwined with an indeterminate sort of quadruped.[8] On the north face, two figures thought to be Patrick and Columba have quadrupeds crouched above their heads, one of whom maybe be grasping its lower limbs in the manner of the cat on the Cross of Scriptures, but due to damage that identification is uncertain. The Durrow cross has a solitary quadruped with a rugose surface that evokes a sheep's wooly coat.

A chariot rider appears high on the east face of the shaft of the Monasterboise Tall cross. On the south arm of the west face, a figure shears a sheep and, on the north arm a figure milks one (Stalley's identifications, 2020: 177). The cap of the cross is carved into the form of a roofed structure. Unfortunately, the scenes on the east and west panels are in poor condition, but, as Stalley notes, what can be discerned does not obviously match Christological expectations (2020: 177). On the east face, a seated or crouching figure holds a hooped or pincer-like object above a quadruped looking backwards. The east side is even more damaged than the west, but one reasonably clear element is a seated human figure at the north edge, which puts it directly opposite the figure on the east side. The western figure holds a hand underneath an eroded shape that fills the upper half of the opposite end. If the linear extension down to the base of the panel is a forelimb, the rest of the shape can be resolved into the neck, head, and rump of a quadruped, which would complete the mirroring between the two sides of the cap.

Any interpretation of this shape is tentative. But, if correct, this panel would also mirror the scene below in which a sheep is milked just to the south of Christ's hand. The posture of the figures is certainly similar. Likewise, the panel from the west face of the capstone has nearly the same composition as the scene to the north of Christ's hand: a figure crouched behind a quadruped (a sheep being sheared). If correctly interpreted, these elements of the Monasterboise Tall cross offer remarkably insistent references to farmyard routines.

Each of these examples can be given a biblical or Christological meaning. But, even if they are warranted, they are executed with remarkably insistent reminders of the life visitors bringing cattle would have left at home. These qualities are a considerable portion of what has previously made them puzzling. They intrude on expectations of what should appear in these sacred realms. Perhaps instead of forcing them into such expectations of opposition between sacred and profane, it would be better to recognize their intrusiveness as the point, as the crossing/dwelling of profane and sacred.

In a similar vein, it is worth noting that not all of the more obvious "wages of sin" iconography is unambiguously horrific. Obviously, the figure on the Cross of Scriptures getting a staff in the eye is not having a pleasant experience. But, equally, neither the cat nor the musician in the panel just above seem afflicted. Perhaps punishment awaits. But that possibility exists in tension with a biological reality of cats. Real cats routinely clean themselves. While human observers might experience sexual associations, the cat is simply performing hygiene. Perhaps the figure really does carry with it an association with the cats on Muiredach's cross.

Such are the counter-currents that emerge when fully engaging with the bodily and mundane practices that would have surrounded the cross. A full ecology of the cross needs to associate with the New Graveyard. Cats and dogs roamed throughout Clonmacnoise just as they roamed through iconography. One can imagine a cat crawling up to sun itself on a cross base. But, most of Clonmacnoise's animals were found downslope in the settlement along the Shannon.

Here we have arrived at a point where the world of our visitor bringing cattle finally gains a notable role in the iconography. Her encounters with Clonmacnoise emerge on the cross iconography. Her animals and all they bring with them are in the sanctuary. Understanding the full significance of such presences requires consideration of exactly how the crosses created sanctuary, and how the sanctuary created a monastic town. All are matters of the tabernacle.

TABERNACLES AND DEER, MONASTERIES AND TOWNS

My first engagement with the nature of sanctuary in early medieval Ireland came in the form of examining the significance of the tabernacle as a symbol for the nature of the sacred in worldly conditions (Soderberg 1993). The topic arose in the context of a set of "house-shaped" shrines often called reliquaries. It was an element of an argument that, instead of simply being reliquaries, the boxes were also likely used as containers for carrying a consecrated host and other elements of the Eucharist from a sanctuary out into the wider world (chrismals).

Tabernacle is a translation of the Hebrew word for "dwelling place." Most basically, in biblical contexts, it refers to the mobile structure that housed the Ark of the Covenant after the Exodus when Israelites traveled the wilderness. The Tabernacle housed the Ark until the construction of Solomon's temple in Jerusalem. In early Christian contexts, the pairing of tabernacle and temple was adapted to conceptualize the structure of the Christian cosmogony, with the mobile tent as a representation of temporal conditions and the fixed temple as a representation of eternal conditions. Bede's *De templo* (Connolly 1995) and *De tabernaculo* (Holder 1994) provide an extended rumination on the relationship of the Church as a sacred community in this world and as an eternal/heavenly phenomenon. Bede writes. "The house of God which king Solomon built in Jerusalem was made as a figure of the holy universal Church . . . and of us as the living stones built upon the foundation of the apostles and prophets, i.e., on the Lord himself" (De templo 1.1, trans. Connolly 1995: 5–6).

Bede's concept builds from a long-standing early Christian trope: the antetype. The term indicates a Platonic foreshadowing in this world of conditions from the next. As McCauley and Stephenson define the term as used by Cyril of Jerusalem: "in theology antetype is the earthly copy of the heavenly reality and model" (1969: 168, note 8). Augustine deploys the concept to define monasticism as "a dim anticipation" of the world to come (Markus 1990: 168). Following this logic, monastery-as-tabernacle becomes an antetype of the "type" community emerging at the end of worldly time. By extension, monasteries are also a type for the surrounding settlements. This layered cosmogony helps explain why it is important to see monasteries as settlement *and sacred* antetype and type. As Tweed's concept of crossing/dwelling emphasizes, the iconography is involved in a cascade of orientations, not absolute divisions. From cattle to cross, all are type and antetype.

My understanding of house-shaped shrines as tabernacles grew from Carol Farr's observation that Bede's conception of the temple and tabernacle also appears in early medieval Irish art (1991, 1997).[9] The "Temptation of Christ" illumination in the *Book of Kells* (Folio 202v) shows Christ on top of a building that is filled with and surrounded by people. A demonic figure flanks Christ. The imagery clearly derives from Luke's description of Satan tempting Christ on the roof of the temple, but Farr argues that the building depicted is better understood as a tabernacle (1991: 131). That association gives the figure of Christ above the building additional significance.

The added significance comes via broader application of antetype concepts to Christ's life and body. In both Bede and Augustine, the architectural imagery of tent and temple is applied to the Eucharist so that, like the tabernacle, the Eucharist becomes an antetype of the eternal Church community. Farr notes that Augustine's commentary on Psalm 90 uses the figure of "Christ the Head" as a representation of the eternal Church and his body as the temporal Church. As did Christ's body, the temporal Church struggles in this world. Farr uses this imagery as the basis for her interpretation of the "Temptation of Christ" illumination in the *Book of Kells*. She argues that the image references this constellation of symbols, with Christ's body blending smoothly into the structure beneath him and, consequently, those in the structure become incorporated into that one body.

The concept of an antetype is central to the iconography of house-shaped shrines. Their most characteristic feature is a roof-shaped lid. But many also reproduce—double—the overall shape with a small house shape at the center of the "ridgepole" of the shrine itself. That "doubling" of house-shape connects these shrines with the Kells folio, making the shrine itself a tabernacle and the ridgepole shape becomes the temple (the eternal state). The article's "big reveal" to seal the argument is a detached ridgepole with a human head in place of the more typical house-shape (National Museum of Ireland, Reg. No. R.2953. See Mahr 1976: plate 18). Given the likelihood that the head references Christ and/or a saint, this fragment neatly replicates the dual architectural and bodily antetypes, which is apt for containers that carried either consecrated hosts or relics out into the world to create sacred communities.

The tabernacle is also repeatedly called "Tent of the Congregation" (e.g., Exodus 40: 2). This association of tabernacle imagery with processes of gathering is also linked to Eucharistic associations with transformation and gathering. Ignatius of Antioch wrote in the second century that, through the Eucharist, churches "gather as unto one shrine" (quoted in Srawley 1949: 232). James Srawley offers that quotation in support of his argument that such conceptions gave rise to the custom of sending consecrated elements between churches as a "pledge of communion" (Srawley 1949: 232). One of the primary sources for early Irish liturgy, the *Book of Stowe*, similarly uses tabernacle imagery for the transformations of gathering in worship (see Pulliam 2020 for discussion). Overbey's approach to relics and shrines draws much the same conclusion, particularly with her emphasis on ways that movement creates the possibility for "unofficial, contradictory, or differential geographies" (2011: 183).

Meghan Constantinou (2010) identifies the same complex of associations in illuminations from the *Book of Deer*, a tenth-century pocket gospel from Scotland (Cambridge University Library, MS. Ii.5.32). In discussing bookshrines (reliquaries for sacred texts), she observes that the gospels were not merely written on flesh—parchment—but were considered the physical manifestation of Christ: the Word made Flesh (John 1:14). As with any relic or a consecrated host, their power is transcending the "boundaries between heaven and earth" (Constantinou 2010: 50–51).

In Tweed's terminology, they mediate crossing and dwelling. The multifaceted use of tabernacles and bodies emphasizes that sacred gatherings are not created by rejecting the body or the temporal realm more generally. The "dim anticipation" Markus describes is a consequence of transformation, not negation. That transformation is part of a charismatic ecology cascading outwards to the wider world.

This "grounded" element of early medieval Irish antetype/type imagery is essential for understanding the Cross of Scriptures and the sacred settlement it created. All of the four Muiredach Master crosses still possessing complete top segments have capstones carved into a shape mirroring the house-shaped shrines and Kells illumination with groups gathering "as unto one shrine." These capstones have long been the subject of speculation. Dorothy Kelly (1991) examined them as indications that stone crosses had wood precursors: the upright end of a wooden cross would have required a cap to avoid rot of the exposed end-grain.) Tomás Ó Carragáin considers their implications for church architecture (2010a: 22, 29–30).

Farr (1991) recognized the link between the tabernacle imagery in the *Book of Kells* and the caps of High crosses. Stalley rejects prior claims that the similarity in shape indicates that high crosses housed relics. Rather, he focuses on the shapes as references to the temple in Jerusalem or other Mediterranean sacred buildings. Yet, he concludes that the capstones remain "puzzling features . . . the origins of which are both obscure and contentious" (2020: 19–21).

One useful means of resolving that puzzle is to anchor the association with the Temple in Jerusalem more deeply in antetype representations. Crosses are deeply affiliated with Christ's body. They have bodies, arms, and heads. The capstone is just above the "head." If, as on house-shaped shrines, the house-shape and Christ's head are symbolically interchangeable as representations of the type, the capstone shape draws Muiredach Master crosses into the same iconography. That possibility certainly resonates with the ways that lower and upper sections of the cross mark distinctions between worldly/temporal and heavenly/eternal states.

It also provides a more successful explanation to the presence of mundane animals above the "base" resisters of the cross. They are not creeping upward because disorderly behavior has broken barriers between base and high. Like gospels, shrines, and relics, they are mediators crossing/dwelling among realms.

One additional element of cross iconography will help demonstrate how fully implicated mundane animals are in the relationship among the different segments of crosses. The replication of deer across different segments helps define the cosmogony of the crosses. As was described above, deer are frequently shown in "hunting" scenes on cross bases. It would be more accurate to call them pursuit scenes. "Hunters" usually appear at the far end of the scene from deer and in no case is a "successful" hunt shown. All the deer on bases are in flight.

For the most part, deer are "base" animals. The only Muiredach Master cross with a deer above its base is Muiredach's cross, where one appears on the lowest panel of the south face of the shaft. Furthermore, the deer in this liminal space that is both above and below is the only captured deer in the group. The panel shows a hunter plunging his spear into the back of a deer and a dog with forelimbs at its neck.

By pairing the capture scene with the pursuit scene on the east face of the base, the Kells Market cross dramatizes the transformation of a deer's body through the stages of the hunt. The deer crosses between realms and is transformed. This pattern holds outside the Muiredach Master group. In another study of twelve deer scenes identified on a wider sample of crosses, pursuit appears only on cross bases and capture only appears on upper segments (Soderberg 2004).[10]

No deer appear above the base on the Cross of Scriptures or the Clonmacnoise South cross. But two other crosses associated with Clonmacnoise do have deer on their shafts. Both the Bealin and the Banagher are stylistically connected with, if not originally from, Clonmacnoise (Edwards 1998). The

Bealin cross (Co. Westmeath) has an inscription stating that the cross was made in the name of Tuathgall, the name of an abbot of Clonmacnoise who died in 811. A captured deer appears on the base of its north shaft face. As with the Kells Market cross, the deer is in the clutches of a dog, but the Bealin dog bites into the leg. The hunter from the Market cross is echoed by a horseman just below the deer. He rides with a pole over his shoulder, which is reminiscent of the hunter's spear on the Kells Market cross or the martial horsemen. But, the Bealin pole also has a transformational element. On the Bealin cross, its top morphs into triskele interlace, suggesting an ecclesiastical association rather martial or secular sporting associations. Like the deer, hunting implements are also transformed on the Bealin cross.

The Banagher cross was discovered in a church yard in the nineteenth century approximately twenty kilometers south of Clonmacnoise (Cooke 1853). Its deer iconography strengthens the religious connotation of the Bealin deer. No dog appears in the Banagher cross, but the deer's leg is caught in a trap. A horseman fills the panel just above the deer. The ecclesiastical marking of this figure is clear. He carries a crosier.

As was discussed in chapter 4, deer had a close identification with monasteries. Their bodies had distinct roles from those of secular settlements. Captured deer scenes on crosses emphasize a sacral transformation of the often chaotic pursuit scenes on the base that matches with the Christological imagery dominating cross iconography. Richard Bailey (1977: 68–71) has argued that the hunted stag should be interpreted as the crucified Christ. A better known version of such symbolism occurs with the later medieval association between Christ and the hunted unicorn. In recalling Bailey's point, Edwards also adds that in Psalm 91, the psalmist pleads to be freed from the huntsman's snare (1998: 115). The sense of transformation from a temporal to an eternal realm is also facilitated by shift from motion to stasis between pursuit and capture scenes. The antetype (secular hunting in this case) foreshadows something that exists outside of time.

Such considerations might appear to have drifted far away from prosaic activities detailed in the New Graveyard excavations. Nothing could be further from the case. If the antetype/type interpretation of high crosses is correct, the analogy with house-shaped shrines requires doubling iconography. But, for all the attention to mirroring and doubling on the Muiredach Master crosses, they offer no mirroring of the capstone shape, raising the question: where is the antetype to the capstone's type? The answer need not appear on the Cross of Scriptures. The cross was surrounded by the living breathing antetype: the settlement. The capstone transforms the settlement into a tabernacle: sacred settlement as dim anticipation.

Here we can settle the question of how activities along the Shannon make Clonmacnoise sacred. The cascade of links between antetype and type do not just mark out a small patch of sacred ground as separate from profane chaos. The capstone makes the settlement antetype, and, in turn, Clonmacnoise becomes a type to the surrounding countryside. This concept is important to understanding monasteries in medieval Ireland because it identifies how people invested the landscape within and around the monastery with meaning. As Overbey observed, pilgrimage would have been a primary sacred practice. In the context of antetype/type conceptions of the sacred, walking cattle to Clonmacnoise becomes equally a sacred—and likely far more common—practice, an effort to become a less dim anticipation.

Chapter 3 concluded with the observation that, when understood via grounded approaches to religion, Wheatley's "material expression of focused sacredness" becomes fuel for urbanism, not merely an instrument for the purveyance of ideology. Such sanctuaries can provide the value system fueling movements, just as alienation and social inequality do from a Weberian perspective. In this sense, the foundation panel on the Cross of Scriptures certainly may reflect the ascendency of elites seeking enhanced control by rebuilding the sanctuary, just as they do by seeking more efficient means of exchange in "decline of the cow" models. Muiredach Master craftsmen may have designed their crosses to block such efforts. But just as instrumental approaches to religion offer insufficient explanations for the miraculous cattle in Adomnán's tale, such explanations are an insufficient explanation for Clonmacnoise as a sanctuary city.

Earlier chapters defined that insufficiency via Veblen's objections to conceptualizing humans as homogeneous and bounded globules of desire. Grounded cognition was presented as a means of establishing an alternative by recognizing how porous the boundaries of individuals are and the fundamental need/desire that state creates for crossing/dwelling, for bundling, for Meeting at Grand Central. As the animals of the crosses demonstrate, Clonmacnoise was a Grand Central. That sanctuary—with its cascade of types and antetypes—drew cattle to Clonmacnoise.

The Weberian city transforms the rural "stranger" into a subordinate via alienation. The concept of a sanctuary city was developed to expand concepts of urbanism to encompass strangers as strangers: "the mores of the ceremonial city were essentially those of the village in more refined form" (Wheatley 1971: 479). These rural visitors can remain strangers finding sanctuary. The cattle afford that process of bundling and crossing/dwelling. Provisioning becomes a generative social dynamic in which strangers bearing their aged worn-out cattle create a sacred settlement, a sanctuary from sanctuaries across the landscape.

REVISITING SANCTUARY FOR STRANGERS

To clarify the significance that such concepts of sanctuary have for understanding the social dynamics of urbanism, a brief consideration of scholarship on sanctuary in medieval Europe is necessary. The goal of this reviews is to establish a fundamental similarity between tales told about urbanism and tales told about sanctuary.

To recap the argument about urbanism: Urbanism requires a theory of strangers (chapter 1). In requiring social solidarity that transforms strangers into co-religionists, Big Gods theories explain strangers away, rather than explaining how people engage with them (chapter 3). Likewise, Weberian models require transformation of rural strangers into hinterland subordinates. Sanctuary cities are best seen as an effort to build a different theory of strangers into urbanism. Crossing/dwelling at Grand Central with leaky minds bundled through charismatic ecologies and awe creates space for strangers in the sanctuary.

The difficulty of seeing sanctuary as space for strangers results from the degree to which medieval European sanctuary has been cast in terms that align with Big Gods theories, Weberian alienation, and Veblen's homogeneous globules. Discourse has been intensely focused on sanctuary as an instrument for adjudicating criminality as different parties vied over the power to determine which criminals merited sanctuary, just as Flann and Coleman seem to vie over the staff. Karl Shoemaker surveys the topic in *Sanctuary and Crime in the Middle Ages 400–1500* (2011). He finds the essence of medieval sanctuary in an exchange between Charlemagne and his teacher Alcuin. Surviving letters record their disagreement about whether a fugitive cleric deserved sanctuary. Alcuin saw a sinner in need of protection. Charlemagne saw a criminal abusing charity to escape prosecution. As Shoemaker writes: "At the heart of this exchange lay a disagreement over the scope of the right of sanctuary in churches within the Carolingian empire" (Shoemaker 2011: 47). He who held it held immense power over others.

Many scholars have made persuasive arguments that such forms of sanctuary evolved in Carolingian contexts. This narrative resonates with the narrative of early medieval urbanism described earlier, in which elites founded towns to secure control over surrounding populations via "gift-exchange." In an earlier time, relationships between people like those discussed above with antetypes were central. Over time, concepts of sanctuary became increasingly defined in terms of offenses against authority. For some scholars, this process marks the beginning of "state-level" institutions for dampening cycles of "tribal" blood feuds. Others cast ecclesiastical and royal powers as opposed forces, with the Church-based sanctuary as a means to circumscribe secular control.

Shoemaker (2011) rejects these dichotomous views and argues that—while ecclesiastical and secular powers might have been at odds over who controlled the right to grant sanctuary—either way the process served to consolidate Carolingian state power. But this view does not escape from instrumental views of sanctuary. The power to define criminal norms fuels control over sanctuary. This "domestication" of sanctuary provides leverage for consolidating medieval states and, in turn, such domestication leads eventually to the extinguishing of ecclesiastical sanctuaries between the end of the Middle Ages and the beginning of the early modern period (e.g., Shoemaker 2011: 123). Here, sanctuary sits firmly within a Weberian social model. Sanctuary is little more than an ideological tool for the consolidation of empire.

This view of sanctuary reflects notions of the sacred as resources to be protected from outsiders and depredations of the profane world generally. The power of such sanctuaries rises from border defense: establishing who deserves and who does not deserve to be within. Accidental murderers remain in. Intentional murderers are out. This perspective articulates well with an instrumental view of the sacred and settlement-based views of monasteries more generally. Whatever is set apart as sacred is a source of communal meaning: a point from which rationalities are constructed and from which order emanates. Power over sacred symbols is power over generative meanings (ideology). As with Weber's model of urbanism and Big God's theories of religion, sanctuary becomes a tool for subordination. Hence, Charlemagne wants to define who is a criminal and Flann wants to move crosses and build a church. All are acting like Veblen's homogeneous globules.

When sanctuary is whittled down to determining who confers protection, the sacred is deconstructed into an instrument of "the larger game of wrong, response, and resolution" (Shoemaker 2011: 50). While the sacred might have considerable consequence, its impact is only indirect since it is a function of larger games that figures such as Charlemagne, Alcuin, Flann, and Coleman conduct.

While such narratives are compelling, they have remarkably little to say about diversity in how sanctuary operated as sacred space. "Wild" or "feral" sanctuary practices are absent or marginal. Instrumental perspectives pass over the rich complexity of sanctuary practices and, consequently, the rich complexity of articulations between sacred and settlement that sanctuaries afford. Sanctuaries appeared throughout the landscape and across demographics. For example, a plowman with his plow is also an example of medieval sanctuary (Morey 1998). Such variations are not a matter of early centuries either. Shannon McSheffrey critiques the identification of sanctuary and crime by demonstrating that in fifteenth- and sixteenth-century London, "most sanctuary dwellers were alien craftsmen rather than criminals" (McSheffrey 2009: 494). McSheffrey makes this observation the foundation for an argument that identifying sanctuary and criminality is an oversimplification of "conceptions of the relationship between law, sin, and mercy" (2009: 508) and an underestimation of the importance of "a shared understanding of sanctuary as holy ground" (2009: 512). In other words, sanctuary was for strangers. Finally, such sanctuary has deep temporal roots. In an Irish context, Charles Doherty (1985) makes a similar set of associations by connecting monastic towns and medieval sanctuary with prehistoric practices of encircling communal gathering spaces with a ditch, a practice extending back into the Iron Age. In advocating that sanctuary must be understood on an evolutionary time-scale, T. B. Lambert (2012) finds that in Anglo-Saxon England sanctuary is entangled with hospitality, age-old and pan-human practices guiding how guests are treated in the household. Instead of a narrowly instrumental reading of Mauss's gift-exchange, sanctuary becomes affiliated with genuine hospitality.

Each of these studies suggests that, while some parties may have been able to "domesticate" sanctuary for a time, its role in human society runs far deeper and wider than that process. In that context, the role of strangers in sanctuary cities is illuminating. The local/stranger dimension has a different logic from the conditional distinctions about criminality. Sanctuary is categorically extended to strangers, as us/them borders are crossed. Strangers are given equal footing as locals. Such concepts of sanctuary retain a quality of hospitality not apparent in dominant perspectives.

Hospitality for those strangers is antithetical to the identification of sanctuary with subordination (in the same way that profligate prosociality is antithetical to mid-twentieth-century biological theories). Strangers are outsiders. Hospitality is explicitly for those who are not part of a community. Hospitality is not primarily about a sibling next door. It is a set of practices for bringing a stranger inside, conditionally granting them access to the same resources as that sibling. Likewise, McSheffrey is interested in sanctuary for alien craftsmen because their presence requires greater attentiveness to "a shared understanding of sanctuary as holy ground" (McSheffrey 2009: 512). In both cases, sanctuary is a process for opening holy ground to outsiders. Strangers taking sanctuary does not subsume participants within sacred meanings in ways implicit in sanctuary for criminals. Sanctuary for strangers creates a space for engagement with those who are not exactly part of the community and its sacra. It breaches communal boundaries to enable external engagements. Sanctuary becomes leaky in a way not associated with sanctuary as a reserved core holding essential symbols/values/valuables. This type of sanctuary creates a different sense of common ground, one not contingent on Weberian subordination.

Chapter 2 observed that the concept of sanctuary cities derives from passages in Joshua and other Deuteronomic histories. For example, Numbers 35:15 (NIV) reads: "These six towns will be a place of refuge for Israelites and for foreigners residing among them, so that anyone who has killed another accidentally can flee there."[11] Similarly, Joshua 20:09 (NIV) reads: "Any of the Israelites or any foreigner residing among them who killed someone accidentally could flee to these designated cities and not be killed by the avenger of blood prior to standing trial before the assembly."[12] Criminality is certainly an important feature of these passages, but both specifically identify sanctuary cities as places for strangers also. According to at least one version of Cogitosus, a defining feature of the sanctuary city of Kildare was the absence of walls. Only sanctuary for strangers can square that quality with its status as "safest city of refuge in the whole land of the Irish for all fugitives" (Connolly and Picard 1987: 26).

Catherine O'Sullivan's *Hospitality in Medieval Ireland* (2004) is illuminating on the articulation of this point with wider social dynamics in medieval Ireland. Her book considers hospitality as an organizing principle in medieval Irish society. Hospitality was certainly used to consolidate control, just as sanctuary for criminals could. But, fundamentally, O'Sullivan views hospitality as a more fundamental guiding value in early medieval Irish society: "the practice of hospitality was an inescapable obligation that for the nexus of people's most important relationships, making it both fundamental and indispensable to the functioning of medieval Irish society" (O'Sullivan 2004: 14).

Obligations to hospitality would have been pervasive. In fact, O'Sullivan notes that travelers in Ireland would not generally have had difficulty finding food or shelter because the obligation to hospitality was more or less mandated for all. It was, of course, also organized along territorial and kin lines, so that travelers were advised in one text to avoid too many visits "on the frontier of a stranger" (2004: 33). And hosts sought standing and advantage via hospitality. But hospitality could not function on such terms alone. Provisions were also necessary to ensure hospitality for strangers. O'Sullivan notes that three groups were specifically charged with "the provision of free and unlimited hospitality: hospitallers, churchmen, and professional learned men (2004: 120).

Her discussion of church hospitality adds yet another element to the iconography of the crosses. The motif of Christ-as-guest was pervasive, which she illustrates with a middle Irish proverb "every guest is Christ" (2004: 167). The biblical associations of such concepts are as deep as those of sanctuary cities: "Do not forget to show hospitality to strangers, for by so doing some people have shown hospitality to angels without knowing it" (Hebrews 13:2 NIV). The motif of Christ-as-guest is matched with the counterpart: Christ-as-host.

Such invocations to profligate hospitality are precisely what is enacted in the story of the farmer who gives hospitality to and receives miraculous cattle in Adomnán's Life of Columba. O'Sullivan provides numerous examples where the profligate hospitality is presented as the type for mundane realms (O'Sullivan 2004: 171). For example, the Life of Ciarán of Clonmacnoise includes a tale that the saint encountered a man on the road who had just been refused hospitality at Ciarán's mother's house. He rushes to her house, throws the food on the ground, and berates her. Similarly, a monastery could lose its legal status for failing to provide hospitality (O'Sullivan 2004: 142). The tales and practices do not invoke the special duty of monasteries to harbor strangers. The profligate nature of "sacred" hospitality is a paradigm to which all hospitality should aspire.

These links between religious figures and profligate hospitality match well with an orientation on sanctuary for strangers, specifically, and grounded approaches to religion, generally. Clonmacnoise is the type of hospitalities to all the surrounding antetypes of hospitality filling its hinterlands. Clonmacnoise's sanctuary is built from crossing/dwelling up through those hospitalities as animals move to their slaughter there.

NOTES

1. See https://sketchfab.com/discoveryprogramme/collections/high-crosses (accessed December 15, 2020).

2. Data tables related to this chapter are available on the book's webpage at rowman.com.

3. N.B. I was unable to identify individual bodies. They appear in the appendix as four single entries. Presumably each has more than one animal.

4. I have not classed these animals as hybrids because their forelimb anatomy is very specifically canine. But the upright posture of these quadrupedal bodies certainly mirrors the bending of a bipedal body into a quadrupedal posture in the Sacrifice of Isaac above.

5. These shapes could be serpents but have not been formally included as animals because they may merge with the shoulders of the canines, making them possibly extensions from their body.

6. Ramsey (2002) views the panel as an expression of the music of the devil.

7. For further discussion of such interpretations, see Soderberg 2004 and Pulliam 2020.

8. N.B. English lacks a gender/age neutral world for a single *Bos taurus*. Here, cattle is used as both singular and plural

9. Swift (1998) reviews the numerous ways that the concept of a tabernacle was used in early medieval Ireland.

10. Interestingly, the Dromiskin cross has a hunting scene on the south arm of its top east face. This location is reminiscent of the sheep that appear on the top sections of the Monasterboise tall cross.

11. International Standard Version: "that is, places of refuge for the Israelis, the resident alien, and any travelers among them. Anyone who kills a person inadvertently may flee there."

12. Contemporary English Version: "These Safe Towns were set up, so that if Israelites or even foreigners who lived in Israel accidentally killed someone, they could run to one of these towns. There they would be safe until a trial could be held, even if one of the victim's relatives came looking for revenge."

Chapter Six

The Animals of Clonmacnoise in a New Millennium

LATE MEDIEVAL IRELAND (~1100 TO ~1600)

By the time of Phase 3 deposits in the New Graveyard (circa 1000 to 1300), Clonmacnoise had been a leading religious, political, economic, and population center for over three hundred years. Worshipers had been circling the Cross of Scriptures for centuries. In the New Graveyard, Phase 3 marks another time of reorganization. A single thick deposit capped Phase 2 deposits across much of the excavation. Structures similar to those of Phase 2 were not rebuilt. The most characteristic features of Phase 3 are the cutting and filling pits down into earlier layers.

As with the ninth century, the twelfth century is a period of profound change in Ireland. Until just a few decades ago, the twelfth century was often seen as the point when Modernity hit Ireland with the appearance of monetary exchange, commercialized agriculture, expansive territorial kingdoms with peasant economies, and urban centers. Many of these changes were specifically associated with the Anglo-Norman conquest that eventually resulted in two-thirds of the island coming under control of various Anglo-Norman rulers. As was discussed in chapter 1, additional research and new theoretical approaches have clarified that most of these changes were well underway, at minimum, by the final centuries of the first millennium. But, even taking account of these changes in perspective, the twelfth century remains a period of tremendous change. As Matthew Stout remarked about ninth-century Ireland, a visitor from the eleventh century would find an unfamiliar landscape in the thirteenth, even if the beginnings of those changes are evident in the eleventh century (and earlier).

Two key events in the twelfth century are reform of the Irish Church and the Anglo-Norman conquest. Church reform is evident in two related processes: the spread of regularized forms of monasticism and enhanced integration of Irish worship into the hierarchical structure of the Western Church. While the organization of the Irish Church in the first millennium is a matter of considerable debate, in the early decades of the twelfth century, a hierarchy of worshipers became established to a new degree. A new diocesan structure emerged to fix the relationship of individual worshipers upward through levels culminating with the pope in Rome. As with Carolingian reforms of the ninth century, one consequence of the increasingly pyramidal organization significantly changed the role of monasteries. In the twelfth-century reforms, monks are specifically prohibited from engaging in baptism, communion, and other liturgical practices (Flanagan 2010: 80–81). Monks are defined as having "left the world" in ways that closed off such practices. Such acts of ministry were located within parishes held within dioceses, which in turn were other ascending levels of ecclesiastical hierarchy. Scholarship over several decades has firmly established that such an organization is not new in the twelfth century. But, in the twelfth century it became established to a new degree.

The changing position of monasteries in Irish society is also evident in the emergence of regularized monastic orders during the twelfth century. Cistercians and a variety of other Continental orders spread across Ireland (e.g., Gwynn and Hadcock 1970, Flanagan 2010). In many ways their presence is a reflection of wider Church reforms. Cistercian monasteries emphasized disengagement from the wider world and operated from a hierarchical structure organized on the pattern of Citeaux and Clairvaux. In addition to following the Rule of St. Benedict, Cistercian monasteries were built from a common pattern, allowing monks from one locale to know the layout of another. In addition to new foundations, existing monasteries also converted to Cistercian and other orders. Emphasizing the profound impact of these changes, Marie Therese Flanagan observes, "it is difficult to point to a major pre-twelfth-century monastery that survived without being transformed into a monastic community following either the Benedictine or Augustinian rules, into a cathedral church, into a parish church, or disappeared altogether" (Flanagan 2010: 161–62). The orientation on leaving the world in such monasteries certainly marginalized monasteries as independent social and ecclesiastical forces.

The monasteries are no less farms than any of the monasteries discussed above. But the transformation associated with Continental orders are as dramatic in this sector of monastic life as any. Cistercian monasteries operated as manorial estates with satellite granges and lay brothers to provide additional labor (G. Stout 2015). These estates brought agricultural changes that intensified production and commodified exchange of agricultural products, including a three field system of crop rotation, new ploughing techniques, and intensified wool production for trade (G. Stout 2015). These innovations spread to the wider landscape during the course of the twelfth century, particularly in areas coming under Anglo-Norman control (McCormick and Murray 2017).

In 1169, three ships under the command of an Anglo-Norman lord with nearly four hundred soldiers were invited by an Irish lord to land at Bannow Bay in Co. Wexford. Through 1170, other lords and military forces arrived. The resulting conquest yielded control of territory from Wexford north to Dublin. In 1171, Henry II formally granted conquered lands to Anglo-Norman lords and led a military campaign that consolidated control over much of the eastern half of Ireland. As Stout observers, "The critical aspect of the Anglo-Norman invasion was not the territory they conquered but how this land, once conquered, was managed" (2017: 267).

In general terms, that management involved instituting royal or other elite control of lands, which were then parceled out to lords who paid fees. Lords, in turn, parceled out lands in return for fees. Feudalism is the common and vexed term for such arrangements. Brian Graham defines two essential qualities to the social and economic obligations implied by that term: (1) appropriation of agricultural surpluses from peasantry (often unfree); (2) a simultaneously hierarchical and decentralized political order in which a king's will reached outward to subject territories only through conceding power to lords ruling those territories (Graham 2000: 127). Graham's description is useful for seeing Anglo-Norman land management as both an elaboration of the social dynamics discussed above in relationship to cattle clientage and something new. Both the scale at which ownership operated and the degree to which ownership is vested in royal figures contrasts sharply with prior periods.

The level of disjunction between periods is clearly marked in settlement patterns. Castles are both practical tools for establishing and symbols for legitimating social inequalities (Creighton 2009). Castles of some form may have been present in pre-Norman Ireland, but the conquest brought a network of castles into the Irish landscape (Barry 2000: 112). They became important settlement nodes in areas fully under Anglo-Norman control, such as Trim (Potterton 2005) and in unstable frontier locales such as Roscommon and Clonmacnoise (Murphy and O'Conor 2008, O'Conor and Manning 2003). Particularly in eastern areas, Anglo-Norman rule also involved establishment of nucleated settlements within lordships in the form of both urban and rural boroughs (Barry 2000: 113). Boroughs were granted special status to attract settlers from Britain. Boroughs often took the form of villages with defined plots and outfields. Moated sites are a third new feature of the Irish landscape in the post-Norman era. They are the defended farmstead of the lesser

Anglo-Norman lords settled in frontier locations demanding additional security (Barry 2000: 116–17).

Rural boroughs, and moated sites attest to ways that the rural landscape was reorganized in the post-Norman period. But, establishment of an urban network was an essential feature of Anglo-Norman Ireland. The more than 300 known urban centers were essential to ensuring the ability of feudal kings to control vassal lords and the goods from the territories they administered. Small urban boroughs were essential for converting agricultural surplus into the currency fueling regional lordships and the larger networks of trade that served higher feudal obligations and international trade networks. (Graham 2000: 129–31). The balance of colonial and indigenous populations in urban settlements remains a matter of debate, but as a key locale for "foreign" practices, they also would have served as major conduits for cultural change.

Gaelic areas, those parts of the island that did not come under direct and/or enduring Anglo-Norman control, represent a significant challenge for understanding post-Norman Ireland. From the time of the conquest, commentators have remarked on the absence of typical Anglo-Norman qualities, such as castles, and the endurance of qualities associated with first millennium Ireland, such as cattle-raiding. In their introduction to *Gaelic Ireland: c1250–c.1650: Land, Lordship and Settlement*, Duffy, Edwards, and Fitzpatrick (2001) pose a crucial question about research on Gaelic Ireland: why has there not been more of it? Their answer is multifaceted, but one pervasive problem is the convergence of colonial and nationalist agendas that have so frequently marginalized or simply snarled interest in what they refer to as "the post-Norman Gaelic world" (2001: 21). Subsequent research has illuminated ways that Gaelic areas tactically borrowed or eschewed elements from Anglo-Norman and wider European worlds depending on local ecology and social conditions (O'Conor 1998, Finan 2004, Brady 2018, Fitzpatrick 2004).

As with urbanization in the first millennium, Clonmacnoise has a curious position amidst the changes of the twelfth century. It became marginalized in the Church reforms. Regularized monastic orders never took hold there. The monastery was also on the border between Gaelic and Anglo-Norman lands. Anglo-Norman forces built a castle adjacent to the monastery early in the thirteenth century. Gaelic forces regained the area after a few decades. By the fourteenth century, settlement at Clonmacnoise declined precipitously, the settlement practices found along the Shannon for six hundred years came to an end. This chapter examines what roles animals had through these pivotal centuries.[1]

NEW GRAVEYARD ANIMALS IN A NEW MILLENNIUM

The Phase 3 assemblage is the largest of all those in the New Graveyard excavations, with over 12,300 identified fragments. At a general level, the prevalence of species remains stable (figure 6.1 and table 6.1). Cattle are the most common animals, followed by pigs, and then sheep/goat. Red deer, dogs, and cats are all more prevalent than in Phase 2, but that shift represents a return to levels associated with Phase 1. As with the previous phases, other than red deer, the bones of wild animals are so rare that little can be said of their prevalence, aside from simple presence or absence. Pine marten makes its first appearance in Phase 3, although other pine marten elements do exist among features not assigned to a specific phase.

The most striking change in Phase 3 is a drop in the prevalence of cattle and a rise in pigs. Bones in Phase 3 tend to be more highly fragmented than in earlier phases (discussed below). In Phases 1 and 2, cattle approached 50 percent of the assemblage. In Phase 3, their prevalence is more even with that of pigs.

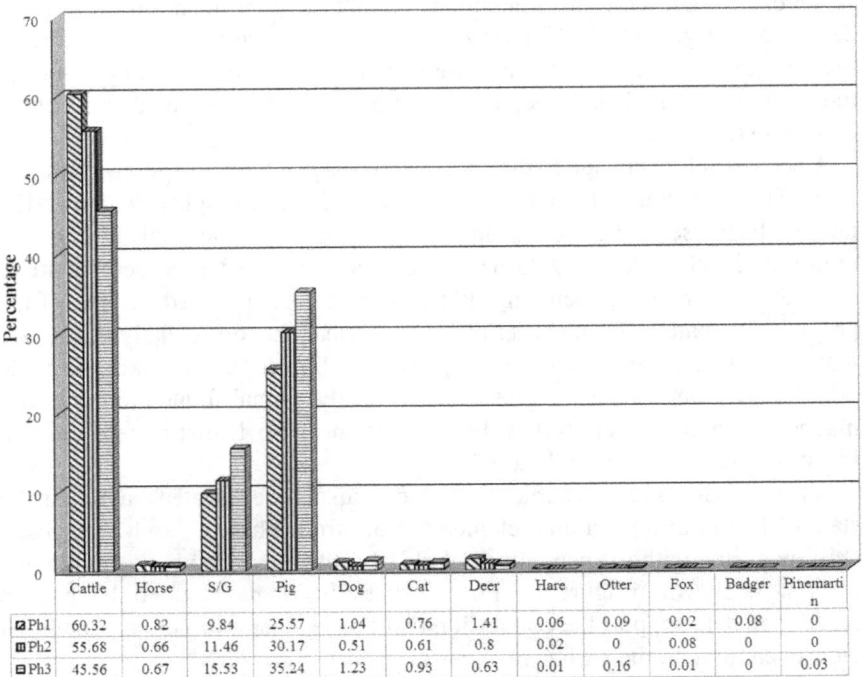

Figure 6.1. Species ratio for all New Graveyard Phases, based on NISP. Created by John Soderberg.

Table 6.1. Statistics on species ratio, based on MNI, for a sample of early medieval Irish sites (after McCormick 1987, McCormick 1991: 43, and McCormick and Murray 2007) and Phases 1 and 2.

	MNI total	Cattle	Sheep/Goat	Pig
Minimum		19	9	8
Maximum		71	51	57
Mean		46	23	31
Standard Deviation		14	13	14
Phase 3 Agg. MNI	384	40	20	41
Phase 2 (agg MNI)	336	44	22	34
Phase 1 (agg MNI)	244	48	21	32
Fishamble St.	1062	35	10	55
Moynagh, sample D	262	40	22	37

As was discussed in chapter 1, beginning in the eighth and ninth centuries, cattle began to lose their central socio-economic position as different value schemes came to prominence. The "decline of the cow" is not evident in Phases 1 and 2, which adds significant support to the regional nature of value schemes through the first millennium. But, the new millennium did bring a degree of marginalization for cattle. The late and relatively small nature of the change suggests that, while Clonmacnoise was responsive to changes in the socio-economic landscape, it is not a point from which the "decline of the cow" emerged.

A second subtle change to the cattle assemblage occurs in age-at-death patterns. The percentage of elderly cattle in Phase 3 is even higher than in earlier phases. In Phase 1, the oldest cattle are 52 percent of the total. In Phase 2, the figure is 68 percent. As shown in figure 6.2, in Phase 3, 76 percent are in the oldest age range. Essentially, Phase 3 has an exaggerated version of the provisioning pattern from earlier phases. Metrical data on sexually diagnostic features indicate that, as with earlier phases, well over 60 percent of the cattle bones were from females. Across all phases, the faunal foundation of Clonmacnoise remains elderly cows. Established in Phase 1, that pattern grew in Phase 2, and even more in Phase 3.

As was discussed in chapter 4, age can also be estimated based on the state of fusion in post-cranial elements. Data from Phases 1 and 2 suggest a shift over time with the percentage of elderly cattle growing between the two phases. As shown in figure 6.3, Phase 3 cattle fusion data extend that pattern and dental data support the conclusion that Phase 3 has a larger percentage of elderly cattle than the earlier two phases.

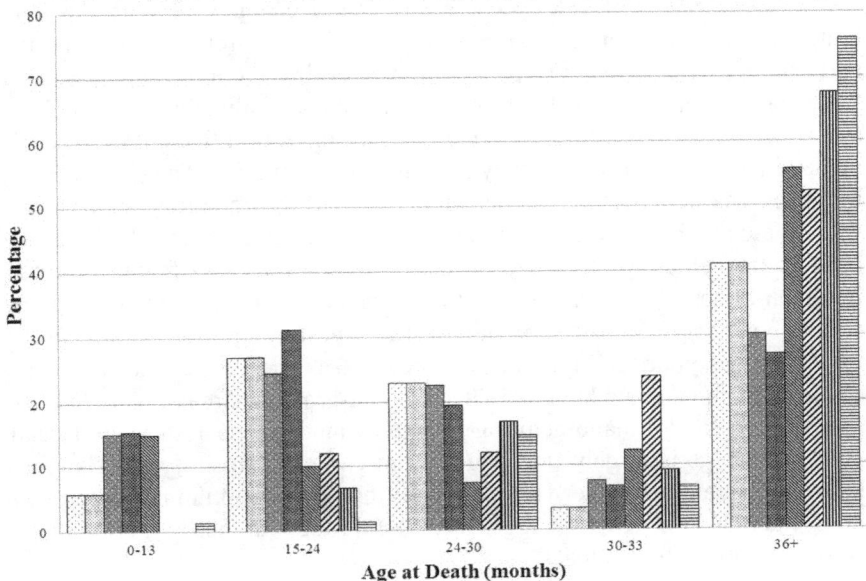

Figure 6.2. Comparison of New Graveyard cattle mortality pattern with those from rural sites (Knowth, Deer Park Farms, Moynagh) and Fishamble St. Created by John Soderberg.

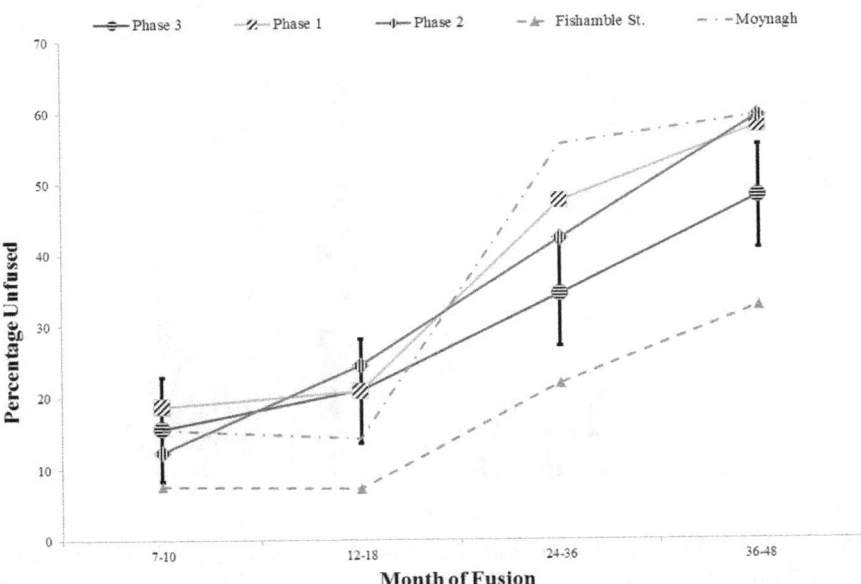

Figure 6.3. Cattle fusion pattern for New Graveyard, Fishamble St., and Moynagh (Fishamble St. and Moynagh after McCormick 1987). Created by John Soderberg.

The proliferation of elderly cattle suggests a changed relationship with hinterland farms, in terms of supply (types of animals released from farms) and/or in terms of demand (types of animals desired). On the supply side of the equation, farms are walking more of their least valuable cattle to Clonmacnoise, which lends further support to the suggestion that cattle were not valued in a radically different way than in earlier centuries. The change is not in types of cattle released. On the demand side of the equation, since elderly cattle yield the toughest meat, epicurean standards seem an unlikely driver of change. But, elderly cattle do yield desirable raw materials for manufacturing: their bones, sinews, and hides. In fact, an argument can be made that the stouter bones of older cattle might have been more sought for manufacturing than those of younger individuals. Likewise, as the prevalence of elderly cattle grew, pigs would have provided a home-grown source of meat (as well as raw materials for manufacturing). As shown in figure 6.4, the age-at-death pattern for pigs is largely unchanged from earlier centuries, with slaughter happening at a much wider variety of ages than is common in farmstead contexts. Such diversity of age suggests culling throughout the year, producing a steady supply of fresh meat.

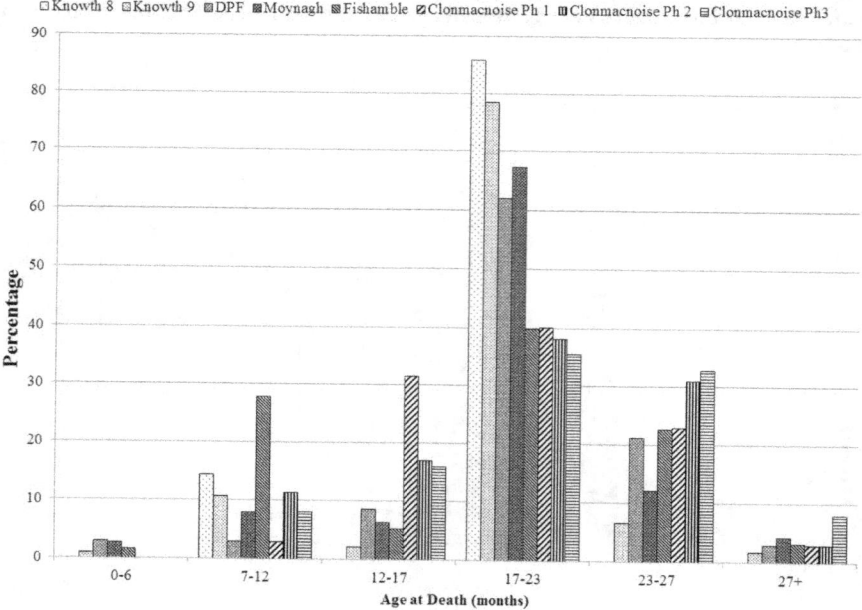

Figure 6.4. Comparison of pig mortality patterns from Knowth, Fishamble St., and Phase 2 (Knowth and Fishamble St. data after McCormick and Murray 2007). Created by John Soderberg.

The goat assemblage also indicates stability across all phases. Goats remain a significant presence, particularly in terms of horn cores. Although sheep horns are somewhat more common in Phase 3 than in earlier phases, the vast majority of sheep/goat horn cores in Phase 3 are from goats, and nearly all the goat horn cores are from females (86 percent). Post-cranial elements suggest goats may be slightly more prevalent in Phase 3 than earlier, mirroring the increased reliance on home-grown animals suggested by the pig assemblage.

Phase 3 is the first of the New Graveyard Phases to yield a large enough sample of mandibles to usefully assess age-at-death profiles, although the likelihood of both sheep and goats being present make detailed conclusions about management strategies impossible. The assemblage is split evenly between animals dying in their second year and those living to their third and beyond. The even distribution suggests a diversified management strategy designed to yield a variety of products, including meat, milk, and wool.

In addition to some change to the species ratio, the Phase 3 assemblage also has a higher rate of fragmentation than earlier phases. Zooarchaeologists examine the frequency with which different skeletal elements are broken (fragmentation rate) for a variety of reasons. Fragmentation rates can assist in determining if an element that appears rare based on counts of relatively complete elements is genuinely rare or if it has merely broken into such small pieces that it only appears rare. In cases such as Clonmacnoise, where the primary agents breaking bones are humans butchering carcasses to access food and raw materials, fragmentation rates are also useful for assessing the intensity of processing (e.g., Outram 2004). Animals bones are usually broken open to access in-bone nutrients such as grease and marrow. The bones themselves are also used as raw material for manufacturing.

Figure 6.5 shows fragmentation rates for all relatively large Phase 3 samples (those with an MNI over 20) in rank order from largest to smallest. Rank order is a helpful way to account for the fact that fragmentation rates vary according to assemblage size, with smaller assemblage having lower rates than larger one. As the slopes for the two linear regression lines suggests, this size-based relationship is similar between Phase 2 and 3. But, taking into account size-based effects, fragmentation rates for the three main species are consistently higher in Phase 3 than in Phase 2.

Figure 6.6 presents fragmentation rates for Phase 3 cattle according to individual elements, with a mean for all at the right. Phase 3 has a higher fragmentation rate by this measure also. The means for individual elements show an interesting pattern: in all cases where the difference between individual elements is 0.4 or greater, the Phase 3 rate is always the higher, and in many cases dramatically higher. Three elements have a 0.5 or greater increase be-

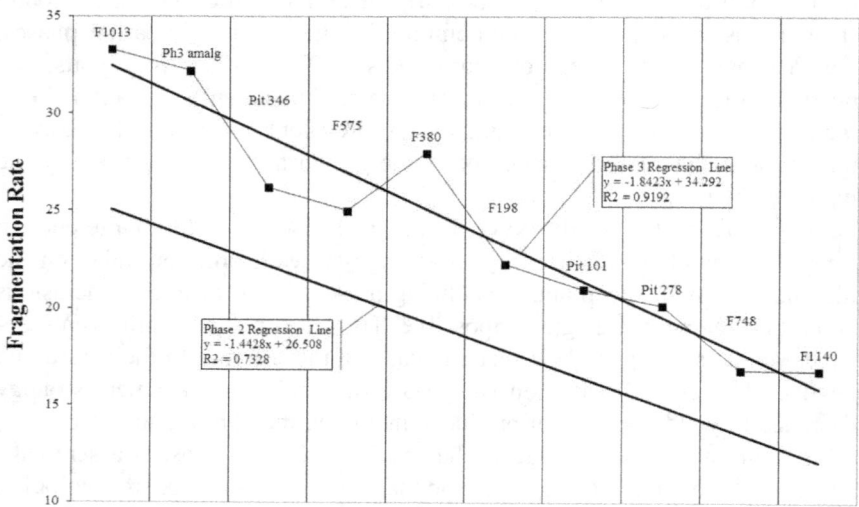

Figure 6.5. Phase 3 fragmentation rates (NISP/MNI) for assemblages from features in Phase 3 with an MNI over 20, in rank order by NISP with the largest at the left. Only bones from cattle, sheep/goats, and pigs are included. Created by John Soderberg.

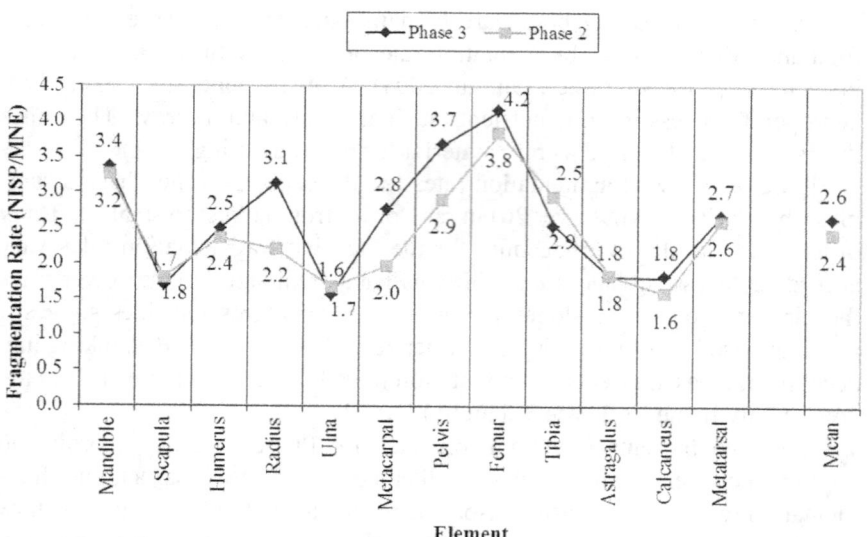

Figure 6.6. Mean rates of fragmentation for cattle elements in Phases 2 and 3. Created by John Soderberg.

tween Phase 2 and 3 (radius, metacarpal, and pelvis). Two elements have a 0.4 difference (femur and tibia). The patterns for sheep/goats and pigs are similar. For each species, the upper portion of the hind-limb is substantially more fragmented in Phase 3, even though, for both phases, the pelvis and femur have high rates. These elements are from carcass segments with the greatest amount of meat and large amounts of in-bone nutrients such as grease and marrow. Since bones in these carcass segments are not particularly useful in manufacturing, these patterns suggest increased effort to extract food from carcasses. The skeletal elements most commonly used for manufacturing are denser and have thicker walls. Cattle metacarpals are particularly prized for these qualities. Cattle metacarpals have among the largest increase between Phase 2 and Phase 3. This change suggests that manufacturing intensity rose as well.

The dog assemblage indicates continuity with earlier periods. As with earlier phases, nearly all of the dog elements are from adults. Only two of ten elements are unfused. The two unfused Phase 3 dog elements—proximal ulna and distal tibia—are elements that fuse earlier than the unfused elements from Phase 2, indicating that these Phase 3 dogs died at a younger age than the Phase 2 individuals. The difference is, however, minor. The fundamental pattern remains unchanged throughout the three New Graveyard phases. The vast majority of the dogs entering the archaeological record are mature individuals. The pattern found at some Irish urban sites in which dogs tend to die when immature does not appear in the New Graveyard faunal assemblage (chapter 4).

The Phase 3 dog assemblage contains six elements that produced an estimated withers height. Two points about these estimates are noteworthy. First, all are within the two size ranges Finbar McCormick identified for early medieval Ireland (1991: 44–45). No evidence of the later medieval break-down in this bimodal distribution is evident in Phase 3. Second, all of the estimates fall into the larger of the two body sizes. No smaller dog elements are present. Interestingly, Phase 2 has only small dogs. Phase 1 is the only New Graveyard phase to have both dog sizes, although some features not yet assigned a phase have dog elements that fall into the range for small dogs.

The cat assemblage has a clearer break with earlier phases in terms of age-at-death. Both Phase 1 and 2 have very few unfused cat elements, suggesting that Clonmacnoise did not develop this feature of an urban economy during the period covered by the first two phases. That pattern changes somewhat in Phase 3. As is shown in figure 6.7, the Phase 3 assemblage has a substantial percentage of unfused elements for those that fuse after the first year. But, while Phase 3 is more similar to the pattern from Fishamble St. than earlier phases, the Phase 3 percentage is still well below what occurs at Fishamble St. As with many of the changes in Phase 3, they echo patterns from coastal urban centers, but in a muted fashion.

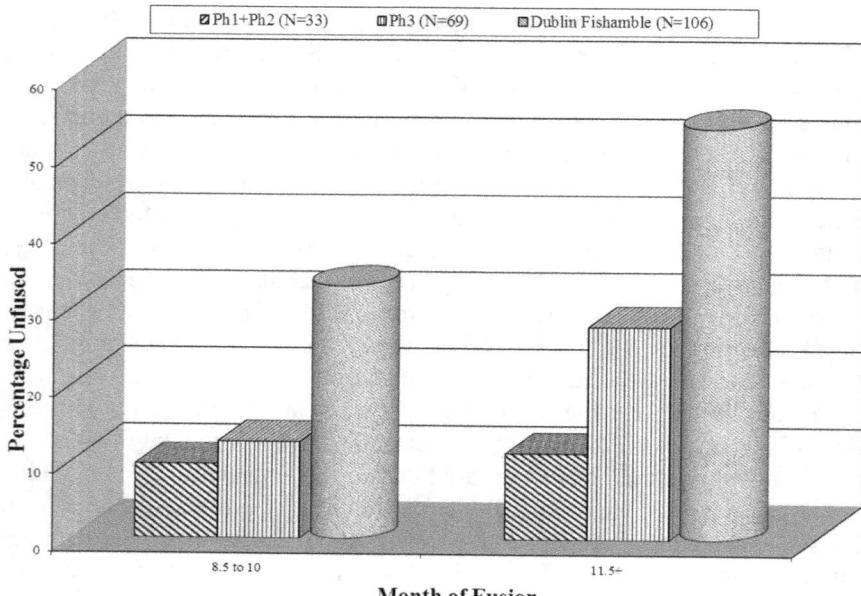

Figure 6.7. Percentage of unfused cat elements for Fishamble St. and the New Graveyard (Fishamble St. data after McCormick 1987). Created by John Soderberg.

Phase 3 also provides interesting data on the muzzle shape of cats and dogs at Clonmacnoise. As was noted in chapter 5, dogs in Phases 1 and 2 have two distinct jaw/snout morphologies. Figure 6.8 plots dog mandibles from all three phases according to the height of the mandible at M_1 (vdD #19) and length of carnassial alveoli (vdD #14). The graph also includes two "unphased" mandibles. One is from a feature without clear association to any phase. The other is from a feature that is between Phases 2 and 3, but not clearly associated with either. The figure shows one group with small measurements for both and another group with much larger measurements for both. While the one "unphased" mandible remains an uncertainty, otherwise, all the very small mandibles derive from Phase 2 or later, presenting the possibility that they represent a dog muzzle shape associated with the latter two occupation phases.

The same bifurcation in dog muzzle shape also appears in New Graveyard cats. As shown in figure 6.9, the mandibles from the first two phases cluster together, with a single exception from Phase 1, which is considerably smaller than the others. Phase 3 contains two mandibles that are of similar proportions. A mandible from an unphased feature is also in this small cluster. Taken as a whole the New Graveyard assemblage forms two clusters in much the same manner as the dog mandibles. Unfortunately, for both the dog and the cat mandibles, the absence of precise ageing data on these mandibles makes it difficult to ascertain the extent to which the clustering is due to age differences, although each of the specimens has only adult dentition.

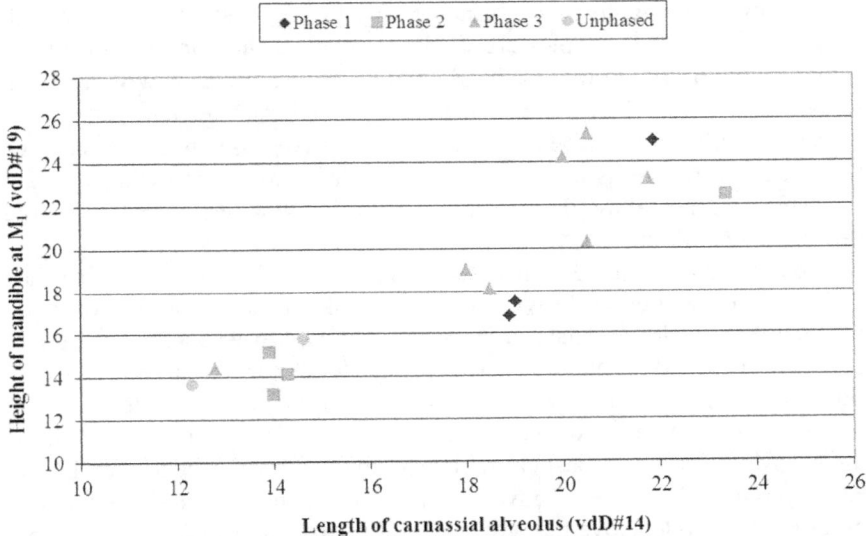

Figure 6.8. Comparison of dog mandible dimensions for all New Graveyard phases. Created by John Soderberg.

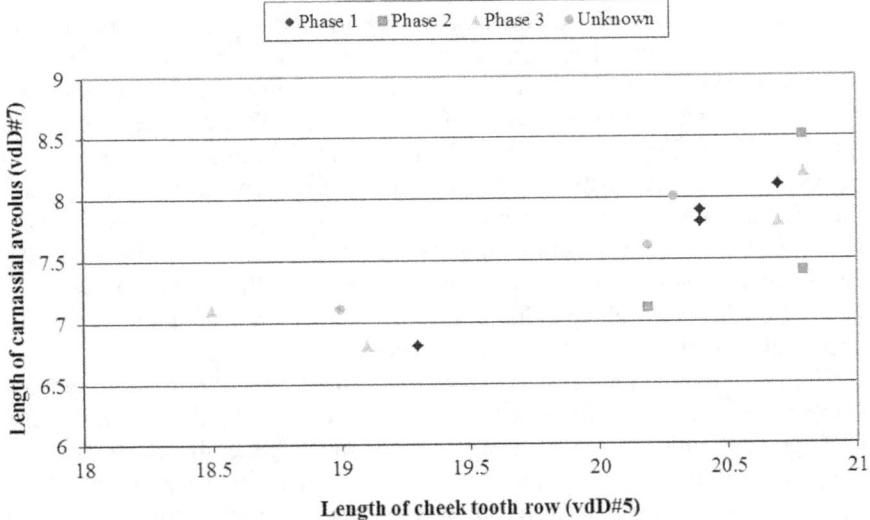

Figure 6.9. Scatter plot of cat mandible dimensions for all New Graveyard phases. Created by John Soderberg.

As with cats and dogs, red deer in Phase 3 return to the very high levels associated with Phase 1. Phase 3 contains 188 deer elements, which is 1.55 percent of the Phase 3 NISP. Given that Phase 3 crosses into the period when fallow deer were introduced into Ireland by Anglo-Normans, it is possible that fallow deer might have appeared in the Phase 3 assemblage, although most of the Phase 3 samples are likely to pre-date the construction of the Anglo-Norman castle on the far side of the site from the New Graveyard. Fiona Beglane has demonstrated that, to date, fallow deer have only been found on settlements with close connections to Anglo-Norman governance (Beglane 2010). No assemblages directly related to castle occupation are available. But no fallow deer were found in the New Graveyard. Only red deer were identified.

The prevalence of red deer in Phase 3 is an order of magnitude higher than their prevalence at either Moynagh or Fishamble St. Some internal variation in red deer prevalence exists in Phase 3 features. Most notably, the assemblage from Pit 278 contains 11 percent red deer. This extraordinarily high figure is essentially the same as that of what is otherwise the feature with the largest concentration of red deer known from early medieval Ireland: the ditch at Moyne, an ecclesiastical settlement in Co. Mayo (McCormick 1987b: 61). Even though the New Graveyard has a prevalence of red deer that is an order of magnitude above the prevalence of Moynagh or Fishamble St., both Pit 278 and the Moyne ditch are an order of magnitude above the typical prevalence in the New Graveyard assemblage. Such patterns solidify the connection of red deer to monastic settlements.

In Phases 1 and 2, the red deer assemblage contained both antler pieces and post-cranial elements. The same is true of the Moyne red deer assemblage. But urban coastal centers have few to no post-cranial elements, even when they have substantial assemblages of antler pieces. This difference presents one of the most important contrasts between Clonmacnoise and urban settlements without a monastic settlement. That difference did not extend into the new millennium. Ninety-one percent of the Phase 3 red deer assemblage is antler. Figure 6.10 illustrates the stark contrast between Phase 3 and the earlier two phases as well as the convergence with Fishamble St. With 91 percent of the assemblage being antler, the phase 3 ratio is more typical of urban settlements such as Dublin or Waterford.

The Pit 278 assemblage offers some clues to why the Phase 3 red deer assemblage is so different from earlier periods. The Pit 278 red deer assemblage is 94 percent antler ($N = 48$). The antler fragments generally consist of partially worked antler such as plates and rings, off-cuts or waste fragments of tines and beams, as well as thin shavings that appear to result from smoothing the surface of the antler. (I excavated a substantial portion of this material.)

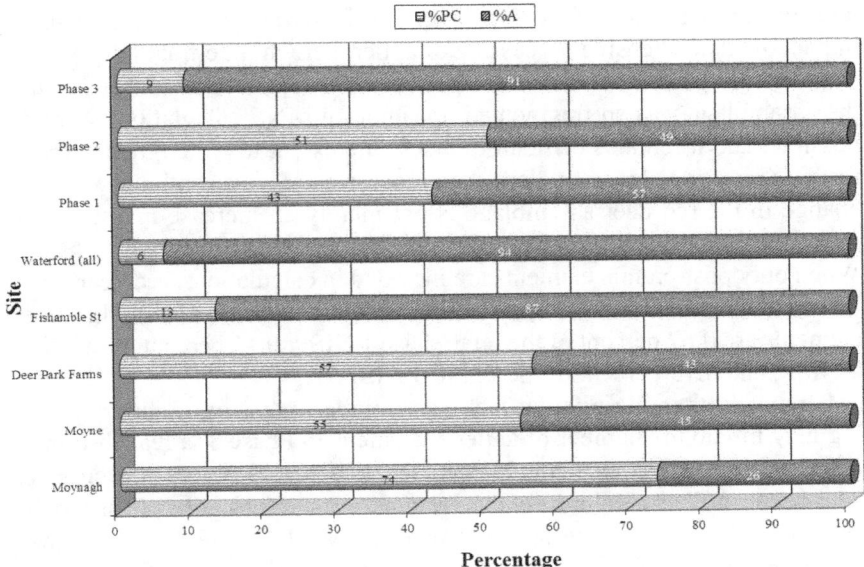

Figure 6.10. Red deer antler to postcranial element ratio for selected Irish sites (Waterford data after McCormick 1997a; Deer Park Farms after McCormick and Murray forthcoming; Moyne after McCormick 1987a; Fishamble St. and Moynagh after McCormick 1987). Created by John Soderberg.

Heather King has described the fill in Pit 278 as representing "the clearing out of a workshop floor" (King 1996: 77). Other pit assemblages have a similarly high concentration of antler. Combined Phase 3 pits produced ninety-seven antler fragments and only four post cranial elements. As at Dublin, the extreme over-representation of antler suggests a strong focus on manufacturing.

Although the percentages are not as high, other types of Phase 3 features indicate that the orientation on antler working was pervasive in Phase 3. With sixty-three antler fragments and thirteen postcranial fragments, the non-pit features of Phase 3 are 83 percent antler. This difference suggests that the pits are more closely associated with antler working than the typical Phase 3 feature; however, the intra-phase variation should not obscure the fact that the change in the prevalence of antler is characteristic of Phase 3 as a whole. Both pit and non-pit assemblages represent a dramatic shift away from the even ratio associated with both Phases 1 and 2.

One additional factor bears consideration before committing to the conclusion that the Phase 3 red deer assemblage reflects a heavy orientation on manufacturing. While antler from all phases is highly fragmented, Phase 3 fragments tend to be smaller than those of earlier phases. Smaller antler pieces suggest that the difference could result from an increased fragmentation rate, rather than a straightforward increase in frequency. To minimize the impact of such extensive processing of antler, here minute fragments such as shavings are only entered as one specimen per feature. Nevertheless, since the assemblage was so fragmented, meaningful MNE calculations were not possible, and it remains difficult to assess the extent to which the difference results from prevalence and/or from processing. Significantly, though, the change in the red deer assemblage is not merely an increase in antler fragments. The postcranial assemblage also changes significantly in Phase 3. When only post-cranial elements are included in calculations, red deer prevalence is still considerably lower than in earlier phases. Post-cranial red deer elements are 0.67 percent of the total Phase 1 NISP, 0.46 percent of the Phase 2 NISP, and 0.13 percent of the Phase 3 NISP.

Ultimately then, despite the fact that a higher intensity of antler processing may inflate the number of antler specimens in Phase 3, a real shift in the nature of the red deer elements entering the archaeological record occurs. Red deer occur in Phase 3 almost exclusively as worked into goods (rings, cylinders, and plaques) or as waste from that process. In Phase 3, red deer have an almost exclusively uni-faceted role. Phase 3 red deer break the pattern of Phases 1 and 2 by becoming more similar to Fishamble St. than Moynagh.

The Phase 3 red deer antler assemblage does maintain one contrast with the Fishamble St. assemblage. The Fishamble St. assemblage contains not only shed antler (McCormick 1987: 151). As was the case in Phases 1 and 2, the Phase 3 assemblage contains both shed and unshed antlers. This aspect of the red deer assemblage represents some continuity with the first two New Graveyard phases in access to carcasses.

The cattle element frequencies from Phase 3 provide some additional support for growing intensity of manufacturing. Typically, the frequency of different carcass segments is well correlated with the food "utility" segment: the concentration of meat, grease, marrow. R^2 values for the correlation of frequency and food utility are commonly 0.7 or higher. Likewise, R^2 values for the correlation of frequency and density of a given bone segment are often below 0.1. In the largest of the pit assemblages (Pit 346), the pattern is reversed, with a relatively high correlation to density ($R^2 = 0.3382$) and with a relatively low correlation to utility ($R^2 = 0.1649$). The change in Pit 346 is due to an unusually high concentration of lower limb elements, particularly proximal metacarpals and proximal metatarsals. The abundance of the proximal ends of these bones (the end closest to the center of the body) is also paired with a dearth of fragments from the distal end (the end closest to the hooves).

Metacarpals and metatarsals are among the densest bones in a cattle skeleton, making them some of the most desirable bones for manufacturing. Similar patterns characterize one other large feature from Phase 3 (F1013).

Most other features produced more typical cattle element frequency patterns, but taken as a whole, the Phase 3 assemblage does have elevated frequency of lower limb segments. A variety of factors are likely responsible for the differences, including processing for marrow and other in-bone nutrients. But, the high number of proximal metacarpals in some assemblages does suggest that manufacturing is a significant factor. Both of the assemblages with large numbers of proximal metacarpals and metatarsals also have even higher percentages of elderly cattle than other Phase 3 assemblages. In Pit 346, 100 percent of the ten dentally-aged specimens were in the oldest category. As was noted earlier, while the meat of such elderly cattle would have been unpalatable, their bones remain sought after for manufacturing.

One final line of evidence for manufacturing bears mentioning. Bone artifacts are registered in bone counts (NISP), assessing them as artifacts is generally outside the parameters of this study; but two trends in the frequency indicated growing intensity of manufacturing with animal bone in Phase 3. First, changes in the prevalence of bone combs matches changes in the prevalence of antler. Of the eight comb fragments from features currently assigned a phase, only one derives from Phase 1 and only two from Phase 2. Five comb fragments (63 percent) derive from Phase 3. While the small sample size and the presence of three comb fragments among unphased features makes definitive conclusions difficult, much the same pattern is evident in the assemblage of pin/needles: 19 percent are from Phase 1, 37 percent from Phase 2, and 44 percent from Phase 3 ($N = 27$). Likewise, the assemblage of other types of worked and/or decorated bone is concentrated in Phase 3: Phase 1 has 32 percent, Phase 2 has 22 percent, and Phase 3 has 46 percent ($N = 54$). If these three categories are combined, Phase 1 contains 26 percent, Phase 2 has 27 percent, and Phase 3 has 47 percent ($N = 89$). By each of these measures, Phase 3 contains a near or an absolute majority of the bone jewelry and tools from features currently assigned a phase. (Only a minority of each artifact type has not been assigned a phase.)

The only category of bone artifact to have a different pattern is "bone points." They taper to a point at one end and widen at the other giving them a head as with tacks, pegs, or pins. They are generally less than two inches long and between one quarter and one eighth of an inch wide. Based on the evidence of partially completed examples, they are made from fragments of cortical bone. Their distribution across the phases is the inverse of the pattern for other bone artifacts: Phase 1 has 44 percent, Phase 2 has 38 percent, while Phase 3 has only 18 percent ($N = 72$). This contrast is interesting in part because these are the least display-oriented category of bone artifacts. Pins, combs, plaques and other types of mounts, motif trial pieces, and items with decoration applied (including one tool handle with an ogham inscription) occur most frequently in Phase 3 features, whereas the bone points decline in frequency with each passing phase. Clearly, this survey of the bone artifacts is at best preliminary; however, it does suggest change in manufacturing in Phase 3 resulting in a growing orientation toward the production of jewelry such as pins and combs.

Other than red deer, Phase 3 contains a total of twenty-nine elements from four different wild species: otter, hare, fox, and pine marten (*Martes martes*), an assemblage that represents 0.23 percent of the Phase 3 NISP. Of the twenty-nine elements identified, thirteen are teeth (10 otter and 3 pine marten). With teeth subtracted, the remaining thirteen elements are 0.13 percent of the Phase 3 NISP. The aggregate MNI value for otter is three (based on distal humeri). The assemblage also contains a left and right maxilla (as well as three other skull fragments), a complete left radius, two complete femurs, and one femur fragment. Hare is represented by a single right pelvis fragment (ischium), and fox by one right second metatarsal. The pine marten assemblage consists of one right mandible with three teeth, and one proximal femur.

These species are not distributed evenly throughout Phase 3 features. Twenty of the twenty-nine elements derive from the fill of Pit 278, the same set of features that produced the unusually high concentration of red deer antlers. Each of these species is prized for its pelt and, as with the red deer in the pit, their presence at Clonmacnoise might best be viewed in the context of manufacturing. Interestingly though, both otter and pine marten are represented by more than just bones from extremities, as one would expect to result from trade in hides. No cutmarks were identified on any elements from these species.

One of these species deserves some additional comment: pine marten (*Martes martes*, Irish *togán*). Commentators on early medieval law texts display some confusion as to how offenses committed by pine martens should be classed. Some texts class them with dogs, calling them *crannchú* (tree dog), while others class them with either the cat or with both cats and dogs (Kelly 1997: 130–31). Interestingly, while pine martens can prey upon small livestock such as poultry, Fergus Kelly notes that the only references to martens in legal documents is in reference to them as pets (1997: 190). This finding is noteworthy because, in faunal assemblages from early medieval Irish sites, chicken and other domestic fowl—the sort of animals susceptible to pine marten predation—are extremely rare. It is only after the twelfth century that domestic game achieves a significant presence (McCormick 1991). The absence of legal provisions for pine marten predation corroborates this conclusion. Pine martens also appear in literary contexts. For example, in the *Táin Bó Cúailgne*, Cú Chulainn kills the pet pine marten of Queen Medb with a stone from his sling (Kelly 1997: 124). I am unaware of any references to pine martens in ecclesiastical sources. McCormick notes that, at least by the thirteenth century, pine martens were exploited for their pelts (1999: 363).

Although some unphased features do contain pine marten, among features for which the phase is known this species only occurs in Phase 3. As its name suggests, this species is associated with woodland areas, its preferred setting for hunting its prey. The presence of postcranial elements in the assemblage conforms well with Valerie Hall's conclusion that the landscape around Clonmacnoise remained a scrubby woodland into the late medieval period (chapter 2). The presence of pine marten limb bones suggests that whole carcasses were arriving at Clonmacnoise, although their exact origin is unclear. Pine marten has also been identified in the Fishamble St. assemblage, Ballinderry II crannog, Co. Meath, and Cahercommaun, Co. Clare (McCormick 1999: 363).

CONCLUSION

The Phase 3 faunal assemblage suggests a complex pattern of continuity and change during the final phase of intensive occupation in the New Graveyard. Fundamentally, Clonmacnoise was provisioned as it had been for centuries. Elderly cattle continued walking to the settlement, where they provided the bulk of the meat and raw materials available to the inhabitants of Clonmacnoise. Pigs and goats remained key locally-produced resources.

Nevertheless, subtle yet significant changes also occurred. Cattle are a somewhat reduced presence, suggesting that Clonmacnoise experienced the complex of socio-economic changes associated with the "decline of the cow" in the new millennium. The argument that marginalization of cattle is associated with the search for "more efficient" exchange media is supported by the presence of coin-hoards at Clonmacnoise from circa 1100 (see chapter 2). But the key question is whether or not Clonmacnoise acted as a fulcrum for advancing commodity exchange. The St. Ciarán's School hoard has a composition of coins and non-numismatic material (hack silver), which is more characteristic of earlier periods when coin-based exchange first emerged (Kenny 1998 and chapter 2). The delayed appearance of the cattle decline and its relatively modest scale also do not favor seeing Clonmacnoise as an "early adopter."

The changes in the cattle slaughter pattern also provide little support for the growth of new means for extracting resources from the hinterland. At Clonmacnoise, the percentage of elderly cattle increases with each phase, reaching an extra-ordinary 76 percent in Phase 3. This trend is a striking contrast to the pattern from Dublin and Waterford. In both cases, excavations on post-eleventh-century features produced faunal assemblages with a *decline* in the percentage of elderly cattle (McCormick and Murphy 1997: 200–201; McCormick 1997a: 823). An increasing number of cattle were arriving at Dublin and Waterford that were still prime sources of meat and that were young enough to retain value for primary productive purposes such as reproduction, milking, and traction. Such changes suggest increased centralization (i.e., ability to extract resources) and/or stronger market-exchange systems (i.e., willingness to release highly valued cattle).

The degree of change in the new millennium at Clonmacnoise is remarkable, but it is in the opposite direction. Change suggests significant changes to the relationship between urban center and hinterland. But the Phase 3 cattle slaughter pattern suggests a "doubling-down" on the practices of previous centuries, particularly when taken in partnership with the increased reliance on goats and pigs.

Understanding the position of Clonmacnoise in the dynamic circumstances of the new millennium becomes more complex when turning to evidence for commodity manufacturing with animal carcasses. Intensive metalworking is likely to have been an important presence at Clonmacnoise well back into the first millennium. Red deer, dogs, and cats provide a vivid illustration of ways that animal-based commodities have a different history. Phases 1 and 2 lack evidence for intensive commodity production typically associated with the red deer, cat, and dog assemblages from urban settlements. The assemblages from the first millennium are similar to those from settlements with a diversified economy, such as Moynagh.

The Phase 3 red deer assemblage breaks this pattern. Phase 3 contains evidence for little else besides the exploitation of red deer for antler working. As was discussed above, more intensive processing of antler may exaggerate the prevalence of antler by creating lots of small antler fragments; however, the change is also apparent in postcranial elements, which are far less common in Phase 3 than earlier phases. The Phase 3 red deer is nearly identical to assemblages from costal urban centers.

Although the contrast with Phase 1 and 2 is less absolute than is the case with red deer, the Phase 3 cat assemblage is a better match with the typical urban assemblage than is true of earlier phases. Only Phase 3 has a significant percentage of unfused cat bones, as found in Fishamble St. and other assemblages. Cats dying at a young age is linked to production of pelts and generally less hospitable conditions in urban locals. Much like the changes in pig prevalence, however, the percentage of unfused cat elements offers a muted form of the pattern from Fishamble St. Also, no Phase 3 cat elements have cutmarks associated with skinning. The Phase 3 dog assemblage remains consistent in its contrast with the coastal urban pattern. The proportion of unfused dog elements is essentially the same as in Phase 2. None of the phases in the New Graveyard show high rates of dogs dying at a young age.

In sum, Phase 3 does not show the wholesale adoption of patterns from coastal urban centers. The change is more piecemeal. Aspects of the Phase 3 faunal assemblage demonstrate the development of an intensive commodity manufacturing orientation. Such manufacturing evidence is usually seen as the socio-economic core of European urbanism (e.g., McCormick 2001, Braudel 1979, Hodges 1982, 1997). Were it not for the evidence of provisioning in the earlier phases, this evidence might suggest that Phase 3 marks the point at which Clonmacnoise becomes urban.

Their disjunction in the New Graveyard assemblage is profoundly important because it underscores that commodity production need not be a precondition for urban development. Furthermore, even in Phase 3, not all faunal signatures of the commodity orientation appear. The contrasts among sites such as Clonmacnoise, Dublin, and Waterford indicate that a spectrum of orientations exists. As urbanism is illuminated by the New Graveyard faunal assemblage, intensive commodity production is secondary, not primary, to the urbanization of Clonmacnoise.

While Phase 3 deposits generally pre-date the Anglo-Norman conquest, circumstances in this final phase of extensive settlement bear upon conceptions about the Anglo-Norman impact on Ireland. The conquest placed Clonmacnoise on a frontier between Norman territory to the east and Gaelic territory to the west. In 1214, an Anglo-Norman castle was constructed on the opposite side of the settlement in an effort to consolidate control of Ireland's midlands (O'Conor and Manning 2003). The effort was largely unsuccessful. The castle was partly demolished by the mid-thirteenth century, and the area came under Gaelic control.

The precise end date for Phase 3 remains a matter of debate. It is tempting to see the advent of the castle as the terminus of Phase 3. The early decades of the thirteenth century were tumultuous, and chronologically diagnostic artifacts suggest eleventh and twelfth century dates for most features. Few artifacts from the New Graveyard suggest substantial occupation after the thirteenth century. Subsequent deposits in the New Graveyard and elsewhere typically take the form of cultivation furrows.

But, Annette Kehnel (1997) argues that the settlement survived well into the thirteenth century, emphasizing that Phase 3 might extend past the foundation of the castle. Whatever its exact terminus, Phase 3 marks conditions leading into the conclusion of intensive settlement at Clonmacnoise. During the course of the thirteenth century, settlement in the area shifted north up the Shannon to Athlone (Bradley 1998). Clonmacnoise became merely "the centre of one of the smallest and poorest dioceses in the country" (Manning 1998: 16).

Kehnel emphasizes that the restoration of Ua Conchobair in Connacht was significant for thirteenth-century Clonmacnoise. Noting the emphasis in texts on correlating Clonmacnoise's functions with prehistoric ceremonial centers, she argues that "The ecclesiastical settlement in its-traditional sense survived the early years of the Anglo-Norman invasion" (Kehnel 1997: 170). She sites this period as one in which the notion that Clonmacnoise was an inheritor of Iron Age ceremonial centers was strong. As was discussed in chapter 1, the sensibility appears in an earlier work, the "Martyrology of Óengus" (circa 800) that defines an origin story for Clonmacnoise and other sanctuary cities. Each is said to have taken the place of one Iron Age ceremonial center and gained sovereignty over secular rulers associated with those places. Clonmacnoise is designated at the successor to Rathcroghan (Chrúachán) in nearby Co. Roscommon: "Chrúachán has vanished along with Ailill, the scion of victory: but fair sovereignty over princes prevails in the settlement of Clonmacnoise." Such continuity seemed important as ties to Connacht grew in the thirteenth century.

Anglo-Norman sources make a number of comments about the consequences of enduring Gaelic control (and the absence of Anglo-Norman control). In 1289, Walter de la Haye recorded that taxes on the lands of Clonmacnoise could not be collected because they "lay uncultivated among the Irish" (Kehnel 1997: 185). Many of the socio-economic transformations associated with Anglo-Norman conquest served to consolidate control over land and other resources in the hands of Anglo-Norman lords to provide for extraction of resources in the form of taxes and rents. De la Haye equates the absence of Anglo-Norman control with inefficient use of the landscape. Although the absence of intensive agriculture in the lands surrounding Clonmacnoise is likely to be a factor in such an assessment, it also likely that people walking cattle in from that landscape bolstered his conclusion.

This perspective also matches with a more deeply rooted sense that Clonmacnoise did not respond well to the changes sweeping the land in the new millennium. The earlier reorganization of the Irish Church is a similar phenomenon in that it also served to establish a more centralized hierarchy, a clearer "chain of command" than characterized the pre-twelfth-century Irish Church. Part of that process involved introduction of regularized Continental forms of monasticism, such as the Cistercians.

None of the continental orders seem to have taken hold at Clonmacnoise. The monastery also appears to have lost out in the power struggles that accompanied the restructuring. Kehnel summarized the reasons (1997: 159): "The lack of adequate secular patronage as well as a certain element of conservatism seem indeed two decisive factors concerning Clonmacnoise's position in the Irish church during the reform of the twelfth century. . . .

[N]either the secular nor the ecclesiastical leaders [of the reform movements] ... were amongst the allies of Clonmacnoise." Scholarly consensus attributes the contrast in the status of Clonmacnoise before and after the twelfth century to a certain lack of nimbleness.

This assessment bears a striking resemblance to the conditions cited by those who reject the possibility that Clonmacnoise could have been an urban settlement circa 700: lack of centralization and inefficient cultural practices. Kehnel cites two reasons that Clonmacnoise became marginalized (Kehnel 1997 158–62): location on a contested frontier and what Aubrey Gwynn colorfully described as being "stout defenders of the Old Irish traditions" (Gwynn 1992: 188).

The Phase 3 faunal assemblage offers an interesting frame for such perspectives. Nothing in the Phase 3 species ratio suggests a dramatic break from past practices. Cattle walked to Clonmacnoise in more or less the same fashion as they had for centuries. No markers for the sorts of changes associated with the Anglo-Norman conquest appear either. The dog remains, for example, show the maintenance of the two distinct body sizes typical of earlier centuries and lost in eastern settlements. No fallow deer were identified.

But, other elements of the assemblage suggest substantial shifts. The red deer assemblage and other aspects of Phase 3 assemblage suggest that commodity manufacturing with animal products became an important feature of Clonmacnoise in ways it had not been earlier. In this way, Phase 3 converges on coastal urban centers such as Dublin. In other ways, Phase 3 also diverges. Dramatic increases in the number of elderly cattle and increased reliance on pigs mark relationships with hinterland suppliers different from later phases at Dublin. The sense that Clonmacnoise was hamstrung by adherence to old ways is not supported by such qualities. The animals of the New Graveyard reflect a complex balance of continuity and innovation in the transition from the early to the later medieval periods.

One element driving the sense of Clonmacnoise in the second millennium as backwards-looking may derive from the colonial dichotomies that were enacted in this landscape in these centuries. As was noted in chapter 1, at least from this period, a tendency exists to see Gaelic peoples as backwards-looking and devoted to inefficient pre-Modern ways, primitives to Anglo-Norman modernities.

Scholars have reconsidered such assumptions and recognized that Gaelic people adopted a strategic approach to Anglo-Norman innovations. For example, Kieran O'Conor writes of Gaelic settlement:

> The processes that led Irish lords to eschew the widespread adoption of true castles in the twelfth, thirteenth and fourteenth centuries show how different this society was in many ways from contemporary western Europe ... [not that]

the Irish were unable to build them. Their methods of territorial and personal defence were a sensible and practical alternative solution, which suited their predominantly pastoral organisation. (1998: 101)

From this perspective, reluctance to change appears to be not so much the product of indigenous primitivism, as a strategic response to defining features of the social and ecological landscape in which Clonmacnoise sat.

Similarly, aspects of the Phase 3 assemblage that diverge from coastal urban centers should not be seen as nostalgic hold-overs from a bygone era. For centuries, Clonmacnoise created sanctuary for strangers by articulating the array of local sanctuaries across the landscape. This process for causing cattle to move to Clonmacnoise is certainly distinct from the processes that caused cattle to flow to Dublin in part because in the first two phases cattle provisioning at Clonmacnoise is not associated with the intensity of commodity-oriented production of goods from animal carcasses that is characteristic of coastal urban centers. Such distinctions do not indicate any absolute opposition of the processes associated with Clonmacnoise with market-based commodity economies. The challenge is explaining how its sanctuary adapted to the dynamics of the new millennium.

Dublin is not profane to Clonmacnoise's sacred. Sanctuary cities are not the antithesis of trade emporia. The distinction concerns the balance of dynamics rising out of historical trajectories. Both are equally Grand Centrals requiring Mauss's curious frame of mind, "one of fear and exaggerated hostility, and of generosity that was likewise exaggerated" (1925 [1990]: 81). The distinctive feature of Clonmacnoise in the account offered here is the centrality of sanctuary for strangers. But, that emphasis does not imply that sanctuary for criminals, instrumental approaches to religion, or any of the other counter-points discussed are absent. Likewise, Dublin or any other town had its sanctuaries for strangers. The zooarchaeology of Phase 3 does indicate that Clonmacnoise retained practices established centuries earlier. The challenge is not figuring out why other alternatives were refused. Clearly some were taken. The challenge is figuring out the utility of maintaining time-tested practices.

NOTE

1. Data tables related to this chapter are available on this book's webpage at rowman.com

Afterword

A curious pattern runs through literature on sanctuary cities. Their cause of death always seems to be Modernity. As conceived by Charles Doherty (1985) monastic towns vanished in the face of market-driven towns such as Dublin circa 900. That pattern follows Wheatley's earlier model. Wheatley considered the social dynamics of his ceremonial centers "an almost universal concept in the traditional world" (Wheatley 1971: 429). Due to Eliade's sense of desacralization, sacred cores disintegrate in the face of Modernity, leaving ceremonial centers trapped in a premodern *illo tempore*.

A similar logic pervades views of sanctuary in medieval Europe. They depend on a fixed chronology in which instrumental forms of sanctuary displace alternative forms as Modernity emerges. Sanctuary for strangers and other such forms are as fully tied to ancient days as Wheatley's ceremonial centers. Much the same approach undergirds Weberian approaches to urbanism. The similarity is particularly clear in the narrowing of Mauss's concept of gift-exchange to an instrument for escaping social conventions that limit an individual's ability to pursue their own ends. In many theories of early medieval European urbanism, as gift-exchanges allow for accumulation of social debts, individuals manipulate exchanges cycles to dissembled them from social constraints. Towns facilitate the process (via establishing control over either long-distance trade in exotic goods or agricultural surplus) and the growth of a new value system to fuel exchange: market economies.

The account of Clonmacnoise as a sanctuary city offered here is an effort to change the antithesis between ancient and modern each of these narratives requires. The social dynamics associated with sanctuary cites are not vestiges of a bygone era lingering through the dawn of Modernity. Mauss's *The Gift* does not offer an account of the transition from embedded to disembedded economies. He certainly accounts for ways that gift-exchange can be co-opted by the utilitarian individualism (Veblen's homogeneous globules) so often seen as the characteristic feature of Modernity. But, he directly rejects views of Modernity as the apotheosis of those globules. He considers humans of all times as possessing "a curious frame of mind, one of fear and exaggerated hostility, and of generosity that was likewise exaggerated" (Mauss 1925 [1990]: 81).

The crucial challenge of enacting such perspective creating an account of how his "generosity" operates under the skin in a way as compelling as utilitarian individualism. The solution offered here works from biological insights on grounded cognition. Helpfully, Sarah Hrdy presents her solution in terms of Maussian generosity. She observes that profligate altruism establishes a key human proclivity: "the point is not to share but to establish and maintain social networks" (Hrdy 2009: 12). Such proclivities can be nourished or subverted in different social circumstances, but they are too deeply embodied to simply recede from social dynamics of any era. Institutions such as sanctuary for criminals and for strangers remain pervasive.

Part of the motivation for calling Clonmacnoise a sanctuary city—as opposed to using the more common and more literal translation "city of refuge"—is to build resonance with modern discourse on sanctuary cities. The animating debates from the edges of Modernity in medieval Europe have not passed from our worlds. We still find ourselves in a curious state of mind, exaggerated in hostility and in generosity.

But, even when that logic is compelling, it can be more difficult to conceive of an extended mind walking into Grand Central Terminal or eighth-century Clonmacnoise. The assumptions surrounding utilitarian individualism are so deeply embedded, it can be difficult to envision alternatives. To clarify the concepts emerging from research surveyed here (and to emphasize that the concepts such as generosity or simulative empathy have little to do with just being nice to others), I would like to end by offering Seamus Heaney's poem "Punishment" as an icon for "others in mind" manifesting itself and the enduring balance Mauss advocated.[1] The poem is also a useful closure for a book on looking back archaeologically. *Punishment* is one of a series of poems inspired by Iron Age Danish bog bodies made famous by P. V. Globe. Heaney draws a parallel between a young girl apparently executed millennia ago and twentieth-century attacks on Irish women who dated British soldiers stationed in Northern Ireland. For Heaney's narrator, all these women represent distinctly *other* individuals, bounded from the narrator by gender, politics, time, and geography. Yet, the narrator's experience is not a contemplation of Otherness. The poem collapses ideological, chronological, and spatial boundaries. The narrator addresses the Iron Age girl and brings her into connection with twentieth-century Irish women punished for dating

British soldiers. They become her "betraying sisters." The narrator becomes complicit, as someone who "stood dumb" before millennia of violence and would only connive

> in civilized outrage
> yet understand the exact
> and tribal, intimate revenge.

Heaney is not merely describing an internal debate "transduced" from life in Northern Ireland and a visit to a bog in Denmark. The others are far more deeply entangled. The narrator's body has a physical encounter with an ancient body that crosses/dwells with encounters from his own life and with other bodies in twentieth-century Northern Ireland. Heaney's simulations of the violence enacted on those bodies are visceral. His experience is not that of Veblen's homogeneous globule unto itself. Willingly or not, the poem's distinctly male speaker crosses and dwells with both ancient and modern women, leaving him to struggle with a revolting internal other and the fact that this internal other is also ineluctably himself. Such is the grounded and enlarged mind. Such is the basis of sanctuary for strangers with its uneasy balance between fear and generosity.

Numerous theories offer a compelling account of religion as fostering within-group coalitional solidarity, a useful tool for competition between groups. Such parochial prosociality is crucial for fueling *Punishment*'s "tribal, intimate revenge." But, that dynamic is not useful for elaborating the larger point the poem makes about the tangled mess of self to other crossings/dwellings that occur. Following parochial prosociality's logic, the empathy Heaney elaborates in *Punishment* seems a bit of a waste, a cul-de-sac on the way to revenge. Others in mind, *Meeting at Grand Central*, sanctuary for strangers, or other perspectives based in simulative empathy are necessary to capture escalating scales of crossing/dwelling.

The key quality of encounters in *Punishment* is that they involve people as close to true strangers as one can imagine: the deceased from a bygone era. Such encounters require the profligate prosociality that builds from simulative cognition. Distinct social dynamics associated with simulation and empathy are needed to encompass the world that the persona of *Punishment* inhabits. Grounded cognition breaks open the boundaries around an individual, moving closer to the idea of personhood found in Heaney's Punishment. Heaney's persona feels a sense of internal other for the girl who died in the bog, the women who dated English soldiers, and the people who attacked them. Cognitive science is supporting the sense that all have become part of him in a fully biological sense. As Philippe Rochat observed, we live with "the particular compulsion of having *others in mind*, the desperate and convoluted human attempt at reconciling first-and third-person perspectives on the self" (2009: 34).Without those dynamics, there is only sectarian conflict among self-contained globules without antecedent or consequence. The animals of Clonmacnoise point us in a similar direction.

The archaeology of religion that they facilitate grows from the observation that humans are built for connection. Theories and discoveries coming out of academic fields ranging from linguistics to neuroanatomy to robotics are challenging long-held views of what constitutes an individual and—perhaps more significantly—the foundational importance of links among individuals. Simply put, we are built for connection. The embodied and materialistic view of religion developed here proceeds from this observation.

A robust understanding of what it means to be "built for connection" begins with the concept of grounded cognition, an umbrella term for a loosely connected set of theories asserting that the physical context of cognition—both in terms of the body and its environment—is essential. People don't escape from their bodies and environments to think. They inhabit them. Simulative models of cognition focus on the role of other people in such unbounded views of the self. It collapses the gaps among agents. Grounded perspectives create ecologies where people extend, as John Teske writes, "into a world from which they are not clearly bounded, including a social world of similarly embodied fellow travelers, our knowledge being intersubjective, composed by knowing each other" (Teske 2013: 760). The ecologies that sustained Clonmacnoise for centuries grew from cattle nurtured in a hinterland and walking to Clonmacnoise.

Bibliography

Albarella, Umberto. 2007. "The End of the Sheep Age: People and Animals in the Late Iron Age. In *The Later Iron Age in Britain and Beyond*, edited by C. Haselgrove and T. Moore. 389–402. Oxford: Oxbow Books.

Anderson, Alan Orr, and M. O. Anderson, editors and translators. 1961. *Adomnán's Life of Columba*. London: T. Nelson.

Anderson, Benedict. 1991. *Imagined Communities: Reflections on the Origin and Spread of Nationalism*. New York: Verso.

Arensberg, Conrad, and Solon Kimball. 1940. *Family and Community in Ireland*. Cambridge, MA: Harvard University Press.

Arponen, Vesa, and Artur Ribeiro. 2014. "Understanding Rituals: A Critique of Representationalism." *Norwegian Archaeological Review* 47, no. 2: 161–179.

Asad, Talal. 1993. "The Construction of Religion as an Anthropological Category." In *Genealogies of Religion: Discipline and Reasons of Power in Christianity and Islam* 27–54. Baltimore, MD: Johns Hopkins University Press.

Ashby, Steven, and Søren M. Sindbæk. 2020. "Crafting the Urban Network" In *Crafts and Social Networks in Viking Towns,* edited by Steven Ashby and Søren M. Sindbæk. 1–30. Oxford: Oxbow Books.

Astill, Grenville, and Annie Grant. 1988. *The Countryside of Medieval England.* London: Basil Blackwell.

Atran, Scott, and Joseph Henrich. 2010. "The Evolution of Religion: How Cognitive By-Products, Adaptive Learning Heuristics, Ritual Displays, and Group Competition Generate Deep Commitments to Prosocial Religion." *Biological Theory* 5: 18–30.

Bader, Christopher D., F. Carson Mencken, and James Parker. "Where Have All the Communes Gone? Religion's Effect on the Survival of Communes." *Journal for the Scientific Study of Religion* 45, no. 1: 73–85.

Bailey, Richard. 1977. "The Meaning of the Viking Age Shaft at Dacre." *Transactions of the Cumberland and Westmorland Antiquarian and Archaeological Society* 77: 61–74.

Banissy, Michael J., and Jamie Ward. 2007. "Mirror-touch Synesthesia is Linked with Empathy." *Nature Neuroscience* 10, no. 7: 815–816.

Baron-Cohen, Simon. 2012. *The Science of Evil: On Empathy and the Origins of Cruelty.* New York: Basic books.

Barrett, Justin L. 2000. "Exploring the Natural Foundations of Religion." *Trends in Cognitive Sciences* 4, no. 1: 29–34.

Barrett, Justin L. 2004. *Why Would Anyone Believe in God?* Walnut Creek, CA: AltaMira Press.

Barry, Terry. 1981. "Archaeological Excavations at Dunbeg Promontory Fort, County Kerry, 1977." *Proceedings of the Royal Irish Academy* 81C: 295–329.

Barry, Terry. 2000. "Rural Settlement in Medieval Ireland." In *A History of Settlement in Ireland*, edited by T. Barry, 110–23. London: Routledge.

Barsalou, Lawrence W. 2008. "Grounded Cognition." *Annual Review Psychology* 59: 617–645.

Barsalou, Lawrence, Aron Barbey, W. Kyle Simmons, and Ava Santos. 2005. "Embodiment in Religious Knowledge." *Journal of Cognition and Culture* 5, nos. 1–2: 14–57.

Bateson, Melissa, Daniel Nettle, and Gilbert Roberts. 2006. "Cues of Being Watched Enhance Cooperation in a Real-world Setting." *Biology Letters* 2, no. 3: 412–414.

Becker, Katharina. 2009. "Iron Age Ireland—Finding an Invisible People." In *Relics of Old Decency: Archaeological Studies in Later Prehistory. Festschrift for Barry Raftery*, edited by Gabriel Cooney, Katharina Becker, John Coles, Michael Ryan, and Susanne Sievers, 353–362. Dublin: Wordwell.

Becker, Katharina. 2012. "Iron Age Ireland: Continuity, Change and Identity." In *Atlantic Europe in the First Millennium BC: Crossing the Divide*, edited by Tom Moore, Xosé-Lois Armada, and X. L. Armada, 449–467. New York: Oxford University Press.

Becker, Katharina, John Ó Néill, and Laura O'Flynn. 2008. *Iron Age Ireland: Finding an Invisible People.* Project report to the Heritage Council. (downloaded August 2010 from http://www.ucd.ie/t4cms/IRON_AGE_IRELAND_Project_16365_PilotWeb.pdf).

Beglane, Fiona. 2010 "Deer and Identity in Medieval Ireland." In *Bestial Mirrors: Animals as Material Culture in the Middle Ages: Using Animals to Construct Human Identities in Medieval Europe*, edited by Aleksander Pluskowski and Mattias Kucera, 77–84. Vienna: Vienna Institute for Archaeological Science.

Bell, Catherine. 1992. *Ritual Theory, Ritual Practice.* New York: Oxford University Press.

Bell, Catherine. 1997. *Ritual: Perspectives and Dimensions.* New York: Oxford University Press.

Bennett, Jane. 2001. *The Enchantment of Modern Life.* Princeton, NJ: Princeton University Press.

Berger, R. 1995. "Radiocarbon Dating of Early Medieval Irish Monuments." *Proceedings of the Royal Irish Academy* 95C: 159–174.

Bering, Jesse M., Katrina McLeod, and Todd K. Shackelford. 2005. "Reasoning about Dead Agents Reveals Possible Adaptive Trends." *Human Nature* 16, no. 4: 360–381.

Berti, Anna, and Francesca Frassinetti. 2000. "When Far Becomes Near: Remapping of Space by Tool Use." *Journal of Cgnitive Neuroscience* 12, no. 3: 415–420.

Bhreathnach, Edel. 2014. *Ireland in the Medieval World, AD 400–1000: Landscape, Kingship and Religion.* Dublin: Four Courts Press.

Binchy, Daniel 1962. "Patrick and his Biographers: Ancient and Modern." *Studia Hibernica* 2: 7–173.

Binford, Lewis R. 1965. "Archaeological Systematics and the Study of Culture Process." *American Antiquity* 31, no. 2: 203–210.

Bintliff, John, 2014. "Sacred Worlds or Sacred Cows? Can We Parameterize Past Rituals?" In *Archaeological Imaginations of Religion*, edited by Thomas Meier and Petra Tillessen, 249–263. Budapest: Archaeolingua Alapítvány.

Blakemore, S-J., Davina Bristow, Geoffrey Bird, Chris Frith, and James Ward. 2005. "Somatosensory Activations During the Observation of Touch and a Case of Vision–Touch Synaesthesia." *Brain* 128, no. 7: 1571–1583.

Boessneck, Joachim. 1969. "Osteological Differences Between Sheep (*Oveis aries Linne*) and Goats (*Capra lircus Linne*)." In *Science in Archaeology*, 2nd edition, edited by D. Brothwell and E. Higgs, 331–358. London: Thames & Hudson.

Boivin, Nicole. 2009. "Grasping the Elusive and Unknowable: Material Culture in Ritual Practice." *Material Religion* 5, no. 3: 266–287.

Bond, K. G. M., 1989. "Clonmacnoise Heritage Zone, Co. Offaly, Ireland: Assessment of Conservation Value Based on Lepidoptera Recorded from 1983 to 1987." *Bulletin of the Irish Biogeographical Society* 12: 63–89.

Bourdieu, Pierre. 1977. *Outline of a Theory of Practice.* Cambridge: Cambridge University Press.

Bourdillon, Jennifer. 1988. "Countryside and Town: The Animal Resources of Saxon Southampton." In *Anglo-Saxon Settlements*, edited by D. Hooke, 177–95. New York: Basil Blackwell.

Bourdillon, Jennifer. 1994. "The Animal Provisioning of Saxon Southampton." In *Environment and Economy in Anglo-Saxon England*, edited by James Rackham, 120–5. York: Council for British Archaeology

Bourdillon, Jennifer, and Jennie Coy. 1980. "The Animal Bones." In *Excavations at Melbourne Street, Southampton, 1971–76, Council for British Archaeology Research Report 33*, edited by P. Holdsworth, 79–121. London: Council for British Archaeology.

Bourke, Cormac. 1980. "Early Irish Hand-Bells." *Journal of Royal Society of Antiquaries of Ireland* 110D: 52–65.

Bourke, Cormac. 2008. "Early Ecclesiastical Hand-Bells in Ireland and Britain." *Journal of the Antique Metalware Society* 16: 22–28.

Bowers, Shauna. 2019. "Number of Visitors to Clonmacnoise Putting Site under 'strain.'" *Irish Times*, Oct 18, 2019 (https://www.irishtimes.com/culture/heritage/number-of-visitors-to-clonmacnoise-putting-site-under-strain-1.4055372).

Boyd, Robert, Peter J. Richerson, and Joseph Henrich. 2011. "The Cultural Niche: Why Social Learning Is Essential for Human Adaptation." *Proceedings of the National Academy of Sciences* 108, no. Supplement 2: 10918–10925.

Boyer, Pascal, and Brian Bergstrom. 2008. "Evolutionary Perspectives on Religion." *Annual Review of Anthropology* 37: 111–130.

Bradley, John. 1988. "The Interpretation of Scandinavian Settlement in Ireland." In *Settlement and Society in Medieval Ireland*, edited by J. Bradley, 49–78. Kilkenny: Boethius Press.

Bradley, John. 1998. "The Monastic Town of Clonmacnoise." In *Clonmacnoise Studies*, edited by Heather King, 42–56. Dublin: Dúchas.

Bradley, John. 2010. "Some Reflections on the Problem of Scandinavian Settlement in the Hinterland of Dublin during the Ninth Century." In *Dublin in the Medieval World: Studies in Honour of Howard B. Clarke*, edited by John Bradley, Alan Fletcher and Anngret Simms, 39–62. Dublin: Four Courts Press.

Brady, Niall. 2006. "Mills in Medieval Ireland: Looking Beyond Design." In *Wind and Water, the Medieval Mill*, edited by Steven Walton, 39–68. Tempe: Arizona State University Press.

Brady, Niall. 2018. "Ethnicity and Archaeology in Later Medieval Ireland: The Challenge of the Gael." In *Reflections: 50 Years of Medieval Archaeology, 1957–2007*, edited by Roberta Gilchrist, 113–130. London: Routledge.

Braudel, Fernand. 1979. *The Wheels of Commerce*, Vol. II, *Civilization and Capitalism 15th–18th Century*. Translated by S. Reynolds. New York: Harper & Row.

Breen, T. C. 1988. "Excavations of a Roadway at Bloomhill Bog, Co. Offaly." *Proceedings of the Royal Irish Academy* 88C: 321–339.

Brown, Peter. 2013. *Through the Eye of a Needle: Wealth, the Fall of Rome, and the Making of Christianity in the West, 350–550 AD*. Princeton: Princeton University Press.

Brück, Joanna. 1999. "Ritual and Rationality: Some Problems of Interpretation in European Archaeology." *European Journal of Archaeology* 2, no. 3: 313–344.

Brück, Joanna. 2005. "Experiencing the Past? The Development of a Phenomenological Archaeology in British Prehistory." *Archaeological Dialogues* 12, no. 1: 45–72.

Brumfiel, Elizabeth and Timothy Earle. 1987. "Specialization, Exchange, and Complex Societies: An Introduction." In *Specialization, Exchange, and Complex Societies*, edited by Elizabeth Brumfiel and Timothy Earle, 1–9. New York: Cambridge University Press.

Bulbulia, Joseph. 2004. "Religious Costs as Adaptations that Signal Altruistic Intention." *Evolution and Cognition* 10, no. 1: 19–38.

Bulbulia, Joseph. 2008. "Meme Infection or Religious Niche Construction? An Adaptationist Alternative to the Cultural Maladaptationist Hypothesis." *Method & Theory in the Study of Religion* 20, no. 1: 67–107.

Bulbulia, Joseph, and Andrew Mahoney. 2008. "Religious Solidarity: The Hand Grenade Experiment." *Journal of Cognition and Culture* 8, nos. 3–4: 295–320.

Bulbulia, Joseph, and Edward Slingerland. 2012. "Religious Studies as a Life Science." *Numen: International Review for the History of Religions* 59: 564–613.

Bulbulia, Joseph, and Marcus Frean. 2010. "The Evolution of Charismatic Cultures." *Method and Theory in the Study of Religion* 22, no. 4: 254–271.
Bulbulia, Joseph, and Richard Sosis. 2011. "Signaling Theory and the Evolution of Religious Cooperation." *Religion* 41, no. 3: 363–388.
Butlin, R. A. 1977. "Urban and Proto-Urban Settlements in Pre-Norman Ireland." In *The Development of the Irish Town*, edited by R. A. Butlin, 11–27. London: Routledge.
Callmer, Johan. 2007. "Urbanization in Northern and Eastern Europe ca. AD 700–1100." In *Post-Roman Towns, Trade, and Settlement in Europe and Byzantium*, vol. 1, edited by Joachim Henning, 233–70. Berlin: Walter de Gruyter.
Campana, Douglas, Pam Crabtree, S. D. DeFrance, Justin Lev-Tov, and Alice Choyke, editors. 2010. *Anthropological Approaches to Zooarchaeology: Colonialism, Complexity and Animal Transformations*. Oxford: Oxbow Books.
Campbell, Ewan, and Adrián Maldonado. 2020. "A New Jerusalem 'At the Ends of the Earth': Interpreting Charles Thomas's Excavations at Iona Abbey, 1956–63." *The Antiquaries Journal* 100: 33–85.
Carbon, Claus-Christian, and Vera M. Hesslinger. 2011. "Bateson et al.'s (2006) Cues-Of-Being-Watched Paradigm Revisited." *Swiss Journal of Psychology* 70, no. 4: 203–210.
Carey, Anne. 2007. *Clonmacnoise*. Available from http://www.excavations.ie.
Carey, Anne. 2008. *Clonmacnoise*. Available from http://www.excavations.ie.
Champion, Matthew. 2015. *Medieval Graffiti: The Lost Voices of England's Churches*. New York: Random House.
Chique, Carlos, Karen Molloy, and Aaron P. Potito. 2017. "Mid-late Holocene Vegetational History and Land-Use Dynamics in County Monaghan, Northeastern Ireland: The Palynological Record of Lough Muckno." *Journal of the North Atlantic* 32: 1–24.
Cho, Francisca, and Richard Squier. 2008. "He Blinded Me with Science: Science Chauvinism in the Study of Religion." *Journal of the American Academy of Religion* 76, no. 2: 420–448.
Clark, Andy. 2011. *Supersizing the Mind: Embodiment, Action, and Cognitive Extension*. Oxford: Oxford University Press.
Clifford, James. 1997. *Routes: Travel and Translation in the Late Twentieth Century*. Harvard University Press.
Clottes, Jean. 2016. *What is Paleolithic Art?: Cave Paintings and the Dawn of Human Creativity*. Chicago: University of Chicago Press.
Comber, Michelle. 2001. "Trade and Communication Networks in Early Historic Ireland." *The Journal of Irish Archaeology* 10: 73–92.
Connolly, Sean. 1995. *Bede: On the Temple, Translated Texts for Historians*. Liverpool: Liverpool University Press.
Connolly, Sean, and Jean-Michel Picard. 1987. "Cogitosus: Life of Saint Brigit." *Journal of the Royal Society of Antiquaries of Ireland* 117: 11–27.
Constantinou, Meghan. 2010. *Books, Book Satchels, and Shrines in the Book of Deer* (Cambridge University Library, MS Ii. 6.32). PhD dissertation, University of Delaware.

Cooke, Thomas. 1853. "The Ancient Cross of Banagher, King's County." *Transactions of the Kilkenny Archaeological Society*, 2, no. 2: 277–280.

Cooney, Gabriel. 2009. "Tracing Lines Across Landscapes: Corporality and History in Later Prehistoric Ireland." In *Relics of Old Decency: Archaeological Studies in Later Prehistory. Festschrift for Barry Raftery*, edited by Gabriel Cooney, Katharina Becker, John Coles, Michael Ryan, and Susanne Sievers, 375–388. Dublin: Wordwell.

Corlett, Christian, and Michael Potterton, editors. 2012. *Life and Death in Iron Age Ireland in the Light of Recent Archaeological Excavations*. Dublin: Wordwell.

Coyne, Frank. 2006. "Excavation of an Early Medieval 'Plectrum-Shaped' Enclosure at Newtown, Co. Limerick." In *Settlement, Industry and Ritual*, edited by Jerry O'Sullivan and Michael Stanley, 63–72. National Roads Authority Monograph Series 3. Dublin: National Roads Authority/Wordwell.

Coyne, Frank, and Tracy Collins. 2003. "Plectrum Shaped Enclosures—a New Site Type at Newtown, Co. Limerick." *Archaeology Ireland* 17, no. 4: 17–19.

Crabtree, Pam. 1994. "Animal Exploitation in East Anglia." In *Environment and Economy in Anglo-Saxon England*, edited by James Rackham, 40–54. York: Council for British Archaeology.

Crabtree, Pam. 2003. "Ritual Feasting in the Irish Iron Age: Re-Examining the Fauna from Dún Ailinne in Light of Contemporary Archaeological Theory." In *Behavior Behind Bones: The Zooarchaeology of Ritual, Religion, Status, and Identity*. 9th ICAZ Conference, Durham, edited by Sharon O'Day, Wim Van Neer, and Anton Ervynck, 62–65. Oxford: Oxbow Books.

Crabtree, Pam. 2016. Zooarchaeology at Medieval Ipswich: From Wic to Regional Market Town. In *Objects, Environment, and Everyday Life in Medieval Europe*. Edited by Ben Jervis, Lee Broderick, Idoia Grau-Sologestoa, 19–39. Turnhout, Belgium: Brepols Publishers.

Crabtree, Pam. 2018. *Early Medieval Britain: The Rebirth of Towns in the Post-Roman West*. Vol. 1. Case Studies in Early Societies. Cambridge: Cambridge University Press.

Creighton, Oliver. 2009. "Castle Studies and the European Medieval Landscape: Traditions, Trends and Future Research Directions." *Landscape History* 30, no. 2: 5–20.

Croix, Sarah, Michael Neiß, and Søren M. Sindbæk. 2019. "The *Réseau Opératoire* of Urbanization: Craft Collaborations and Organization in an Early Medieval Workshop in Ribe, Denmark." *Cambridge Archaeological Journal* 29, no. 2: 345–364.

Cronk, Lee. 1994. "Group Selection's New Clothes." *Behavioral and Brain Sciences* 17, no. 4: 615–616.

Cronk, Lee, and Beth L. Leech. 2012. *Meeting at Grand Central: Understanding the Social and Evolutionary Roots of Cooperation*. Princeton, NJ: Princeton University Press.

Crumley, Carole. 1995. "Heterarchy and the Analysis of Complex Societies." In *Heterarchy and the Analysis of Complex Societies*, edited by Robert Ehrenreich, Carol Crumley and Janet Levy, 1–7. Arlington, VA: American Anthropological Association.

Culley, Elisabeth V. 2008. "Supernatural Metaphors and Belief in the Past: Defining an Archaeology of Religion." In *Belief in the Past: Theoretical Approaches to the Archaeology of Religion*, edited by David Whitley and Kelley Hays-Gilpin, 67–84. Walnut Creek, CA: Left Coast Press.

Curta, Florin. 2006. "Merovingian and Carolingian gift giving." *Speculum* 81, no. 3: 671–699.

Daffy, Sean. 2002. "A Site for Sore Eyes: A Hiberno-Roman Curative Cult at Golden, Co. Tipperary." *Archaeology Ireland* 16, no. 2: 8–9.

Danziger, Eve. 2017. "Toward an Anthropology of Intersubjectivity." *HAU: Journal of Ethnographic Theory* 7, no. 2: 451–455.

Darwin, Charles. 1871. *The Descent of Man and Selection in Relation to Sex*. London: John Murray.

Dawkins, Richard. 1976. *The Selfish Gene*. New York: Oxford University Press.

Day, Rachel L., Kevin N. Laland, and F. John Odling-Smee. 2003. "Rethinking Adaptation: The Niche-Construction Perspective." *Perspectives in Biology and Medicine* 46, no. 1: 80–95.

Deacon, Terrence. 1997. *The Symbolic Species*. New York: Norton.

de Certeau, Michael. 1984. *The Practice of Everyday Life*. Translated by S. Rendall. Berkeley, CA: University of California Press.

Devane, Caitríona. 2013. "The History of Kilbegly and its Environs." In *The Mill at Kilbegly, an Archaeological Investigation on the Route of the M6 Ballinasloe to Athlone National Road Scheme*, edited by Neil Jackman, Caitríona Moore, and Colin Rynne, 97–114. Dublin: National Roads Authority/Wordwell.

Devlin, Gary, and Rob Shaw. 2017. "The Digital Documentation of High Crosses." *Archaeology Ireland* 31, no. 3: 30–31.

de Waal, Frans. 2008. "Putting the Altruism Back into Altruism: The Evolution of Empathy." *Annual Review Psychology* 59: 279–300.

de Waal, Frans. 2013. *The Bonobo and the Atheist: In Search of Humanism among the Primates*. New York: W. W. Norton.

Doherty, Charles. 1980. "Exchange and Trade in Early Medieval Ireland." *Journal of the Royal Society of Antiquaries of Ireland* 110: 67–89.

Doherty, Charles. 1984. "The Use of Relics in Early Ireland. In *Irland und Europa: Die Kirche im Fruhmittelalter*, edited by Proinséas Ní Catháin and Michael Richter, 89–101. Stuttgart: Klett-Cotta.

Doherty, Charles. 1985. "The Monastic Town in Early Medieval Ireland." In *The Comparative History of Urban Origins in Non-Roman Europe*, edited by Howard B. Clarke and Anngret Simms, 45–75. Oxford: British Archaeological Reports.

Doherty, Charles. 1991. "The Cult of St. Patrick and the Politics of Armagh in the Seventh Century." In *Ireland and Northern France AD 600–850*, edited by Jean-Michel Picard, 53–94. Dublin: Four Courts.

Doherty, Charles. 2000. "Settlement in Early Ireland: A Review." In *A History of Settlement in Ireland*, edited by T. Barry, 50–80. London: Routledge.

Doherty, Charles. 2005. "Kingship in Early Ireland." In *The kingship and Landscape of Tara*, edited by Edel Bhreathnach, 3–31. Dublin: Four Courts Press.

Dolan, Brian. 2014. "Beyond Elites: Reassessing Irish Iron Age Society." *Oxford Journal of Archaeology* 33, no. 4: 361–377.

Donald, Merlin. 2011. "The First Hybrid Minds on Earth." In *Religious Narrative, Cognition and Culture: Image and Word in The Mind of Narrative*, edited by Armin Geertz and Jeppe Sinding Jensen, 67–96. New York: Routledge.

Doran, Linda. 2004. "Medieval Communication Routes through Longford and Roscommon and Their Associated Settlements." *Proceedings of the Royal Irish Academy* 104C: 57–80.

Dornan, Jennifer. 2002. "Agency and Archaeology: Past, Present and Future Directions." *Journal of Archaeological Method and Theory* 9, no. 2: 303–329.

Douglas, Mary. 1990. "No Free Gifts." Foreword to Marcel Mauss ([1925] 1990) *The Gift: the Form and Reason for Exchange in Archaic Societies*, translated by W. D. Halls, vii–xviii. London: Routledge.

Dowling, Ger. 2014. "Landscape and Settlement in Late Iron Age Ireland: Some Emerging Trends." In *Late Iron Age and 'Roman' Ireland*, edited by Cahil Wilson, Ger Dowling, Michael Ann Bevivino and Philippa Barry, Discovery Programme Reports 8, 151–174. Dublin: Wordwell.

Dowling, Ger. 2015. "Exploring the Hidden Depths of Tara's Hinterland: Geophysical Survey and Landscape Investigations in the Meath–North Dublin Region, Eastern Ireland." *Proceedings of the Prehistoric Society* 81, 61–85.

Dubisch, Jill, and Michael Winkelman, editors. 2005. *Pilgrimage and Healing*. Tempe: University of Arizona Press.

Duby, George. 1968. *Rural Economy and Country Life in the Medieval West*. Columbia: University of South Carolina Press.

Duby, George 1974. *The Early Growth of the European Economy: Warriors and Peasants from the Seventh to the Twelfth Century*. Ithaca, NY: Cornell University Press.

Duffy, Patrick, David Edwards, and Elizabeth Fitzpatrick, editors. 2001. *Gaelic Ireland: Land, Lordship and Settlement, c. 1250–c. 1650*. Dublin: Four Courts.

Duignan, Michael. 1944. "Irish Agriculture in Early Historic Times." *Journal of the Royal Society of Antiquaries of Ireland* 74: 124–145.

Duke, Sean. 1998. "Irish Bridge Sheds Light on Dark Ages." *Science* 279 (January 23): 480.

Durkheim, Emile. 1965 [1915]. *Elementary Forms of Religion*. New York: Free Press.

Edwards, Nancy. 1990. *The Archaeology of Early Medieval Ireland*. London: B. T. Batsford.

Edwards, Nancy. 1998. "A Group of Shafts and Related Sculpture from Clonmacnoise and Its Environs." In *Clonmacnoise Studies*, vol. 1, edited by Heather King, 101–18. Dublin: Dúchas.

Emerson, Thomas, and Timothy R. Pauketat. 2008. "Historical-Processual Archaeology and Culture Making: Unpacking the Southern Cult and Mississippian Religion." In *Belief in the Past: Theoretical Approaches to the Archaeology of Religion*. Edited by David S. Whitley and Kelley Hays-Gilpin, 167–188. New York: Routledge.

Etchingham, Colmán. 2006. "Pastoral Provision in the First Millennium: A Two-Tier Service?" In *The Parish in Medieval and Early Modern Ireland: Community, Territory and Building*, edited by Elizabeth FitzPatrick and Raymond Gillespie, 79–90. Dublin: Four Courts.

Etchingham, Colmán. 2011. "Organization and Function of an Early Irish Church Settlement: What Was Glendalough?" In *Glendalough: City of God*, edited by Charles Doherty, Linda Doran and Mary Kelly, 22–53. Dublin: Four Courts Press for the Royal Society of Antiquaries.

Farr, Carol. 1991. "Liturgical Influences on the Decoration of the Book of Kells." In *Studies in Insular Art and Archaeology*, edited by Catherine Karkov and Robert Farrel, 127–41. Oxford, Ohio: American Early Medieval Studies..

Farr, Carol. 1997. *The Book of Kells: Its Function and Audience*. Toronto: University of Toronto Press.

Ferguson, Leland. 1992. *Uncommon Ground: Archaeology and Early African America, 1650–1800*. Washington, DC: Smithsonian Books.

Finan, Thomas. 2004. *A Nation in Medieval Ireland? Perspectives on Gaelic National Identity in the Middle Ages*, BAR British Series 367. Oxford: Archaeopress.

Finley, Moses. 1970. "Aristotle and Economic Analysis." *Past and Present* 47: 3–25.

Finley, Moses. 1973 [1985]. *The Ancient Economy*, 2nd ed. Berkeley: University of California Press.

Fitzgibbon, Bernadette M., Peter G. Enticott, Anina N. Rich, Melita J. Giummarra, Nellie Georgiou-Karistianis, and John L. Bradshaw. 2012. "Mirror-Sensory Synaesthesia: Exploring 'Shared' Sensory Experiences as Synaesthesia." *Neuroscience and Biobehavioral Reviews* 36, no. 1: 645–657.

Fitzpatrick, Elizabeth. 2004. *Royal Inauguration in Gaelic Ireland c. 1100–1600: A Cultural Landscape Study*. Dublin: Boydell Press.

Fitzpatrick, Elizabeth. 2009. "Native Enclosed Settlement and the Problem of the Irish 'Ring-fort'." *Medieval Archaeology* 53, no. 1: 271–307.

Fitzpatrick, Elizabeth and Caimin O'Brien. 1998. *The Medieval Churches of County Offaly*. Dublin: Government of Ireland.

Flanagan, Marie Therese. 2010. *The Transformation of The Irish Church in the Twelfth and Thirteenth Centuries*. Boydell & Brewer.

Fleming, Robin. 2010. *Britain after Rome: The Fall and Rise, 400–1070* (Vol. 1). London: Penguin Global.

Fogelin, Lars. 2007a. "The Archaeology of Religious Ritual." *Annual Review of Anthropology* 36, no. 1: 55–71.

Fogelin, Lars. 2007b. "History, Ethnography, and Essentialism: the Archaeology of Religion and Ritual in South Asia." In *The Archaeology of Ritual*, edited by Evangelos Kyriakidis, 23–42. Los Angeles: Costen Institute of Archaeology.

Fogelin, Lars. 2008. "Delegitimizing religion: The Archaeology of Religion as. . . Archaeology. In *Belief in the Past: Theoretical Approaches to the Archaeology of Religion*, edited by David Whitley and Kelley Hays-Gilpin, 139–142. Walnut Creek, CA: Left Coast Press.

Forstmann, Matthias, and Pascal Burgmer. 2015. "Adults are Intuitive Mind-Body Dualists." *Journal of Experimental Psychology: General* 144, no. 1: 222–235.

Fowles, Severin. M. 2013. *An Archaeology of Doings: Secularism and the Study of Pueblo Religion.* Santa Fe, NM: SAR Press.

Fredengren, Christina. 2002. *Crannogs: A Study of People's Interaction with Lakes, with Particular Reference to Lough Gara in the North-West of Ireland.* Dublin: Wordwell.

Fredengren, Christina, Meriel McClatchie, and Ingelise Stuijts. 2004. "Connections and Distance: Investigating Social and Agricultural Issues Relating to Early Medieval Crannogs in Ireland." *Environmental Archaeology* 9: 173–178.

Galen, Luke. 2016. "Big Gods: Extended Prosociality or Group Binding?" *Behavioral and Brain Sciences* 39: 29–30.

Gallese, Vittorio, and Alvin Goldman. 1998. "Mirror Neurons and the Simulation Theory of Mind-reading." *Trends in Cognitive Sciences* 2, no. 12: 493–501.

Gallese, Vittorio, and Corrado Sinigaglia. 2011. "What Is So Special about Embodied Simulation?" *Trends in Cognitive Sciences* 15, no. 11: 512–519.

Garrow, Duncan. 2012. "Odd Deposits and Average Practice. A Critical History of the Concept of Structured Deposition." *Archaeological Dialogues* 19, no. 2: 85–115.

Geary, Patrick. 1986. "Sacred Commodities: The Circulation of Medieval Relics. In *The Social Life of Things,* edited by A. Appadurai, 169–191. Cambridge: Cambridge University Press.

Geary, Patrick. 1988. *Before France and Germany: The Creation and Transformation of the Merovingian World.* New York: Oxford University Press.

Gell, Alfred. 1998. *Art and Agency: An Anthropological Theory.* Oxford: Clarendon Press.

Geraghty, Shiobhán. 1996. *Viking Dublin: Botanical Evidence from Fishamble Street.* Dublin: Royal Irish Academy for the National Museum of Ireland and the Royal Irish Academy.

Giacometti, Antione. 2006. "Living in the Landscape." *Archaeology Ireland* 20, no. 2: 36–39.

Gibson, D. Blair. 2012. *From Chiefdom to State in Early Ireland.* Cambridge. Cambridge University Press.

Gilchrist, Roberta 2020. *Sacred Heritage: Monastic Archaeology, Identities, Beliefs.* Cambridge: Cambridge University Press.

Glob, P.V. 1969. *The Bog People: Iron-Age Man Preserved.* London: Faber.

Graeber, David. 2001. *Towards An Anthropological Theory of Value: The False Coin of Our Own Dreams.* New York: Palgrave Macmillan.

Graham, Brian. 1987. "Urban Genesis in Early Medieval Ireland." *Journal of Historical Geography* 13, no. 1: 3–16.

Graham, Brian. 2000. "Urbanization in Ireland during the High Middle Ages, c. 1100 to c. 1350." In *A History of Settlement in Ireland,* edited by T. Barry, 124–39. London: Routledge.

Grant, Annie. 1991. "Economic or Symbolic? Animals and Ritual Behavior." In *Sacred and Profane: Proceedings of a Conference on Archaeology, Ritual, and Religion Oxford, 1989,* edited by Paul Garwood, David Jennings, Robin Skeates, and Judith Toms, 109–114. Oxford: Oxford University Committee for Archaeology.

Green, Patrick. 1992. *Medieval Monasteries*. Leicester University Press.
Gregory, Chris. 1982. *Gifts and Commodities*. Cambridge, MA: Academic Press.
Grierson, Phillip. 1959. "Commerce in the Dark Ages: A Critique of the Evidence." *Transactions of the Royal Historical Society* 9: 123–140.
Grogan, Eoin. 2009. *Rath of the Synods: Tara, Co. Meath, Excavations by Séan Ó Ríordáin*. Dublin: Wordwell.
Gudeman, Stephen. 2001. *The Anthropology of Economy*. New York: Blackwell.
Guthrie, Stewart. 1993. *Faces in the Clouds: A New Theory of Religion*. Oxford: Oxford University Press.
Gwynn, Aubrey. 1992. *The Irish Church in the Eleventh and Twelfth Centuries*, edited by Gerard O'Brien. Dublin: Four Courts.
Gwynn, Aubrey, and Neville Hadcock. 1970. *Medieval Religious Houses: Ireland*. London: Longman.
Haidt, Jonathan. 2001. "The Emotional Dog and Its Rational Tail: A Social Intuitionist Approach to Moral Judgment." *Psychological Review* 108: 814–834.
Hall, Valerie. 2005. "The Vegetation History of Monastic and Secular Sites in the Midlands of Ireland over the Last Two Millennia." *Vegetation History and Archaeobotany* 15: 1–12.
Hall, Valerie, and Dmitri Mauquoy. 2005. "Tephra-Dated Climate-And Human-Impact Studies during the Last 1500 Years from a Raised Bog in Central Ireland." *The Holocene* 15, no. 7: 1086–1093.
Hall, Valerie, John Pilcher, and Finbar McCormick. 1993. "Tephra-Dated Lowland Landscape History of the North of Ireland, AD 750–1150." *New Phytologist* 125: 193–202.
Hamilton, William. 1964. "The Genetical Evolution of Social Behavior." *Journal of Theoretical Biology* 7: 1–52.
Hamilton-Dyer, Sheila. n.d. *Bird and Fish Bones from Clonmacnoise, New Graveyard Excavations*. Unpublished report.
Hamilton-Dyer, Sheila. 2007. "Exploitation of Birds and Fish in Historic Ireland: A Brief Review of the Evidence." In *Environmental Archaeology in Ireland*, edited by Eileen Murphy and Nikki Whitehouse, 102–18. Oxford: Oxbow Books.
Harbison, Peter. 1979. "The Inscriptions on the Cross of the Scriptures at Clonmacnois, County Offaly." *Proceedings of the Royal Irish Academy* 79C: 177–188.
Harbison, Peter. 1995. *Pilgrimage in Ireland: the Monuments and the People*. Syracuse: Syracuse University Press.
Hardin, G. 1968. "The Tragedy of the Commons." *Science* 162: 1243–1248.
Hare, Brian. 2017. "Survival of the Friendliest: *Homo sapiens* Evolved via Selection for Prosociality." *Annual Review of Psychology* 68: 155–186.
Harney, Lorcan. 2017. "Christianising Pagan Worlds in Conversion-Era Ireland: Archaeological Evidence for the Origins of Irish Ecclesiastical Sites." *Proceedings of the Royal Irish Academy* 117C: 103–130.
Harrison, Neil A., Tania Singer, Pia Rotshtein, Ray J. Dolan, and Hugo D. Critchley. 2006. "Pupillary Contagion: Central Mechanisms Engaged in Sadness Processing." *Social Cognitive and Affective Neuroscience* 1, no. 1: 5–17.

Hatting, Tove. 1990. "Cats from Viking Age Odense." *Journal of Danish Archaeology* 9: 179–193.
Hawkes, Christopher F. 1954. "Archaeological Theory and Method: Some Suggestions from the Old World." *American Anthropologist* 56: 155–168.
Hawkes, Gillian. 1999. "Beyond Romanization: The Creolization of Food: A Framework for the Study of Faunal Remains from Roman Sites." *Papers from the Institute of Archaeology* 10: 89–95.
Heald, A. 2001. "Knobbed Spearbutts of the British and Irish Iron Age: New Examples and New Thoughts." *Antiquity* 75: 689–696.
Hencken, Hugh. 1950. "Lagore Crannog: An Irish Royal Residence of the 7th to 10th Centuries AD." *Proceedings of the Royal Irish Academy* 53C: 1–247.
Henrich, Joseph. 2009. "The Evolution of Costly Displays, Cooperation and Religion: Credibility Enhancing Displays and Their Implications for Cultural Evolution." *Evolution and Human Behavior* 30, no. 4: 244–260.
Henrich, Joseph, and Richard McElreath. 2007. "Dual-Inheritance Theory: The Evolution of Human Cultural Capacities and Cultural Evolution." In *Oxford Handbook of Evolutionary Psychology*, edited by Robin Dunbar, Ian MacDonald Dunbar, and Louise Barrett, 123–135. Oxford: Oxford University Press.
Henry, Françoise. 1980. "Around an Inscription: The Cross of the Scriptures at Clonmacnoise," *Journal of the Royal Society of Antiquaries of Ireland* 110: 36–46.
Herbert, Máire. 1988. *Iona, Kells, and Derry: The History and Hagiography the Monastic Familia of Columba*. Oxford: Clarendon Press.
Herva, Vesa-Pekka. 2009. "Living (with) Things: Relational Ontology and Material Culture in Early Modern Northern Finland." *Cambridge Archaeological Journal* 19, no. 3: 388–397.
Hesse, Brian, and Paula Wapnish. 1985. *Animal Bone Archeology: From Objectives to Analysis*. Washington, DC: Taraxacum.
Heyes, Cecilia. 2010. "Where Do Mirror Neurons Come From?" *Neuroscience and Biobehavioral Reviews* 34, no. 4: 575–583.
Hill, J. D. 1995. *Ritual and Rubbish in the Iron Age of Wessex*, British Archaeological Reports, British Series 242. Oxford: British Archaeological Reports.
Hodges, Richard. 1982. *Dark Age Economics: The Origins of Towns and Trade, AD 600–1000*. London: Duckworth.
Hodges, Richard. 1997. *Light in the Dark Ages: The Rise and Fall of San Vincenzo al Volturno*. London: Duckworth.
Hodges, Richard. 2012. *Dark Age Economics: A New Audit*. London: Bristol University Press.
Hodges, Richard, and David Whitehouse. 1983. *Mohammed, Charlemagne and the Origins of Europe*. Ithaca, NY: Cornell University Press.
Hoffmann, Robert. 2013. "The Experimental Economics of Religion." *Journal of Economic Surveys* 27, no. 5: 813–845.
Højbjerg, Christian 2007. *Resisting State Iconoclasm Among the Loma of Guinea*. Carolina Academy of Ritual Studies. Durham, NC: Carolina Academic Press.
Holder, Arthur. 1994. *Bede: The Tabernacle, Translated Texts for Historians*. Liverpool: Liverpool University Press.

Holmes, Matilda. 2014. *Animals in Saxon and Scandinavian England: Backbones of Economy and Society*. Leiden: Sidestone Press.
Hrdy, Sarah Blaffer. 2011. *Mothers and Others*. Cambridge MA: Harvard University Press.
Hull, Graham, and Michelle Comber. 2008. "Caherconnell, Co. Clare and Cashel Chronology." *Archaeology Ireland* 22, no. 4: 30–33.
Hvass, Steen. 1979. "The Viking Age Settlement at Vorbasse, Central Jutland." *Acta Archaeologica* 50: 137–172.
Iacoboni, Marco. 2009. "Imitation, Empathy, and Mirror Neurons." *Annual Review of Psychology* 60: 653–670.
Iacoboni, Marco, Istvan Molnar-Szakacs, Vittorio Gallese, Giovanni Buccino, John C. Mazziotta, and Giacomo Rizzolatti. 2005. "Grasping the Intentions of Others with One's Own Mirror Neuron System." *PLoS Biol* 3, no. 3: 529–535.
Inglis, David. 2016. "Durkheimian and Neo-Durkheimian Cultural." *The SAGE Handbook of Cultural Sociology*: 60–76. Thousand Oaks, CA: SAGE Publications.
Ingold, Tim. 1998. "From Complementarity to Obviation: On Dissolving the Boundaries between Social and Biological Anthropology, Archaeology, And Psychology." Zeitschrift für Ethnologie 123: 21–52. JSTOR.
Ingold, Tim. 2007. *Lines: A Brief History*. London: Routledge.
Ingold, Tim. 2011. *Being Alive: Essays on Movement, Knowledge and Description*. London: Routledge.
Inomata, Takeshi. 2006. "Plazas, Performers, and Spectators: Political Theaters of the Classic Maya." *Current Anthropology* 47, no. 5: 805–842.
Insoll, Timothy. 2004. *Archaeology, Ritual, Religion*. New York: Routledge.
Irons, William. 1996. "Morality as an Evolved Adaptation," In *Investigating the Biological Foundations of Morality*, edited by James Hurd, 1–34. Lewiston: Edwin Mellon Press.
Irons, William. 2001. "Religion as a Hard-to-Fake Sign of Commitment." In *Evolution and the Capacity for Commitment*, edited by Randolph Nesse, 292–309. New York: Russell Sage Foundation.
Jaski, Bart. 2000. *Early Irish Kingship and Succession*. Dublin: Four Courts.
Johnson, Matthew. 1996. *An Archaeology of Capitalism*. Cambridge, MA: Blackwell.
Johnston, Susan, Pam Crabtree, and Douglas Campana. 2014. "Performance, Place and Power at Dún Ailinne, a Ceremonial Site of the Irish Iron Age." *World Archaeology* 46, no. 2: 206–223.
Jones, Andrew. 2007. *Memory and Material Culture*. Cambridge: Cambridge University Press.
Jones, Siân. 1997. *The Archaeology of Ethnicity: Constructing Identities in the Past and Present*. New York: Routledge.
Kantner, John, and Kevin J. Vaughn. 2012. "Pilgrimage as Costly Signal: Religiously Motivated Cooperation in Chaco and Nasca." *Journal of Anthropological Archaeology* 31, no. 1: 66–82.
Kapogiannis, Dimitrios, Aron K. Barbey, Michael Su, Giovanna Zamboni, Frank Krueger, and Jordan Grafman. 2009. "Cognitive and Neural Foundations of Re-

ligious Belief." *Proceedings of the National Academy of Sciences* 106, no. 12: 4876–4881.
Kavanagh, Rhoda. 1988. "The Horse in Viking Ireland." In *Settlement and Society in Medieval Ireland: Studies Presented to Francis Xavier Martin O.S.A.*, edited by John Bradley: 89–121. Kilkenny: Boethius Press.
Keegan, Mark. 2011a/b. *Clonmacnoise*. Available from http://www.excavations.ie.
Kehnel, Annette. 1997. *Clonmacnoise—The Church and Lands of St. Ciarán: Change and Continuity in an Irish Monastic Foundation (6th to 16th Century)*. Vita Regularis: Ordungen und Deutungen religiosen Lebens im Mittelalter, vol. 8. Munster: Lit Verlag.
Kehnel, Annette. 1998. "The Lands of St Ciarán." In *Clonmacnoise Studies*, vol. 1, edited by Heather King, 11–18. Dublin: Dúchas.
Kelly, Dorothy. 1991. "The Heart of the Matter: Models for Irish High Crosses." *The Journal of the Royal Society of Antiquaries of Ireland*: 105–145. Dublin: Royal Society of Antiquaries of Ireland.
Kelly, Fergus. 1988. *A Guide to Early Irish Law*. Dublin: Dublin Institute for Advanced Studies.
Kelly, Fergus. 1997. *Early Irish Farming*. Dublin: Dublin Institute for Advanced Studies.
Kenny, M. 1998. "A Hoard of Hiberno-Norse Coins from Clonmacnoise, Co. Offaly," in *Clonmacnoise Studies*, vol. 1, edited by Heater King, 133–148. Dublin: Dúchas.
Kenward, H. K., A. Hall, E. P. Allison, and J. Carrott, 2011. "Environment, Activity and Living Conditions at Deer Park Farms: Evidence from Plant and Invertebrate Remains." In *Deer Park Farms: the Excavation of a Raised Rath in the Glenarm Valley, Co. Antrim*, edited by C. J. Lynn and J. A. McDowell, 498–547. Northern Ireland Archaeological Monographs 9. Belfast. HMSO and Environment and Heritage Service.
Kerr, Thomas. 2007. *Early Christian Settlement in North-West Ulster*. BAR British Series 430. Oxford. Archaeopress.
Kerr, Thomas, Finbar McCormick, and Aidan O'Sullivan. 2013. *The Economy of Early Medieval Ireland, The Early Medieval Archaeology Project (EMAP): Project Report 2013*. UCD School of Archaeology, and School of Geography, Archaeology and Palaeoecology, Queens University Belfast.
Kerr, Thomas, Graeme T. Swindles, and Gill Plunkett. 2009. "Making Hay While the Sun Shines? Socio-Economic Change, Cereal Production and Climatic Deterioration in Early Medieval Ireland. *Journal of Archaeological Science* 36, no. 12: 2868–2874.
Keysers, Christian, and Valeria Gazzola. 2009. "Expanding the Mirror: Vicarious Activity for Actions, Emotions, and Sensations." *Current Opinion in Neurobiology* 19, no. 6: 666–671.
King, Heather. 1991. "Clonmacnoise New Graveyard, Clonmacnoise." In *Excavations 1990: Summary Accounts of Archaeological Excavations in Ireland*, edited by Isabell Bennett. Dublin: Wordwell.

King, Heather. 1992a. "'Clonmacnoise New Graveyard, Clonmacnoise," in *Excavations 1991: Summary Accounts of Archaeological Excavations in Ireland*, edited by Isabell Bennett, 40–41. Dublin: Wordwell.

King, Heather. 1992b. "Moving Crosses." *Archaeology Ireland* 6, no. 4: 22–23.

King, Heather. 1993. "New Graveyard at Clonmacnoise." In *Excavations 1992: Summary Accounts of Archaeological Excavations in Ireland*, edited by Isabell Bennett, 53–54. Dublin: Wordwell.

King, Heather. 1994. "New Graveyard, Clonmacnoise." In *Excavations 1993: Summary Accounts of Archaeological Excavations in Ireland*, edited by Isabell Bennett, 66–67. Dublin: Wordwell.

King, Heather. 1995. "New Graveyard, Clonmacnoise." In *Excavations 1994: Summary Accounts of Archaeological Excavations in Ireland*, edited by Isabell Bennett. Dublin: Wordwell.

King, Heather. 1996. "New Graveyard, Clonmacnoise." In *Excavations 1995: Summary Accounts of Archaeological Excavations in Ireland*, edited by Isabell Bennett, 76–77. Dublin: Wordwell.

King, Heather. 1997a. "Burials and High Crosses at Clonmacnoise (Ireland)," in *Death and Burial in Medieval Europe, Papers of the "Medieval Europe Brugge 1997" Conference* vol. 2, edited by G. De Boe and F. Verhaeghe, 127–131. Brugge: Zelik.

King, Heather. 1997b. "New Graveyard, Clonmacnoise," in *Excavations 1996: Summary Accounts of Archaeological Excavations In Ireland*, edited by Isabell Bennett, 92–93. Dublin: Wordwell.

King, Heather. 1998. *New Graveyard, Clonmacnoise*. Available from http://www.excavations.ie.

King, Heather. 2001. "Excavation of the High Cross in the Medieval Market Place of Kells." In *From Megaliths to Metal: Essays in Honour of George Eogan*, edited by Helen Roche, Eoin Grogan, John Bradely, John Coles, and Barry Raftery, 233–242. Oxford: Oxbow Books.

King, Heather. 2002. *Clonmacnoise*. Available from http://www.excavations.ie.

King, Heather. 2003. *Clonmacnoise*. Available from http://www.excavations.ie.

King, Heather. 2004. *Clonmacnoise*. In *Ancient Europe 8000 B.C.–A.D. 1000: Encyclopedia of the Barbarian World*, edited by Peter Bogucki and Pamela Crabtree, 456–59. New York: Thompson/Gale.

King, Heather. 2008. "An Ogham-Inscribed Antler Handle from Clonmacnoise." *Peritia* 20: 315–322.

King, Heather. 2009. "The Economy and Industry of Early Medieval Clonmacnoise: A Preliminary View." In *The Archaeology of the Early Medieval Celtic Churches*, edited by Nancy Edwards, 333–349. Society for Medieval Archaeology Monograph 29. Leeds: Maney Publishing.

Kinsella, Jonathan. 2010. "A New Irish Early Medieval Site Type? Exploring the 'Recent' Archaeological Evidence for Non-Circular Enclosed Settlement and Burial Sites." *Proceedings of the Royal Irish Academy* 110C: 89–132.

Kirsh, David and Paul Maglio. 1994. "On Distinguishing Epistemic from Pragmatic Action." *Cognitive Science* 18, no. 4: 513–549.

Krämer, Ulrike M., Bahram Mohammadi, Nuria Doñamayor, Amir Samii, and Thomas F. Münte. 2010. "Emotional and Cognitive Aspects of Empathy and Their Relation to Social Cognition—An fMRI-Study." *Brain Research* 1311: 110–120.

Lakoff, George. 2003. "How the Body Shapes Thought: Thinking with an All-Too-Human Brain." In *The Nature and Limits of Human Understanding*, edited by A. J. Sanford, 49–74. Edinburgh: T. & T. Clark.

Lakoff, George, and Mark Johnson. 1980. *Metaphors We Live By*. Chicago: University of Chicago Press.

Lakoff, George, and Mark Johnson. 1999. *Philosophy in the Flesh: The Embodied Mind and Its Challenge to Western Thought*. New York: Basic Books.

Lambert, T. B. 2012. "The Evolution of Sanctuary in Medieval England." In *Legalism: Anthropology and History*, edited by P. Dresch and H. Skoda, 115–144. Oxford: Oxford University Press.

Leone, M. 1988. "The Georgian Order as the Order of Capitalism in Annapolis, Maryland." In *The Recovery of Meaning in Historical Archaeology*, edited by Mark Leone and Parker Potter, 235–261. Washington, DC: Smithsonian Institution.

Lewis, James. 2006. "Cortical Networks Related to Human Use of Tools." *Neuroscientist* 12: 211–231.

Lewis-Williams, David. 2002. *A Cosmos in Stone: Interpreting Religion and Society through Rock Art*. Lanham, MD: AltaMira Press.

Lewis-Williams, David and Jean Clottes. 1998. "The Mind in the Cave—The Cave in the Mind: Altered Consciousness in the Upper Paleolithic." *Anthropology of Consciousness* 9, no. 1: 13–21.

Longo, Matthew, and Stella Lourenco. "Space Perception and Body Morphology: Extent of Near Space Scales with Arm Length." *Experimental Brain Research* 177, no. 2: 285–290.

Lucas, A. T. 1989. *Cattle in Ancient Ireland*, edited by John Bradley. Kilkenny: Boethius Press.

Lyman, R. Lee, and Michael J. O'Brien. 1998. "The Goals of Evolutionary Archaeology: History and Explanation." *Current Anthropology* 5: 615–652.

Lynn, C. J. 1994. "Houses in Rural Ireland, AD 500–1000." *Ulster Journal of Archaeology*: 81–94.

Lyons, Susan. 2018. "Pioneering New Approaches to Woodland Ecology and Human Activity in Medieval Ireland (c. AD 500–1550): An Investigation Using Archaeological Charcoal." PhD diss., University College Cork.

Mac Airt, Seán, and Gearóid Mac Niocaill, editors. 1983. *The Annals of Ulster (to A. D. 1131)*. Dublin: Institute for Advanced Studies.

Macaulay, David. 1979. *Motel of the Mysteries*. New York: Houghton Mifflin Harcourt.

Macaulay, David. 2010 [1973]. *Cathedral: The Story of Its Construction*. New York: Houghton Mifflin Harcourt.

McAnany, Patricia A., and E. Christian Wells, editors. 2008. "Toward a Theory of Ritual Economy." In *Dimensions of Ritual Economy*, 1–16. Bingley, UK: Emerald Group Publishing Limited.

McBrearty, Sally, and Alison S. Brooks. 2000. "The Revolution That Wasn't: A New Interpretation of the Origin of Modern Human Behavior." *Journal of Human Evolution* 39, no. 5: 453–563.

McCauley, Leo, and Anthony Stephenson. 1969. *The Works of Saint Cyril of Jerusalem*. Vols. 61, 64, The Fathers of the Church. Washington, DC: The Catholic University of America Press.

McClatchie, Meriel, Finbar McCormick, Thomas R. Kerr, and Aidan O'Sullivan. 2015. "Early Medieval Farming and Food Production: A Review of the Archaeobotanical Evidence from Archaeological Excavations in Ireland." *Vegetation History and Archaeobotany* 24, no. 1: 179–186.

McClung, Lisa Coyle. 2013. "The Late Iron-Age Lull—Not So Late-Iron Age After All!" *Emania* 21: 73–83.

McClung, Lisa Coyle, and Gill Plunkett. 2020. "Cultural Change and the Climate Record in Final Prehistoric and Early Medieval Ireland." *Proceedings of the Royal Irish Academy*. 120C: 1–30.

McCormick, Finbar. 1983. Dairying and Beef Production in Early Christian Ireland: The Faunal Evidence. In *Landscape Archaeology in Ireland*, edited by Terence Reeves-Smyth and Fred Hamond, 253–67. Oxford: British Archaeological Reports.

McCormick, Finbar. 1984a. The Animal Bones from Drogheda. *Proceedings of the Royal Irish Academy* 84C: 209–215.

McCormick, Finbar. 1984b. Appendix I: The Animal Bones. In Lynch, Ann. "Excavations of the Medieval Town Defences at Charlotte's Quay, Limerick." *Proceedings of the Royal Irish Academy*. 84C: 322–331.

McCormick, Finbar. 1987a. *Stockrearing in Early Christian Ireland*. PhD, Archaeology, Queen's University of Belfast, Belfast.

McCormick, Finbar. 1987b. "Appendix 1: The Animal Bones." In Con Manning, "Excavation at Moyne graveyard." *Proceedings of the Royal Irish Academy* 87C: 60–68.

McCormick, Finbar. 1988. "The Domesticated Cat in Early Christian and Medieval Ireland." In *Keimelia: Studies in Medieval Archaeology and History in Memory of Tom Delaney*, edited by Geroid Mac Niocaill and Patrick Wallace, 218–228. Galway: Galway University Press.

McCormick, Finbar. 1991. "The Effect of the Anglo-Norman Settlement on Ireland's Wild and Domesticated Fauna." In *Animal Use and Culture Change*, edited by Pam Crabtree and Kathleen Ryan, 41–52. Philadelphia: University of Pennsylvania.

McCormick, Finbar. 1995. "Cows, Ringforts and the Origins of Early Christian Ireland." *Emania* 13: 33–37.

McCormick, Finbar. 1997a. "The Animal Bones." In *Late Viking Age and Medieval Waterford: Excavations 1986–92*, edited by Maurice Hurley, Orla Scully, and Sarah McCutcheon. Waterford: Waterford Corporation.

McCormick, Finbar. 1997b. "Farming and Food in Medieval Lecale." In *Down—History and Society*, edited by Lindsay Proudfoot. Dublin: Geography Publications.

McCormick, Finbar. 2002a. "The Animal Bones from Tara." In *Discovery Programme Reports 6*: 103–116.

McCormick, Finbar. 2002b. "The Distribution of Meat in a Hierarchical Society: The Irish Evidence." In *Consuming Passions and Patterns of Consumption*, edited by Preston Miracle and Nicky Milner, 25–31. Cambridge: McDonald Institute for Archaeological Research.

McCormick, Finbar. 2005. "Archaeology: The Horse in Early Ireland." In *The Irish Draught Horse: A History*, edited by Mary McCGrath and Joan Griffith, 85–104. Cork: Collins Press.

McCormick, Finbar. 2007. "The Horse in Early Ireland." *Anthropozoologica* 42, no. 1: 85–104.

McCormick, Finbar. 2008. "The Decline of the Cow: Agricultural and Settlement Change in Early Medieval Ireland." *Peritia* 20: 210–225.

McCormick, Finbar. 2012. "Cows, Milk and Religion: The Use of Dairy Produce in Early Societies." *Anthropozoologica* 47, no. 2: 99–113.

McCormick, Finbar. 2014. "Agriculture, Settlement and Society in Early Medieval Ireland." *Quaternary International* 30: 119–130.

McCormick, Finbar, and Eileen Murphy. 1997. "Mammal Bones." In *Archaeological Excavations at Patrick, Nicholas and Winetavern Streets*, edited by Claire Walsh, 199–218. Dingle: Brandon Book Publishers.

McCormick, Finbar, and Emily Murray. 2007. *Knowth and the Zooarchaeology of Early Christian Ireland. Excavation at Knowth 3*. Dublin: Royal Irish Academy.

McCormick, Finbar, and Emily Murray. 2011. "The Animal Bones from Deer Park Farms" In *Deer Park Farms: The Excavation of a Raised Rath in the Glenarm Valley, Co. Antrim*, edited by Lynn, C. J. and McDowell, J. A., 469–488. Belfast: HMSO and Environment and Heritage Service.

McCormick, Finbar, and Emily Murray. 2017. "The Zooarchaeology of Medieval Ireland." In *The Oxford Handbook of Zooarchaeology*, edited by Umberto Albarella, 195–213. Oxford: Oxford University Press.

McCormick, Finbar, Thomas R. Kerr, Meriel McClatchie, and Aidan O'Sullivan. 2011. "The Archaeology of Livestock and Cereal Production in Early Medieval Ireland, AD 400–1100." In *Reconstructing the Early Medieval Irish Economy*, EMAP Report 5.1: Irish National Strategic Archaeological Research (INSTAR) programme 2011.

McCormick, Michael. 2001. *Origins of the European Economy: Communications and Commerce AD 300–900*. Cambridge University Press.

McCorriston Joy. 2011. *Pilgrimage and Household in the Ancient Near East*. Cambridge: Cambridge University Press.

McDermott, Conor. 1995. "A Paved Way in Bloomhill Bog, Counties Westmeath and Offaly." In *Blackwater Survey and Excavations: Artefact Deterioration in Peatlands, Lough More, Co. Mayo*, edited by Aonghus Moloney et al., 59–66. Dublin: Department of Archaeology, University College Dublin.

McDonald, Nicola, ed. 2014. *Medieval Obscenities*. Rochester, NY: Boydell & Brewer Ltd.

McErlean, Thomas, and Norman Crothers. 2007. *Harnessing the Tides: The Early Medieval Tide Mills at Nendrum Monastery, Strangford Loch*. Norwich: Environment & Heritage Service/The Stationery Office.

McGettigan, Frances, and Kevin Burns. 2001. "Clonmacnoise: A Monastic Site, Burial Ground and Tourist Attraction." *Cultural Attractions and European Tourism*, edited by Greg Richards. 135–158. Oxon UK: CABI Publishing.

McSheffrey, Shannon. 2009. "Sanctuary and the Legal Topography of Pre-reformation London. *Law and History Review* 27, no. 3: 483–514.

Maddox, Melanie. 2016. "Re-conceptualizing the Monastic Town" *Journal of the Royal Society of Antiquaries of Ireland* 146: 21–32.

Madgwick, Richard, Vaughan Grimes, Angela L. Lamb, Alexandra J. Nederbragt, Jane A. Evans, and Finbar McCormick. 2019. "Feasting and Mobility in Iron Age Ireland: Multi-isotope Analysis Reveals the Vast Catchment of Navan Fort, Ulster." *Scientific reports* 9, no. 1: 1–14.

Mahr, Adolf. 1976. *Christian Art in Ancient Ireland: Selected Objects Illustrated and Described*. New York: Hacker Art Books.

Malafouris, Lambros. 2007. "The Sacred Engagement: Outline of a Hypothesis about the Origin of Human 'Religious Intelligence.'" In *Cult in Context: Reconsidering Ritual in Archaeology*, edited by David Barrowclough and Caroline Malone. Oxford: Oxbow Books.

Maltby, Mark. 1979. *The Animal Bones from Exeter, 1971–1975*, Exeter Archaeological Reports, vol. 2. Sheffield: University of Sheffield, Department of Prehistory and Archaeology.

Manning, Conleth. 1985. *Clonmacnoise*. Available from http://www.excavations.ie.

Manning, Conleth. 1986. "Archaeological Excavations at a Succession of Enclosures at Millockstown, Co. Meath." *Proceedings of the Royal Irish Academy* 86C: 135–381.

Manning, Conleth. 1987. "Excavation at Moyne Graveyard, Shrule, Co. Mayo." *Proceedings of the Royal Irish Academy* 87C: 37–70.

Manning, Conleth. 1989. "'Clonmacnois,' Clonmacnoise," Available from http://www.excavations.ie.

Manning, Conleth. 1990. "'Clonmacnois,' Clonmacnoise," Available from http://www.excavations.ie.

Manning, Conleth. 1992. "The Base of the North Cross at Clonmacnoise." *Archaeology Ireland* 6, no. 2: 8–9.

Manning, Conleth. 1994a. "The Earliest Plans of Clonmacnoise." *Archaeology Ireland* 8, no. 1: 18–20.

Manning, Conleth. 1994b. "Revealing a Personal Inscription." *Archaeology Ireland* 8: 24–26.

Manning, Conleth. 1995. "Clonmacnoise Cathedral—The Oldest Church in Ireland?" *Archaeology Ireland* 9, no. 4: 30–33.

Manning, Conleth. 1998. "Clonmacnoise Cathedral." In *Clonmacnoise* Studies, vol. 1, edited by Heather King, 57–86. Dublin: Dúchas.

Manning, Conleth. 1998. *Clonmacnoise*, 2nd edition. Dublin: Stationary Office.

Manning, Conleth and Fionnbarr Moore. 1991. "An Ogham Stone Find from Clonmacnoise." *Archaeology Ireland* 5, no. 4: 10–11.

Marean, Curtis. 2015. "An Evolutionary Anthropological Perspective on Modern Human Origins." *Annual Review of Anthropology* 44: 533–556.

Markus, Robert. 1990. *The End of Ancient Christianity*. Cambridge: Cambridge University Press.
Marshall, Jenny, and Claire Walsh. 2005. *Illaunloughan Island: An Early Medieval Monastery in County Kerry*. Dublin: Wordwell.
Mauss, Marcel. 1925 [1990]. *The Gift: The Form and Reason for Exchange in Archaic Societies*, W. D. Halls trans. London: Routledge.
Meier, Thomas, and Petra Tillessen. 2014. "Archaeological Imaginations of Religion: an Introduction from an Anglo-German Perspective." In *Archaeological Imaginations of Religion*, edited by Thomas Meier and Petra Tillessen, 11–248. Budapest: Archaeolingua Alapítvány.
Migne, J. P. 1849. "Sanctae Brigidae Virginis Vita A Cogitoso Adornata." In *Patrologiae Cursus Completus*. Paris.
Miller, Emma. 2009. "Faunal Analysis." In *N6 Kinnegad to Kilbeggan Dual Carriageway Archaeological Excavation Final Report E2723 Clonfad 3, Co. Westmeath*, vol. 2, edited by Paul Stevens. Dublin: National Roads Authority/Wordwell.
Moloney, Aonghus. 1998. "From East and West, Crossing the Bogs at Clonmacnoise." In *Clonmacnoise Studies*, vol. 1, edited by Heather King, 7–10. Dublin: Duchás.
Monk, Mick, and Orla Power. 2012. "More than a Grain of Truth Emerges from a Rash of Corn-Drying Kilns." *Archaeology Ireland* 26, no. 2: 38–41.
Moore, Fionnbarr. 1996. "Ireland's Oldest Bridge." *Archaeology Ireland* 10, no. 4: 24–27.
Moreland, John. 2000 (2010). "Concepts of the Early Medieval Economy." In *Archaeological Theory and the Middle Ages*, edited by John Moreland, 75–115. London: Duckworth.
Morey, James. 1998. "Plows, Laws, and Sanctuary in Medieval England and in the Wakefield 'Mactacio Abel.'" *Studies in Philology* 95, no. 1: 41–55.
Mosko, Mark. 2015. "Unbecoming Individuals: The Partible Character of the Christian person." *HAU: Journal of Ethnographic Theory* 5, no. 1: 361–393.
Murphy, Denis, ed. 1896 [1993]. *The Annals of Clonmacnoise: Being Annals of Ireland from the Earliest Period to A.D. 1408*, translated into English A.D. 1627 by Conall Mageoghagan. Lampeter: Llanerch Publishers.
Murphy, Donald. 1999. *Clonmacnoise*. Available from http://www.excavations.ie.
Murphy, Donald. 2000. *Clonmacnoise*. Available from http://www.excavations.ie.
Murphy, Donald. 2001. *Clonmacnoise*. Available from http://www.excavations.ie.
Murphy, Donald. 2003. "Excavation of an Early Monastic Enclosure at Clonmacnoise." In *Clonmacnoise Studies*, vol. 1, edited by Heather King, 1–34. Dublin: Duchás.
Murphy, Donald. 2008. *Clonmacnoise*. Available from http://www.excavations.ie.
Murphy, Donald. 2019. *Clonmacnoise*. Available from http://www.excavations.ie.
Murphy, Margaret, and O'Conor Kieran. 2008. *Roscommon Castle: A Visitor's Guide*. Roscommon County Council.
Mytum, Harold. 2003. "Surface and Geophysical Survey at Clonmacnoise: Defining the Extent of Intensive Monastic Settlement." In *Clonmacnoise Studies*, vol. 2, edited by H. King, 35–58. Dublin: Dúchas.

Newman, Conor. 1998. "Reflections on Making A 'Royal Site' in Early Ireland." *World Archaeology* 30, no. 1: 127–141.

Newman, Conor. 2007. "Procession and Symbolism at Tara: Analysis of Tech Midchúarta (the 'Banqueting Hall') in the Context of the Sacral Campus." *Oxford Journal of Archaeology* 26, no. 4: 415–438.

Newman, Conor. 2008. "Environment and Ritual in a Late Iron Age Context: An Example from Raffin Fort, Co. Meath, Ireland." In *Charcoals from the Past: Cultural and Palaeoenvironmental Implications: Proceedings of the Third International Meeting of Anthracology*, Cavallino-Lecce (Italy), June 28–July 1, 2004, edited by Girolamo Fiorentino. BAR Int. Ser. #1807, 75–92. Oxford: British Archaeological Reports.

Newman, Conor, and A. Halpin. 2006. *Ireland: An Oxford Archaeological Guide to Sites from Earliest Times to A.D. 1600.* Oxford: Oxford University Press.

Newman, Conor, Michael O'Connell, Mary Dillon, and Karen Molloy. 2007. "Interpretation of Charcoal and Pollen Data Relating to a Late Iron Age Ritual Site in Eastern Ireland: A Holistic Approach." *Vegetation History and Archaeobotany* 16: 349–365.

Noë, Alva. 2009. *Out of Our Heads: Why You Are Not Your Brain, and Other Lessons from the Biology of Consciousness.* New York: Macmillan.

Norenzayan, Ara. 2013. *Big Gods: How Religion Transformed Cooperation and Conflict.* Princeton: Princeton University Press.

Norenzayan, Ara, Azim Shariff, Will Gervais, Aiyana Willard, Rita McNamara, Edward Slingerland, and Joseph Henrich. 2016. "The Cultural Evolution of Prosocial Religions." *Behavioral and Brain Sciences* 39: 1–65.

Norenzayan, Ara, and Will Gervais. 2012. "The Cultural Evolution of Religion." In *Creating Consilience: Integrating Science and the Humanities*, edited by Edward Slingerland and Mark Collard, 243–265. Oxford: Oxford University Press.

Norenzayan, Ara, Will Gervais, and Kali Trzesniewski. 2012. "Mentalizing Deficits Constrain Belief in a Personal God." *PLoS ONE* 7, no. 5: e36880.

Norenzayan, Ara, and Azim F. Shariff. 2008. "The Origin and Evolution of Religious Prosociality." *Science* 322: 58–62.

North, Douglass. 2008. "Institutions and the Performance of Economies over Time." In *Handbook of New Institutional Economics*, edited by Ménard, Claude, and Mary M. Shirley, 21–30. Dordrecht: Springer

Ortman, Scott. 2000. "Conceptual Metaphor in the Archaeological Record: Methods and an Example from the American Southwest." *American Antiquity* 65, vol. 4: 613–645.

Ortman, Scott. 2008. "Architectural Metaphor and Chacoan Influence in the Northern San Juan." In *Archaeology without Borders: Contact, Commerce, and Change in the US Southwest and Northwestern Mexico*, edited by Lauri Webster and Maxine McBrinn, 227–255. Boulder: University Press of Colorado.

Oosthuizen, Susan. 2016. "Recognizing and Moving on from a Failed Paradigm: The Case of Agricultural Landscapes in Anglo-Saxon England c. AD 400–800." *Journal of Archaeological Research* 24, no. 2 (2016): 179–227.

O'Brien, Caimin, and David Sweetman. 1997. *Archaeological Inventory of County Offaly*. Dublin: The Stationary Office.

O'Brien, Elisabeth. 1992. "Pagan and Christian Burial in Ireland During the First Millennium AD: continuity and change." In *The Early Church in Wales and the West: Recent Work in Early Christian Archaeology, History and Place-Names*, edited by Nancy Edwards and Alan Lane, 130–137. Oxford: Oxbow Books.

O'Brien, Elisabeth. 2003 "Burial Practices in Ireland: First to Seventh Centuries A.D." In *Sea Change: Orkney and Northern Europe in the Later Iron Age, A.D.300–800*, edited by J. Downes and A. Ritchie, 63–72. Angus: Pinkfoot Press.

O'Brien, Elizabeth, and Edel Bhreathnach. 2011. "Irish Boundary Ferta, Their Physical Manifestation and Historical Context" In *Tome: Studies in Honour of Thomas Charles-Edwards*, edited by Fiona Edmonds and Paul Russell, 53–64. Woodbridge: The Boydell Press.

O'Brien, Elizabeth. 2020. *Mapping Death: Burial in Late Iron Age and Early Medieval Ireland*. Dublin: Four Courts Press.

O'Brien, William. 2002. "Megaliths in a Mythologised Landscape: South-West Ireland in the Iron Age." In *Monuments and Landscape in Atlantic Europe*, edited by Chris Scarre, 152–176. London: Routledge.

O'Brien, William. 2009. "Hidden 'Celtic' Ireland: Indigenous Iron Age Settlements in the South-Western Peninsulas." In *Relics of Old Decency: Archaeological Studies in Later Prehistory. Festschrift for Barry Raftery*, edited by Gabriel Cooney, Katharina Becker, John Coles, Michael Ryan, and Susanne Sievers, 437–448. Dublin: Wordwell.

Ó Carragáin, Éamonn. 2011. "High Crosses, the Sun's Course, and Local Theologies at Kells and Monasterboice." In *Insular and Anglo-Saxon Art and Thought in the Early Medieval Period*, edited by Colum Hourihane, 149–174. University Park, PA: Penn State University Press.

Ó Carragáin, Tomás. 2009. "Cemetery Settlements and Local Churches in Pre-Viking Ireland in Light of Comparisons with England and Wales." *Proceedings of the British Academy* 157: 329–366.

Ó Carragáin, Tomás. 2010a. *Churches in Early Medieval Ireland: Architecture, Ritual and Memory*. New Haven, CT: Yale University Press.

Ó Carragáin, Tomás. 2010b. "From Family Cemeteries to Community Cemeteries in Viking Age Ireland?" In *Death and Burial in Early Medieval Ireland in Light of Recent Archaeological Excavations*, edited by C. Corlett and M. Potterton. Dublin: Wordwell.

Ó Carragáin, Tomás. 2014. "The Archaeology of Ecclesiastical Estates in Early Medieval Ireland: A Case Study of the Kingdom of Fir Maige." *Peritia* 24–25: 266–312.

Ó Carragáin, Tomás. 2015. "Is There an Archaeology of Lay People at Early Irish Monasteries?" *Bulletin du centre d'études médiévales* 8: 2–17.

O'Connell, Aidan. 2013. *Harvesting the Stars: A Pagan Temple at Lismullin, Co. Meath*. Dublin: NRA Scheme Monographs.

O'Conor, Kieran, and Conleth Manning. 2003. "Clonmacnoise Castle." In *Clonmacnoise Studies*, vol. 2, edited by Heather King, 137–165. Dublin: Dúchas.

Ó Cróinín, Dáibhí. 1995. *Early Medieval Ireland*. New York: Longman Publishing.

O'Donnell, Lorna. 2018. "Into the Woods: Revealing Ireland's Iron Age Woodlands Through Archaeological Charcoal Analysis." *Environmental Archaeology* 23, no. 3: 240–253.

O'Driscoll, James, Patrick Gleeson, and Gordon Noble. 2020. "Re-imagining Navan Fort: New Light on the Evolution of a Major Ceremonial Centre in Northern Europe" *Oxford Journal of Archaeology* 39, no. 3: 247–273.

Ó Floinn, Raghnall. 1995. "Clonmacnoise: Art and Patronage in the Early Medieval Period." In *From the Isles of the North: Early Medieval Art in Ireland and Britain*, edited by Cormac Bourke, 251–60. Belfast: HMSO.

Ó Floinn, Raghnall. 1998. "The Archaeology of the Early Viking Age in Ireland." In *Ireland and Scandinavia in the Early Viking Age*, edited by Howard B. Clarke, Máire Ní Mhaonaigh and Raghnall Ó Floinn, 131–65. Dublin: Four Courts Press.

Ó Floinn, Raghnall. 2000. "Freestone Hill, Co. Kilkenny: A Re-assessment." In *Seanchas: Studies in Early and Medieval Irish Archaeology, History and Literature in Honour of Francis J. Byrne*, edited by A. P. Smyth, 12–29. Dublin: Four Courts Press.

Ó Floinn, Raghnall, and Heather King. 1998. "Archaeological Investigations at St Ciarán's National School." In *Clonmacnoise Studies*, vol. 1, edited by Heather King, 12–29. Dublin: Dúchas.

O'Keeffe, Tadhg. 2000. *Medieval Ireland: An Archaeology*. Charleston, SC: Tempus.

Ó Lochlainn, Colm. 1940. "Roadways in Ancient Ireland." In *Féilsgribhin Eóin Mhic Néill*, edited by John Ryan, 465–474. Dublin: At the Sign of the Three Candles.

O'Loughlin, Tom. 2005. "Map and Text: A Mid Ninth–Century Map for the Book of Joshua." *Imago Mundi*, 57, no. 1: 7–22.

Ó Ríordáin, Sean. 1942. *Antiquities of the Irish Countryside*. Cork: Cork University Press.

Ó Ríordáin, Seán P., and J. Ryan. 1941/1942. "The Excavation of a Large Earthen Ring-Fort at Garranes, Co. Cork." *Proceedings of the Royal Irish Academy* 47C: 77–150.

O'Sullivan, Aidan. 1998. *The Archaeology of Lake Settlement in Ireland*, Discovery Programme Monographs 4. Dublin: Royal Irish Academy.

O'Sullivan, Aidan. 2009. "Early Medieval Crannogs and Imagined Islands." In *Relics of Old Decency: Archaeological Studies in Later Prehistory. Festschrift for Barry Raftery*, edited by Gabriel Cooney, Katharina Becker, John Coles, Michael Ryan, and Susanne Sievers, 79–87. Dublin: Wordwell.

O'Sullivan, Aidan, and Collin Breen. 1996. "An Early Christian Wooden Bridge on the River Shannon at Clonmacnoise, Co.Offaly." *Newswarp: The Newsletter of the Wetland Archaeology Research Project* 20 (November): 23–5.

O'Sullivan, Aidan, and Donal Boland. 1997. *Clonmacnoise: Early Medieval Bridge*. Available from http://www.excavations.ie.

O'Sullivan, Aidan, and Donal Boland. 1999. "Medieval Irish Engineers Conquer the River Shannon." *Discovering Archaeology* 1, no. 1: 33–37.

O'Sullivan, Aidan and Collin Breen. 2007. *Maritime Ireland: An Archaeology of Coastal Communities*. Stroud: Tempus.

O'Sullivan, Aidan, Niall Brady, and Donal Boland. 1998. Clonmacnoise: *Early Medieval Wooden Bridge*. Available from http://www.excavations.ie.

O'Sullivan, Aidan, and Triona Nicholl. 2011. "Early Medieval Settlement Enclosures in Ireland: Dwellings, Daily Life and Social Identity." *Proceedings of the Royal Irish Academy* 111C: 59–90.

O'Sullivan, Aidan and Finbar McCormick. 2017. "Early Medieval Ireland: Investigating Social, Economic and Settlement Change, AD 400–1100" *Stories of Ireland's Past Knowledge Gained from NRA Roads Archaeology*, edited by Michael Stanley, Rónán Swan, and Aidan O'Sullivan, 101–132. Dublin: Transport Infrastructure Ireland.

O'Sullivan, Aidan, Finbar McCormick, Thomas R. Kerr, and Lorcan Harney. 2014. *Early Medieval Ireland AD 400–1200: The Evidence from Archaeological Excavations*. Dublin: Royal Irish Academy.

O'Sullivan, Catherine. 2004. *Hospitality in Medieval Ireland, 900–1500*. Dublin: Four Courts Press.

Outram, Alan K. 2004. "Identifying Dietary Stress in Marginal Environments: Bone Fats, Optimal Foraging Theory and the Seasonal Round." *Colonisation, Migration and Marginal Areas: A Zooarchaeological Approach*, edited by Mondini, Mariana, Sebastián Munoz, and Stephen Wickler, 74–85. Oxford: Oxbow Books.

Overbey, Karen. 2012. *Sacral Geographies: Saints, Shrines and Territory in Medieval Ireland*. Chicago: Brepols.

Parkes, Hilda and Fraser Mitchell. 2000. "Vegetation History at Clonmacnoise, Co. Offaly." *Biology and Environment: Proceedings of the Royal Irish Academy* 100B, no. 1: 35–40.

Patterson, Nerys. 1994. *Cattle Lords and Clansmen: Social Structure of Early Ireland*. Notre Dame: University of Notre Dame Press.

Patterson, Nerys. 1995. "Clans Are Not Primordial: Pre-Viking Irish Society and the Modeling of Pre-Roman Societies in Northern Europe." In *Celtic Chiefdom, Celtic State*, edited by Betina Arnold and Blair Gibson, 129–36. New York: Cambridge University Press.

Pauketat, Timothy R. 2012. *An Archaeology of the Cosmos: Rethinking Agency and Religion*. New York: Routledge.

Pauketat, Timothy, and Susan Alt. 2004. "The Making and Meaning of a Mississippian Axe-head Cache." *Antiquity* 78, no. 302: 779–797.

Pauketat, Timothy, Susan Alt, and Jeffery Kruchten. 2017. "The Emerald Acropolis: Elevating the Moon and Water in the Rise of Cahokia." *Antiquity* 91, no. 355: 207–222.

Pavao-Zuckerman, Barnet. 2007. "Deerskins and Domesticates: Creek Subsistence and Economic Strategies in the Historic Period." *American Antiquity* 72, no. 1: 5–33.

Pavao-Zuckerman, Barnet, and Vincent LaMotta. 2007. "Missionization and Economic Change in the Pimería Alta: The Zooarchaeology of San Agustín de Tucson." *International Journal of Historical Archaeology* 11, no. 3: 241–268.

Peirce, Charles S. 1982. *Writings of Charles S. Peirce: A Chronological Edition, Volume 1: 1857–1866*. Bloomington: Indiana University Press.

Piff, Paul K., Pia Dietze, Matthew Feinberg, Daniel M. Stancato, and Dacher Keltner. 2015. "Awe, the Small Self, and Prosocial Behavior." *Journal of Personality and Social Psychology* 108, no. 6: 883.

Pilcher, John, and Valerie Hall. 2001. *Flora Hibernica*. Cork: Collins Press.

Pinker, Steven. 2003. "Language as an Adaptation to the Cognitive Niche." In *Studies in the Evolution of Language*, edited by Morten H. Christiansen and Simon Kirby 16–37. Oxford: Oxford University Press.

Pirenne, Henri. 1925. *Medieval Cities: Their Origin and the Revival of Trade*. Princeton, NJ: Princeton University Press.

Pitts, Martin. 2008. "Globalizing the Local in Roman Britain: An Anthropological Approach to Social Change." *Journal of Anthropological Archaeology* 27: 493–506.

Plummer, Charles, ed. and trans. 1910. *Vitae sanctorum Hiberniae*, 2 vols, Oxford: Oxford University Press.

Plummer, Charles, ed. and trans. 1922. *Bethada ndem nErenn: Lives of Irish saints*. Oxford: Oxford University Press.

Plummer, Charles, editor and translator. 1925. *Irish Litanies, Text and Translation*. London: Henry Bradshaw Society.

Pluskowski, Aleksander, editor. 2007. *Breaking and Shaping Beastly Bodies*. Oxford: Oxbow Books.

Polanyi, Karl. 1944. *The Great Transformation*. New York: Reinhart.

Polanyi, Karl. 1968. "Aristotle Discovers the Economy" In *Primitive, Archaic, and Modern Economies*, edited by G. Dalton, 78–115. Garden City, NJ: Beacon Press.

Plunkett, Gil. 2007. "Pollen Analysis and Archaeology in Ireland." In *Environmental Archaeology in Ireland*, edited by Eileen Murphy and Nicki Whitehouse, 221–240. Oxford: Oxbow Books.

Potterton, Michael. 2005. *Medieval Trim: History and Archaeology*. Dublin: Four Courts Press.

Potts, Richard, and Tyler Faith. 2015. "Alternating High and Low Climate Variability: The Context of Natural Selection and Speciation in Plio-Pleistocene Hominin Evolution." *Journal of Human Evolution* 87: 5–20.

Premack, David, and Guy Woodruff. 1978. "Does the Chimpanzee Have a Theory of Mind?" *Behavioral and Brain Sciences* 1, no. 4: 515–526.

Prendergast, Frank. 2012. "The Lismullin Enclosure: Design Beyond the Obvious in the Iron Age." In *Encounters Between Peoples*, edited by Bernice Kelly, Niall Roycroft, and Michael Stanley, 15–30. Dublin: National Roads Authority.

Preucel, Robert. 2008. *Archaeological Semiotics*. Oxford: Blackwell.

Proffitt, Dennis. 2006. "Embodied Perception and the Economy of Action." *Perspectives on Psychological Science* 1, no. 2: 110–122.

Price, Neil. 2008. "Bodylore and the Archaeology of Embedded Religion: Dramatic License in the Funerals of the Vikings." In *Belief in the Past: Theoretical Approaches to the Archaeology of Religion*, edited by David Whitley and Kelley Hays-Gilpin, 143–165. Walnut Ceek CA: Left Coast Press.

Prummel, Wietske. 1983. *Excavations at Dorestad 2: Early-Medieval Dorestad, an Archaeozoological Study*. Amersfoort: ROB.

Pulliam, Heather. 2020. "Between the Embodied Eye and Living World: Clonmacnoise's Cross of the Scriptures." *The Art Bulletin* 102, no. 2: 7–35.
Purzycki, Benjamin Grant, Omar Haque, and Richard Sosis. 2014. "Extending Evolutionary Accounts of Religion beyond the Mind: Religions as Adaptive Systems." In *Religion, and Cognitive Science: Critical and Constructive Essays*, edited by Fraser Watts and Léon Turner, 74–91. Oxford: Oxford University Press.
Quin, Annette. 2003. *Clonmacnoise*. Available from http://www.excavations.ie.
Raftery, B. 1994. *Pagan Celtic Ireland*. London: Thames & Hudson.
Ramsey, Greer. 2002. "The Triple Pipes on Irish High Crosses: Identification and Interpretation." *Ulster Journal of Archaeology* 6: 26–36.
Ray, Celeste, and Manuel Fernández-Götz, editors. 2019. *Historical Ecologies, Heterarchies and Transtemporal Landscapes*. New York: Routledge.
Renfrew, Colin. 1985. *The Archaeology of Cult: The Sanctuary at Phylakopi*. London: The British School of Archaeology at Athens.
Renfrew, Colin. 1998. "Mind and Matter: Cognitive Archaeology and External Symbolic Storage." In *Cognition and Material Culture: The Archaeology of Symbolic Storage*, edited by Colin Renfrew and Christopher Scarre, 1–6. Cambridge: McDonald Institute for Archaeological Research.
Renfrew, Colin. 1994. "The Archaeology of Religion." In *The Ancient Mind: Elements of Cognitive Archaeology*, edited by Colin Renfrew and Ezra Zubrow, 47–54. Cambridge: Cambridge University Press.
Renfrew, Colin. 2001. "Symbol before Concept: Material Engagement and the Early Development of Society" In *Archaeological Theory Today*, edited by Ian Hodder, 122–140. Cambridge: Polity Press.
Renfrew, Colin. 2004 "Towards a Theory of Material Engagement." In *Rethinking Materiality: The Engagement of Mind with the Material World*, edited by Elizabeth DeMarrais, Chris Gosden, and Colin Renfrew, 23–32. Cambridge: McDonald Institute for Archaeological Research.
Renfew, Colin. 2007. "Ritual and Cult in Malta and Beyond: Traditions of Interpretation." In *Cult in Context: Reconsidering Ritual in Archaeology*, edited by David Barrowclough and Caroline Malone. Oxford: Oxbow Books.
Renfrew, Colin. 2012. "Towards a Cognitive Archaeology." In *Archaeological Theory Today*, 2nd edition, edited by Ian Hodder, 124–145. Cambridge: Polity Press.
Renfrew, Colin. 2013. "Centres of congregation." *NEO-LITHICS: The Newsletter of Southwest Asian Neolithic Research* 2, no. 13: 30–34.
Richards, Colin, and Julian Thomas. 1984. "Ritual Activity and Structured Deposition in Later Neolithic Wessex." In *Neolithic Studies: A Review of Some Current Research*, edited by Richard Bradley and Julie Gardiner, 189–218. Oxford: British Archaeological Reports.
Richerson, Peter, and Robert Boyd. 2005. *Not by Genes Alone: How Culture Transformed Human Evolution*. Chicago University of Chicago Press.
Rizzolatti, Giacomo and Laila Craighero. 2004. "The Mirror-Neuron System." *Annual Review of Neuroscience* 27: 169–192.
Robb, John. 1998. "The Archaeology of Symbols." *Annual Review of Anthropology* 27: 329–346.

Rochat, Philippe. *Others in Mind: Social Origins of Self-Consciousness*. Cambridge: Cambridge University Press, 2009.

Roe, Helen. 1965. "The Irish High Cross: Morphology and Iconography." *The Journal of the Royal Society of Antiquaries of Ireland* 95, nos. 1/2: 213–226.

Rosati, Massimo. 2016. *Ritual and the Sacred: A Neo-Durkheimian Analysis of Politics, Religion and the Self*. New York: Routledge.

Russell, Ian, and Stephen Harrison. 2011. "Woodstown 6—Viking Age Enclosed Settlement and Grave." In *Cois tSiúire: Nine Thousand Years of Human Activity in the Lower Suir Valley: Archaeological Excavations on the N25 Waterford City Bypass*. Dublin: National Roads Authority, 53–72.

Ryan, John. 1940. "The Abbatial Succession at Clonmacnoise." In *Féilsgribhin Eóin Mhic Néill*, edited by John Ryan, 490–507. Dublin: At the Sign of the Three Candles.

Sapolsky, Robert M. 2017. *Behave: The Biology of Humans at Our Best and Worst*. London: Penguin Books.

Sharp, Richard, translator and editor. 1995. *Adomnán's Life of Columba*. London: Penguin Books.

Schlinger, Henry D. 2009. "Theory of Mind: An Overview and Behavioral Perspective." *The Psychological Record* 59, no. 3: 435–448.

Seaver, Matthew, Edward Bourke, Ian W. Doyle, Linda Fibiger, Denise Keating, Susan Lyons, Caitríona Moore, and Emily Murray. 2016. *Meitheal: The Archaeology of Lives, Labours and Beliefs at Raystown, Co. Meath*. Dublin: Transport Infrastructure Ireland.

Serjeantson, Dale. 1989. "Animal Remains and the Tanning Trade." In *Diet and Crafts in Towns: The Evidence of Animal Remains from the Roman to the Post-Medieval Periods*, edited by Dale Serjeantson and Tony Waldron, 129–46. Oxford: British Archaeological Reports.

Sheehan, John. 1998. "Early Viking Age Silver Hoards from Ireland and their Scandinavian Elements." In *Ireland and Scandinavia in the Early Viking Age*, edited by Howard B. Clarke, Máire Ní Mhaonaigh, and Ragnall Ó Floinn, 166–202. Dublin: Four Courts Press.

Sheehan, John. 2009. "A Peacock's Tale: Excavations at Caherlehillan, Kerry, Ireland." In *The Archaeology of the Celtic Churches*, edited by Nancy Edwards, 191–206. The Society for Medieval Archaeology Monograph 29. Leeds: Maney.

Sheehan, John. 2014. "Caherlehillan, Co. Kerry: Ritual, Domestic and Economic Aspects of a Corcu Duibne Ecclesiastical Site." In *The Church in Early Medieval Ireland in the Light of Recent Archaeological Excavations*, edited by Chris Corlett and Michael Potterton, 247–258. Dublin: Wordwell

Shiota, Michelle, Dacher Keltner, and Amanda Mossman. 2007. "The Nature of Awe: Elicitors, Appraisals, and Effects on Self-Concept." *Cognition and Emotion* 21, no. 5: 944–963.

Shoemaker, Karl. 2011. *Sanctuary and Crime in the Middle Ages, 400–1500*. New York: Fordham University Press.

Silverman, Helaine. 2016. "An Andeanist's Perspective on the Newark Earthworks." In *The Newark Earthworks: Enduring Monuments, Contested Meanings*, edited by

Lindsay Jones and Richard D. Shiels, 97–110. Charlottesville, VA: University of Virginia Press.

Simpson, Linzi. 1999. "Forty Years A-Digging: A Preliminary Synthesis of Archaeological Investigations in Medieval Dublin." In *Medieval Dublin I: Proceedings of the Friends of Medieval Dublin Symposium*, edited by Seán Duffy, 11–68. Dublin: Four Courts Press.

Skeates, Robin. 2007. "Religious Experience in the Prehistoric Maltese Underworld." In *Cult in Context: Reconsidering Ritual in Archaeology*, edited by David Barrowclough and Caroline Malone, 90–96. Oxford: Oxbow Books.

Skousen, Jacob. 2018. "Rethinking archaeologies of pilgrimage." *Journal of Social Archaeology* 18, no. 3: 261–283.

Slingerland, Edward. 2008. "Who's Afraid of Reductionism? The Study of Religion in the Age of Cognitive Science." *Journal of the American Academy of Religion* 76, no. 2: 375–411.

Smith, Barbara. 2009. *Natural Reflections: Human Cognition at the Nexus of Science and Religion*. New Haven, CT: Yale University Press.

Smith, Carol A. 1976. "Exchange Systems and the Spatial Distribution of Elites: The Organization of Stratification in Agrarian Societies." In Regional Analysis, edited by Carol Smith, 309–374. New York: Academic Press.

Smith, Jonathan Z. 1987. *To Take Place: Toward Theory in Ritual*. Chicago: University of Chicago Press.

Snell, Daniel, Jack Sasson, and John Baines. 1995. "Methods of Exchange and Coinage in Ancient Western Asia." *Civilizations of the Ancient Near East*, vol. 3, edited by Jack Sasson, 1487–1497. London: Scribner.

Soderberg, John. 1993. "A Lost Cultural Exchange: Reconsidering the Bologna Shrine's Origin and Use." *The Proceedings of the Thirteenth Annual Harvard Celtic Colloquium* 13: 156–165.

Soderberg, John. 2001. "Feeding Communities: Monasteries and Urban Development in Early Medieval Ireland." In *Shaping Communities: The Archaeology and Architecture of Monasticism*, edited by Sheila McNally, 67–77. British Archaeological Reports International Series 941.

Soderberg, John. 2003. "Feeding Community: Urbanization, Religion, and Zooarchaeology at Clonmacnoise, an Early Medieval Irish Monastery." PhD thesis, Department of Anthropology, University of Minnesota, Minneapolis.

Soderberg, John. 2004. "Wild Cattle: Red Deer in the Religious Texts, Iconography, and Archaeology of Early Medieval Ireland." *International Journal of Historical Archaeology* 8, no. 3: 167–183.

Soderberg, John. 2006. "Clientage and Social Hierarchy in Early Medieval Ireland: An Archaeological Perspective." *Proceedings of the Harvard Celtic Colloquium* 19: 396–433.

Soderberg, John, and Jennifer Immich. 2010. "Animal Contact: Livestock Approaches to Understanding Social Boundaries in Later Medieval Roscommon." In *Medieval Lough Cé: History, Archaeology, and Landscape of Medieval Lough Cé*, edited by Thomas Finan, 97–118. Dublin: Four Courts Press.

Soderberg, John. 2013. "Between Britain and Spain: Ireland in Roman Period Europe" In *Rome beyond its Frontiers: Imports, Attitudes and Practices*, edited by Peter Wells, 71–86. Portsmouth RI: JRA.

Soderberg, John. 2017a. "Anthropological Civitas and the Possibility of Monastic Towns in Early Medieval Ireland." *Journal of the Royal Society of Antiquaries of Ireland* 144–145: 45–59.

Soderberg, John. 2017b. "Ceremonial Complexity: The Roles of Religious Settlements in Medieval Ireland." In *European Archaeology as Anthropology: Essays in Memory of Bernard Wailes*, edited by Pam Crabtree and Peter Bogucki, 195–224. Philadelphia: University of Pennsylvania Museum Press.

Soderberg, John. 2021. "Animals Make the Man: Violence and the Colonial Project in Derricke's Image of Irelande." In *John Derricke's The Image of Irelande: with a Discoverie of Woodkarne Texts and Contexts* edited by Thomas Herron, Denna Iammarino and Maryclaire Moroney, 49–64. Manchester: Manchester University Press.

Sofaer, Joanna R. 2006. *The Body as Material Culture*. Cambridge: Cambridge University Press.

Soler, Montserrat, Frank Batiste, and Lee Cronk. 2014. "In the Eye (and Ears) of the Beholder: Receiver Psychology and Human Signal Design." *Evolutionary Anthropology: Issues, News, and Reviews* 23, no. 4: 136–145.

Sosis, Richard, and Bradley J. Ruffle. 2004. "Ideology, Religion, and the Evolution of Cooperation: Field Experiments on Israeli Kibbutzim." *Socioeconomic Aspects of Human Behavioral Ecology Research in Economic Anthropology* 23: 89–117.

Sosis, Richard, and Candace Alcorta. 2003. "Signaling, Solidarity, and the Sacred: The Evolution of Religious Behavior." *Evolutionary Anthropology: Issues, News, and Reviews: Issues, News, and Reviews* 12, no. 6: 264–274.

Sosis, Richard, and Eric R. Bressler. 2003. "Cooperation and Commune Longevity: A Test of the Costly Signaling Theory of Religion." *Cross-Cultural Research* 37, no. 2: 211–239.

Spector, Jane D. 1993. *What This Awl Means: Feminist Archaeology at a Wahpeton Dakota Village*. St. Paul, MN: Minnesota Historical Society Press.

Srawley, James. 1913 [1947]. *The Early History of the Liturgy*. Cambridge: Cambridge University Press.

Stalley, Roger. 1996. *Irish High Crosses*. Dublin: Country House.

Stalley, Roger. 2007. "Artistic Identity and the Irish Scripture Crosses," In *Making and Meaning in Insular Art*, edited by Rachel Moss, 153–166. Dublin: Four Courts.

Stalley, Roger. 2014. "Irish Sculpture of the Early Tenth Century and the Work of the 'Muiredach Master': Problems of Identification and Meaning." *Proceedings of the Royal Irish Academy* 114C: 141–179.

Stalley, Roger. 2020. *Early Irish Sculpture and the Art of the High Crosses*. London: Paul Mellon Centre for Studies in British Art.

Stein, Gil. 1998. "Heterogeneity, Power, and Political Economy: Some Current Research Issues in the Archaeology of Old-World Complex Societies." *Journal of Archaeological Research* 6, no. 1: 1–44.

Stevens, Paul. 2009. "For Whom the Bell Tolls: The Monastic Site at Clonfad 3, Co. Westmeath." *Creative Minds: Production, Manufacturing and Invention in Ancient*

Ireland, edited by Michael Stanley, Ed Danaher, and James Eogan, 85–94. Dublin: Wordwell.

Stevens, Paul. 2012. "Clonfad—an industrious monastery." In *Settlement and Community in the Fir Tulach Kingdom: Archaeological Excavation on the M6 & N52 Road Schemes*, edited by Paul Stevens and John Channing, 107–134. Dublin: Wordwell.

Stevens, Paul. 2015. "The Early Medieval Church in Ireland and Its Impact on Transformations in the Irish Economy." In *Dying Gods—Religious Beliefs in Northern and Eastern Europe in the Time of Christianisation*, edited by Christiane Ruhmann and Vera Brieske, 121–143. Stuttgart: Konrad Theiss Verlag.

Stokes, Margaret. 1898. *The High Crosses of Castledermot and Durrow*. Dublin: Hodges and Figgis.

Stokstad, Marilyn. 2004. *Medieval Art*. Boulder, CO: Westview.

Stout, Geraldine. 2015. "The Cistercian Grange: A Medieval Farming System." In *Agriculture and Settlement in Ireland*, edited by Margaret Murphy and Matthew Stout, 28–68. Dublin: Four Courts Press.

Stout, Geraldine, and Matthew Stout. 1992. "Patterns in the Past: County Dublin 500 BC–1000 AD." In *Dubin City and County: From Prehistory to Present*, edited by F. H. A. Aalen and Kevin Whelan, 5–14. Dublin: Geography Publications.

Stout, Geraldine, and Mathew Stout. 2008. *Excavations of an Early Medieval Secular Cemetery at Knowth Site M, County Meath*. Dublin: Wordwell.

Stout, Geraldine, and Mathew Stout. 2011. "Early landscapes: from prehistory to plantation." In *Atlas of the Irish Rural Landscape*, edited by F. H. A. Aalen, K. Whelan and Matthew Stout, 31–65. Cork: Cork University Press.

Stout, Matthew. 1997. *The Irish Ringfort*. Dublin: Four Courts Press.

Stout, Matthew. 2017. *Early Medieval Ireland: 431–1169*. Wordwell.

Strathern, Marilyn. 1988. *The Gender of the Gift: Problems with Women and Problems with Society in Melanesia*. Berkeley: University of California Press.

Strathern, Marilyn. 1992. "Qualified Value: The Perspective of Gift." In *Barter, Exchange and Value: An Anthropological Approach*, edited by Caroline Humphrey and Stephen Hugh-Jones, 169–191. Cambridge: Cambridge University Press.

Stutz, Aaron J. 2014. "Embodied Niche Construction in The Hominin Lineage: Semiotic Structure and Sustained Attention in Human Embodied Cognition." *Frontiers in Psychology* 5: 1–19.

Sutton, John. 2010. "Exograms and Interdisciplinarity: History, the Extended Mind, and the Civilizing Process." In *The Extended Mind*, edited by Richard Menary, 189–225. Cambridge: MIT Press.

Swenson, Edward. 2011. "Stagecraft and the Politics of Spectacle in Ancient Peru." *Cambridge Archaeological Journal* 21, no. 2: 283–313.

Swenson, Edward. 2015. "The Archaeology of Ritual." *Annual Review of Anthropology* 44: 329–345.

Swift, Cathy. 1998. "Forts and Fields: A Study of 'Monastic Towns' in Seventh and Eighth Century Ireland." *The Journal of Irish Archaeology* 9: 105–125.

Swift, C., 2003. "Sculptors and Their Customers: A Study of Clonmacnoise Grave-Slabs." In *Clonmacnoise Studies*, vol. 2, edited by H. King. Dublin: Dúchas, 105–123.

Sykes, Naomi. 2005. "Hunting for the Anglo-Normans: Zooarchaeological Evidence for Medieval Identity." In *Just Skin and Bones? New Perspectives on Human-Animal Relations in the Historical Past*, edited by Aleksander Pluskowski, 71–78. Oxford: Archaeopress.

Sykes, Naomi. 2006. "The Impact of the Normans on Hunting Practices in England." In *Food in Medieval England: Diet and Nutrition*, edited by Christopher Woolgar, Dale Serjeantson and Tony Waldron, 162–175. Oxford: Oxford University Press.

Sykes, Naomi. 2007. "Taking Sides: the Social Life of Venison in Medieval England." In *Breaking and Shaping Beastly Bodies*, edited by Aleksander Pluskowski, 149–160. Oxford: Oxbow Books.

Tainter, Joseph. 1988. *The Collapse of Complex Societies*. New York: Cambridge University Press.

Tarlow, Sarah. 2012. "The Archaeology of Emotion and Affect." *Annual Review of Anthropology* 41: 169–185.

Teske, John. 2013. "From Embodied to Extended Cognition." *Zygon* 48, no. 3: 759–787.

Thomas, Richard. 2007. "Chasing the Ideal? Ritualism, Pragmatism and the Later Medieval Hunt in England." In *Breaking and Shaping Beastly Bodies*, edited by Aleksander Pluskowski, 125–148. Oxford: Oxbow Books.

Throop, Jason, and Charles Laughlin. 2002. "Ritual, Collective Effervescence and the Categories: Toward a Neo-Durkheimian Model of the Nature of human Consciousness, Feeling and Understanding." *Journal of Ritual Studies*: 40–63.

Tilley, Christopher. 2004. *The Materiality of Stone: Explorations in Landscape Phenomenology*. London: Routledge.

Tomasello, Michael, Malinda Carpenter, Josep Call, Tanya Behne, and Henrike Moll. 2005. "Understanding and Sharing Intentions: The Origins of Cultural Cognition." *Behavioral and Brain Sciences* 28, no. 5: 675–691.

Tooby, John, and Irven DeVore. 1987. "The Reconstruction of Hominid Behavioral Evolution through Strategic Modeling." *The Evolution of Human Behavior: Primate Models*, edited by Warren Kinzey, 183–237. Albany: State University of New York.

Tremlin, Todd. 2006. *Minds and Gods: The Cognitive Foundations of Religion*. Oxford: Oxford University Press.

Trigger, Bruce. 2008. "Early Cities: Craft Workers, Kings, and Controlling the Supernatural." In *The Ancient City: New Perspectives on Urbanism in the Old and New World*, edited by Joyce Marcus and Jeremy Sabloff, 53–66. Santa Fe: SAR Press.

Trivers, Robert. 1971. "The Evolution of Reciprocal Altruism." *Quarterly Review of Biology* 46: 35–57.

Turbridy, Mary, ed. 1987. *The Heritage of Clonmacnoise*. Dublin: Environmental Science Unit, Trinity College.

Turbridy, Mary. 1998. "The Pre-Monastic Environment at Clonmacnoise." In *Clonmacnoise Studies*, vol. 1, edited by Heather King, 1–6. Dublin: Duchás.

Turner, Victor. 1967. *The Forest of Symbols: Aspects of Ndembu Ritual*. Ithaca, NY: Cornell University Press.

Tweed, Thomas. 2006. *Crossing and Dwelling: A Theory of Religion*. Cambridge, MA: Harvard University Press.

Valante, Mary. 1998. "Reassessing the Irish 'Monastic Town.'" *Irish Historical Studies* 31: 1–18.
Valante, Mary. 2008. *The Vikings in Ireland: Settlement, Trade and Urbanization*. Dublin: Four Courts Press.
Van Dyke, Ruth. 2007. *The Chaco Experience: Landscape and Ideology at the Center Place*. Santa Fe: School of Advanced Research Press.
Van Dyke, Ruth. 2018. "From Enchantment to *Agencement*: Archaeological Engagements with Pilgrimage." *Journal of Social Archaeology* 18, no. 3: 348–359.
Veblen, Thorstein. 1898 [2010]. "Why Economics is Not an Evolutionary Science." *Quarterly Journal of Economics* 12, no. 4: 373–397.
Wailes, Bernard. 1995. "A Case Study of Heterarchy in Complex Societies: Early Medieval Ireland and its Archaeological Implications." In *Heterarchy and the Analysis of Complex Societies*, edited by Robert Ehrenreich, Carol Crumley, and Janet Levy, 55–69. Arlington, VA: American Anthropological Association.
Wallace, Patrick F. 1992. *The Viking Age Buildings of Dublin*. Dublin: Royal Irish Academy.
Wallace, Patrick. 2004. "The Big Picture: Mapping Hiberno-Norse Dublin." In *Surveying Ireland's Past: Multidisciplinary Essays in Honour of Anngret Simms*, edited by H. B. Clarke, Jacinta Prunty, and Mark Hennessy, 13–40. Dublin: Geography Publications.
Wallace, Patrick. 2008. "Archaeological Evidence for the Different Expressions of Scandinavian Settlement in Ireland, 840–1100." In *The Viking World*, edited by Stefan Brink and Neil Price, 434–438. London: Routledge.
Wallace, Patrick. 2016. *Viking Dublin: The Wood Quay Excavations*. Dublin: Irish Academic Press.
Wallis, Neill, and Meggan Blessing. 2015. "Ritualized Deposition and Feasting Pits: Bundling of Animal Remains in Mississippi Period Florida." *Cambridge Archaeological Journal* 25, no. 1: 79–98.
Walsh, Fintan. 2012. "Iron Age Sanctuary Enclosure, Boundary Ditch and Kilns at Kilmainham, Co. Meath." In *Life and Death in Iron Age Ireland in the Light of Recent Archaeological Investigations*, edited by Christian Corlett and Michael Potterton, 303–312. Dublin: Wordwell.
Warner, Richard. 1988. "The Archaeology of Early Historic Kingship." In *Power and Politics in Early Medieval Britain and Ireland*, edited by Stephen Driscoll and M. R. Nieke, 47–68. Edinburgh: Edinburgh University Press.
Warner, Richard. 2009. "Clogher in Late Prehistory" In *Relics of Old Decency: Archaeological Studies in Later Prehistory. Festschrift for Barry Raftery*, edited by Gabriel Cooney, Katharina Becker, John Coles, Michael Ryan, and Susanne Sievers, 507–518. Dublin: Wordwell.
Weber, Max. 1958. *The City*. Glencoe, Ill.: Free Press.
Weber, Max. 1964. *The Theory of Social and Economic Organization*. New York: Free Press.
Webster, Jane. 2001. "Creolizing the Roman Provinces." *American Journal of Archaeology*: 209–225.

Wells, Peter. 1984. *Farms, Villages, and Cities. Commerce and Urban Origins in Late Prehistoric Europe*. Ithaca, NY: Cornell University Press.
Wells, Peter. 1999. *The Barbarians Speak: How the Conquered Peoples Shaped Roman Europe*. Princeton, NJ: Princeton University Press.
Wells, Peter. 2005. "Creating an Imperial Frontier: Archaeology of the Formation of Rome's Danube Borderland." *Journal of Archaeological Research* 13: 49–88.
Wheatley, Paul. 1971. *The Pivot of the Four Quarters*. Chicago: Aldine Publishing Co.
Whitehouse, Harvey. 2002. "Modes of Religiosity and the Cognitive Science of Religion." *Method and Theory in the Study of Religion* 16, no. 3: 321–335.
Whitehouse, Harvey. 2004. *Modes of Religiosity: A Cognitive Theory of Religious Transmission*. Walnut Creek, CA: AltaMira Press.
Whitley, David. 2008. "Cognition, Emotion, and Belief: First Steps in an Archaeology of Religion." In *Belief in the Past: Theoretical Approaches to the Archaeology of Religion*, edited by David Whitley and Kelley Hays-Gilpin, 85–103. Walnut Creek, CA: Left Coast Press.
Whitley, David. 2009. *Cave Paintings and the Human Spirit: The Origin of Creativity and Belief*. Amherst NY: Prometheus Books.
Whitley, David, and Kelley Hays-Gilpin, editors. 2008. *Belief in the Past: Theoretical Approaches to the Archaeology of Religion*. Walnut Creek, CA: Left Coast Press.
Wickham, Chris. 2005. *Framing the Early Middle Ages: Europe and the Mediterranean, 400–800*. Oxford: Oxford University Press.
Williams, George. 1968. *Group Selection*. New York: Idine.
Williams, Maggie. 1999. "Warrior Kings and Savvy Abbots: The Sacred, the Secular, and the Depiction of Contemporary Costume on the Cross of the Scriptures, Clonmacnoise." *AVISTA Forum* 12, no. 1: 4–11.
Wilson, David. 2003. *Darwin's Cathedral: Evolution, Religion, and the Nature of Society*. Chicago: University of Chicago Press.
Wiseman, Rob. 2015. "Interpreting Ancient Social Organization: Conceptual Metaphors and Image Schemas." *Time and Mind* 8, no. 2: 159–190.
Woods, David. 2010. "Crowd-Control in Sixth-Century Clonmacnoise (Admnán, VC 1.3)." *Ériu* 60: 131–136.
Zahavi, Amotz. 1975. "Mate selection: A Selection for a Handicap." *Journal of Theoretical Biology* 53, no. 1: 205–214.
Zahavi, Amotz, and Avishag Zahavi. 1997. *The Handicap Principle: A Missing Part of Darwin's Puzzle*. Oxford: Oxford University Press.
Zedeño, María Nieves. 2008. "Bundled Worlds: The Roles and Interactions of Complex Objects from the North American Plains." *Journal of Archaeological Method and Theory* 15, no. 4: 362–378.

Index

Adomnán's, Life of Columba, 1, 62, 99
   miraculous cattle, 1–4, 13–14, 19, 81, 100, 110, 180
   Columba's visit to Clonmacnoise, 70
altruism, biological theories of, 97, 208
Anglo-Norman. *See* twelfth century
awe and the small self, 109–10, 176

Bell, Catherine, 85–87
Big Gods theories, 98–99, 176
   critique of, 99–100, 102, 108

cattle, theories of value about, 39–43
Caherlehillan, 31–33, 78, 116, 126, 135
callows, Shannon River, 59, 61, 77
charismatic ecologies, 108–9, 110, 144, 176
Christianity, appearance in Ireland, 28–30
clientage, 2–3, 34, 39–43, 51, 62, 100, 110, 185
Clonfad, 128
Clonmacnoise, archaeology of:
Car Park, 71–72
Castle, 64, 74, 79, 186, 196, 203
Clonmacnoise Bridge, 68–69
   ecology and landscape, 57–61
High Crosses, 67–68
New Graveyard, 72–77
palynology, 60–61
pre-monastic history, 61–62
St. Ciarán's Church, 71
St. Ciarán's School, 66–67
Steeple Garden, 67
Tourist Office, 69–70
Wastewater System, 70–71
Crabtree, Pamela:
   Anglo-Saxon England, 9, 43
   urbanism, 9–11, 19, 116, 137–8
   Iron Age Ireland, 26
Cross of Scriptures, Clonmacnoise, 64–65, 68, 80–81, 141–82
Chruachan. *See* Rathcroghan
Church reform in the twelfth century. *See* twelfth century
Curta, Florin, 7, 19, 81

de Waal, Frans, 101–3
decline of cattle, 36, 39–42, 46, 120, 121, 166, 175, 188, 201
Deer Park Farms, 36, 45, 130, 132, 189, 197
Doherty, Charles: 9, 44, 52, 64, 82, 137, 178
domnach/domnaig (pl.), 29
Dún Ailinne, 25

eskers, Eiscir Riada, 60

fertae, 27
Fishamble Street excavations, Dublin, 49–51
  cats, 193–4, 202
  cattle, 122–6, 188–90
  deer, 134, 196–8
  pigs, 129–31
  pine martin, 201
  sheep and goats 132
Fowles, Severin, 92, 95
Freestone Hill, 27, 29

Garranes, 29
Gaelic. *See* twelfth century
The Gift. *See* Mauss, Marcel
Graeber, David, 7, 13–20, 42, 81, 84, 88, 93, 95, 100
Grierson, Philip, views on Mauss, 7–14, 18, 21n3, 47–48, 85
grounded cognition, 102–5, 107–8, 113n5, 167–8, 175, 208–10

Hodges, Richard, 8–9, 15, 42, 47, 51,
Hrdy, Sarah, 101–2, 104, 208

Iron Age Lull, 25–26, 28, 35
irregular enclosures, 37

Kehnel, Annette, 59, 62–64, 203–5
Knowth, 45, 120, 127–8, 130–31, 189, 190

Mauss, Marcel, 7–14, 17–20, 42, 47, 54, 85–6, 91, 100, 102, 105–6, 110, 206–8
McCormick, Finbar. *See* decline of cattle; Fishamble St. excavations
Meeting at Grand Central, 106–7, 109–10, 175, 209

Nendrum, 33
North Cross, Clonmacnoise, 67–68, 81, 158

Patterson, Nerys, and the paradox of clientage, 40–41, 43, 110
Pauketat, Timothy, 86, 88–89, 91
pilgrimage, 60, 62, 87–89, 93–94, 146, 175
post-Roman urbanism, theories about, 5–20, 29, 83, 116–117, 138
provisioning and zooarchaeology, 50–51, 116–7, 125–8, 129–32, 135–39, 140n7, 175–76, 188, 203, 206

Rathcroghan, 25, 204
ringforts and related enclosures, 34–43, 127, 135
  multi–vallate, 35
  raised raths, 45–46, 50, 76
Roman era Ireland, 26–30

sanctuary cities, theories about, 5–6, 9–12, 19–20, 32, 51–55, 57, 64, 82, 85, 89, 126, 137–39, 142, 145, 175–180, 206
sanctuary, medieval concepts of, 177–180
settlement cemeteries, 33–34, 37, 127, 129–131, 133, 136, 139n4
Shannon River, 58–59, 73, 75
South cross, Clonmacnoise, 68, 81, 150, 158–160, 174
Spector, Janet, 1, 4, 6, 13

tabernacle, and type/antetype imagery, 170–73, 175
Theuws, Frans, 7, 10–12, 15, 19–20, 27, 33, 54, 81, 88–89, 110, 138–39
tuath, 38, 40, 63
Tweed, Thomas, 89–91, 100, 111
twelfth century, changes in Ireland:
  Anglo-Norman, era in Ireland, 30, 44–45, 64, 183–86, 196, 203–5
  Church reform, 64, 183–84, 186, 204
  Gaelic identities, 186, 203–5

urbanism. See sanctuary cities, post–Roman urbanism

Veblen's globules, 14–19, 42, 84, 100–102, 104–5, 175–77, 208, 210

Weber, Max, 8, 49–54. 55n6, 85, 108, 137, 139, 175–77, 179, 207

West Cross, Clonmacnoise. *See* Cross of Scriptures

Wheatley, Paul, 53–55, 82–83, 139, 175, 207

About the Author

John Soderberg teaches archaeology in the Department of Sociology and Anthropology at Denison University. His main research interest is the intersection of religion and economies in the Middle Ages. He has excavated sites in Ireland, Scotland, and Wales. He received his PhD from the University of Minnesota and MA from the Irish Studies Program at Boston College.

www.ingramcontent.com/pod-product-compliance
Lightning Source LLC
Chambersburg PA
CBHW061710300426
44115CB00014B/2631